SEMEIA 64

THE RHETORIC OF PRONOUNCEMENT

Editor: Vernon K. Robbins

©1994
by the Society of Biblical Literature

SEMEIA 64

Copyright © 1993 by the Society of Biblical Literature

All rights reserved. No part of this work may be reproduced or transmitted in any form or by any means, electronic or mechanical, including photocopying and recording, or by means of any information storage or retrieval system, except as may be expressly permitted by the 1976 Copyright Act or in writing from the publisher. Requests for permission should be addressed in writing to the Rights and Permissions Office, Society of Biblical Literature, 825 Houston Mill Road, Atlanta, GA 30329, USA.

ISSN 0095-571X
ISBN 1-58983-111-X

Printed in the United States of America
on acid-free paper

CONTENTS

Contributors to this Issue V

Introduction: Using Rhetorical Discussions of the Chreia to Interpret Pronouncement Stories
Vernon K. Robbins VII

I. MEDITERRANEAN LITERATURE AND THE NEW TESTAMENT

1. Paradigms in Homer, Pindar, the Tragedians, and the New Testament
Øivind Andersen and Vernon K. Robbins 3

2. Authorizing Humor: Lucian's *Demonax* and Cynic Rhetoric
R. Bracht Branham 33

3. Rhetorical Argumentation in Early Rabbinic Pronouncement Stories
Alan J. Avery-Peck 49

4. Rhetorical Argumentation in the Hadith Literature of Islam
R. Marston Speight 73

II. EXPANSION AND ELABORATION IN SYNOPTIC STORIES

5. Biblical Sources for Pronouncement Stories in the Gospels
Miriam Dean-Otting and Vernon K. Robbins 95

6. Conflict and Rhetoric in Mark 2:23-28
Rod Parrott 117

7. Rhetoric, Purity, and Play: Aspects of Mark 7:1-23
Gregory Salyer 139

8. A Socio-Rhetorical Analysis of Simon of Cyrene: Mark 15:21 and Its Parallels
Brian K. Blount 171

III. LITERARY AND SOCIAL STUDIES OF PRONOUNCEMENT

9. The Story of Zacchaeus as Rhetoric: Luke 19:1-10
   Robert C. Tannehill 201

10. Hospitality and Characterization in Luke 11:37-54: A Socio-Narratological Approach
    David B. Gowler 213

11. Cursing Fig Trees and Robbers' Dens: Pronouncement Stories Within Social-Systemic Perspective. Mark 11:12-25 and Parallels
    Douglas E. Oakman 253

IV. RESPONSES

12. The Chinese Box: Method within Method
    Bernard Brandon Scott 275

13. Persuasive Pronouncements: An Evaluation of Recent Studies on the Chreia
    Burton L. Mack 283

14. Telling the Other Story: A Literary Response to Socio-Rhetorical Criticism of the New Testament
    Mark Ledbetter 289

CONTRIBUTORS TO THIS ISSUE

Øivind Andersen
 Department of Classics
 University of Trondheim
 N-7055 Dragvoll-Trondheim
 Norway

Alan J. Avery-Peck
 Department of Religious Studies
 College of the Holy Cross
 Worcester, MA 01610

Brian K. Blount
 Princeton Theological Seminary
 CN 821
 Princeton, NJ 08542-0803

R. Bracht Branham
 Department of Classics
 404 Humanities Building
 Emory University
 Atlanta, GA 30322

Miriam Dean-Otting
 Department of Religion
 Kenyon College
 Gambier, OH 43022-9623

David B. Gowler
 Department of Philosophy and
 Religion
 Chowan College
 Murfreesburo, NC

Mark Ledbetter
 Department of Religion and
 Philosophy
 1500 East Fairview Avenue
 Huntingdon College
 Montgomery, AL 36106-2148

Burton L. Mack
 Claremont Graduate School
 Institute for Antiquity and
 Christianity
 831 Dartmouth
 Claremont, CA 91711

Douglas E. Oakman
 Religion Department
 Pacific Lutheran University
 Tacoma, WA 98447

Rod Parrott
 Disciples Seminary Foundation
 P.O. Box 1177
 Claremont, CA 91711

Vernon K. Robbins
 Department of Religion
 312 Physics Building
 Emory University
 Atlanta, GA 30322

Gregory Salyer
 Department of Religion and
 Philosophy
 1500 East Fairview Avenue
 Huntingdon College
 Montgomery, AL 36106-2148

Bernard Brandon Scott
 Phillips Graduate Seminary
 University of Tulsa
 600 South College
 Tulsa, OK 74104

R. Marston Speight
 National Council of Churches of
 Christ in the USA
 Interfaith Relations, Christian-
 Muslim Concerns
 Hartford Seminary
 77 Sherman St.
 Hartford, CT 06105

Robert C. Tannehill
 Methodist Theological School in
 Ohio
 P.O. Box 630
 Delaware, OH 43015

INTRODUCTION:
USING RHETORICAL DISCUSSIONS OF THE CHREIA
TO INTERPRET PRONOUNCEMENT STORIES

Vernon K. Robbins
Emory University

Five of the authors who have contributed to this volume wrote an initial version of their essay during the final years of the second phase (1981-87) of the SBL Pronouncement Story Work Group.[1] During this phase,[2] the importance of the study of the rhetorical chreia—a form containing speech and/or action attributed to a specific person—was becoming more and more evident (Robbins 1988b). The first volume of ancient texts discussing the chreia, edited by Ronald F. Hock and Edward N. O'Neil, was not available in published form, since it became available only as the work of the Group came to an end (Hock and O'Neil). Nor was the work on synoptic Gospel texts by Mack and Robbins available, since it did not appear until 1989 (Mack and Robbins). Information from some of these materials was available, however, through written communications to members of the Group by its Director, Vernon Robbins. The first major task of the second phase of the work came to fruition in the publication of a collection of more than 1500 pronouncement stories in a collection entitled *Ancient Quotes and Anecdotes* (Robbins 1989). The second and final task comes to fruition in the publication of the essays in this volume.

After the term of the Work Group ended, I began to solicit additional papers for the volume and to edit or request revisions of the earlier papers. It has been a major challenge to produce a unified volume of essays, since the authors who produced the essays were selected because of their specialties rather than their agreement on a unified approach to pronouncement stories. The individuals who have allowed their work to be published in this volume, however, were willing to see their insights placed in a context of interpretation informed by Greco-Roman rhetorical practices.

---

[1] Øivind Andersen, Miriam Dean-Otting, Alan J. Avery-Peck, R. Marston Speight, and Rod Parrott.
[2] For the results of the first phase, see Tannehill, 1981.

The first part of the volume contains four essays focusing on some aspect of Mediterranean literature that holds potential significance for interpreters of New Testament literature. The initial essay, co-authored by Øivind Andersen and Vernon K. Robbins, addresses the issue of the "paradigm" in New Testament literature, which was the term Martin Dibelius used for the pronouncement story. The analysis of paradigms in Homer's *Iliad* and the survey of the use of the paradigmatic tradition in Pindar and the tragedians reveals both the inappropriateness of calling pronouncement stories paradigms and the absence of an overall study of paradigms in New Testament literature. The essay points the way forward by analyzing the function of each Homeric paradigm in the specific portion of the speech in which it occurs. The essay by R. Bracht Branham exhibits an interpretation of a pronouncement story in Lucian's *Demonax* in the context of Cynic rhetoric. The specific way in which pronouncements in Mediterranean literature use wordplay, wit, inversion, and the unexpected becomes fully evident in this study. Alan J. Avery-Peck's essay presents an analysis of all of the pronouncement stories considered by Gary G. Porton to be present in the Tannaitic strata of rabbinic literature. A major result of this study is an exhibition of the kind of chreia which is best called an "argumentative chreia." This kind of chreia does not contain a sequence of argumentation like Hermogenes' chreia elaboration, but it contains at least one argumentative figure, like an argument from enthymeme, contrary, analogy, example, or authoritative testimony. More will be said about this at the conclusion of this essay. R. Marston Speight's essay pursues a comment made by Rudolf Bultmann about analogies between stories in the gospels and stories in Islamic literature. This investigation displays the usefulness of knowledge about the chreia for approaching various literary collections in which the action and speech of authoritative personages play a special role.

The second part of the volume contains four essays that present new insights in two major arenas for interpreters who use discussions of the chreia in their analysis of New Testament literature. New clarity has emerged on the relation between expanded ($\dot{\epsilon}\pi\epsilon\kappa\tau\epsilon\dot{\iota}\nu\epsilon\iota\nu$; Hock and O'Neil: 100-103) and elaborated ($\dot{\epsilon}\rho\gamma\alpha\sigma\dot{\iota}\alpha$; Hock and O'Neil: 176-177) chreiai in the *Progymnasmata*. The clarity is a result of analysis of a wide range of chreia-like stories in Mediterranean literature with the aid of insights from the *Progymnasmata* and of close attention to Theon's comments about elaboration of the chreia in his eighth exercise (Hock and O'Neil: 106-107). For those interested in the details about abbreviated, expanded, and elaborated chreiai in the *Progymnasmata*, a summary that incorporates the new information serves as a conclusion to this introductory essay.

The first arena of new insights concerns the order of argumentation in chreiai. Stories containing chreia expansion and stories containing chreia elaboration use an order of argumentation virtually reversed from one another. The reason for this is simple, but it has taken some years of scholarship to clarify it. An expanded chreia contains a sequence designed to complete the story with a dramatic finish. This design produces a delay of the statement and/or its rationale to the end of the story. This means that an expanded chreia often contains an enthymematic conclusion, either in the form of a chreia statement and a rationale at the end or in the form of a rationale at the end that provides an enthymematic premise for a statement that occurred somewhere earlier in the story. The major characteristic of a chreia elaboration, in contrast, is to bring a thesis and its rationale to the beginning of a unit (with the aid of an abbreviated chreia) and to create a flow of argumentation out from that enthymematic beginning.

The second arena of new insights occurs in the essays in the second part, which uncover two levels of elaboration (ἐργασία) of chreiai. "First-level elaboration" provides "arguments for each part of the chreia" using "topics" of various kinds, like obscurity, pleonasm, ellipsis, impossibility, implausibility, falsity, unsuitability, uselessness, shamefulness (Hock and O'Neil: 102-107), feasiblility, according to nature and the customs of all peoples, easy, praiseworthy, pious, necessary, advantageous, etc. (Hock and O'Neil: 71-74). If the argumentative figures of contrary, analogy, example and authoritative testimony do appear, they are likely to be embedded in these other topics and will not provide the dominant context for the order of the elaboration. "Second-level elaboration," in contrast, presents a sequence of rhetorical and argumentative figures that approximate a complete argument (Hock and O'Neil: 176-177; Mack and Robbins: 51-65; Mack: 41-47). The second level of elaboration regularly contains an introduction—a statement with its rationale and restatement—usually accompanied by an argument from the contrary—an argument containing some combination of analogy, paradigm, and/or authoritative judgment—and a conclusion.

An essay co-authored by Miriam Dean-Otting and Vernon K. Robbins begins the second part of the volume by investigating a series of gospel units using basic insights from the *Progymnasmata* about expanded and elaborated chreiai. The essay reveals that the synoptic Gospels contain "artistic" uses of biblical verses both in expanded and elaborated chreiai. This means that quotations are not simply brought into stories in extended "inartistic" form, but these quotations are abbreviated and modified in "artistic" ways to give them their particular function in the argument. While abbreviated rhetorical selection and/or verbal modification occurs in all instances where biblical wording is incorporated, the kinds of modification vary. In abbreviated and expanded chreiai, the tendency is to select and modify biblical wording in such a manner that it receives the form of a maxim, sometimes with and sometimes without an epilogue (Aristotle II.xxi.3-6). Long strings of verbatim biblical wording, however, are almost never brought into abbreviated or expanded chreiai, since efficient use of words in these contexts is desirable to move the language to a dramatic conclusion. In elaborated chreia, on the other hand, extended strings of verbatim biblical verses are possible, although entire clauses may be omitted from these verbal strings to give them a rhythm and wording that fits their new context.

Within the larger investigation of the uses of verbatim wording of scripture in chreiai, this study displays the manner in which expanded chreiai and elaborated chreiai contain a reverse order of argumentation. The Matthean version of Jesus' meal with tax collectors (9:10-13) is an expanded chreia in which a clause from written testimony creates at the end a deductive line of reasoning that is typical of the beginning of a chreia elaboration. Instead of beginning a chreia elaboration, however, this reasoning ends the expanded chreia. A detailed analysis of the use of biblical quotations in the three synoptic versions of the chreia about plucking grain on the Sabbath follows. Here one sees a fascinating interplay of modes of argumentation characteristic of expanded and elaborated chreiai. After this, the essay contains an analysis of Mark's version of Jesus' discussion of marriage and divorce (10:1-12), which again contains a combination of expansion and elaboration techniques. The final section of the paper analyzes the use of scriptural quotations in the first thirteen verses of Jesus' debate with the Pharisees in Mark 7:1-23, which uses extensive wording from scripture in the context of "second-level elaboration."

Rod Parrott's essay argues the case for understanding "the grainfield incident" in Mark 2:23-28 as a chreia elaboration that presents the argument in inverted order. Since the inversion occurs as a result of the dramatic sequence of the story, this is an "expanded" story. Nevertheless, the expansion has produced the argumentative steps of an elaboration. Parrott's essay goes on to distinguish between fights, games, and debates, and analyzes the Markan version of the elaborated chreia about the grainfield incident as an interplay of a fight and a game. More must be said about these results at the end of this essay.

Gregory Salyer's essay investigates the two different levels of elaboration of a chreia in the first and second parts of Jesus' debate with the Pharisees in Mark 7:1-23. Mark 7:14-23 contains a division of a chreia statement in v. 15 into two parts, with an argument for the first part in vv.

17-19 and the second part in vv. 20-23. In each instance, the elaboration amplifies the chreia statement without adding a significantly new argumentative figure. The initial part of Jesus' argument, however, begins in a manner consonant with Hermogenes' display of second-level elaboration. In this instance, new argumentative figures of citation of ancient authority, example, contrary, and conclusion are used in this elaboration. After analysis of the rhetorical nature of both levels of argumentation, the essay contains a social and ideological interpretation of the argument, which concerns the Jewish purity system based on temple purity and the people's relation to it.

Brian Blount's essay analyzes the Simon of Cyrene episode in the synoptic gospels with insights both from Theon's discussion of the "diegema," a brief narrative, and from discussion of chreia elaboration in the *Progymnasmata*. The Markan and Matthean versions formulate the Simon episode as a narrative that evokes a call to discipleship; the Lukan version makes the episode part of a larger scene in which Jesus censures the daughters of Jersualem for being implicated in the actions of the people of Jerusalem against him.

The third part of the volume contains three essays that investigate synoptic Gospel units with some combination of literary and social perspectives. Robert Tannehill's essay investigates the Zaccheus story in the context of the language and reasoning of Lukan discourse. David Gowler's essay uses a socio-narratological approach to analyze characterization and social dynamics of hospitality in the Lukan account of the dinner in a Pharisee's house when Jesus does not wash his hands before dinner. The final essay by Douglas Oakman uses tools from the social sciences to explore the seemingly inconsistent feature in the Cursing of the Fig Tree episode where Jesus looks for figs even though "it was not the season for figs." The volume concludes with responses by Bernard Brandon Scott, Burton L. Mack, and Mark Ledbetter.

Results

The essays in this volume were solicited and edited for the purpose of advancing our ability to use insights about the chreia in our interpretations of New Testament literature. The progress has been encouraging. Prior to this volume, it was obvious that ancient rhetoricians had observed two levels of rhetorical amplification of the chreia: expansion (ἐπεκτείνειν; Hock and O'Neil: 100-101) and elaboration (ἐργασία; Hock and O'Neil: 176-177). This basic insight informed the production of *The Chreia in Ancient Rhetoric. Volume I. The Progymnasmata* (Hock and O'Neil), *Patterns of Persuasion in the Gospels* (Mack and Robbins), and *Rhetoric and the New Testament* (Mack). These studies have made it obvious that earlier scholars were mistaken to think of chreiai as existing only in abbreviated form. Chreiai may be expanded or elaborated, either moderately or extensively, with the result that a chreia may contain argumentative steps that move toward or actually present a complete argument.

Some of the conclusions may not be as explicit as one might wish in the essays in this volume, since they emerged in the process of editing. I offer the following summary in the hope of moving the discussion yet another step forward.

1. *Chreia recitation* (ἀπαγγελία)

It is important to remind ourselves that variations among chreiai regularly result simply from individual "recitations" which produce particular written versions of them. This terminology comes from Theon (Hock and O'Neil: 94-95), and it seems obvious that the writers of the gospels felt free to present their own recitations of chreiai (Robbins 1991).

2. *Abbreviated chreiai*

Even an abbreviated chreia may contain argumentative figures. The essays by Alan J. Avery-Peck and R. Marston Speight especially bring this to light. Theon observed the following rhetorical and argumentative figures in chreiai when he explained the manner in which they could be expressed (προσφέρονται; Hock and O'Neil: 82-93):

(1) in the manner of a maxim (γνωμολογικῶς);
(2) in the manner of an explanation (ἀποδεικτικῶς);
(3) with wit (κατὰ χαριεντισμόν);
(4) in the manner of a syllogism (συλλογιστικῶς);
(5) in the manner of an enthymeme (ἐνθυμηματικῶς);
(6) with an example (κατὰ παράδειγμα);
(7) in the manner of a wish (εὐκτικῶς);
(8) in a symbolic manner (συμβολικῶς);
(9) in a figurative manner (τροπικῶς);
(10) with double entendre (κατὰ ἀμφιβολίαν);
(11) with a change of subject (κατὰ μετάληψιν);
(12) with combinations of the above forms.
              (Theon, Hock and O'Neil: 88-93)

The studies by Avery-Peck and Speight make it clear that any rhetorical or argumentative figure may be present in an abbreviated chreia—even those, perhaps especially those, displayed by Hermogenes' chreia elaboration. A chreia is a rhetorical form. This means that it contains some kind of language that has an attractive, authoritative, or logically persuasive quality. There has not been enough investigation of the rhetorical qualities of short statements themselves, but perhaps we are at a stage where this kind of investigation can move forward.

3. Expanded chreiai

Since a chreia is a rhetorical form, one of its major characteristics is its potential for modification. A chreia can be adapted to function in very different ways—beginning an argument, ending an argument, winning a person to a particular side of an argument, separating allies from one other, uniting divided groups, or furnishing amusement for one purpose or another. If a chreia is to have this range of functions, it must be highly adaptable. For this reason, Theon discusses the primary modifiable aspects of a chreia at some length (Hock and O'Neil: 94-103). Not only can these aspects be presented in every case and number; they can be expanded or abbreviated internally, and positive or negative comments may be added to them. Chreia modification can take the form of:

(a) inflexion (κλίσις);
(b) commentary (ἐπιφωνεῖν);
(c) objection (ἀντιλέγειν);
(d) expansion (ἐπεκτείνειν);
(e) abbreviation (συστέλλειν).
(Theon, Hock and O'Neil: 94-103)

Chreia modification covers a wide range of phenomena as a result of the potential rhetorical and argumentative figures in it. A chreia may simply contain amplification that adds no new argumentative figures, or it may add argumentative figures to a point where it approximates a complete argument. It would be helpful to have terminology to refer to these different phenomena. I recommend the following:

(a) Amplified chreiai: expanded chreiai that contain amplification which has the nature of the beginning of a speech. An amplified chreia may contain any combination of a statement, a rationale, and a restatement. The expanded chreia Theon composed in his *Progymnasmata* contains amplification, both in the setting and in the saying (Hock and O'Neil: 100-103). The saying contains an exhortation, a direct address, and an amplified rationale for the exhortation. There is no major argumentative figure in it; thus it is simply an amplified chreia.

(b) Expanded argumentative chreiai: any chreia with an argumentative figure in it may properly be called an "argumentative chreia." An argumentative figure puts forth a constituent of an argument. Thus, an expanded argumentative chreia will contain some combination of contrary, analogy, example, and/or wording from written testimony, but it will not set them forth in a manner that approximates a complete argument. In his seventh exercise, Theon discusses refutation that focuses on basic grammatical, logical, or social issues like obscurity, pleonasm, ellipsis, impossibility, implausibility, falsity, unsuitability, uselessness, and shamefulness (Hock and O'Neil: 101-105). These kinds of statements would be natural in expanded argumentative chreiai.

(c) Elaborated chreiai: an argumentative chreia that approximates a complete argument. Parrott's essay makes the case that Mark's version of "the grainfields incident" in Mark 2:23-28 is such a chreia. An elaborated chreia will arrange some combination of argument from analogy, example, and/or citation of authoritative testimony in an order that approximates a complete argument.

4. Elaboration

(a) First-level elaboration: "first-level elaboration" provides arguments for individual parts of a chreia. Theon indicates that this level of elaboration should use "topics," and it seems clear that these would be topics like the ones he lists for the refutation and the thesis (Hock and O'Neil: 71-75, 102-105). In other words, at this level, an elaboration is likely to contain embellishments, contrasts, lists, and inferences based on topics like plausible, shameful/honorable; pious, etc. If it contains argumentative figures like those that move toward a complete argument, those figures will be embedded in units that provide arguments for individual parts of the chreia. Salyer's essay analyzes first-level elaboration in the final part of Jesus' debate with the Pharisees in Mark 7:14-23.

(b) Second-level elaboration: elaboration beginning with a chreia that establishes an enthymematic context out of which flow the constituents of a complete argument. The beginning point of the elaboration regularly contains praise, statement, and rationale, possibly with restatement. The argument that ensues regularly contains argument from contrary, analogy, example, and/or authoritative testimony, with some kind of conclusion.

5. Language context for chreiai

Many, perhaps most, of the readers of this introduction are aware that the particular nature of a chreia emerges in a specific language context. Yet a review of this context may be helpful in the framework of this volume. Chreia discourse concerns speech and/or action attributed to a specific person. Therefore, discourse which allows the personage behind it to disappear is not chreia discourse. Because of the particular nature of chreia discourse, Theon divides chreiai into three major types: sayings-chreiai, action-chreiai, and mixed-chreiai. Expanded or elaborated chreiai, and first-level and second-level elaboration, may develop out of any of these types.

The sayings–chreia (λογικὴ χρεία) either presents a statement (ἀπόφασις) or a response (ἀπόκρισις). Therefore, there are two species of sayings–chreiai: statement (ἀποφαντικόν) and response (ἀποκριτικόν). In a statement–chreia, the statement–chreia is either unprompted (καθ' ἑκούσιον ἀπόφασις) or arising out of a specific circumstance (κατὰ περίστασιν ἀπόφασις). The important thing in the statement-chreia appears to be the absence of any speech prior to the attributed statement in the chreia. A response-chreia, according to Theon, may occur in five forms:

(1) a response to a simple question (τὸ κατ' ἐρώτησιν ἀποφαντικόν), which means that the question only requires that a person answer with yes or no;

(2) a response to an inquiry (τὸ κατὰ πύσμα ἀποφαντικόν), which means that a question that requires more than a yes or no has been given an answer which contains neither an explanation of the reason for the answer nor any other advice or comment;

(3) an explanatory response to a question (τὸ κατ' ἐρώτησιν αἰτιῶδες ἀποφαντικόν), which means that the answer contains some explanation, advice, or other comment in addition to the answer;

(4) a responsive chreia (τὸ ἀποκριτικόν, ambiguously bearing the same name as this class of chreia) which contains an explicit or implied remark other than a question, to which a response is made;

(5) a double chreia (τὸ διπλοῦν), which contains statements of two characters, either one of which creates a chreia.

(Theon, Hock and O'Neil: 84-87)

The second main class is the action-chreia (πρακτικὴ χρεία), which either may be active (ἐνεργητική) or passive (παθητική). An active action–chreia shows some aggressive act (ἐνέργεια), while a passive action–chreia points to something experienced or suffered (πάθος τι). The third main class is mixed. This class, according to Theon, contains both sayings and actions, but makes its point with the action (Hock and O'Neil: 88-89).

Theon's discussion, not only of sayings and actions but also of the manner in which chreiai are expressed, signals the unusual importance of this form for analysis of New Testament literature in general and gospel literature in particular. In the setting of action and/or speech attributed to someone, this kind of language interweaves people and their actions with meanings, intentions, and hopes. Chreia language is embodied language in action; thus it has special significance for religious literature that claims a fusion of divine wisdom and power with human thought, action, and being. This volume of essays is offered to its readers with the hope of further elucidating this significance.

WORKS CONSULTED

Aristotle
    1926   *The "Art" of Rhetoric*. Ed. J.H. Reese. Loeb Classical Library. London: William Heinemann.

Hock, Ronald F. and Edward N. O'Neil
    1986   *The Chreia in Ancient Rhetoric. Volume I. The Progymnasmata*. Atlanta: Scholars.

Mack, Burton L.
    1990   *Rhetoric and the New Testament*. Minneapolis: Fortress.

Mack, Burton L. and Vernon K. Robbins
    1989   *Patterns of Persuasion in the Gospels*. Sonoma: Polebridge.

Porton, Gary G.
    1981   "The Pronouncement Story in Tannaitic Literature: A Review of Bultmann's Theory." *Semeia* 20: 81-99.

Robbins, Vernon K.
    1988a   "The Chreia." Pp. 1-23 in *Greco-Roman Literature and the New Testament*. Ed. David E. Aune. Atlanta: Scholars.
    1988b   "Pronouncement Stories from a Rhetorical Perspective." *Forum* 4,2: 3-32.
    1989   *Ancient Quotes and Anecdotes: From Crib to Crypt*. Sonoma: Polebridge.
    1991   "Writing as a Rhetorical Act in Plutarch and the Gospels." Pp. 157-186 in *Persuasive Artistry: Studies in New Testament Rhetoric in Honor of George A. Kennedy*. Ed. Duane F. Watson. Sheffield: JSOT.

Tannehill, Robert (ed.)
    1981   *Pronouncement Stories. Semeia* 20. Chico: Scholars.

I
MEDITERRANEAN LITERATURE AND THE NEW TESTAMENT

Paradigms in Homer, Pindar, the Tragedians, and the New Testament

Øivind Andersen
University of Trondheim
and
Vernon K. Robbins
Emory University

ABSTRACT

This essay demonstrates that Martin Dibelius turned scholarship in the wrong direction when he applied the word paradigm (*das Paradigma*) to the pronouncement stories in the synoptic gospels. An exhibition of the functions of paradigms (*paradeigmata*) in the *Iliad*, with the additional information about their role in the writings of Pindar, the Greek tragedians, and the New Testament, moves interpretation of the New Testament toward an appropriate use of the term and concept. The key is to understand that paradigms' function in the domain of inductive argumentation: they make their case by appeal to a particular example (παράδειγμα). In order for paradigms to function effectively, they must have some kind of authoritative quality: an important person did it, it was an important moment in a larger scenario, or it was a special circumstance, which revealed something important. The New Testament contains a significant number of paradigms, and New Testament scholarship awaits a systematic analysis of their function in early Christian discourse.

Introduction

On the one hand, the effect of this essay for New Testament studies is negative, since it demonstrates that Martin Dibelius turned scholarship in the wrong direction when he applied the word paradigm (*das Paradigma*) to the pronouncement stories in the synoptic gospels (Dibelius 1919). On the other hand, the exhibition of the functions of paradigms (*paradeigmata*) in the *Iliad*, with the additional information about their role in the writings of Pindar, the Greek tragedians, and the New Testament can move interpretation of the New Testament toward an appropriate use of the term and concept. The key is to understand that paradigms function in the domain of inductive argumentation: they make their case by appeal to a particular example (παράδειγμα). In an inductive argument an example or a set of examples makes a conclusion probable. In a deductive argument such as a syllogism, if the syllogism is valid and the premises are true, then the conclusion is necessarily true. Since a deductive premise is itself based on a number of specific examples, paradigms have an intricate relation to deductive reasoning. Paradigms themselves, however, function inductively: they support arguments by presenting one particular example. It is necessary, then, for a paradigm to have some special kind of authoritative quality: an important person did it, it was an important moment in a larger scenario, or it was a special circumstance, which revealed something important (Fiore: 26-44; Cosby: 93-105).

Our investigation has a significant relation to Burton Mack's analysis of arguments from analogy in Mark 4:1-34 (Mack and Robbins: 143-60). In Mark 4, different analogies (*parabolai*) function as a thesis, a rationale, a contrary, a judgment, an example, and an analogy to support the other analogies. Analogies, in contrast to paradigms, present ordinary occasions, circumstances that people know about by observing them regularly, by doing them at least occasionally, or by seeing the results of their having been done by someone else. Analogies, then, present occasions like planting grain, sewing cloth, presenting sacrifices in the temple, and the like. Mack's study shows that analogies have an amazing plasticity of function—it appears that they can function in every domain of argumentation. The range of functions for paradigms is likely to be more limited, since they present special rather than ordinary circumstances. Nevertheless, the data in this essay suggests that the range of functions for paradigms is remarkable. This investigation looks carefully only at the range of functions of paradigms in Homeric argumentation, but it presents basic data about paradigms in Pindar, the Greek tragedies, and the New Testament. The procedure will be: (a) to present and discuss the major functions of paradigms in the *Iliad*; (b) to discuss briefly the manner in which Pindar, Sophocles, Aeschylus, and Euripides use the Homeric paradigms; and (c) to reflect briefly on the implications of the functions of paradigms for interpretation of the New Testament.

THE FUNCTIONS OF PARADIGMS IN *THE ILIAD*

This initial section concerns Homer's *Iliad* and the so-called "*mythological* paradigms" in that epic. The term "mythological" in this connection has a wide application. First, it covers stories about the previous life and internal struggle of the gods at Mt. Olympus, such as Zeus hurling Hephaestus to earth. Second, there are the more numerous incidents about non-Trojan matters, such as the Calydonia boar-hunt and the exploits of Heracles. Third, the term "mythological" may refer to

Trojan material outside the scope of the narrative proper to the *Iliad*. Fourth, the term may refer to episodes in the so-called *"paradeigmata oikeia"* which recount the past life of the characters themselves or their ancestors.

A mythological paradigm in the *Iliad* may be defined as a myth introduced as a precedent or pattern. All of the paradigms in Homer are interwoven in speeches and are part of a more extensive communicative exchange of words and actions. Ironically, this indeed is the situation Dibelius envisioned for the pronouncement stories. Rather than interpret them in their contexts in the gospels, he postulated a function for them in speeches, that is, in Christian sermons (Dibelius 1935: 17-23; Mack and Robbins: 3-6, 10-16). We use the term "ironically," because Dibelius disavowed any use of insights from classical literature for the study of early Christianity (Dibelius 1935: 6).

In rhetorical terms, when a speaker in the *Iliad* articulates a mythological paradigm as a precedent, that person presents a paradigm as a "recitation" (Theon, Hock and O'Neil: 95). In Theon's terms, the form being recited is more akin to a *diegesis* (narrative) than a chreia, since usually there is no speech in a paradigm. But whether or not the paradigm contains speech, the recitation of it may be abbreviated or expanded (Theon, Butts: 311, 319-21). Since each paradigm occurs in a speech in the *Iliad*, a major issue is its function in the speech. Our investigation highlights the following functions:

1. Confirmation of the Authority (*ethos*) of the Speaker
2. Rationale or Confirmation of the Rationale for a Hortatory (Protreptic) Thesis
    A. Addressed to a Human
    B. Addressed to a God or Goddess
3. Contrary in Support of a Dissuasive (Apotreptic) Thesis
4. Rationale for the Speaker's Disposition toward Action
5. Confirmation of the Speaker's Understanding of a Situation
    A. In the Past
    B. In the Present

We will discuss each function in turn and present at least one example of it from the *Iliad*.

1. Confirmation of the Authority (ethos) *of the Speaker*

A paradigm that confirms the authority of the speaker appears in the first book of the *Iliad*, where Nestor tries to make Agamemnon and Achilles come to terms with each other. In this instance, the thesis is: "allow yourself to be persuaded by me." In other words, the context is the beginning of a speech, where the concern of the speaker is to establish his or her own *ethos*. In this rhetorical environment, the speaker can exercise authority either in an exhortative thesis that means "trust me" or in a thesis of self-attribution that means "I am qualified to speak authoritatively to you." Before launching his proposal for compromise (1.274-284), and after a short introduction (1.254-258), Nestor introduces and supports an exhortative thesis:

> Homer, *Iliad* 1.259-274 (quoted here and below from Lattimore's translation)
> **Introduction**
>> *Exhortative Thesis*: Yet be persuaded
>> *Rationale using Comparison*: Both of you are younger than I am.
>
> Yes, and in my time I have dealt with better men than
> you are, and never once did they disregard me.
>> *Amplification of the Rationale*: Never
>
> yet have I seen nor shall see again such men as these were,
> men like Peirithoös, and Dryas, shepherd of the people,
> Kaineus and Exadios, godlike Polyphemos,
> or Theseus, Aigeius' son, in the likeness of the immortals.
> These were the strongest generation of earth-born mortals—
> the strongest, and they fought against the strongest, the beast men
> living within the mountains, and terribly they destroyed them.
> **Paradigmatic Confirmation of the Rationale**
> I was of the company of these men, coming from Pylos,
> a long way from a distant land, since they had summoned me.
> And I fought single-handed, yet against such men no one
> of the mortals now alive upon earth could do battle. And also
> these listened to the counsels I gave and heeded my bidding.
> **Conclusion**
>> *Exhortation*: Do you also obey,
>> *Rationale*: since to be persuaded is better.

A confirmation is a restatement that adds an additional dimension to the initial statement (Rhet ad Her 2.19.28). A paradigmatic confirmation recites a paradigm that confirms the initial statement. By presenting a recitation of the occasion when he sailed out and fought among the great men, Nestor confirms his assertion that none of them disregarded him.

Another instance in which a paradigm confirms the authority of the speaker occurs when Diomedes responds to Agamemnon's request for constructive proposals from anybody who feels like making one, young man or old:

Homer, *Iliad* 14.113-125

Introduction

Thesis of Self-Attribution: That man is here,
Exhortative Amplification of the Thesis: we shall not look far for him, if you are willing to listen, and not be each astonished in anger against me because by birth I am the youngest among you.
Rationale: I also can boast that my generation is of an excellent father, Tydeus, whom now the heaped earth covers over in Thebe.

Paradigmatic Confirmation of the Rationale

For there were three blameless sons who were born to Portheus,
and their home was in Pleuron and headlong Kalydon. Agrios
was first, then Melas, and the third was Oineus the horseman,
the father of my father, and in valour beyond the others.
But Oineus stayed in the land, while my father was driven and settled
in Argos. Such was the will of Zeus and the other immortals.
He married one of the daughters of Adrestos, and established
a house rich in substance, and plenty of wheat-grown acres
were his, with many orchards of fruit trees circled about him,
and many herds were his. He surpassed all other Achaians
with the spear.

Conclusion

Appeal: If all this is true, you must have heard of it.
Recapitulation: Therefore you could not, saying that I was base and unwarlike by birth, dishonour any word that I speak, if I speak well.

The paradigms a speaker recites to confirm the authority of the speaker are, necessarily, epideictic in nature. Their purpose is to elicit approval of the speaker through praise of virtuous achievement. If people accept the truth of the appeal, they are in a ready state of mind to listen carefully to a deliberative (symbouleutic) thesis which will follow, that is, a thesis that gives advice for or against a certain kind of action (Aristotle, Rhet 1.3.3-6). The story of Phoenix's youth (9.447-484), which is told by Phoenix to Achilles to remind Achilles (and inform the audience) of Phoenix's background and so to give his subsequent appeal to Achilles due weight, also belongs to this type of function. In each instance the paradigm supports the *ethos* of the speaker.

The function of a paradigm that supports the *ethos* of the speaker is related to the praise Hermogenes discusses at the beginning of the elaboration of the chreia (Hock and O'Neil: 177). The purpose of the praise is to establish the virtuous character of the one who spoke the chreia. In other words, the concern is the *ethos* of the speaker of the chreia, and it is especially important in the introduction of a speech for a speaker to use praise of virtuous achievements as a means of establishing confidence within the audience (Aristotle, Rhet. 1.2.3, 9.33). When Nestor and Diomedes speak, they include praise in the statement before the recitation of the paradigm. In both instances, the purpose of the paradigm is to establish confidence in the *ethos* of the speaker himself.

2. *Rationale or Confirmation of the Rationale for a Hortatory (Protreptic) Thesis*

In other instances, a speaker uses a paradigm to support an exhortation to act in a specific way. Since there are differences in the tone and procedure of the rhetoric according to whether the exhortation is a directive to a person or a plea addressed to a god or goddess, we separate the analysis of these different situations. Nevertheless, both situations feature hortatory language, language that functions as deliberative (symbouleutic) or advisory rhetoric (Aristotle, Rhet 1.3.3-8).

Here we enter the general rhetorical environment of Hermogenes' elaboration of the chreia, since that elaboration ends with an exhortation toward a certain kind of action. Yet there is a difference in the sequence of argumentation. Hermogenes begins with an attributed maxim and ends with an exhortation. The Homeric argumentation, in contrast, begins and ends with exhortation. This means that the Homeric argumentation does not attempt to make its case on the basis of generalized principles but bases its argumentation on specific mythological instances from which generalized principles may perhaps be deduced.

A. *Addressed to a Human*

The story of Niobe, told by Achilles to Priam in the last book of the *Iliad*, presents an excellent instance of a paradigm functioning as a rationale for a hortatory thesis addressed to a human. Priam has come to ransom the dead Hector, and when the deal has been made, Achilles exhorts him to have a meal with him:

Homer, *Iliad* 24.601-619
Introduction
   Hortatory Thesis: Now you and I must remember our supper.
Paradigmatic Rationale
For even Niobe, she of the lovely tresses, remembered
to eat, whose twelve children were destroyed in her palace,
six daughters, and six sons in the pride of their youth, whom Apollo
killed with arrows from his silver bow, being angered
with Niobe, and shaft-showering Artemis killed the daughters;
because Niobe likened herself to Leto of the fair colouring
and said Leto had borne only two, she herself had borne many;
but the two, though they were only two, destroyed all those others.
Nine days long they lay in their blood, nor was there anyone
to bury them, for the son of Kronos made stones out of

the people; but on the tenth day the Uranian gods buried them.
But she remembered to eat when she was worn out with weeping.
And now somewhere among the rocks, in the lonely mountains,
in Sipylos, where they say is the resting place of the goddesses
who are nymphs, and dance beside the waters of Acheloios,
there, stone still, she broods on the sorrows that the gods gave her.

Conclusion

Recapitulation: Come, then, we also, aged magnificent sir, must remember to eat.

This paradigm provides the rationale, directly, for Achilles' exhortation to Priam. Achilles does not try to present a more generalized rationale, like "When people eat, they acquire energy and comradeship that carries them through the severest of circumstances." This level of deduction could easily emerge from the Homeric situation, and this is the level of deduction Hermogenes displays in his rationale:

> For the most important affairs generally succeed because of toil, and once they have succeeded, they bring pleasure (Hock and O'Neil: 177).

But the Homeric argumentation remains one level removed from the deductive rhetorical environment of Hermogenes' elaboration of the chreia, namely, it remains at the level of argumentation from one particular occasion. In this inductive environment, a paradigm can function directly as the rationale for a hortatory thesis.

This means that the overall action and speech in the Homeric context play a role in the argumentation. Achilles, in response to Priam's prayer, has finally brought himself to lay the body of Hector on a couch and to place it on a wagon. He then returns to Priam and says: "Your son is given back to you, aged sir, as you asked it. He lies on a bier. When dawn shows you yourself shall see him as you take him away. Now you and I must remember our supper" (24.599-601). When the story of Niobe is told, he ends: "Come then, we also, aged magnificent sir, must remember to eat, and afterwards you may take your beloved son back to Ilion, and mourn for him; and he will be much lamented" (24.618-620). The meal shall not put an end to mourning; on the contrary, as in the case of Niobe, there will be time forever to mourn after supper. (Surely, the salient point of Niobe's eating is an invention by the poet of the *Iliad* for the sake of the argument — a reminder that we not only are in fiction, but are dealing with fictitious paradigm). There is no room for any reaction on the part of Priam, for Achilles "sprang to his feet," slaughtered a lamb and prepared food. The two of them eat, "but when they had taken their fill of gazing one on the other" (24.633), Priam asks for a bed to be made ready for him. The paradigm of Niobe seems to have made any further discussion superfluous. It has provided a sufficient rationale for the hortatory thesis, and it leads directly to the preparation of the meal, to the reciprocal contemplation by the two men, and to Priam himself taking an initiative to further community. In Achilles' speech, then, we see a specific authoritative example serving as the rationale for a hortatory thesis.

A second instance of this kind of rationale for action may be found in King Agamemnon's words to Diomedes as Agamemnon musters the army before the first day of battle. In this instance, however, a rationale is stated prior to the recitation of the paradigm. The paradigm functions as a confirmation of the rationale rather than as the initial statement of the rationale (see Rhet ad Her 2.19.28). But the rationale still is not a generalized statement; it is simply an initial statement about Diomedes' father which the paradigm amplifies. This means that the rationale itself remains at the level of inductive argumentation, stating its case on the basis of one instance.

Agamemnon's speech occurs in the following context: having just had a rather rough exchange with Menestheus and Odysseus, King Agamemnon proceeds to where Diomedes and his companion Sthenelos stand, with war chariots and horses all around them. The king, as soon as he sees them, starts to rebuke Diomedes:

Homer, *Iliad* 4.372-400

Introduction

Questions Implying a Hortatory Thesis: Ah me, son of Tydeus, that daring breaker of horses,
why are you skulking and spying out the outworks of battle?
Paradigmatic Rationale: Such was never Tydeus' way, to lurk in the background,
but to fight the enemy far ahead of his own companions.
So they say who had seen him at work,
Qualification: since I never saw nor
encountered him ever; but they say he surpassed all others.
Paradigmatic Confirmation of the Rationale
Once on a time he came, but not in war, to Mykenai
with godlike Polyneikes, a guest and a friend, assembling
people, since these were attacking the sacred bastions of Thebes,
and much they entreated us to grant him renowned companions.
And our men wished to give them and were assenting to what they asked for
but Zeus turned them back, showing forth portents that crossed them.
Now as these went forward and were well on their way, and came
to the river Asopos, and the meadows of grass and the deep rushes,
from there the Achaians sent Tydeus ahead with a message.
He went then and came on the Kadmeians in their numbers
feasting all about the house of mighty Eteokles.

> There, stranger though he was, the driver of horses, Tydeus,
> was not frightened, alone among so many Kadmeians,
> but dared them to try their strength with him, and bested all of them
> easily, such might did Pallas Athene give him.
> The Kadmeians who lash their horses, in anger compacted
> an ambuscade of guile on his way home, assembling together
> fifty fighting men, and for these there were two leaders,
> Maion, Haimon's son, in the likeness of the immortals,
> with the son of Autophonos, Polyphontes stubborn in battle.
> On these men Tydeus let loose a fate that was shameful.
> He killed them all, except that he let one man get home again,
> letting Maion go in obedience to the god's signs.

Conclusion
> *Recapitulation:* This was Tydeus, the Aitolian;
> *Proverbial Paraphrase:* yet he was father
> to a son worse than himself at fighting, better in conclave!

Again we notice that the recitation of the paradigm is epideictic in nature: Agamemnon praises the great deeds of Diomedes' father Tydeus. In contrast to the first group of paradigms where the epideictic recitation supports the *ethos* of the speaker, however, these support, as we have seen, an exhortation to act.

This particular paradigm that Agamemnon tells to Diomedes draws attention to itself in the context of an analysis of pronouncement stories, since everything in the recitation aims at the pregnant words of the last sentence, which are even more effectively antithetical in the Greek original: "yet he was father to a son worse than himself at fighting, better in conclave." This emphasis on a final saying, however, appears to be an accidental resemblance, since it is unusual for a Homeric paradigm to have such a poignant ending. The purpose of the final words, indeed, is to incite Diomedes to action, and in this regard it reminds one of a pronouncement story. But this feature is not characteristic of other Homeric paradigms.

Diomedes does not react in words to Agamemnon's challenge. He accepts the reprimand—in fact he seems to presuppose that part of the role of a king is to provoke his men thus (4.412ff). In addition, the scene gives an ironic cast to the exploits during the battle that soon will ensue (Book 5, "The Aristeia of Diomedes"). Diomedes' companion Sthenelos, son of Capaneus who, along with Tydeus, was one of the seven against Thebes, points out to the king that, in the end, the sons ("epigons") were more successful than their fathers in obeying the gods and so conquering Thebes. For our concern, however, the lesser success of the father is irrelevant. Sthenelus' "correction" highlights the quality of both the father and the son, adding richer dimensions to the overall episode. Our primary concern is Agamemnon's recitation of the paradigm, for it confirms the statement that Diomedes should act because his father acted.

B. *Addressed to a God or Goddess*

A special kind of hortatory function occurs in a context where someone appeals to a god or goddess for help. In these instances, the paradigm supports a plea to the god or goddess to repeat what has been done before. A clear instance is Diomedes' praying to Athena at the beginning of his great exploits on the battlefield:

Homer, *Iliad* 5.115-118

Introduction:

Exhortation: Hear me now,
Atrytone, daughter of Zeus of the aegis:
Paradigmatic Rationale for the Exhortation
if ever before in kindliness you stood by my father
through the terror of fighting, be my friend now also, Athene;

Conclusion

Exhortation: grant me that I may kill this man and come within spearcast,
who shot me before I could see him,
and now boasts over me, saying
I cannot live to look much longer on the shining sunlight.

The important and distinctive feature in this kind of appeal lies in the power of the argument that the thing now hoped for has been performed once already by the person addressed. It is not so much the "what" as the "that" which counts. As in the instances where the speaker addresses a human, so in these instances praise plays an important role. But now, the praise applies directly to the one being addressed rather than to someone else.

A similar incident occurs in the remark of Achilles to his mother, Thetis, when he asks her to go to Olympus to move Zeus to steer things in his favor:

Homer, *Iliad* 1.393-407

Introduction:

Exhortation: You then, if you have power to, protect your own son, going to
Olympus and supplicating Zeus,
if ever before now either by word you comforted Zeus' heart or by action.
Paradigmatic Rationale for the Exhortation
Since it is many times in my father's halls I have heard you
making claims
Paradigmatic Confirmation of the Rationale

when you said you only among the immortals
beat aside shameful destruction from Kronos' son the dark-misted
that time when all the other Olympians sought to bind him,
Hera and Poseidon and Pallas Athene. Then you,
goddess, went and set him free from his shackles, summoning
in speed the creature of the hundred hands to tall Olympus,
that creature the gods name Briareus, but all men
Aigaios' son, but he is far greater in strength than his father.
He, rejoicing in the glory of it, sat down by Kronion,
and the rest of the blessed gods were frightened and gave up binding him.

Introduction:
    Exhortation: Sit beside him and take his knees and remind him of these things now....

In this instance Achilles includes the praise in the recitation of the confirming paradigm: "you only among the immortals beat aside shameful destruction from Kronos' son." Achilles has often heard her tell how she, of all the gods, stood by Zeus when the others wanted to have him fettered in irons (1.397-406). By thus reminding her of her relations with Zeus, Achilles can all the easier persuade her and provide her with an argument to use when she approaches Zeus (1.406-407; cf. 1.503-510).

3. Contrary in Support of a Dissuasive (Apotreptic) Thesis

If advice (deliberative, symbouleutic rhetoric) is designed to persuade a person to undertake a certain action, as in the discussion above, the rhetoric is hortatory (protreptic), but if it is designed to dissuade a person from performing a certain action, it is dissuasive (apotreptic) (Aristotle, Rhet 1.3.3). Paradigms occur in the *Iliad* in both kinds of situations, so we will now turn to one that features dissuasion.

A paradigm in the service of dissuasion exists in the story of Meleager, told by Phoenix in the Presbeia (9.529-599) as a part of his great effort to make Achilles change his mind and take up arms again. We summarize the story as told by Phoenix:

Summary of Homer, *Iliad* 9.529-599
Phoenix first takes us to the war between the Couretes and the Aetolians around Calydon (529-532), before giving the background of the conflict; viz., that Artemis in anger had sent a boar to ravage the territory of the Aetolians and that Meleager had killed it. After this event, strife arose between the Curetes and the Aetolians over the spoils. As long as Meleager fought for the Aetolians, everything went well. It then happened, however, that he got angry at this mother and stayed at home with his wife Cleopatra (550-556, with the excurses on her parents, Idas and Marpessa, 557-566). Phoenix explains the reason why Meleager became angry and stayed at home: he was furious at his mother because she had cursed him and

delivered her son up to die for killing her brother (567-572). Meleager remained adamant even in the face of increasingly intense supplication; only when the city was in uttermost peril was he moved by Cleopatra to take up arms again (687-596). He eventually saved the city, even if it was too late for him to get the gifts that had originally been promised him (597-599).

Initially the paradigm has a positive ring, since Meleager apparently serves as a model of action for Achilles, as is clear from Phoenix's introduction:

Homer, *Iliad* 9.524-528

Introduction
Thus it was in the old days also, the deeds that we hear of
from the great men,
    Thesis: when the swelling anger descended upon them.
The heroes would take gifts; they would listen, and be persuaded.

Paradigmatic Confirmation of the Thesis
For I remember this action of old, it is not a new thing,
and how it went; you are all my friends, I will tell it among you.

As the story proceeds, it is not simply a positive confirmation of the thesis, but it functions as an argument from the contrary. Phoenix ends on a very strong note, warning Achilles not to copy Meleager, who fought too late to be awarded gifts:

Homer, *Iliad* 9:598-605

Conclusion
    Recapitulation: yet these no longer would make good
their many and gracious gifts; yet he drove back the evil from them.
    Dissuasive Thesis: Listen, then; do not have such a thought in your mind; let not the spirit within you turn you that way dear friend. It would be worse
to defend the ships after they are burning. No, with gifts promised
go forth.
    Rationale: The Achaians will honour you as they would an immortal.
    Recapitulation of the Contrary: But if without gifts you go into the fighting
where men perish,
your honour will no longer be as great, though you drive back the battle.

Achilles does not accept Phoenix's advice. Rather, he corrects him and invalidates the point that he makes of the paradigmatic story—that one will be lacking in honor if one fights too late. He does not dispute the story of Meleager as such, but he challenges its relevance for himself. He fastens on the word "honor" ($\tau\iota\mu\acute{\eta}$) and claims for himself an honor that goes beyond that which can be obtained by fighting:

Homer, *Iliad* 9.606-610
   Then in answer to him spoke Achilles of the swift feet:
   Phoenix my father, aged, illustrious, such honour is a thing
   I need not. I think I am honoured already in Zeus' ordinance
   which will hold me here beside my curved ships as long as life's wind
   stays in my breast, as long as my knees have their spring beneath me.

Hermogenes' elaboration of a chreia exhibits the importance of a rationale in support of a thesis (Hock and O'Neil: 177). The addition of a rationale to a thesis forms a rhetorical syllogism, which rhetoricians since Aristotle call an enthymeme (Kennedy: 7, 16-17, 49-51; Mack and Robbins: 58, 60, 78-79, 120-123, 125-126, 199-200). In an enthymeme, the rationale provides a premise for the thesis: "Do this because ...." After Hermogenes presents the rationale, he presents the argument from the contrary, and now we see the potential for this next step in an environment of dissuasive argumentation. Since the argument from the contrary works together with the rationale to support an initial thesis (Rhet ad Her 4.43.56-57; cf. 4.18.25-26), it can be especially important in an argument against a certain kind of action. As Phoenix attempts to dissuade Achilles, the rationale he presents in the form of a paradigm turns out to be an argument from the contrary: "Do not do this, because Meleager did it once with bad result."

4. Rationale for the Speaker's Disposition toward Action

Another function for a paradigm is as a rationale for the speaker's disposition toward his own action. This kind of function for a paradigm occurs in Hephaestus' story of his own (literal) downfall at the end of the first book of the *Iliad*. In this instance, the overall environment is dissuasive argumentation as he tries to calm down his mother Hera who is so upset with Zeus. But the point of our interest is the particular rationale he presents and the means by which he defends the rationale. His rationale is based on his own personal circumstance: "Sorry though I be I shall not be able to do anything"; and he confirms his rationale with a paradigm:

Homer, *Iliad* 1.586-594

Introduction

   Dissuasive Thesis: Have patience, my mother, and endure it, though you be saddened,
   Rationale presenting the Speaker's Disposition toward Action: for fear that, dear as you are, I see you before my own eyes
   struck down, and then sorry though I be I shall not be able to do anything.

Paradigmatic Confirmation of the Rationale
It is too hard to fight against the Olympian.
There was a time once before now I was minded to help you,

and he caught me by the foot and threw me from the magic threshold,
and all day long I dropped helpless, and about sunset
I landed in Lemnos, and there was not much life left in me.

Conclusion

After that fall it was the Sintian men who took care of me.

Another instance occurs in the story of Lycurgus, told by Diomedes to Glaucus to explain why he is not willing to fight with him if he be a god:

Homer, *Iliad* 6.128-142

Introduction

Thesis about the Speaker's Own Disposition toward Action: But if you are some one of the immortals come down from the bright sky,
know that I will not fight against any god of the heaven,

Paradigmatic Rationale for the Speaker's Disposition

since even the son of Dryas, Lykourgos the powerful, did not
live long; he who tried to fight with the gods of the bright sky,
who once drove the fosterers of rapturous Dionysos
headlong down the sacred Nyseian hill, and all of them
shed and scattered their wands on the ground, stricken with an ox-goad
by murderous Lykourgos, while Dionysos in terror
dived into the salt surf, and Thetis took him to her bosom,
frightened, with the strong shivers upon him at the man's blustering.
But the gods who live at their ease were angered with Lykourgos,
and the son of Kronos struck him to blindness, nor did he live long
afterwards, since he was hated by all the immortals.

Conclusion

Recapitulation: Therefore neither would I be willing to fight with the blessed gods;
Contrary: but if you are one of those mortals....

In this instance, the paradigm takes the role of the rationale. The reason for this relation, of rationale to thesis appears to lie in the personal form of the apodosis of the thesis: "...I will not fight against any god of the heaven." Instead of the thesis being a general maxim, then, it moves into the arena of the personal action of the speaker himself. This means that the thesis functions in the domain of personal example, and a paradigm, since it also functions in the domain of personal example, can readily function as its rationale.

The reader will notice that the paradigms in the last two instances support an apotreptic argument, that is, they contribute to the attempt to dissuade someone. This means, therefore, that this function has a kinship with the function of the Meleager paradigm discussed in the previous section. There is, however, an essential difference in the structure of the argument. The last two paradigms support the speaker's personal rationale for his argument ("I shall not be able to do anything"; "I would not fight against any god of the heaven"). When a paradigm functions as the rationale for a hortatory or dissuasive argument, the story itself bears the weight of the argument; that is, the story itself rather than one's opinion or predisposition about one's own action provides the rationale (Priam should eat because Niobe ate, Diomedes should act because his father Tydeus acted, Achilles should *not* do as Meleager did because Meleager did *not* receive the gifts). In the instances where paradigms support one's own personal disposition toward action, however, the paradigm provides a rationale for that disposition rather than for the hortatory or dissuasive thesis about the other person's action. In light of this, support for a personal disposition is akin to the next function we will discuss, namely one in which the paradigm confirms one's understanding of a situation. The essential difference in the next type is that the situation is not one that involves a choice of action, but only of reaction.

5. *Confirmation of the Speaker's Understanding of a Situation*

When the mythological precedent is used as a means of confirming one's understanding of a situation, it will often at the same time suggest a course of action and so have the effect of an argument. But the main function of the myth under this heading is the appeal to a general situation on the basis of one or more mythological incidents. The myth may be used as a means of understanding something that has taken place in the past or that happens presently. In either case, the mythological paradigm teaches reaction rather than action.

A. *In the Past*

A clear instance of myth functioning to confirm the speaker's understanding of a past situation is present in the story of Ate ("Blindness" or "Folly") told by Agamemnon (19.72-144) in explanation of his behavior towards Achilles in the episodes that make up the beginning of our *Iliad*:

Homer, *Iliad* 19.87-133

Introduction

Thesis: yet I am not responsible
Paradigmatic Rationale: but Zeus is, and Destiny, and Erinys the mist-walking
who in assembly caught my heart in the savage delusion
on that day I myself stripped from him the prize of Achilles.
Yet what could I do?
Generalized Rationale: It is the god who accomplishes all things

> *Paraphrase of Paradigmatic and Generalized Rationales*: Delusion is the eldest daughter of Zeus, the accursed
> who deludes us all; her feet are delicate and they step not
> on the firm earth, but she walks the air above men's heads
> and leads them astray. She has entangled others before me.
>
> **Paradigmatic Confirmation of the Rationales**
>
> (Summary of 19.95-133)
> Even Zeus was one day beguiled by Ate. On the day when Alcmene was to give birth to Heracles Zeus proudly announced that one of his own blood would be born to reign over Argos. Hera saw her chance and had Zeus in his folly swear a mighty oath to confirm it (95-113). Hera then hurried to Argos, where the wife of Sthenelus, son of Perseus, was with child. Hera made her deliver Eurystheus two months early, while the labor of Alcmene was checked. Then she triumphantly told Zeus that there had in fact been born someone of his own stock, by the line of Perseus, who was to be ruler of the Argives (96-124). Then Zeus in sudden anger flung Ate from heaven, wherefrom she came to the world of men. Even so Zeus had to see his dear Son, Heracles, toil for Eurystheus (125-133).

Agamemnon has obviously been the victim of Ate, just as Zeus once was a victim of the same Ate. The myth is his frame of reference. Agamemnon maintains that he is not to blame. That Zeus one day was beguiled by Ate is his model for understanding what really went on in the quarrel with Achilles.

B. *In the Present*

In other instances, a mythological paradigm may be used to confirm the speaker's understanding of a present situation. This function is well represented by the consolation speech by Dione to Aphrodite in the fifth book (5.382-415), after the goddess of love has tried her hand in battle and has been wounded in the wrist by Diomedes. Dione relates the wounding of her daughter to a number of (more or less) similar cases to help her bear her plight:

> Homer, *Iliad* 5.382-403
>
> **Introduction**
>
> *Hortatory Thesis*: Have patience, my child, and endure it, though you be saddened.
> *Paradigmatic Rationale*: For many of us who have our homes on Olympus endure things
> from men, when ourselves we inflict hard pain on each other.
>
> **Paradigmatic Confirmation of the Rationale**
>
> Ares had to endure it when strong Ephialtes and Otos,
> sons of Aloeus, chained him in bonds that were too strong for him,

and three months and ten he lay chained in the brazen cauldron;
and now might Ares, insatiable of fighting, have perished,
had not Eëriboia, their stepmother, the surpassingly lovely,
brought word to Hermes, who stole Ares away out of it
as he was growing faint and the hard bondage was breaking him.
Hera had to endure it when the strong son of Amphitryon
struck her beside the right breast with a tri-barbed arrow,
so that the pain he gave her could not be quieted. Hades
the gigantic had to endure with the rest the flying arrow
when this self-same man, the son of Zeus of the aegis,
struck him among the dead men at Pylos, and gave him to agony;
but he went up to the house of Zeus and to tall Olympus
heavy at heart, stabbed through and through with pain, for the arrow
was driven into his heavy shoulder, and his spirit was suffering.
But Paiëon, scattering medicines that still pain,
healed him, since he was not made to be one of the mortals.

Conclusion
Brute, heavy-handed, who thought nothing of the bad he was doing,
who with his archery hurt the gods that dwell on Olympus!

In this story, and the one before it, we see the process by which inductive argumentation and deductive argumentation work hand in hand. In the first story, Agamemnon juxtaposed a paradigmatic rationale, "but Zeus is (responsible), and Destiny, and Erinys the mist-walking...," with a more generalized rationale, "The god accomplishes all things." The second statement is more generalized, because it does not limit itself to: "The god accomplished *this event*." To confirm this line of reasoning, Agamemnon presents a specific case when Opus was beguiled by Ate. It is informative that Agamemnon does not try to assert and confirm a yet more generalized form of argumentation, like, "Gods can accomplish anything." His concern lies with one specific case, namely, "I am not responsible [for a specific act that I did]." In support of his thesis about the specific case, he presents a partially generalized rationale: "The god accomplishes all things" and immediately confirms it with one specific case: "even Zeus was one day beguiled by Ate."

In the second story, Dione presents a rationale based on a number of cases: "For many of us who have our homes on Olympus endure things from men, when ourselves we inflict hard pain on each other" (*Iliad* 5.384-385). This rationale does not move to the level of a fully generalized principle like, "All Olympic gods hurt one another." Rather, it is a paradigmatic rationale based on a number of cases. What is needed to confirm such a rationale, then, is a list of those cases. Dione's recitation contains precisely this: (a) when Otus and Ephialtes chained Ares; (b) when Amphitryon's mighty son shot Hera with an arrow; and (c) when the same mighty son pierced Hades' shoulder with an arrow. In both instances, one concerned with a past event and one with a present event, one or more paradigms are recited to confirm the speaker's understanding of a particular situation. The speaker articulates his understanding, presents a partially generalized rationale to support his view, then recites one or more paradigms to confirm his rationale.

Our investigation of Homeric paradigms has shown that a paradigm is a summary of a significant situation in the past that is placed in a speech at a particular point to establish the *ethos* of the speaker or support the thesis or some part of the argument. A paradigm, in other words, performs a function in a speech. This is how Martin Dibelius understood a paradigm, so his rhetorical understanding of a paradigm was correct. The problem lies in the assertion that the early Christian stories that we call pronouncement stories functioned as paradigms, since they do not have this function in the Gospels. Dibelius' designation of the pronouncement stories as paradigms presupposes the existence of "the early Christian sermon" as a context for the pronouncement stories, and for this purpose he posited a sermon containing the four basic parts of the speech as Aristotle described them (Mack and Robbins: 3-6). There is one paradigm in the pronouncement stories, namely Jesus' summary of David's taking of the showbread for himself and his associates (Mark 2:25-26 par.; see Dean-Otting and Robbins in this volume). But the stories themselves are not paradigms, but abbreviated, expanded, or elaborated chreiai.

Confusion between paradigms and chreiai can easily exist, since a speaker can also use chreiai in a speech. The difference is that a chreia is a form, albeit a rhetorical form, while a paradigm is a function. The evidence that a paradigm is a function becomes clearer when we extend the investigation to Pindar and the tragedians, for in this literature simply a reference to a particular person may be a paradigm. This is of special interest, since the essential characteristic of a chreia is that it is a statement or action attributed to a particular person (Hock and O'Neil: 83). This means that a chreia is a form that may stand on its own. A chreia may be used in a speech, and used as a paradigm, but a chreia is not at base a function but a form. For the evidence, we will turn first to Pindar, then to the tragedians.

Paradigms in Pindar

In the choral lyrics of Pindar, myths may be summarized in an exuberant way in order to lend luster to the addressee of the poem or to the occasion of the poem (cf. e.g., *Pythian* 6.27-46), or, on the contrary, there may be just hints, like: "You, son of Diodotos, matched the warrior

Meleagros, and matched Hektor and Amphiaraos, when you breathed out your youth in all its flower-time..." (*Isthmian* 7.31-34). The mythological person has been so invested with meaning that he or she has become a symbol of prowess, and so it suffices to mention the name.

Pindar's choral odes in celebration of the victors in the great panhellenic games (from the first half of the fifth century B.C.) are full of mythology. Often the place of the victory and its presiding deity, or the home-town of the victor, or the kind of competition in which he was victorious will spark off some more or less densely compressed version of a myth. These myths are sometimes developed through what seem to us rather free associations; for example in Nemean VII, apropos the "recompenses for labour that are found in echoing words of song":

(15) But I hold that the name of Odysseus
Is more than his sufferings
Because of Homer's sweet singing;

For on his untruths and winged cunning
A majesty lies.
Art beguiles and cheats with its tales,
And often the heart of the human herd is blind.
If it could have seen the truth,
Aias would not, in wrath about armour,
Have driven a smooth sword through his breast.
After Achilles he was the strongest in battle
Of all who were sent in fast ships
To fetch his wife for brown-haired Menelaos
By the speeding breath of the straight West Wind

To Ilos' city. To all comes
The wave of death and falls unforeseen
Even on him who foresees it.
        (Nemean VII, 21-32, tr. Bowra)

This is typical of Pindar's way of composing; a few lines further he goes on to speak of the fate of Neoptolemus, the son of Achilles. Both Ajax and Neoptolemus are connected with Aegina, the native island of Sogenes, the young victor who is celebrated here. The mythical allusions have obvious relevance as frames of reference. It is also possible to sort out a number of mythical allusions or stories that are paradigmatic in a somewhat stricter sense. But a neat classification and cataloguing of myths in Pindar is hardly feasible in the present context. We propose to give only a sample of typical instances here.

When Pindar sings in honor of Hagesidamus of Western Locri, he as usual finds reason to glorify the city. There then follows a brief allusion to

Heracles and an exhortation underpinned by a mythological comparison, before the poet pauses with one of his numerous *gnomai*:

> (16) For Simplicity rules the city
> Of the Lokrians in the West,
> And their care is for Kalliopa
> And brazen Ares.
> —Even prodigious Herakles
> Was routed in battle with Kyknos.
> Let Hagesidamos, who has won in the boxing at Olympia,
> Thank Ilas as Patroklos thanked Achilles.
> One born to prowess
> May be whetted and stirred
> To win huge glory
> If a God be his helper.
> (Olympian X, 14=22, tr. Bowra)

The abrupt allusion to Heracles may be a tactful hint that the victor only succeeded in spite of severe difficulties, which has a mythical precedent. All the more reason then to thank the trainer Ilas, just as Patroclus thanked Achilles.

The seventh Isthmian—which opens, incidentally, with the poet heaping myth upon myth about Thebes, the famous home-town of the victor Strepsiadas—also provides examples of myth being used as paradigm:

> (17) You, son of Diodotos, matched
> The warrior Meleagros, and matched
> Hektor and Amphiaraos,
> When you breathed out your youth in all its flower-time
>
> In the foremost press of the fighters,
> Where the bravest kept up the struggle of battle
> In desparate hopes.
> (Isthmian VII, 31-36, tr. Bowra)

While these are concise cases of parallel figures, the poet later makes use of the paradigm for the sake of illustration or corroboration of a general insight:

> (18) If a man peers at what is afar,
> He is too small to reach
> The bronze-floored home of the Gods.
> Winged Pagasos threw off
>
> His master Bellerophon
> When he wished to come to the sky's dwellings

And the company of Zeus.
A most bitter end
Awaits what is sweet in despite of right
   (Isthmian VII, 43-48, tr. Bowra)

Another example is that of Antilochus in the ode to Xenocrates of Acragas, brother of the tyrant Theron; Xenocrates won the chariot-race in Delphi in 490 B.C. Here Pindar is in fact more interested in the son of the victor, young Thrasyboulos, whom he exhorts to honour his parents for the length of their days by "quoting" some words of Chiron to Achilles. He then continues:

(19) Antilochus was a warrior long ago
Who kept this purpose.
For he died for his father,
Braving the murderous Memnon, prince of the Ethiopian host.
– Nestor's chariot was held
(An arrow of Paris pierced his horse): and Memnon
Came on with mighty spear.
And the old Messenian, shaken at heart,
Cried upon his son.
That cry cast forth

Did not fall to the ground.
There he stood fast, a more than man,
And paid his death for the rescue of his father:
And gained, through his tremendous deed,
Among younger generations,
This fame, that he of the men of old
Was best son to this father.
   It was long ago:
Of men now, Thrasyboulos has come nearest
To what a father would have,

And follows in all
His uncle's paths of splendour.
   (Pythian VI, 27-46, tr. Bowra)

The above sample could be multiplied quantitatively, even if we collected only the instances of mythology that had in some limited sense a paradigmatic use. Qualitatively, however, we would not get any further. Formally, the paradigmatic use of myth in Pindar ranges from bare allusion (16) to relatively straightforward and complete stories (19). Sometimes there is direct speech: the Antilochus story (19) follows the sentence spoken by Chiron; in Pythian VIII, the character of Amphiaraus compares Alcmaeon, the victorious leader of the sons of the Seven against

Thebes, with Adrastus, who saw the death of his son. But a fundamental difference between Pindar and Homer lies exactly in this, that paradigms in Homer are used by the characters, while in Pindar they are only adduced by the poet. In the highly dramatized Homeric epic, the paradigm has a function in the plot—the mimesis of reality that is acted out in front of us. In the victory ode, Pindar as a real poet talks to real persons. It may be interesting to note in this connection that in the *Iliad*, a speaker (Agamemnon) only once (4.274f) has to refer to hearsay, while Pindar refers much more often to how "the saying goes."

As to function, it may be briefly said that the paradigm in Pindar a) provides a parallel and so a mythical standard; b) is used to underpin an exhortation or a warning; and c) is used to illustrate or corroborate a maxim.

GREEK TRAGEDY

We proceed now to Greek tragedy, but in only the most cursory manner. There are obvious differences in the way the three tragedians employ mythological paradigms, but the tendency is towards the use of the mythical precedent less as an argument than as a means of reflection. This is especially so in the cases (e.g., Aeschylus' *Choephoroe* 602-622; Sophocles' *Antigone* 944-987) where the chorus comments on the action or the suffering of the protagonist, but even in dialogue there is rather little use of myth as an argument, and more in the way of simple parallelism. At the same time, the plasticity and narrative vividness of the myths are ever decreasing. In fact, mythological matter may not lend itself easily to crystallization in distinct situations. For gods and heroes are, after all, rather distant characters.

Without further justification of criteria chosen and decisions made, we will present a list of mythological paradigms in the extant works of each of the three tragedians, placing those paradigms that occur in lyrical (not only choral) passages to the left and those in the *rhesis* or dialogue to the right. We shall also indicate briefly to which person(s) the example refers.

a. *Survey of paradigms*

AESCHYLUS

	Lyrical	*Dialogue*
Agamemnon	1022ff Asclepius	870 Geryon
	1140ff Aedon	1040f Heracles
		1629f Orpheus
Choephoroe	602ff Althaea, Scylla,	

	Lyrical	*Dialogue*
	Lemnians	
	831 Perseus	
Eumenides		441 Ixion
		640ff Zeus
		717f Ixion
Supplices	57ff Aedon	214 Apollo
Prometheus	425ff Atlas	345ff Atlas, Typhos

SOPHOCLES

Electra	147ff Niobe, Aedon	
	837ff Amphiaraus	
Antigone	823ff Niobe	
	944ff Danae, Lycurgus, Cleopatra	
Trachiniae	497ff Zeus, Poseidon, Hades	
Philoctetes	676ff Ixion	

EURIPIDES

Alcestis	903ff ("somebody")	357ff Orpheus
		1118 Gorgo
Medea	1282ff Ino	543f Orpheus
		1342f Scylla
Hippolytus	545ff Iole, Semele	337 Pasiphae
		451ff Zeus, Eos
Hecuba		886f Danaids, Lemnians
Supplices	1078f Oedipus	
Hercules	1016ff Danaids, Procne	1297f Ixion
		1315ff Zeus
Troades		948ff Zeus
Electra		856 Gorgo
Helena	375ff Callisto, Merops's daughter	
Phoenissae		455f Gorgo
		1185 Ixion
		1675 Danaids
Orestes		1520 Gorgo
		588ff Penelope, Telemachus
Iphigenia in Aulidi		1211 Orpheus
Bacchae		337ff Actaeon

In Aeschylus, Sophocles, and Euripides there are 14, 6, and 24 places respectively where paradigms occur (Hodler). The greater number in Euripides is a result, partially, of a greater number of extant plays. Nevertheless, Sophocles is somewhat sparing in comparison with both Aeschylus and Euripides. While Aeschylus uses slightly more paradigms in dialogue than in lyrical passages, and Euripides amplifies this preference, Sophocles is unique in that all his paradigms occur outside of the dialogue proper, either in choral songs or in parts of the plays where the chorus is involved.

There is a wide range of uses and forms in the different instances in the table. In many places there is only the barest reference, and no mythological story; for example, in the three instances from the *Phoenissae*, here quoted in context:

> (20) Refrain fierce look and passion's story breath:
> The Gorgon's severed head thou seest not;
> Thou seest thine own brother hither come...
> (21)   From the ladder flew
> His limbs abroad wide-whirling slingstone-like:
> Heavenward his hair streamed, earthward rained his blood:
> Hands, feet – Ixion on his wheel seemed he –
> Whirled round. To earth he fell, a corpse flameblasted.
> (22) That night shall prove me one of Danaus' Daughters
>   (*Phoenissae*, 454ff, 1182ff, 1675, tr. Way)

Or take the first instance from the *Eumenides*:

> (23) a solemn supplicant in the manner of Ixion
>   (*Eumenides* 441, tr. Lloyd-Jones)

Or Clytaemnestra's comparison of Agamemnon with a mythical monster:

> (24) And if he had been dead, as many stories reported,
> then with three bodies, like a second Geryon,
> he could have claimed to receive a threefold cloak of earth...
>   (*Agamemnon* 869ff, tr. Lloyd-Jones)

A number of Euripidean paradigms, especially in dialogue, are of this short and allusive type, while he also has a few longer ones; e.g., *Medea* 1282ff and *Hippolytus* 545ff. In Aeschylus most examples also amount to less than three verses, although he has two long ones, *Choephoroe* 602ff and above all *Prometheus* 345ff, running into 27 verses. In Sophocles, on the other hand, all paradigms or clusters of paradigms are at least six verses long.

Another peculiarity with Sophocles is that, with one exception (*Electra* 147ff), all his mythological paradigms are presented as straightforward narratives. There are instances of this in Aeschylus (e.g. *Choeph.* 602ff) and in Euripides too, particularly in those cases where the poet takes his time (e.g. *Hipp.* 545ff; *Alcestis* 903ff; *Medea*, 1282ff). But in the two latter poets, we also often find cases of simple identification (see items 22 and 24 above), rhetorical question, sheer exclamation, and comparison.

PARADIGMS IN THE NEW TESTAMENT

When we turn to the New Testament, we find paradigms from the Bible functioning in ways similar to the paradigms in Homer, Pindar, and the Greek tragedians. The account of Plucking Grain on the Sabbath contains perhaps the most notable instance of a paradigm in a pronouncement story (Mark 2:23-28 par.; Mack and Robbins: 107-141). From the perspective of this essay, it is striking that the David paradigm is Jesus' opening statement to the Pharisees in all of the accounts. Can the function of the paradigms in the Homeric tradition help the interpreter to ascertain the function of the paradigm in Jesus' response? The opening statement could be, as in the speech of Nestor or Diomedes, a confirmation of the *ethos* of the speaker. If this is the case, the Pharisees' statement means "By what authority have you given the disciples permission to pluck grain on the sabbath?" and Jesus' response means "My ancestor David took the bread of the Presence from the house of God on the sabbath, and both he and those with him ate it." The paradigm functions, then, as an authoritative precedent for Jesus, Son of David.

Another alternative would be for the paradigm to function as a confirmation of the speaker's understanding of the situation, in the manner of Agamemnon's telling about Ate or Dione's recounting of the sufferings of Ares, Hera, and Hades. In this instance, Jesus does not hear the Pharisees' statement as a direct challenge to his own authority but as a misunderstanding of the situation. With the David paradigm, Jesus explains that this is the kind of situation that can naturally arise when a leader and his associates are traveling around together, away from the provisions made available through hospitality in a household. Jesus' speech acquires additional complexity when it ends with "The Son of man is lord even of the sabbath." At this point, Jesus has introduced a generalized rationale, like "It is the god who accomplishes all things," in Agamemnon's speech where he defends his taking of the girl Chriseis from Achilles. Jesus' response not only confirms the *ethos* of Jesus and explains Jesus' understanding of the situation, but it also provides a rationale for the disciples' action when they are with Jesus.[1] For the purposes of this essay, it is most important to see that the term paradigm applies to Jesus' recital of the David incident in his elaborated response to the Pharisees. The overall story is an elaborated chreia, not a paradigm, as Dibelius would have it. Jesus' abbreviated recitation of the David incident is a paradigm that Jesus introduces in his discourse.

In the Lukan version of the Beelzebul Controversy (Luke 11:14-36; cf. Matt 12:38-42), an even more extensively elaborated chreia, Jesus introduces a series of paradigms to respond to the request for a sign: Jonah, the Queen of the South, and the men of Nineveh. For a rhetorical analysis of the function of these paradigms in Jesus' speech, see Mack-Robbins: 185-191. Suffice it to say here that the basic function of the paradeigmata is to provide a rationale for giving only the sign of Jonah to this generation (Edwards).

Another well-known instance of a paradigmatic argument occurs in the opening sermon of Jesus in Luke 4:16-30. Again, the paradigms provide a rationale, in this instance a rationale for not healing in one's own country. Elijah healed only the son of a widow of Zarephath in the land of Sidon, not anyone in Israel; and Elisha cleansed only Naaman the Syrian, not any lepers in Israel (Luke 4:24-27).

The speeches in Acts also contain paradigms. The most extensive use of paradigmatic argumentation occurs in Stephen's speech, where he recites the exploits of Abraham (7:2-8), the patriarchs (7:9-16), Moses (7:17-44), Joshua (7:45), David (7:46), and Solomon (7:47). The speech introduces an elaborated paradigmatic rationale by Stephen in response to the charge that he speaks "against this holy place and the law" (7:13).

The most well-known paradigms in Pauline discourse occur in Romans 4 and Galatians 3, where Paul introduces God's reckoning of Abraham as righteous prior to his circumcision as a rationale for faith as the means by which a Gentile receives the grace of God. The use of personal example in the Pauline letters and the Pastorals has also been well exhibited by Benjamin Fiore's excellent study (Fiore: 164-231). In addition, the epistle to the Hebrews has an extensive paradigmatic argument in chapter 11, which Michael Cosby has analyzed at length (Cosby). The epistle of James introduces Abraham as a paradigmatic rationale, but in this instance the emphasis is on works as a completion of faith (2:18-24). In the same context, the epistle introduces the reception by Rahab the

---

[1] The rationale is nurtured into a rhetorical syllogism, an enthymeme, when the story adds the saying about the sabbath being made for man (see Mack-Robbins: 123-129).

harlot of the messengers sent by Joshua as a completion of a life of faith (2:25).

Conclusion

The import of the preceding analysis is the correction of a misunderstanding in investigation of the Gospels that has prevented a full-scale study of paradigmatic argumentation in the New Testament. Paradigms are arguments from example. Thus, the term is appropriate when the emphasis lies on rhetorical function. Appropriate reference to the form of the recitation of an incident will discuss it as a narrative (*diegesis*) or a chreia. Either a narrative or a chreia may function in someone's discourse as a paradigm; that is, as an argument from example. A paradigm, therefore, is an inductive argument. Narratives or chreiai, on the other hand, are forms which may function paradigmatically or may provide an overall context for paradigmatic argumentation.

At present, many obvious investigations of the New Testament in the context of Mediterranean literature are waiting in the wings. Interpreters of New Testament epistles during the last two decades have progressively enriched analysis of their texts in the context of Mediterranean society and culture, and rhetorical investigations have been an important part of this expansion of the boundaries. A similar expansion of insights still awaits most of the units in the Gospels. Interpreters need to investigate the Gospels in the context of Homeric literature, Pindar, the tragedians, Plato's dialogues, the writings of Plutarch, etc., in order to acquire a base for understanding Christianity in the kind of diverse cultural situation that confronts it in our contemporary world. Paradigmatic argumentation is one means of expanding our understanding. Early Christians were unwilling to use the same incidents and people in their arguments that many people were using in Mediterranean society. This is part of their resistance as a subculture or counterculture. The way in which they engage in paradigmatic argumentation, however, has amazing similarities with the way in which paradigmatic argumentation was being employed throughout Mediterranean culture. It will serve New Testament interpreters well to engage in broader analyses that exhibit the distinctive aspects of early Christian argumentation in the setting of Mediterranean society and culture. If they do not, interpreters impose a ghettoized ideology on New Testament texts and on early Christianity (see Smith: 70-71).

WORKS CONSULTED

Aristotle
    1926   *The "Art" of Rhetoric*. Trans. J. H. Freese. Loeb Classical Library. Cambridge: Harvard University Press.

Butts, James R.
    1987   "The *Progymnasmata* of Theon: A New Text with Translation and Commentary." Ann Arbor: University Microfilms International.

Cosby, Michael R.
    1988   *The Rhetorical Composition and Function of Hebrews 11: In Light of Example Lists in Antiquity*. Macon, GA: Mercer University Press.

Dibelius, Martin
    1919   *Die Formgeschichte des Evangeliums*. Tübingen: J.C.B. Mohr.
    1935   *From Tradition to Gospel*. Trans. B. L. Wolf. New York: Charles Scribner's Sons.

Fiore, Benjamin
    1986   *The Function of Personal Example in the Socratic and Pastoral Epistles*. Analecta Biblica 105. Rome: Biblical Institute Press.

Hock, Ronald F. and Edward N. O'Neil
    1986   *The Chreia in Ancient Rhetoric. Vol. I. The Progymnasmata*. Atlanta: Scholars.

Hodler, G.
    1956   *Untersuchungen zum Gebrauch mythologischer Beispiele in der attischen Tragödie*. Diss. Heidelberg.

Kennedy, George A.
    1984   *New Testament Interpretation through Rhetorical Criticism*. Chapel Hill: North Carolina Press.

Lattimore, Richard
    1951   *The Iliad of Homer*. Chicago: University of Chicago Press.

Mack, Burton L. and Vernon K. Robbins
    1989   *Patterns of Persuasion in the Gospels*. Sonoma: Polebridge.

Pindar
    1964   *Pindar*. Trans. C. M. Bowra. Oxford: Clarendon.

[Ps. Cicero]
    1954   *Rhetorica ad Herennium*. Trans. H. Caplan. Loeb Classical Library. Cambridge: Harvard University Press.

Robbins, Vernon K.
    1988a   "The Chreia." Pp. 1-23 in *Greco-Roman Literature and the New Testament: Selected Forms and Genres*. Ed. David E. Aune. Sources for Biblical Study 21. Atlanta: Scholars.

1988b   "Pronouncement Stories From a Rhetorical Perspective." *Foundations and Facts Forum* 4,2: 3-32.

Smith, Jonathan Z.
1990   *Drudgery Divine: On the Comparison of Early Christianities and the Religions of Late Antiquity.* Chicago: University of Chicago Press.

AUTHORIZING HUMOR: LUCIAN'S DEMONAX AND CYNIC RHETORIC

R. Bracht Branham
Emory University

ABSTRACT

Lucian's Demonax comprises a collection of humorous anecdotes about an eclectic Cynic philosopher and contains very little continuous narrative. This paper argues that the text reflects the deliberate choice of a rhetorical style cultivated above all by the Cynics, which systematically exploits the comic resources of surprise and incongruity and takes as its characteristic vehicle the chreia or pointed anecdote. Wit has an enthymematic character: it requires the audience to perform an act of mental collaboration that can be variously described as bridging a logical gap; moving between alien codes, frames of reference, or universes of discourse; or, in Koestler's classic formulation, "bisociating" divergent matrices of meaning. Demonax uses wit Lucianically to provoke his interlocutors to consider themselves and their situations from unexpected and often incongruous perspectives.

> Men practice rhetoric with speeches. They practice philosophy by being silent, by being playful, and, yes by Zeus, by being the butt of jokes and the jester.
> Plutarch, *Symposiaka*

Lucian's *Demonax* may well strike a modern reader as an oddity. Its title, ΔΗΜΩΝΑΚΤΟΣ ΒΙΟΣ or *The Life of Demonax*, leads us to expect a biographical account and yet it contains almost no continuous narrative. Instead, after a brief introduction, the work consists of a collection of short, jocular anecdotes about an Athenian philosopher whom Lucian claims to have known personally. It is in fact the primary source for Demonax's life (Jones: 91–92). But no attempt is made to join one story to the next, nor is the sage ever shown, like Socrates in Plato or Xenophon, discoursing philosophically on the immortality of the soul or tying hapless interlocutors in logical knots. The argument of this paper is that the *Demonax*'s formal oddity, unlike all Lucian's other works, reflects the deliberate choice of a rhetorical style cultivated above all by the Cynics, which systematically exploits the comic resources of surprise and incongruity and takes as its characteristic vehicle the *chreia,* or pointed anecdote. I wish first to highlight some of the salient features of Cynic rhetoric as they bear on the *Demonax* and Dio Chrysostom's *Diogenes* (Or.8) and then to explore how and why these authors chose to avail themselves of this particular tradition. Seen in this light both works emerge as interesting examples of the literary adaptation of a popular rhetorical procedure and as a point of intersection between oral and written performance.

That the comic *chreia* was the hallmark of the Cynic style can be confirmed by surveying the anecdotes preserved about the sect's founder, Diogenes of Sinope, in Diogenes Laertius. Almost everything we know of him is expressed in the form of anecdotes. This in itself is not distinctive since chreiai are told of philosophers and wise men generally. But it has long been recognized, even by casual readers, that the stories told about Diogenes are simply funnier than those Diogenes Laertius reports about other philosophers. D. R. Dudley takes this as an indication that the stories about him may well be true, but the opposite inference is equally possible (Dudley: 29 n. 2; for the best account of the *chreia* traditions about philosophers see Kindstrand: 217 ff.). The humor of the Cynic traditions about Diogenes reflect the polish of a self-consciously rhetorical practice which made optimal use of the argumentative resources of the short but memorable anecdote. Indeed, Cynic rhetoric drew praise on formal grounds from as discerning a critic as Demetrius, who notes in particular the importance of humor for the Cynic style (κυνικὸς τρόπος)[1]. If we ask why the comic anecdote would have been so assiduously cultivated by Diogenes' followers, several reasons seem obvious: Cynicism was from its inception a popular philosophy opposed to the learned theoretical teachings of Plato, and, later, of Zeno and Epicurus. What form would be better

---

[1] Demetrius shows himself keenly aware of the rhetoric of humor. While discussing the graces (χάριτες) of the elegant (γλαφυρός) style, he observes that the most potent grace (ἡ δυνατωτάτη χάρις) is created by introducing humor into an otherwise noncomic context; he cites as an example a jest of Xenophon made at the expense of a dour Persian (Demetrius: 134–5). Demetrius admires this technique precisely because the writer produces an effect ostensibly at odds with his material. He touches on the κυνικὸς τρόπος explicitly in two passages. In the first (Demetrius: 170), he notes the affinity between the pointed humor of Crates' encomium of the lentil and that of anecdotes and maxims generally (χρεία, γνώμη). Later (Demetrius: 259–61) in discussing the stylistic sources of forcefulness (δεινότης), Demetrius observes that it is created in comedy and Cynic literature by the element of playfulness (ἐκ παιδιᾶς); he cites as examples a line of Crates' "Cynic epic" and a *chreia* about Diogenes at the Olympics: "At the conclusion of the hoplite race Diogenes ran up and proclaimed himself victor over all mankind—in nobility of character (καλοκἀγαθίᾳ)." Demetrius observes that the *chreia* creates laughter (γελᾶται) and astonishment (θαυμάζεται), and has a gentle bite (ὑποδάκνει). He then quotes another *chreia* about Diogenes and observes that its wit is covertly pointed and significant (ἡ κευθομένη ἔμφασις). This complexity of effect, he says, is why the whole genre (εἶδος) of Cynic discourse (λόγος) is like a dog that wags its tail and bites at the same time. Cf. Lucian, *Bis Accusatus* 33. (All references to Lucian's text are to M. D. Macleod's OCT editions.)

suited to propagate such a philosophy than anecdotes that were short enough to be easily remembered and made memorable and significant by their calculated use of comic incongruity and surprise? The perspectives enabled by humor dovetail with central Cynic themes in ways that are hardly incidental. It is this which makes "Cynic rhetoric" a recognizable generic category, distinguished by its serious use of humor as a heuristic device. From this practice of "serious jesting" evolved a set of techniques—unexpectedness, emphasis, implicitness (the techniques of wit as analyzed by Koestler: 82-86)—by which humor was made a means of perception. This mode of writing is sometimes associated with the σπουδογέλοιος, or seriocomic performer, a term applied explicitly by Strabo to the Cynic Menippus (16.2.24 Kramer's ed.).

When I speak of Cynic rhetoric, therefore, I refer to a style of performance preserved in the chreiai about Cynics like Diogenes or Crates and elaborated formally by such writers as Dio Chrysostom and Lucian. Like any *chreia*, the Cynic anecdote may make its point through significant acts as well as words. The informing assumptions of Cynic rhetoric also form the theme of many Cynic chreiai: παρρησία, "freedom of speech," and ἀναίδεια, "freedom from shame in action," or simply "shamelessness." It was this freedom from shame or social constraint (νόμος) in speech and action that set the Cynic preacher apart from his fellows as one who had the gumption to tell embarrassing truths and was willing to risk social ostracism rather than conform to rules which he taught were nothing more than conventional prejudice (νόμος = δόξα). It was probably this antinomian tendency at the heart of Cynicism that led to the cultivation of the rhetorical possibilities of humor as a way of making the Cynic perspective accessible and persuasive to a larger audience.[2]

The defining qualities of the Cynic style are epitomized in the figure of Diogenes as preserved by tradition: a self-dramatizing iconoclast who would teach anyone who would listen, by paradox, hyperbole and subversive wit. In Theon's terms, most of the chreiai about him are oral (λογικαί) and voluntary (ἀποφαντικαί), placing him in a context to which his remark is a response. Though he is not infrequently answering a question, he is shown more typically reacting spontaneously to something he has seen or heard. (By contrast, almost all the stories about Demonax present him responding to a specific question. The questioner himself is often identified.) If we attempt to classify the form of the sayings themselves according to rhetorical categories, we could find examples of

---

[2] The rise of Cynicism was accompanied by the development of new forms of satiric and parodic literature. Unfortunately, these are poorly documented. See, however, A. A. Long: 636–9, and Martin Drury: 851–4; cf. Branham: chap. 1. For the Menippean tradition, see Relihan.

most of the standard types used by Theon (e.g., syllogistic, symbolic, witty, wishful, etc.), but that will tell us little, given the size of the collection. Theon himself cites and classifies the following *chreia*: On seeing a youth, who was the son of an adulterer, in the act of throwing stones, Diogenes the Cynic said: "Stop boy, you may unwittingly hit your father" (Butts: 3.135–38; see also Hock and O'Neil: 92). Theon calls Diogenes' remark an example of a mixed type, both symbolic and witty. But it is what makes a remark witty and how that wit functions thematically that makes Diogenes' chreiai rhetorically interesting. In this case the wit resides in using the apparently unrelated fact of the boy's birth to reproach his stone throwing. Usually the implications of Diogenes' witticisms are more specifically philosophical. This example is representative, however, in that it is the incongruous nature of Diogenes' connections that produces the recurring and self-consciously comic character of his chreiai. All true wit has an enthymematic character: it requires the audience to perform an act of mental collaboration that can be variously described as bridging a logical gap; moving between alien codes, frames of reference, or universes of discourse; or, in Koestler's classic formulation, bisociating divergent matrices of meaning (the themes of Koestler: chaps. 1–4; cf. also Cohen: 120–36). His analysis of this process convinced Koestler that humor exemplified "the logical pattern" of inventive thinking generally. In whatever language we choose to describe it, it is precisely this feature that distinguishes the chreiai about Diogenes.

One of Diogenes' favorite tactics was to teach by example, using immediate experience to dramatize a question or subvert a theoretical quandary: Once he lit a lamp in broad daylight and walked about saying, "I am looking for a human being" (ἄνθρωπος D.L. 6.41). After Plato had elaborated a definition of man in terms of genus and differentia as a "featherless biped," Diogenes walked in with a plucked chicken saying, "Here is Plato's man!" (D.L. 6.40). When confronted with a theoretical question, Diogenes would shift the argument to another plane by rejecting the question's premise: Thus when asked, perhaps by the Atheist Theodorus, if he believed in the gods, he retorted, "Of course—when I see how they hate you!" (D.L. 6.42). Similarly, when asked where he saw good men in Greece he replied wryly: "Good men nowhere, good boys in Sparta" (D. L. 6.27). In each of these examples the humor is deliberately provocative: It is used to raise questions about what it is to be human or a good man, or to cast doubt on the utility of theoretical disputes on the existence of the gods or the proper definition of *homo sapiens*. While any of these anecdotes would repay detailed analysis, my point here is merely to emphasize the purposeful nature of Cynic humor. Although Dudley recognizes that Diogenes' "shamelessness" (ἀναίδεια) was philosophically motivated, he fails to see that the traditions about him make wit essential to his chief didactic method, his much-vaunted παρρησία ("freedom of speech"): "the finest thing in the world" (D. L. 6.69).

Cynic rhetoric developed a distinctive set of terms and gestures reflecting its thematic emphasis on such characteristic values παρρησία and ἀναίδεια. The distinguishing traits of Cynic practice are preserved not only in many brief chreiai about Diogenes or Crates, but even in the polished orations of the sophistic moralist, Dio Chrysostom. Dio's treatment of familiar Cynic *topoi*, such as "Diogenes at the Games," (Or 8; cf. Malherbe: Epistle 38 of Diogenes; cf. also note 1), serves to illustrate how acutely aware skillful practitioners were of utilizing a traditional style of performance suited to their own rhetorical purposes. The impact of Dio's piece is distorted if divorced from the basic conventions of Cynic jesting. It recounts Diogenes' visit to the Isthmian games, a traditional locus for generalizing about human life in light of the athletes' trials and the motley diversity of the crowd thronging to see them. In Dio's account Diogenes uses this occasion to develop the theme of the Cynic as agonist, using the traditional but inherently improbable and comic idea of Heracles as a paradigmatic Cynic (27–35). Part of what makes Diogenes' diatribe interesting is the rhetorical challenge of finding similarities between the disparate terms of his comparison; it is also this feature which makes his mode of argument comic. The process of developing the metaphor gives scope to the moral tenets of Cynic discourse as Diogenes defines the old hero's labors as distinctly Cynic achievements. But it is the final act of his performance which will pull most readers up short, just as, Dio reports, it did the original audience: after completing his praise of Heracles, Diogenes abruptly squats (καθεζόμενος) and does "something disgraceful" (ἐποίει τι τῶν ἀδόξων; 36) before the crowd. This might seem a distinctly odd way to conclude a moral homily, but it makes perfect sense in the context of Cynic rhetoric. What may seem an incomprehensible bit of buffoonery or tasteless clowning is actually crucial to the interpretation of Dio's entire oration. It works on several levels. First, it alludes to Heracles' final exploit as just recounted by Diogenes, the cleaning of the Augean stables, which the orator interprets as anticipating his own healthy disrespect for common opinion (δόξα; 35). Both the comparison of the lowly Cynic to the ancient hero and the public act of defecation strike at the arbitrary, provisional nature of conventional categories, "lifting their pressure for a moment and suggesting other ways of structuring reality." These are deliberately structured Cynic incongruities and as much a part of the movement as the Cynic knapsack (πήρα). As Mary Douglas argues of the joker generally, the Cynic jester "appears to be a privileged person who can say certain things in a certain way which confers immunity [i.e., παρρησία]. . . . Safe within the permitted range of attack, he lightens for everyone the oppressiveness of social reality, demonstrates its arbitrariness by making light of formality in general, and expresses the creative possibilities of the situation (Douglas: 110, 107; for the joke-like structure of some NT parables, see 99-100)." Specifically, the surprise ending validates Diogenes' role as a Cynic preacher by dramatizing his commitment to say what is true and to act according to nature, undeterred by shame, society's revenge on the non-conformist. It is precisely his willingness to make himself an object of ridicule, to engage in unseemly, shameful, or ridiculous acts, that empowers Diogenes as a Cynic moral authority. Otherwise he would just be another philosopher haranguing crowds. His shocking peroration is an act of philosophical jesting directed at the audience. It is an action *chreia* of an unmistakably Cynic kind and serves as a kind of signature authenticating the Cynic nature of the speech.

No work could be better suited to complement the argument that Lucian is best understood as an heir of seriocomic or Cynic traditions as we have characterized them here than his portrait of his teacher, the philosopher Demonax. The *Demonax* connects Lucian directly to the philosophical practice of serious jesting and provides an opportunity to examine the particular stamp which he gives it. Formally Boswell's portrait of Johnson is the closest thing in English to the *Demonax*. Like Johnson—once called by a friend "the Demonax of the present age" (Boswell: 40)—the philosopher appears in a series of dramatized moments rather than a continuous narrative. Lucian's decision to use detached incidents, or chreiai, as his medium rather than a connected narrative, as in his accounts of the pagan renegades Alexander and Peregrinus, shows that his subject is not Demonax's career but his way of life (βίος) or character. This is best revealed by letting Demonax appear in his own words unlike the satiric target Alexander of Abonoteichus, for example, who is never allowed to speak for himself. Lucian knew that character "must be manifested in the concrete" (Rader: 28) to be memorable and that the uniqueness of a character is best displayed in expressive moments. The conventional vehicle for sayings of wise men, the pointed anecdote (or *chreia*), was perfectly suited for this purpose. It places Demonax in a rhetorical frame used especially with idealized figures and associated in particular with Diogenes and the Cynics (cf. Theon 1.40–43: Butts' ed.). It thus allows Lucian to use a series of discrete episodes to construct a model of the rhetorical uses of humor exemplifying a comic method and moral stance clearly indicative of his own.³ He gives the collection a biographical shape by beginning with a brief narration of Demonax's education and philosophical temperament and concluding with chreiai about his attitude toward death. The *Demonax* probably represents the first instance in which many of the chreiai it contains passed from oral to written performance.⁴

If Aristotle is right when he says the comic genres tend to represent men as worse than they are in making them appear funny, then presenting an image of authority, a source of admiration, poses an interesting rhetorical problem for writers whose heroes are laughable. It is one that Plato and the followers of Diogenes solved by emphasizing the comic qualities of their heroes but presenting them as instrumental to a larger purpose that may well seem absurd when viewed through a conventional lens. Lucian is deliberately following their lead when he seeks to embody the oxymoronic ideal of a "comic authority figure" in Demonax. His express purpose is twofold: to preserve the memory of Demonax among the best men and through him to provide a contemporary pattern (κανών; 2) by which men can shape themselves (αὐτοὺς ῥυθμίζειν; 2). Thus the *Demonax* as a whole is epideictic. It is meant to commemorate a particular life as it embodied an iterable ideal. After briefly sketching Demonax's upbringing and philosophical temper, his indifference to the things conventionally regarded as good (3), Lucian turns to the philosopher's role models (4): Although Demonax was too intellectually wary to commit himself to the doctrines of a particular philosophical sect,⁵ he is said to have most in common with Socrates and Diogenes. Lucian stresses, however, that Demonax eschews the exhibitionism of Diogenes' antics and the hauteur of Socratic irony, which, as Aristotle remarks, was sometimes felt to be disdainful (*Rhet.* 2.1380a). Instead we are shown Demonax adapting Cynic license (παρρησία) and Socratic techniques of irony to fit his own philosophical style, in which wit is used as a delicate weapon for puncturing the windy self-concepts of his interlocutors.

Thus, if Demonax takes Socrates and Diogenes as his models, it is less for the specific content of their philosophies than for their success in

---

3 I am not concerned here with the historicity of Lucian's portrait, but with the qualities of the character whom he presents as his teacher and exemplar. Cf. K. Funk's notion of *Demonax* as Lucian's *Idealbild* (Funk: 558–574).

4 Lucian chose to retain the *chreiai*, so closely tied to oral performance, presumably to preserve the live traditions about Demonax in circulation in the Athens of his day (cf. Jones: 93). This method of preserving the philosopher's image lends his portrait an air of authenticity. It may also explain why the wit of the *Demonax* often seems less sophisticated than Lucian's own creations.

5 Cf. *Demonax* 62: "Asked which of the philosophers was most of his taste, he said, `I admire them all; Socrates I revere, Diogenes I admire, Aristippus I love.'" (Fowlers trans.). Not a single *chreia* identifies Demonax with a point of doctrine.

expressing ethical perspectives in highly idiosyncratic comic styles. Like Diogenes or the Socrates of Plato's *Symposium*, Demonax makes of himself a didactic instrument which issues naturally in a comic mode. Every anecdote Lucian tells represents an attempt to preserve and examine distinctive aspects of Demonax's unassuming didactic style. Before assessing the portrait that emerges from the collection as a whole, I will analyze how Lucian establishes Demonax's *ethos* in the only extended *chreia* he recounts, that of Demonax's trial, which serves as a bridge between the introductory narrative (1–10) and the collection of shorter chreiai.

Demonax's "Apology" shows the sage at a dramatic moment, playing the role assigned to the philosopher-hero by tradition, but easily evading its tragic potential. Thus the repeated allusions to Socrates concentrated in this passage are used to mark differences in their responses to similar situations as well as to enhance Demonax's stature and to suggest the injustice of the charges against him. If we break it down into its constituent parts, the *chreia* of the trial embodies in narrative form conventional features of judicial rhetoric (cf. Mack and Robbins). Assuming that there actually was a trial, we can imagine that there would originally have been numerous versions of the incident reflected in various chreiai. Lucian's version is clearly a polished amalgam (one paragraph in the original) which serves his aims at this juncture in his biography by enlarging upon certain thematically significant points in the action, in the manner of an expanded *chreia*:[6]

1) Proem of Praise:
> Accordingly Demonax was regarded with reverence (ἐθαύμαζον) at Athens, both by the collective Assembly and by the officials; he always continued to be a person of great consequence in their eyes.

2) Statement of Case; Comparison to Socrates:
> And this though most of them had been at first offended with him, and hated him as heartily as their ancestors had Socrates. Besides his candor and independence (παρρησία καὶ ἐλευθερία), there had been found Anytuses and Meletuses to repeat the historic charge: 1) he had never been known to sacrifice; and 2) he made himself singular by avoiding initiation at Eleusis.

---

[6] For the expanded *chreia*, see Theon, Hock and O'Neil: 100; for the use of praise to open a *chreia*, see Hermogenes on "elaboration" (*ergasia*), Hock and O'Neil: 176.

3) Refutation of Charges by Challenging the *Stasis*, or Issue, of the Case; Facts Admitted but Justified by Redefining their Quality:7

> A) On this occasion he showed his courage by appearing in a garland and festal attire, and then pleading his cause before the people with a dash of unwanted asperity (τραχύτερον) infused into his ordinarily moderate tone. On the count of never having sacrificed to Athena, "Men of Athens," he said, "there is nothing wonderful in this (μὴ θαυμάσητε); it was only that I gave the goddess credit for being able to do very well without sacrifices from me."

> B) And in the matter of the Mysteries, his reason for not following the usual practice was this: if the Mysteries turned out to be bad, he would never be able to keep quiet about it to the uninitiated, but must dissuade them from the ceremony; while if they were good, his *philanthropia* would tempt him to divulge them.

4) Spontaneous Acquittal; Malice Converted to Veneration:
The Athenians, stone in hand already, were at once disarmed, and from that time onward paid him honor and respect, which ultimately rose to reverence (θαυμάζειν).

5) Reproach as Epilogue; Argument from Example:
Yet he had opened his case with a bitter enough (τραχυτέρῳ) reproof: "Men of Athens, you see me garlanded; proceed to sacrifice me, then; your former offering [i.e., Socrates] was deficient in this formality." (ET in Lucian 1905: *Dem.* 11)

---

7 Cf. Kennedy: 18–19: "A speaker in planning a speech, or a critic in analyzing it, was encouraged to define the stasis, or basic issue of the case. There are four main forms of stasis: fact (also known as conjecture), definition, quality and jurisdiction... The question is one of quality if the facts and definitions are admitted by all parties, but the action is justified on other grounds."

Lucian's presentation of Demonax's trial exhibits a surprising complexity in its use of verbal repetition and rhetorical structure to support its central argument—that Demonax is rightly regarded as a modern Socrates. Demonax is compared to Socrates by Lucian twice (in section 2 above):

1) for his ἐλευθερία and παρρησία;
2) for having accusers like Anytus and Meletus.

In addition, Demonax explicitly compares himself to Socrates in the epilogue (section 5). His trial is, therefore, offered as a reenactment or refiguring of that of Socrates, but the overtly drawn parallels mask some equally significant differences. Of course, the political dimension to the case against Socrates, expressed in the charge of "corrupting the young," is absent; rather the analogy with Socrates is that in accusing Demonax of not sacrificing or joining the mysteries the Athenians are charging him with standing outside the bounds of community—of illicit individualism. Lucian explicitly states that the motive of the attack was social and not religious: Demonax's freedom of conduct had excited the people's hatred (μῖσος), just as Socrates' had (πρὸ αὐτοῦ). But that freedom is defined in the specifically Cynic terms of παρρησία and ἐλευθερία. This is where an element of subterfuge emerges in the rhetorical conflation of Demonax with Socrates. For while Socrates is effectively used to valorize Demonax, their responses to the charge of religious misconduct actually serve to distinguish them. According to both Xenophon and Plato, Socrates was pious, observed the customary rituals, and urged his friends to consult Delphi on difficult matters. Consequently, he denied the charge that he did not recognize the gods of the state. In his first response (section 3), however, Demonax questions the need to sacrifice in an open challenge to traditional religious belief. In his second response (section 3), which is reported rather than quoted, Demonax's rhetorical strategy becomes clear. While conceding the factual basis of the charges against him—unlike Socrates—he seeks to redefine the quality of his actions so as to make them acceptable to the jury (see note 7). (Thus if he does not sacrifice, it is because he thinks the gods have no need of what he can offer; if he does not join the mysteries, it is because his φιλανθρωπία would compel him to divulge the truth about them.)

Both Demonax's responses are clearly meant to portray his willingness to tell the truth regardless of the consequences (παρρησία), but the second, which is decisive in winning over the jury, is also a demonstration of φιλανθρωπία, a subordinate Cynic virtue associated above all with Crates (see Dudley: 42-44)—not Socrates. The success of Demonax's deceptively simple defense is dramatized, as the spontaneous response of the jury to his evident φιλανθρωπία converts their hatred to veneration (θαυμάζειν); the peripeteia thus returns us to the very terms of praise used to introduce Demonax in the proem (ἐθαύμαζον), which the trial itself had called into question. Similarly artful is the way the people are said to take on qualities ascribed to Demonax in the preceding section (πρᾶος) as they are converted to his point of view.

If this analysis is correct, then the comparison with Socrates is used in part as rhetorical cover for Lucian's celebration of the more properly Cynic conception of freedom embodied in Demonax. That this is, in fact, the argumentative tendency of the episodes seems confirmed by the epilogue (section 5). At first the epilogue may seem puzzling: Why does Lucian put this incident, which came at the beginning of the trial, at the end of his account? The epilogue does, of course, serve to recapitulate the salient themes of the trial by digressing to its starting point, but it is not simply a summation. It shifts the emphasis from Demonax's φιλανθρωπία and the people's admiration for him (section 4) back to a more emphatically Cynic style of confrontational truth-telling (παρρησία). Thus, like the first direct quotation of Demonax (section 3), his remarks in the epilogue are termed τραχύτερον ("rather rough"). The context of the quotation is equally significant: Demonax compares himself directly to Socrates, reproaches the jury and parodies the charges against him by appearing at his trial in the guise of an animal wreathed for sacrifice. By ending on this note of Cynic theatricality, Lucian is acknowledging the distinctively Cynic cast of his hero even as he claims Socratic authority for his divergence from communal norms.[8]

One way to establish the authority of a marginal figure is to pit him against the established authorities, to contrast his *ethos* with theirs. The Demonax who appears wearing a garland at his own trial is notably free of any trace of self-seriousness (ἀλαζονεία). Indeed, he gets into trouble precisely through a failure to take "serious things" seriously as his attitude toward the Mysteries shows (11, 34). This, paradoxically, is made the immediate source of his authority. The words for laughing and smiling appear repeatedly in the stories about him. Thus when asked if he is worried about being eaten by birds and dogs after his death (the nightmare of the epic hero) he replies that he will be glad to be of use (66; cf. 35). Similarly, when the sophist Favorinus asked him what philosophical school he preferred, inviting him to identify himself as a "serious"

---

[8] A trial before his fellow citizens had become a kind of rite of passage authenticating the philosopher's claim to his title. It may well be a dramatic means of representing the process whereby a Cynic, by definition an outsider, came in time to be regarded as an unofficial moral authority in Athens: It thus establishes a focal image of Demonax, different facets of which form the subjects of the briefer *chreiai* which follow.

philosopher, he replied, "Who told you I was a philosopher?" (13). This natural antipathy to taking one's role too seriously leads Demonax to point out embarrassing incongruities to those who abuse the authority of their positions. Thus when he saw a Spartan beating a slave he remarked dryly, "Stop treating him as your equal!" (46). This is a complex bit of wit. First, it ridicules the Spartans by alluding to their notorious custom of submitting to flagellation to inure themselves to hardship. Second, it suggests that whoever beats his slave is himself no better than a slave. In requiring the reader or auditor to fill in these steps to appreciate the humor of the story, it functions, as does any joke worth laughing at, like an enthymeme. We "get the point" of the joke when we recognize and interpret what is implicit in the story. Similarly, when a depilated Roman proconsul was about to punish a Cynic severely for having called him a catamite, Demonax intervened in defense of Cynic license ($\pi\alpha\rho\rho\eta\sigma\iota\alpha$). When the proconsul asked him to propose an alternative punishment for a second offense, Demonax retorted, "Depilate him!" (50). In this exchange the moral authority of the official, sanctioned by law ($\nu\acute{o}\mu o\varsigma$), is deftly appropriated by the philosopher empowered by $\pi\alpha\rho\rho\eta\sigma\iota\alpha$.

Implicit in Demonax's method is Dr. Johnson's advice: "A man should pass a part of his time with the laughters, by which means anything particular or ridiculous might be presented to his view and corrected (cited by Vance: 210)." Thus most of the *Demonax* is devoted to anecdotes that dramatize the philosopher as an interesting example of the seriocomic type, a specialist in the techniques of comic deflation. Demonax's wit is, therefore, usually tendentious, but it can also be purely playful, "wit for its own sake."[9] His forte is not Cynic denunciation or shrewd Socratic questioning, but the one-liner in the tradition of Diogenes. Much of his humor is verbal and works through puns and word play (15, 17, 19, 21, 29, 30, 31, 47–49, 54, 56). As noted above, he is shown characteristically making a reply, not asking a question. His only working assumption, one which he shares with Diogenes and Socrates, is that most people he meets are in some sense *poseurs*. His practice applies Plato's theory (*Philb.* 48–50) that one becomes comic through a lapse in self-knowledge; as though wearing the ring of Gyges with reverse effect, the respect in which the comic figure is risible tends to be invisible to himself (Bergson: 71).

---

9 Cf. S. Freud (688–90): "It is easy to guess the character of the witticism by the kind of reaction that wit exerts on the hearer. Sometimes wit is `wit for its own sake' and serves no other particular purpose: then again it places itself at the service of such a tendency; i.e., it becomes tendentious. Only that form of wit which has such a tendency runs the risk of ruffling people who do not wish to hear it.... `Harmless' or `abstract' wit should in no way convey the same meaning as `shallow' or `poor' wit.... A harmless jest, i.e., a witticism without a tendency, can also be very rich in content and express something worthwhile."

Demonactean wit seeks to expose these blind spots by calling attention to the discrepancy between solipsistic fantasies and public realities. For example, when the wealthy sophist, Herodes Atticus, was ostentatiously mourning the death of his favorite slave, Polydeuces, he continued to have the dead man's chariot prepared and his dinner served as if he were still alive. When he heard that Demonax had arrived with a message from Polydeuces, Herodes assumed that he was falling in with his pretense like everyone else, but Demonax's message was: "Polydeuces is unhappy with you for not coming to join him at once" (24). Similarly, a muscular Roman soldier who had just given a demonstration of his prowess with the sword on a post asked Demonax what he thought of his swordsmanship: "Excellent—if you have a wooden adversary" (38).

All the prominent qualities of Demonax as he is presented in the anecdotes, the purposeful application of wit, verbal play and ridicule, his detachment, self-deprecating humor, and aversion to ἀλαζονεία, correspond to common characteristics of Lucian's varied authorial stances. Demonax uses wit Lucianically to provoke his interlocutors to consider themselves and their situations from unexpected and often incongruous perspectives. The recurring theme of the anecdotes is the philosopher's resistance to deception, particularly self-deception. The most frequent targets of his witticisms are those who arrogate illusory powers and beguile themselves and others with inflated self-images. Of particular significance is Demonax's skepticism which on several occasions pits him against theorists, prophets, and magicians, the preeminent ἀλαζῶνες of the day (22, 23, 27). Significantly, the vast majority of his barbs are aimed at sophists, philosophers, and religious figures (12, 14, 19, 25, 28–9, 31, 33, 36, 44, 48, 53, 56), and secondly, at representatives of officialdom, wealthy aristocrats, and Roman officers (15, 18, 32, 38, 41, 50, 51).

Although Demonax expresses his admiration for Thersites as a prototypical Cynic (61), Lucian is careful to distinguish his comic style from the noisome abuse of Cynic street preachers in the story of his encounter with the infamous Cynic, Peregrinus Proteus. Peregrinus reproaches the jocular Demonax for his obvious lack of seriousness, for his habit of jesting and laughing with everyone (ὅτι ἐγέλα τὰ πολλὰ καὶ τοῖς ἀνθρώποις προσέπαιζε 21), and accuses him of "not acting like a real Cynic" (οὐ κυνᾷς). Alluding to the misanthropic tendencies inherent in the harsher examples of the Cynic style (κυνικὸς τρόπος) and the root meaning of "Cynic" ("dog-like") Demonax replies simply οὐκ ἀνθρωπίζεις, "you aren't really human." As Sartre argues, echoing Rabelais: "Laughter is proper to man because man is the only animal that takes itself seriously: hilarity denounces false-seriousness in the name of true-seriousness."[10] It is an argument which Lucian and Demonax would obviously have appreciated. In Demonax, Lucian presents the Socratic tradition persisting in an esoteric role in which humor becomes a means of satire and refutation, reflecting the discovery, not only of the resources of humor as a rhetorical instrument, but as a source of insight: For "all humor and much intelligence entails an ability to think on two planes at once" (Redfern: 2). The *chreia* is Lucian's vehicle for illustrating why this is so.

WORKS CITED

Aristotle
    1983   *Aristotle. Vol 12. The Parts of Animals.* Ed. and Trans. A. L. Peck. LCL. Cambridge: Harvard University Press.

Bergson, H.
    1956   "Laughter." Pp. 61-190 in *Comedy*. Ed. W. Sypher. Baltimore: Johns Hopkins University Press.

Boswell, James
    1904   *Boswell's Life of Johnson*, Vol. 4. Ed. G. B. Hill. New York: Harper Bros.

Branham, R. Bracht
    1989   *Unruly Eloquence: Lucian and the Comedy of Traditions.* Cambridge: Harvard University Press.

Butts, J. R.
    1986   "The *Progymnasmata* of Theon: A New Text with Translation and Commentary." Ph.D. Dissertation. Claremont Graduate School.

Caws, P.
    1984   "Flaubert's Laughter." *Philosophy and Literature* 8.2: 167-180.

Cohen, T.
    1983   "Jokes." Pp. 120–36 in *Pleasure, Preference and Value*. Ed. E. Schaper. Cambridge: Cambridge University Press.

Demetrius
    1902   *De Elocutione = Demetrius on Style*. Ed. W. Rhys Roberts. Cambridge: Cambridge University Press.

Douglas, Mary
    1975   "Jokes." Pp. 90-104 in *Implicit Meanings*. London: Rutledge & Kegan Paul.

---

[10] Sartre: 821. Cited and trans. P. Caws: 173–4. Cf. Rabelais's preface to *Gargantua*; cf. also Bergson: 62; Aristotle (3.10 [673a]): "... no animal but man ever laughs."

Drury, Martin
1985   "Appendix of Authors and Works." Pp. 719-892 in *The Cambridge History of Classical Literature, I. Greek Literature*. Eds. P. E. Easterling, B. M. W. Knox. Cambridge: Cambridge University Press.

Dudley, D. R.
1937   *A History of Cynicism*. London: Metheun.

Freud, S.
1938   "The Tendencies of Wit." Pp. 688-708 in *The Basic Writings of Sigmund Freud*. Trans. A. A. Brill. New York: Modern Library.
1907   "Idealbild: Untersuchungen über die Lucienische `Vita Demonactis'." *Philologus* Supplementband 10: 558–574.

Hock, R. F. and E. N. O'Neil (eds.)
1986   *The Chreia in Ancient Rhetoric. Volume I: The Progymnasmata*. Atlanta: Scholars.

Jones, C. P.
1986   *Culture and Society in Lucian*. Cambridge: Harvard University Press.

Kennedy, G. A.
1984   *New Testament Interpretation through Rhetorical Criticism*. Chapel Hill: University of North Carolina Press.

Kindstrand, J. F.
1986   "Diogenes Laertius and the `Chreia' Tradition." *Elenchos* 7.1–2: 217-243.

Koestler, A.
1964   *The Act of Creation*. London: Hutchinson.

Long, A.A.
1985   "Post-Aristotelian Philosophy." Pp. 622-642 in *The Cambridge History of Classical Literature, I. Greek Literature*. Eds. P. E. Easterling, B. M. W. Knox. Cambridge: Cambridge University.

Lucian
1905   *The Works of Lucian Samosata*. Trans. H. W. and F. G. Fowler. Oxford: Clarendon.
1972-80 *Opera*. Vols. 1-4. Ed. M.D. Macleod. Oxford: Oxford University Press.

Mack, B. L. and V. K. Robbins
1989   *Patterns of Persuasion in the Gospels*. Sonoma, Ca.: Polebridge.

Malherbe, A. J.
1977   *The Cynic Epistles: A Study Edition*. Missoula, Mt.: Scholars.

Rader, R.
1985   "Literary Form in Factual Narrative." Pp. 25-52 in *Boswell's Life of Johnson: New Questions, New Answers*. Ed. J. A. Vance. Athens, Ga.: University of Georgia Press.

Redfern, W. P.
1985   *Puns*. Oxford: Basil Blackwell.

Relihan, J.
    1993   *Ancient Menippean Satire*. Baltimore: Johns Hopkins University Press.

Sartre, Jean Paul
    1971   *L'idiot de la Famille: Gustave Flaubert de 1821 à 1857*, Vol. 1. Paris: Gallimard.

Vance, J. A.
    1985   "The Laughing Johnson and the Shaping of Boswell's *Life*." Pp. 204-227 in *Boswell's Life of Johnson: New Questions, New Answers*. Ed. J. A. Vance. Athens, Ga.: University of Georgia Press.

Rhetorical Argumentation in Early Rabbinic Pronouncement Stories

Alan J. Avery-Peck
College of the Holy Cross

ABSTRACT

Rabbinic pronouncement stories do not contain Hermogenes' full model of chreia elaboration in which all eight basic modes of argumentation appear. However they do use the types of argument treated by Hermogenes which include: praise of the one who spoke or acted; the chreia (thesis); rationale; statement of the contrary; analogy; example; statement from authority; and conclusion with exhortation. Statements of the contrary and statements of authority appear most frequently in early rabbinic pronouncement stories. This is the case because the rabbinic stories concentrate on questions of religious law and correct behavior under the law.

This article examines the use in rabbinic pronouncement stories of the forms of argumentation described by Hermogenes of Tarsus (Mack and O'Neil: 153-181). In the chapter "On the Chreia" in his *Progymnasmata*, Hermogenes advanced previous discussions of rhetorical art by evaluating eight basic modes of argumentation. Hermogenes saw these forms not as independent exercises but as elements to be united in a set order, so as to create a "full and coherent confirmation" (Mack: 51) of a chreia as thesis. For their part, the rabbinic pronouncement stories primarily use a single mode of argumentation. They do not, that is, comprise the complete elaboration of the chreia that Hermogenes described. Still, all of the rabbinic pronouncement stories use the types of argument discussed by Hermogenes and common within hellenistic rhetoric. These examples therefore allow us to examine the rabbinic use of the chreia form and to determine the extent to which the rabbinic patterns of argumentation conform to usages familiar from Greco-Roman rhetoric in general.

This analysis supports the contention of advocates of rhetorical criticism, who hold that, within broad historical and geographical limits, rhetorical art remains the same from literature to literature. While "colored by the traditions and conventions of the society in which it is applied," rhetoric, this is to say, "is also a universal phenomenon which is conditioned by the basic workings of the human mind and heart and by the nature of all human society" (Kennedy: 10). Analysis of rabbinic pronouncement stories supports this thesis by highlighting the dimensions in common between the rhetorical patterns found in rabbinic and other hellenistic writings.

To accomplish this purpose, this analysis focuses on an easily identifiable literary form that occurs twenty-three times in the early rabbinic literature and that appears widely in the gospels and in other hellenistic literatures.[1] The pronouncement form consists of "a brief narrative in which the climactic (and often final) element is a pronouncement that is presented as a particular person's response to something said or observed on some specified occasion in the past" (Tannehill:1). In this form, all rhetorical movement is towards the concluding memorable comment or maxim, which dominates the pronouncement story as a whole. This suggests that a basic function of the pronouncement story is to highlight the unique personality of the individual who makes that statement, showing that individual to be a model to be imitated or, at times, to be shunned.

The question in the following is whether or not the pronouncement stories that appear in the early rabbinic literature can be understood within the typology and categories of rhetorical analysis defined by Hermogenes and Aelius Theon of Alexandria (Hock and O'Neil). To answer this question, the twenty-three early rabbinic pronouncement stories[2] are arranged and discussed according to the classificatory scheme Hermogenes describes as integral to the elaboration of the chreia.[3] This schema consists of eight categories: 1) introduction/praise, 2) thesis/chreia, 3) rationale, 4) statement of the contrary, 5) analogy, 6) example, 7) statement from authority, and 8) conclusion/exhortation. The stories are organized according to this scheme, and further are evaluated from the perspective of their rhetorical character. This involves a description of their primary compositional attributes, evaluation of the presence of

---

[1] The stories were identified by Porton, 1981:81-99. Porton located these pericopae in order to test Rudolph Bultmann's theory of the relationship between the rabbinic literature and the Gospels' *apophthegmata*. Contrary to Bultmann's claim, Porton found that "the relevant Jewish texts do not provide a large number of good parallels to the selections from the Christian Bible which Bultmann analyzed" (1981:96).

[2] To identify these stories, Porton (1981) only examined documents that belong to the earliest stratum of the rabbinic literature. Since the evidence indicates that later editors created or, at least, reformulated materials that concerned early figures, it would be misleading to employ late pericopae in order to draw conclusions about the use of a literary convention in Tannaitic times. Studies that evaluate early and late rabbinic stories attributed to or about specific rabbinic figures make this explicit. See, e.g., Neusner and Avery-Peck, 1982b:87-98 and 1982a:194-214; Gary Porton's study of the Tannaitic master Ishmael (1976-1982); and Jacob Neusner's study of Yohanan b. Zakkai (1970).

[3] When more than one story appears in a single category, the items are presented in order of increasing rhetorical complexity.

expansion or abbreviation, and, finally, a noting of the extent to which there is elaboration, marked by the uniting of several distinct compositional attributes within a single story.

THE EARLY RABBINIC PRONOUNCEMENT STORIES

I. *Introduction/Praise*

The standard hellenistic speech began with an introduction through which the speaker "was to acknowledge the speech-situation in such a way as to establish his right to address the audience about the matter at hand" (Mack: 53). In two rabbinic pronouncement stories, the primary focus is upon such an encomium, which introduces an individual who is to serve as a model for the Jewish community. In both stories, the individual represents such a model because he acted with extreme piety, in accordance with rabbinic precepts.

> Sifre Numbers 13:1
>
> **Situation**
>
> One time Sabta of Ulan hired his donkey to a gentile woman. When she reached the edge of the territory, she said to him: "Wait until I enter the temple of the territory's idol." When she came out, he said to her: "Wait for me until I enter and do as you have done." She said to him: "Is it possible that you, a Jew, [will enter and serve the idol]!?" He entered, [uncovered himself], and wiped himself on the nose of Peor.
>
> **Conclusion with Praise**
>
> Then all the gentiles laughed and said: "No man has served [Peor] like this before!"

In this action-chreia [Theon: 205, 20], Sabta not only refrains from idol worship but goes so far as to deface an object of idolatry. The conclusion expresses with wit [Theon: 206, 10] a final, approving comment in the mode of the commentary, *epiphonesis*, described by Theon [212, 13].[4] This use of irony in placing praise of Sabta in the mouths of gentiles highlights the story's polemical intent. By commending Sabta, the gentiles themselves admit to the irrational character of idol-worship. This enhances the epideictic force of the story, which strengthens belief in Israelite religion.

---

[4] "It is also possible for those who approve of what has been fittingly and concisely said in a *chreia* to comment that it is true or noble or advantageous or that the saying has also appealed to other men of distinction."

Tosefta Berakhot 3:20

Situation

They said about R. Haninah b. Dosa that he was praying when a lizard bit him. Even so, he did not stop praying. His students went and found it dead.

Thesis

They said: "Woe to the man whom a lizard bites; woe to the lizard that bites Ben Dosa."

This story presents the encomium in the mode of a commentary, *epiphonesis*, in the manner of a maxim [Theon: 206, 10]. An unidentified "they" both describes the setting and delivers the praise of the story's main character, Haninah b. Dosa. Haninah is commended for his fervor and concentration during prayer.

2. *Thesis/Chreia*

Thesis-stories describe an action or situation and briefly indicate a resolution. Both Rabbinic examples concern basic legal principles that, once stated, are assumed to be correct. Like the preceding two stories, the first story here exhibits only the primary attributes of the chreia. The second, by contrast, shows some internal expansion, in which the story is developed by the presence of more than one basic rhetorical element normally found in the chreia.

Mishnah Berakhot 1:1

Situation

One time [Gamaliel]'s sons returned [after midnight] from a wedding feast. They said to him: "We have not yet recited the *Shema*."

Thesis

He said to them: "If the morning star has not yet risen, you [still] are obligated to recite [it]!"

This unit falls within Theon's description of chreiai in which responses are "based neither on a simple question nor on an inquiry; rather, they contain some remark to which the response is made" [204, 10]. Since it is after midnight, Gamaliel's sons express concern that they have lost the opportunity to recite the Shema-prayer, required every evening. But they do not specifically ask their father what they should do. Gamaliel responds anyway with a brief statement in the manner of a (legal) maxim [Theon: 206, 10]. Within its larger context in Mishnah Berakhot 1:1, this maxim buttresses an encompassing legal principle, expressed conditionally, as casuistic rather than apodictic law: if one fails to perform on time a religious obligation to which he is subject until midnight, then, if the morning star has not yet risen, he may still perform the required act.

> Sifre Deuteronomy 80
>
> **Situation**
>
> One time R. Judah b. Bethyra, R. Mattyah b. Harash, R. Hananyah b. Ahai, R. Joshua and R. Yonatan were leaving the land [of Israel]. When they reached Palton, they recalled the land and they stood erect while their eyes shed tears. They rent their garments and recited this verse:
>
> **Maxim**
>
> *"[You shall indeed cross the Jordan to enter and to make the land your own that the Lord your God is giving you.] You shall possess it and shall live in it and you must keep and observe all the laws..."* (Dt. 11:31).
>
> **Conclusion**
>
> They said: "Living in the land is equal to observing all of the [other] commandments [stated] in the Torah."

This is a saying-chreia, in which the point is made through words, not actions [Theon: 202, 20]. The maxim, cited from Scripture, captures the significance of the rabbis' situation upon leaving the land of Israel. The conclusion forms an *epiphonesis*, which approves the truth of the scriptural verse [Theon: 212, 10]. The rabbinic authorities, that is, respond to Dt 11:31 by saying, "Having experienced departure from the land of Israel, we can personally attest to the truth of the cited statement, that living in the land is equal to observing all of the commandments." The authorities reach this conclusion by treating the words *"You shall live in the land and you shall keep and observe all the laws"* to mean *"By living in the land you will be keeping all of the commandments."*[5] At the same time, by making explicit the meaning of the preceding statement, the conclusion represents somewhat of a paraphrase. We might therefore argue that this story moves into what Hermogenes [7, 10] calls the elaboration, which begins with a paraphrase of the chreia itself.

3. *Rationale*

In these examples the concluding thesis explains the situation, establishing a "primary proof or basic argument" (Mack: 58). This form of

---

[5] While functioning as a reminiscence, this *chreia* also exemplifies standard rabbinic reliance upon the interpretation of Scripture. Still, this example is different from the stories in section 7, in which the argument depends upon a statement from authority. The present example relies upon a rabbinic interpretation of Scripture, not upon a presentation of Scripture as an ultimate authority in itself.

chreia makes explicit the grounds for the conclusion, explaining the situation, not simply responding to it [Theon: 207,1-7].

> Mishnah Berakhot 1:3
>
> **Situation**
>
> R. Tarfon said: "I was going on the road and I reclined to recite the [evening] *Shema* according to the words of the House of Shammai, and [in doing so] I placed myself in danger from robbers."
>
> **Thesis with Rationale**
>
> They said to him: "You deserved to lose your life, for you transgressed the words of the House of Hillel."

As at M. Ber. 1:1, so here the chreia is a maxim that responds to a remark, specifically, a description of what happened to Tarfon. The maxim is in the manner of an explanation, indicating why Tarfon found himself in danger. As in so many of the rabbinic stories, the underlying issue concerns adherence to the law and, as in this case, the definition of that law.

> Tosefta Nedarim 5:15
>
> **Situation**
>
> It happened to Hananyah b. Hananyah that his father dedicated him to be a Nazarite. [The father] brought him before Rabban Gamaliel, [and] Rabban Gamaliel examined him to see if he were of age.
>
> **Thesis with Rationale**
>
> [Hananyah] said to him: "Why are you worried? [Are you worried that] I am [already of age and therefore not] under my father's authority? [If] I am under my father's authority, behold, I am a Nazarite [as a result of his dedication]. [But] if I am under my own authority, behold, I [dedicate myself and still] am a Nazarite from this moment [forward]."
>
> **Conclusion with Praise**
>
> [Gamaliel] stood and kissed him on the head. He said: "I am certain that you will be an authoritative teacher in Israel before you die."
>
> **Postscript**
>
> And he did become a teacher in Israel before his death.

In this saying-chreia, Hananyah's *thesis with rationale* responds to the circumstance described in the short statement of situation. The response is "in the manner of a syllogism" [Theon: 207, 5], exploring alternatives as a means of searching for a reason. This chreia is internally expanded with Gamaliel's praise of Hananyah b. Hananyah for his willingness to fulfill his father's wish (*epiphonesis*) and the postscript, which supports the argument of the whole by indicating that Gamaliel spoke correctly.

> Sifre Deuteronomy 43
>
> **Situation**
>
> And one time Rabban Gamaliel, R. Joshua, R. Eleazar b. Azariah and R. Aqiba entered Rome. They heard a din from Petilon, 120 miles away. They began crying, but R. Aqiba laughed. They said to him: "Aqiba, why are we crying, but you are laughing?" [Aqiba] said to them: "And you, why are you crying?"
>
> **Thesis with Rationale**
>
> They said to him: "Should we not cry? For the gentile idolaters, who offer sacrifices to [false] gods and prostrate themselves before idols, sit in peace and ease. But the House that was the footstool of our God is burned with fire and has become a dwelling place for beasts of the field."
>
> **Thesis with Rationale**
>
> [Aqiba] said to them: "It is even for that reason that I laugh. If [God] acted thus towards those who anger him, [giving the idolaters in Petilon peace and ease], how much the more [will He act in this way] towards those who do His will, [so that Israel eventually will also dwell in peace]."

This is an example of Theon's double-chreia [205, 10], with "statements of two characters, either one of which creates a chreia of one character." This is set up by the two questions in the statement of situation. The first *thesis with rationale* comprises a saying-chreia based on Aqiba's question ("And you, why are you crying?" "For the gentile idolaters...sit in peace and ease"). The second *thesis with rationale* comprises a saying-chreia based on the other rabbis' question ("...why are you laughing" "...If [God] acted thus towards those who anger him...."). Based on Aqiba's concluding statement, we see that the story's rhetoric is epideictic, strengthening belief in a positive, continuing relationship between the people of Israel and God.

4. *Statement of the Contrary*

In hellenistic rhetorical form, a statement of the contrary is used to test the validity of an argument. The point is that, "If the opposite set of relationships also makes sense, or is recognized as a plausible statement, this judgment serves to support the original contention" (Mack: 59). This relationship is clear in an example from Hermogenes:

> For everyday occurrences do not require labors, and their end is most unpleasant, but in the case of worthwhile matters it is just the opposite (7, 20-8, 1) (cited by Mack: 59).

Hermogenes places this category after the chreiai involving rationales since, when contrary statements are present, they normally are exploring rationales. This is the case even if, as in the rabbinic examples, the rationale is not explicitly stated. Further, in these rabbinic pericopae, the parallel between the contrasting statements is not made explicit. Still, as we shall see, the point of these arguments and their rhetorical force are quite strong and similar to their hellenistic counterparts.

> Mishnah Berakhot 2:6
>
> **Situation**
>
> [Gamaliel] washed on the first night after his wife had died.
>
> **Question**
>
> His students said to him: "Did you not teach us, our Rabbi, that a mourner is forbidden to wash?
>
> **Thesis with Rationale, in the form of a Contrary**
>
> He said to them: "I am not like other men, for I am of feeble health."

The form of a question and answer concerning an action (whether or not a mourner should wash) is characteristic of the chreia.[6] The law is correctly stated in the question. Gamaliel responds with a contrary "in the manner of an explanation" [Theon: 206, 15] which explains the exception. The contrary is acceptable only because of Gamaliel's health. As in the following two examples, the thesis in the form of a contrary highlights an aspect of Gamaliel's character. He was extremely pious yet not to a fault.

The extent to which a chreia such as this, depending upon an argument from the contrary, was familiar in hellenistic rhetoric is clear from the description in Cicero's *Rhetorica ad Herennium* (4.18.25-26), which describes well this and the following materials from Mishnah Berakhot:

> This figure ought to be brief and completed in an unbroken period. Furthermore, it is not only agreeable to the ear on account of its brief and complete rounding-off, but by means of the contrary statement it also forcibly proves what the speaker needs to prove; and from a statement which is not open to question it draws a thought which is in question, in such a way that the inference cannot be refuted, or can be refuted only with much the greatest difficulty.[7]

As Cicero describes, so in the rabbinic examples, the brief contrary statement is not easily refuted. The argument that "I am not like other men," or, in the following, "Tabi was not like other slaves," is phrased as fact, not logical deduction, so that it is countered only with great

---

[6] Hermogenes, *On the Chreia*, 7,1. See Mack and O'Neil 1986:175.

[7] Translation: Loeb Classical Library

difficulty. The students, that is, can hardly be expected to argue that Gamaliel is in fact just like all other people or that he has incorrectly evaluated his slave's personal traits. They therefore cannot respond to his explanation of the actions he performed as a result of these facts.

> Mishnah Berakhot 2:7
>
> **Situation**
>
> And when Tabi, his slave, died, [Gamaliel] received consolation because of him.
>
> **Question**
>
> His students said to him: "Did you not teach us, our Rabbi, that one does not receive consolation on account of slaves?"
>
> **Thesis with Rationale, in the form of a Contrary**
>
> He said to them: "Tabi was not like other slaves: He was ritually fit."

By explaining why he acted in a manner contrary to the law, Gamaliel proves that the law itself is correct. This expanded chreia again shows Gamaliel to constitute a special case.

> Mishnah Berakhot 2:5
>
> **Situation**
>
> There was an incident concerning Rabban Gamaliel, who recited the *Shema* on the night of his wedding.
>
> **Question**
>
> His students said to him: "Did you not teach us, our Rabbi, that the groom is exempt from reciting the *Shema* on the night of his marriage?"
>
> **Thesis with Rationale, in the form of a Contrary**
>
> He said to them, "I will not listen to you so that I would remove the kingdom of Heaven from me for even one hour!"

The students again question Gamaliel's actions, claiming that he contradicts his own teaching. His indication of the contrary both explains his actions and indicates that the statement of law cited in his name is correct. Bridegrooms are exempt from reciting the *Shema*. But Gamaliel is not a usual bridegroom, content to follow the law's letter. Thus, he is not breaking the law but, rather, acting with piety beyond what is expected. The underlying message that, just as there are reasons for each and every rule, so there are reasons for rejecting a particular law, is powerfully expressed through each of the units discussed here concerning Gamaliel.

Tosefta Hagiga 2:1

Situation

One time R. Yohanan b. Zakkai was riding on his donkey, and Eleazar b. Arak was close behind him. [Eleazar] said to him: "Rabbi, teach me one section of the Maaseh Merkavah."

Thesis

[Yohanan] said to him: "No! Thus I have said to you previously, that they do not teach about the Merkavah to an individual unless he is a sage who understands his own knowledge."

Contrary

[Eleazar] said to him: "Now I wish to discuss with you." [Yohanan] said to him: "Speak." R. Eleazar b. Arak opened [his discourse] and expounded the Maaseh Merkavah. R. Yohanan b. Zakkai got down from his donkey and wrapped himself in his prayer shawl, and both of them sat on a stone under an olive tree, and he discussed before him.

Conclusion with Praise

[Yohanan] stood and kissed him on his head and said: "Blessed is the Lord, the God of Israel, who gave a son to Abraham, our father, who knows [how] to understand and to explain the glory of our Father in heaven. There are those who expound well but do not live well. But Eleazar b. Arak expounds well and lives well. Happy are you, Abraham our father, for Eleazar b. Arak, who knows [how] to understand and to explain the glory of our Father in heaven, came out of your loins."

This is an expanded chreia [Theon: 219, 15], in which the contrary and conclusion elaborate the first question and response. The conclusion exhibits the basis for Yohanan's original response. A knowledgeable sage may expound on esoteric knowledge; an ignorant one may not. Since Eleazar b. Arak proves himself to be extremely knowledgeable, he earns Yohanan's praise.

5. *Statement from Analogy*

The analogy is one of the most basic methods of formulating a supporting argument. In the Greco-Roman literature, analogies from the natural and social orders are preferred (Mack: 59). The one rabbinic example in this category is similar, depending on the notion that wisdom is learned from and expressed in actions. Unlike this example, however, the Rabbis use analogies primarily in legislative activity. They accomplish this by extending existing rules to new, analogous situations. That approach often yields tightly structured arguments, in which two authorities disagree concerning the most appropriate analogy. Since such legal discussions must be resolved through recourse to a different form of argument, the other analogies that occur within the corpus of rabbinic pronouncement stories are discussed elsewhere, under the heading that represents the primary rhetorical type of the argument.[8]

> Sifre Deuteronomy 13
>
> **Situation**
>
> *Choose wise, understanding [and experienced] men* (Dt. 1:13). This is the question Arios asked R. Yose: [Arios] said to him: "Which is a wise man?"
>
> **Thesis/Chreia**
>
> [Yose] said to him: "He who practices that which he teaches. Or perhaps [such a person] is [referred to] rather [as] an understanding man?"
>
> **New Situation**
>
> [Arios] said to him: "*Understanding men* is already said [in the above verse]. What is the difference between a wise man and an understanding man?"
>
> **Thesis with Analogy**
>
> [Yose said to him:] "A wise man is similar to a rich [gold] smith. When [others] bring him [gold] to examine [lit.: see], he examines [it]. When [others] do not bring him [gold] to examine, he takes out his own [gold] and examines [it]. An understanding man is similar to a poor [gold] smith. When [others] bring him [gold] to examine, he examines [it]. When [others] do not bring him [gold] to examine, he must sit and be idle."

This expanded chreia evinces a rudimentary level of elaboration, moving from a basic form of argumentation, the thesis, to a more persuasive one, the analogy. Through his analogy, Yose apparently convinces Arios of his position: A wise person practices what he preaches. This person differs from an understanding one in that he alone puts his knowledge to work in his own life. The question and answer format hides an underlying polemic. Yose points out that rabbis (rich men), who carry out their knowledge in all aspects of everyday life, are superior to pagan philosophers (poor men), who teach but have no overall theory of proper day-to-day behavior, such as is represented by rabbinic law.

6. *Statement from Example*

Like the analogy, the example is an extremely powerful form of proof. Indeed Aristotle says that the example and the rhetorical syllogism are "the two primary forms of rhetorical logic and proof."[9] In the rabbinic use of this form, as in other hellenistic usages, "the example comes from the arena of history, and is about some well-known person." As a result, "the

---

[8] See below, Sifre Numbers 75 (section 6) and Tosefta Pisha 4:13 (section 7).
[9] *Rhet*. I.ii.8-9; II.xx.1; II.xxv.8; cited by Mack 1989:60.

argument confirms the validity of the general rule in terms of a specific and precedent case" (Mack: 60).

Sifre Deuteronomy 38

Situation

One time R. Eliezer and R. Zadoq were reclining at a feast for the son of Rabban Gamaliel. Rabban Gamaliel mixed a glass [of wine] for R. Eliezer, but he did not wish to accept it. R. Joshua accepted it. R. Eliezer said to him: "What is this, Joshua? Is it right that we should recline and Gamaliel beRabbi should stand and serve us?"

Thesis with Example from Authority

R. Joshua said to him: "Leave him alone that he might serve [us]. Abraham, the greatest one of the world, served the ministering angels, even though he thought that they were Arab idolaters, for it is said, *And he lifted his eyes and looked and behold three men stood in front of him* (Gen. 18:2). And is it not an *a fortiori* [argument]? Now if Abraham, the greatest one of the world, served the ministering angels, and he thought that they were Arab idolaters, should not Gamaliel beRabbi serve us?"

This response to an inquiry [Theon: 203, 10] sets out a question of law, whether or not a great rabbi should be allowed to serve an equal or lesser master. The example from authority points out that even Abraham served others. By analogy, Joshua can rationalize his and Gamaliel's actions. Note the similarity of this story to common exegetical pericopae in which an *a fortiori* argument based on a passage from Scripture serves to describe permitted or forbidden behavior. This passage belongs here, however, and not below with statements from authority, since Abraham is adduced as an example of proper behavior. The argument focuses upon his behavior, not primarily upon Scripture as an authoritative source of information.

Mekhilta Ishmael Vayassa 1

Situation

Again it happened that a student went [before the ark to lead the service] in the presence of R. Eliezer, and [the student] lengthened his prayers. [Eliezer]'s students said to him: "Our Rabbi, you saw that so-and-so lengthened his prayers." ....

Thesis with Example from Authority

[Eliezer] said to them: "He did not lengthen [them] more than Moses, for it is said: *So I fell down before the Lord forty days...* (Deut. 9:25)."

Conclusion

For R. Eliezer used to say: "There is a time to shorten [one's prayers] and a time to lengthen [them]."

The students object to the action of someone who lengthened his prayers. Eliezer defends that person by appealing to the example of Moses, viewed by the rabbinic movement as the paradigmatic rabbi. The conclusion expands the chreia with a rationale that explains the example and thereby responds directly to the students' question.

> Sifre Numbers 75
>
> **Situation: Legal Analogy**
>
> *[And the sons of Aaron], the priests, [shall blow the trumpets]* (Num. 10:3). "Whether blemished or unblemished"—the words of R. Tarfon. R. Aqiba says, "*Priests* is said here, and *priests* is said elsewhere (Lev. 1:11). Just as *priests* which is said elsewhere [refers to] unblemished [priests] and not to blemished [ones], also here [*priests* refers to] unblemished [priests] and not to blemished [ones]."
>
> **Thesis with Example**
>
> R. Tarfon said to him: "How long will you rake [words] together and bring them against us, Aqiba?" He was unable to bear up. "I swear by the life of my children that I saw Simon, my mother's brother, who girded his feet [for he was a cripple], standing and blowing the trumpets."
>
> **Contrary Thesis**
>
> [Aqiba] said to him: "Yes, [but] perhaps [he did this only] on New Year, the Day of Atonement, or in the Jubilee year?"
>
> **Conclusion A: With Praise**
>
> [Tarfon] said to him: "You are not refuted. Happy are you, Abraham, our father, for Aqiba has come out of your loins.
>
> **Conclusion B: Statement of the Contrary**
>
> "Tarfon saw and forgot, [but] Aqiba explained [it] on his own and made [it] agree with the law.
>
> **Conclusion C: In the Manner of a Maxim**
>
> "Behold, anyone who separates himself from you, [Aqiba], it is as if he separated himself from his own life."

Interesting in this expanded chreia is the interplay among the several already familiar forms. The legal analogy that comprises the situation is refuted by an example of how matters actually have been done in the past (thesis with example). Aqiba wins the argument by showing that Tarfon has misrepresented the example. Aqiba's contrary thesis functions as in the pericopae above in section 4. The fact that what Tarfon describes occurred only on the listed days proves all the more that it cannot occur on other occasions. At the end, Tarfon praises Aqiba, as we have come to expect, for his prowess in matters of law. This expanded conclusion displays several rhetorical features already familiar to us.

7. Statement from Authority

This form shows that recognized authorities support the proposition being advanced. The rabbinic examples adduce the most prominent sources available, prior rabbinic masters or Scripture itself.

Sifra 45c

Situation

It once happened that one of the students was rendering [legal] decisions in [Eliezer's] presence. [Eliezer] said to his wife, Imma Shalom: "He will no longer live after the end of the Sabbath." And when he died after the Sabbath, sages entered and said to [Eliezer]: "Rabbi, you are a prophet!"

Contrary Thesis with Authority

He said to them: "I am neither a prophet nor the son of a prophet. However, thus I received from my teachers, that anyone who renders legal decisions in the presence of his teacher deserves death."

In a chreia based upon a response to a remark [Theon: 203, 15], Eliezer corrects the sages' misunderstanding of how he knew that the student would die. His knowledge came from rabbinic lore (citation of ancient authority, Theon: 212, 20), not prophetic abilities. The story thus proposes that rabbinic knowledge is tantamount to, or perhaps more powerful than, prophetic insight.

Tosefta Kelim Baba Batra 1:2-3

Situation

One time a certain woman who had woven a garment in cultic cleanness came before R. Ishmael for [him] to examine her [concerning whether or not the garment indeed was to be deemed clean]. She said to him: "Rabbi, I know that the garment was not rendered unclean; however, it was not in my heart to guard it [from uncleanness]." As a result of the examination of her which R. Ishmael conducted, she said to him: "Rabbi, I know that a menstruating woman entered and pulled the cord [so that she conveyed uncleanness to the garment by her shaking the web] with me."

Thesis with Authority

Said R. Ishmael: "How great are the words of sages, for they used to say: "If one did not intend to guard it [in cleanness], it is unclean."

Here again rabbinic sages are shown to be exemplary authorities for the determination of correct practice.

Sifra 58b-c

Situation

A certain student said before R. Aqiba: "I must say what I have learned: [When a woman at childbirth bears a male] she shall be unclean seven days....And on the eighth day [the flesh of his foreskin] shall be circumcised (Lev. 12:2-3).

Thesis

"One might think [that he should be circumcised] fifteen days [after his birth, that is] the eighth [day] after [her] seven days [of uncleanness. However] Scripture says, 'On that day,' [which proves that circumcision is on the eighth day after birth]."

Statement from Authority

R. Aqiba said to him: "You sink in mighty waters and bring up clay in your hands. For is it not already said: *"And a son eight days old you shall circumcise, all the males forever* (Gen. 17:12)?"

The explicit statement of Gen. 17:12, that males must be circumcised on the eighth day, shows that the student's innovative exegesis of Lev. 12:2-3 is entirely unnecessary. The concluding statement from authority is a "refutation for uselessness" [Theon: 214, 5], which shows that the thesis is entirely unnecessary. The refutation is supported by a citation of authority.

Sifra 94a

Situation

One time an ulcer formed on the leg of Joseph b. Pakas, and he asked the doctor to operate. He said to him: "Let me know when [you] finish the operations and [the leg] remains [hanging] as if by a hair." The doctor [finished the operation and] left [the leg hanging] as if by a hair, and he made this known to him.

Thesis with Rationale

[Joseph] called to his son, Nahunyah. He said to him: "Hunyah, my son, until now you have been obligated to care for me. From now on, go away, for one does not defile [himself] by the limb of a living person, even his father's."

Thesis from Authority

And when the matter came before the sages, they said that it was said [concerning him]: *"There is a righteous man who perishes in his righteousness* (Lam. 7:15), [which means], the righteous one is lost, and his righteousness [is lost] with him."

Joseph b. Pakas defends his position, that his son must leave his side, with his own rationale "in the manner of an explanation" [Theon: 206, 15] ("one does not defile [himself] by the limb of a living person"). Sages refute this view "for unsuitability" [Theon: 215, 10] on the basis of an authoritative citation. Their point, that "one can be, so to speak, too righteous" (Porton: 93), is phrased "in the manner of a maxim" [Theon: 206, 10].

Sifre Deuteronomy 322

Situation

One time [when] there was a war in Judea, a commander of horsemen ran after an Israelite on a horse in order to kill him, but he did not reach him. Before he reached him, a snake bit [the commander] on the heel.

Thesis with Rationale

[The Israelite] said to him: "Because we are strong, you are delivered into our hands.

Thesis with Authority

"'Were it not that their rock had sold them'" (Dt 32:34).

Two rhetorical elements, a rationale "in the manner of an explanation" supported by a statement of authority, work together to express a thesis concerning the predicament of the Israelite people. The point is ironic. As the thesis with rationale indicates, the Israelites actually are stronger than the Romans. The Israelites' defeat is explained by the fact that they had angered God (Porton: 93). Dt 32:34, cited at the end of the story, proves this.

Tosefta Shebuot 3:6

Situation

One time R. Reuben spent the Sabbath in Tiberias, and one philosopher found him. He said to him: "Which is the one who is hated in the world?" [Reuben] said to him: "The one who denies his Creator." [The philosopher] said to him: "How [does he deny Him]?"

Thesis with Authority

[Reuben] said to him: *"Honor your father and your mother. Do not murder. Do not bear false witness against your neighbor. Do not covet.*

Conclusion

"Behold, a man does not deny a thing until he denies [its] essential part. And a man commits a sin only after he has denied [the existence of] the one who commanded concerning it."

Reuben's response to the philosopher's question depends upon the authority of Scripture. The deeper point of the story, however, is inherent in its setting, which has a pagan philosopher question a rabbi. The point is that philosophers respect rabbis, politely asking them questions and accepting their answers.

Tosefta Pisha 4:13

Situation

One time the 14th [of Nisan] fell on the Sabbath. They asked Hillel the Elder: "Does the Passover offering override the Sabbath?"

Thesis, A

He said to them: "And do we have only one Passover offering in the year which overrides the Sabbath? We have more than 300 Passover offerings in the year, and they [all] override the Sabbath."

New Situation

The whole courtyard collected against him.

Thesis with Analogy, B

He said to them: "The continual offering is a community sacrifice and the Passover offering is a community sacrifice. Just as the continual offering, which is a community sacrifice, overrides the Sabbath, so the Passover offering, which is a community offering, overrides the Sabbath.

Thesis with Analogy, C

"Another matter: It is said concerning the continual offering 'its season' (Num 28:2), and 'its season' (Num 9:2) is said concerning the Passover offering. Just as the continual offering—concerning which 'its season' is said—overrides the Sabbath, so the Passover offering—concerning which 'its season' is said—overrides the Sabbath.

Thesis with Analogy, D

"And furthermore [it is an] *a fortiori* [argument]. Since the continual offering, which does not produce liability to extirpation, overrides the Sabbath, the Passover offering, which does produce liability to extirpation—how much the more should it override the Sabbath!

Thesis with Authority, E

"And further, I have received from my masters [the tradition] that the Passover offering overrides the Sabbath, and not [merely] the first Passover offering [overrides the Sabbath], but [also] the Passover offering of the individual [overrides the Sabbath]."

New Situation

They said to him: "What will be the rule for the people who do not bring knives and Passover offerings to the Sanctuary [before the Sabbath, so as to prevent themselves from needing to do forbidden labor on the Sabbath itself]?"

Thesis with Rationale

He said to them: "Leave them alone. The holy spirit is upon them. If they are not prophets, they are the disciples of prophets."

This chreia, expanded through a series of questions and responses [Theon: 213, 10], is a good example of the cumulative impact of the bringing together of several different types of argument. The rejection of Hillel's initial thesis leads him to present three additional theses that make use of analogies. But his position ultimately is accepted only when he adduces an antecedent source of authority. The elaboration of the argument here thus parallels Hermogenes' description, beginning with an analogy and turning afterwards to a statement from authority. As in the preceding examples, the authority cited here is the rabbinic masters represented in the inherited tradition.

Hillel's appeal to antecedent authorities causes his opponents too to resort to a different type of argument (new situation, "with a change of subject," Theon: 209, 5). Hillel's ruling, a response to an inquiry [Theon: 203, 10], is challenged because it potentially will lead to transgressions. Hillel responds with a syllogism [Theon: 207, 5] that rationalizes his view. His opponents do not correctly understand the situation. Subject to the holy spirit, the people naturally will do the correct thing. This final thesis and rationale strikingly parallel Hillel's previous reference to authority at D. Having proven that he speaks with the authority of the heritage of rabbinic masters, rationales stated in Hillel's own voice take on the authority of that same heritage. His views in general are authoritative, that is, because he always follows past teachers.

8. *Conclusion/Exhortation*

An exhortation indicates why it is necessary to heed the argument being presented (Mack: 61). One rabbinic example works powerfully to suggest why people should not murder.

> Mishnah Avot 2:6
>
> **Situation**
>
> Also [Hillel] saw a skull floating on the face of the water.
>
> **Thesis with rationale**
>
> He said to it: "Because you drowned [others], they drowned you.
>
> **Conclusion/Exhortation**
>
> "And in the end, they that drowned you shall be drowned."

Hillel responds to the situation described in the first line of this pronouncement story, showing off his perceptive understanding of human nature. By indicating Hillel's perceptiveness, the rationale strengthens the concluding statement, which, in indicating what will happen to murderers, exhorts people to proper behavior.

The Corpus as a Whole

The following synopsis indicates the overall distribution of the rabbinic stories within Hermogenes' taxonomy.

Synopsis:
The Early Rabbinic Pronouncement Stories

I. Introduction/praise: 8.69%
Sifre Numbers 13:1
Tosefta Berakhot 3:20

II. Thesis/Chreia: 8.69%
Mishnah Berakhot 1:1*
Sifre Deuteronomy 80* (expansion)

III. Rationale: 13.04%
Mishnah Berakhot 1:3*
Sifre Deuteronomy 43 (expansion)
Tosefta Nedarim 5:15 (expansion)

IV. Statement of the Contrary: 17.39%
Mishnah Berakhot 2:6* (expansion)
Mishnah Berakhot 2:7* (expansion)
Mishnah Berakhot 2:5* (expansion)
Tosefta Hagiga 2:1 (expansion)

V. Analogy: 4.34%
Sifre Deuteronomy 13 (rudimentary elaboration)

VI. Example: 13.04%
Sifre Deuteronomy 38*
Mekhilta Ishmael Vayassa 1* (expansion)
Sifre Numbers 75* (expansion)

VII. Statement from Authority: 30.43%
Sifra 45c*
Tosefta Kelim Baba Batra 1:2-3*
Sifra 58b-c* (expansion)
Sifra 94a (expansion)
Sifre Deuteronomy 322* (expansion)
Tosefta Shebuot 3:6 (expansion)
Tosefta Pisha 4:13* (elaboration)

VIII. Conclusion/Exhortation: 4.34%
Mishnah Avot 2:6 (expansion)

(* = Legal or exegetical materials)

The rabbinic corpus is concentrated in categories IV and VII, which account for 47.82% of the total. Statements from authority, category VII, are the largest single group, comprising 30.43% of the whole. We find particularly little use of the introduction form, of the thesis/chreia, or of the conclusion/exhortation.[10] Those categories concentrate notably upon personality and unchallenged opinion. Since fourteen of the twenty-three units focus on legal issues, and since a central focus of the Rabbinic literature is on proof of specific legal propositions, the absence of these other concerns is not entirely unexpected.

In light of these facts, the Rabbinic emphasis on statements from authority and statements of the contrary also should not surprise us. Eight of the eleven stories in these categories concern issues of law. Disputes that underlie statements of the contrary as well as appeals to a prior authority therefore are quite natural. The same can be said for the other larger categories, the rationale and example. In the former, a Rabbinic authority's view is substantiated through a reasoned explanation. In the latter pericopae, all of which concern legal issues, examples of actual practice serve to support the statement of law under consideration.

The distribution of stories within Hermogenes' categories thus confirms an assessment of the interests and concerns of early Rabbinic Judaism, derived from a purely substantive evaluation. The synoptic table shows that this literature has minimal interest in aspects of personality *per se*. Nor does it exhibit a great concern for human ethics, heroism, or patriotism, which are normally the central issues in the introduction/praise story, the thesis/chreia, and the conclusion/exhortation. The focus of the Rabbis, rather, is upon questions of religious law (the concern of fourteen of the twenty-three stories listed here) and correct behavior under the law. The rabbinic literature highlights the personality of a rabbi or presents an unexamined statement of belief only to the extent that, in specific cases, these matters shed light on the creation and implementation of the legal system.

At the same time we must recognize that, while subject to interpretation within the rhetorical categories developed by Theon and Hermogenes, the rabbinic evidence does not suggest a knowledge of or conscious attempt to utilize those patterns. This is particularly apparent from the fact that we have found almost no evidence of the elaboration of the chreia described by Hermogenes. Clear elaboration occurs in only one example, Tosefta Pisha 4:13, a long pericope in which Hillel and anonymous authorities debate the rule for sacrificing the Passover offering on the Sabbath. Here elaboration occurs as a result of the presentation of a

---

[10] The slim number of examples of the Analogy is misleading, since other analogies appear within different categories.

dialogue between the disputing parties, not, it seems, as the conscious work of authors familiar with the concept of the complex chreia. The overall results of this study therefore are mixed. On the one hand, we see the extent to which rhetorical forms and usages familiar from the Greco-Roman world can be identified as well within the rabbinic literature. At the same time, we see the limits of the comparative approach used here. We find no evidence of significant procedural overlap in the use of a rhetorical form or in the application of a rhetorical model.

Conclusion

Evaluation of rabbinic pronouncement stories within Hermogenes' rhetorical scheme instructs us concerning the varied rhetorical functions of the pronouncement story and also directs our attention to the salient characteristics of the rabbinic examples and of the early rabbinic literature as a whole. Our analysis, that is, permits identification of important attitudes within the early rabbinic movement and allows isolation of the social and philosophical ideologies of the individuals who created the rabbinic literature. This assessment of that literature therefore achieves positive results, illustrating the value of rhetorical criticism in general. On the one hand, we see how rhetorical form and content determine meaning. On the other, we now recognize the degree to which rhetorical forms have a comparable significance across diverse literatures. Significantly, in the case at hand, rhetorical evaluation of a small portion of a literature substantiates an understanding gained through evaluation of the content and interests of the corpus as a whole.[11]

We find that rhetorical patterns found in rabbinic pronouncement stories reflect some of the patterns found elsewhere in hellenistic literature. The rabbinic pericopae at once speak as pieces of the rabbinic corpus of which they are a part and exhibit rhetorical traits shared with other contemporary literatures. The details of their rhetoric, however, are highly distinctive. This ability to highlight both the shared features and the distinctive traits of the literatures subject to evaluation comprises, of course, the central value of rhetorical analysis.

---

[11] This study's conclusions regarding the early rabbinic movement's disinterest in the personality of individual masters parallels conclusions reached by William Green on the basis of formal and substantive analysis of the rabbinic corpus as a whole. See Green 1978.

WORKS CONSULTED

Avery-Peck, Alan J.,
    1983   "Classifying Early Rabbinic Pronouncement Stories." *SBL Seminar Papers* 22:223-244.
    1991   "Rhetorical Analysis of Early Rabbinic Pronouncement Stories." *Hebrew Annual Review* 13:1-24.

Bultmann, Rudolph
    1968   *The History of the Synoptic Tradition*. Revised Ed. Translated by John Marsh. New York: Harper and Row.

Green, William S.
    1978   "What's in a Name? The Problematic of Rabbinic 'Biography.'" Pp. 77-96 in *Approaches to Ancient Judaism: Theory and Practice*. Ed. W.S. Green. Missoula: Scholars.

Hock, Ronald F. and Edward O'Neil
    1986   "The Chreia Discussion of Aelius Theon of Alexandria." Pp. 82-107 in *The Chreia in Ancient Rhetoric. Vol. I. The Progymnasmata*. Ed. Ronald Hock and Edward O'Neil. Atlanta: Scholars.

Kennedy, George A.
    1984   *New Testament Interpretation through Rhetorical Criticism*. Chapel Hill: The University of North Carolina Press.

Mack, Burton
    1989   "Elaboration of the Chreia in the Hellenistic School." *Patterns of Persuasion in the Gospels*. Ed. Burton Mack and Vernon Robbins. Sonoma: Polebridge.

Mack, Burton and Edward O'Neil
    1986   "Hermogenes of Tarsus." Pp. 153-181 in *The Chreia in Ancient Rhetoric. Vol. I. The Progymnasmata*. Ed. Ronald Hock and Edward O'Neil. Atlanta: Scholars.

Neusner, Jacob
    1970   *Development of a Legend: A Life of Yohanan ben Zakkai*. Second ed. Leiden: E.J. Brill.

Neusner, Jacob and Avery-Peck, Alan J.
    1982a   "The Quest for the Historical Hillel." *Judaica* December, 1982:194-214 and Pp. 45-63 in *Formative Judaism: Religious, Historical and Literary Studies*. Ed. Jacob Neusner. Chico: Scholars.
    1982b   "Literature and Society: The Unfolding Conventions on Hillel." Pp. 87-98 in *Formative Judaism: Religious, Historical and Literary Studies*. Ed. Jacob Neusner. Chico: Scholars.

Porton, Gary G.
    1981   "The Pronouncement Story in Tannaitic Literature: A Review of Bultmann's Theory." *Semeia* 20:81-99.

1976-82　　*The Traditions of Rabbi Ishmael.* 4 vols. Leiden: E.J. Brill.

Robbins, Vernon K.
1981　　"Classifying Pronouncement Stories in Plutarch's *Parallel Lives.*" *Semeia* 20:29-52.

Tannehill, Robert C.
1981　　"The Pronouncement Story and its Types." *Semeia* 20:1-13.

Rhetorical Argumentation in the Hadith Literature of Islam

R. Marston Speight
National Council of the Churches
of Christ in the U.S.A.

ABSTRACT

This study examines rhetorical argumentation in the Muslim hadith, which are authoritative traditions of Muhammad and his followers. Most of the hadith are epideictic because they display Muhammad's ethos as prophet, governor, judge, and honored leader. They have a deliberative and judicial function since they regulate Muslim behavior. The rhetorical elements of thesis/rationale, contrary, and judgment (citation of written authority) appear in the hadith discussed below.

Introduction

Next to the Qur'ān no body of literature is more influential in the Muslim community than that of the hadith, or the authoritative traditions. This material is not easily accessible to readers who do not know Arabic, although several important collections have been translated into Western languages.[1]

The idea expressed in Islam by the word *hadith* grew out of the notion of *sunna*, meaning "a level path," and, by extension, behavior which conforms to well-established patterns, for example, venerated ancestral customs. Muslims speak of the *sunna* of the Prophet Muhammad, which means the example of the Prophet as a model for humankind. A particular account of any aspect of the Prophet's example is called *hadith*. Aside from this religious meaning the word signifies "report," "conversation" or "narration." The word *hadith* has a plural, *ahādīth*, but the singular form is also used as a collective noun. For the sake of simplicity only the one form, *hadith*, will be used in this study, expressing both the singular and

---

[1] Some that have been translated into English are: Al-Bukhari 1979; Muslim 1971-75; Abu Dawud 1984. The best general introduction in English to the Hadith literature is Robson 1971. Other introductions are: Goldziher 1971; Guillaume 1966; Ṣiddīqī 1961.

the plural sense. The Companions of Muhammad collected reports, or hadith, of:

1. Words pronounced by the Prophet giving his opinions, judgments and reactions with reference to a variety of social, moral, political, legal, and theological concerns;
2. Events that occurred during the Prophet's life, in the course of which his actions were carefully observed by onlookers;
3. Events and situations in the life of Muslims and others, concerning which the Prophet asked or answered questions, or made remarks.

To these were added during the first centuries of Islam a large number of stories and pronouncements of a historical, biographical, cultic, or legal nature, which were attributed to the Companions of Muhammad and to the generation of Muslims following that of the Companions.

Hadith texts became a basic source of doctrine and practice in Islam. They were preserved and transmitted for the purpose of providing the community of Muslims with authoritative information regarding the interpretation of the Qurʾān and the ways of fulfilling the duties of private, social, and cultic life. They became a source for historical information on the life of Muhammad and his Companions as well as on the initial expansion of Islam, and they constitute a lively record of the early development of Islamic thought.

From the beginning the reports were transmitted orally, but very early they were also written down, at least in some circles. By the first quarter of the eighth century A.D., collections of hadith began to be compiled in a systematic way. By the ninth century the search for and transmission and preservation of hadith became one of the most respected tasks of Muslim scholars. That century was the era of the authoritative collections. These were not prepared upon the order of any central authority, but owe their existence to the personal initiative of their compilers. Later their collections recommended themselves to the community by virtue of their intrinsic worth. From an enormous fund of material, the compilers chose reports that they considered to be authoritative according to the criteria of the science of hadith criticism. The most important collectors, with the titles of their works are:

1. Muḥammad ibn Ismāʿīl al-Bukhārī (d. 870), *Al-Jāmiʿ al-Ṣaḥīḥ (The Authentic Collection)*.
2. Muslim ibn al-Ḥajjāj (d. 875), *Al-Ṣaḥīḥ (The Authentic)*.
3. Sulaymān Abū Dāʾūd al-Sijistānī (d. 888), *Al-Sunan (The Norms)*.

4. Abū ʿĪsā al-Tirmidhī (d. 892), *Al-Jāmiʿ (The Collection)*.
5. Aḥmad ibn ʿAlī al-Nisāʾī (d. 915), *Al-Sunan (The Norms)*.
6. Ibn Māja al-Qazwīnī (d. 887), *Al-Sunan (The Norms)*.

These and numerous other collections have been published in many editions. There are voluminous commentaries on the great Six Collections, as they are called. Other books written for the study of hadith are lexicons of rare words, biographical encyclopedias of the transmitters, specialized treatises on various aspects of hadith criticism and legal manuals.

Hadith take the form of short unconnected pieces, each of which is preceded by its chain of authorities. The reports were formulated to be told and recited aloud, and after being recorded in writing they did not undergo literary recomposition. The material retains the distinctive characteristics of oral composition: lively narrative, simple, vigorous, and conversational style, concrete and colorful language, minimal description, use of formulas, stereotyped expressions, and frequent repetition.

Although the primary concerns of Muslim scholarship have been to use the hadith in Qurʾān exegesis, historical research, jurisprudence, and edificatory literature, there developed as early as the ninth century a tradition of rhetorical study of hadith. A classic work of this period, *Kitāb Taʾwīl Mukhtalif al-Ḥadīth (A Treatise on Divergent Hadith)*, by Ibn Qutayba (d. 889), illustrates a practical purpose which characterized some rhetorical analysis of the reports; that is, the effort to reconcile or otherwise explain apparently contradictory reports. The Muslim literary critics were often concerned with interpreting the meaning of the texts for the performance of duty, rather than dealing with their aesthetic value. Another preoccupation was to demonstrate by rhetorical analysis the truth of the doctrine which affirms the inimitability of the Qurʾān and, by extension, the inimitability of the Prophet's words, since it was through him that the Qurʾān was revealed. The inspiration of the Qurʾān is, to Muslims, on a different and higher level than that of the hadith, but Muhammad's person establishes a link between the two. A modern work of this kind, showing aesthetics at the service of doctrine, is *Iʿjāz al-Qurʾān wa-l-Balāgha al-Nabawīya (The Inimitability of the Qurʾān and the Rhetoric of the Prophet)*, by Muṣṭafā al-Rafīʿī (d. 1937). The figures of speech in the hadith attracted attention in Islamic history. An important book from the tenth century is *Al-Majāzāt al-Nabawīya (The Prophetic Figures of Speech)*, by Al-Sharīf al-Raḍī. Throughout the extensive commentaries on hadith may be found occasional remarks about the rhetoric of the reports in question, intermingled with grammatical, legal, historical, and doctrinal information. Non-Muslim scholars have been preoccupied with historical features of the material, trying to demonstrate the degree of its authenticity and how it casts light on the evolution of Islamic thought.[2]

In this study I am undertaking an approach to the hadith that I have not seen elsewhere, except in fragmentary ways. I am analyzing the complete report rhetorically, from its statement of situation to its dialogue or action, and finally to its pronouncement, the heart of the hadith. It is this latter that usually receives attention from critics, to the neglect of the overall rhetorical setting in which it is laid.

The literary forms of hadith are of a number of kinds, such as sermons, extended narratives, historical reminiscences, prayers, commands, judgments, affirmations, and promises, to name a few.[3] Using the insights and terminology of the hellenistic rhetoricians, however, a large number of the texts can be grouped together as answering to the description of a chreia, that is, "a brief statement or action with pointedness attributed to a definite person or something analogous to a person" (Quoted from Theon in Mack and Robbins 1989:11). The reference to hellenistic rhetoric in the case of hadith is appropriate for two reasons: First, without distorting the analysis we are able to bring the Islamic material into the continuum of an ongoing comparative study being carried on by scholars in hellenistic, biblical, and rabbinic literature. Second, although Arabic rhetoric and literary theory owe nothing fundamental to the Greeks, the extensive cross-cultural exchanges during the flowering of the Islamic Empire resulted in the borrowing from Hellenism of a number of literary motifs, conventions, and definitions (Schaade: 981). So the use of Greek terminology in describing Islamic texts is not as foreign as it might seem. The ease with which hellenistic terms can be used to describe Islamic stories may be explained by the statement of George A. Kennedy:

> Though rhetoric is colored by the traditions and conventions of the society in which it is applied, it is also a universal phenomenon which is conditioned by basic workings of the human mind and heart and by the nature of all human society (Kennedy 1984: 10).

The broad definition of a chreia given above encompasses those hadith which contain only an introductory formula and a pointed saying attributed to a particular person, corresponding to Theon's "unprompted statement," (Robbins 1988:5) or a chreia having no specific situation described. There are literally hundreds of such texts in the hadith literature. However, in this study I have restricted the choice of material to

---

[2] Examples of recent books of this kind are: van Ess 1975; Graham 1977; Juynboll 1983; Powers 1986; Wansbrough 1978.

[3] A description of these may be found in Speight 1970.

those texts which contain situations and a minimum of narrative and conversation. These correspond to the "response" type of chreia, with statements (or actions) arising "out of specific circumstances" (Robbins 1988: 6). There is an abundance of material of this kind. It is to these stories that Rudolf Bultmann made reference in his study of the synoptic Gospels when he wrote, "...in the tradition of Islam there are also apophthegmatic items which would repay study" (Bultmann: 42, n.1).

THE RHETORIC OF HADITH

As might be expected from what has already been said about hadith, this material conforms in large part to the Greek category of plain or simple style, with occasional examples of forceful style (Kennedy 1963: 12, 281). The general impression left by hadith is that of oral expression, artless and direct in its impact, concerned with many apparently minor aspects of life, as well as with weighty matters, and integrated by the overall purpose of transmitting the normative example (sunna) of the Prophet to members of the community which was formed by the effort of his life. Muhammad's example as reported in the hadith functions in two general ways, 1) to nurture Muslim piety, and 2) to regulate Muslim behavior. In serving these functions the hadith exhibit clearly the three sorts of rhetoric described by the Greeks: epideictic, deliberative, and judicial (Kennedy 1984:19). The three kinds overlap in the texts to a considerable degree, and given the central figure of Muhammad in the literature, there is a sense in which nearly all hadith are epideictic, that is, they serve to display his ethos (Kennedy 1984:15) as prophet, governor, judge, and honored leader. At the same time the function of regulating Muslim behavior is served by deliberative and judicial rhetoric, since elements of persuasion, exhortation, and other argumentation are employed to insure the effectiveness of the stories in showing the way for the community to conduct itself. Recent studies of Aelius Theon of Alexandria and Hermogenes of Tarsus (Hock and O'Neil) have brought to light useful information for analysis of a chreia and the argumentation in it. The following hadith will illustrate various aspects of rhetoric associated with the chreia and show that the material issuing from Muslim traditionists (muḥaddithūn) fits into the mold of rhetoric in the ancient world.

ACTION STORY

1. **Situation-Introduction**
Qays b. abī Ḥazm said: The Messenger of God was preaching and he saw my father in the sun.

Action-Response

So he bade him, or signaled to him, to come into the shade. (Ṭayālisī, 1298)

This first example illustrates the purely epideictic nature of many hadith. There is no argumentation involved. The statement of the situation provides the introduction to the story. A brief description sets the stage for the action-pronouncement. Qays, the primary guarantor, gives a reminiscence of a minor scene from the Prophet's life, the memory of which affected him personally. The time was during the adult career of Muhammad and the interaction was with one of his associates. The audience was an assembly of listeners to the Prophet. The occasion was a congregational gathering of Muslims, probably on a Friday at noon, according to the custom. Qays was not present because he did not know the Prophet personally, but became a Muslim after Muhammad's death.

The ethos of the Prophet is seen in the word, "amara," translated, "bade," and expressing authority. Although the action may have involved words (unless the version, "signaled," is preferred), the overall pronouncement is one of action rather than words.[4] There is no speaker in the story, only an actor, the Prophet. The circumstance calling forth the pronouncement action is the sight of Qays' father standing or sitting in the sun. Unexpressed but implicit in the act is the sympathy of a great man who can single out an uncomfortable or overly scrupulous or timid man in a group and respond to him by putting him at ease. So, restrained pathos is part of the rhetorical picture. It is also to be noted that the broad circumstantial setting, recurring often in the hadith literature, of a group of listeners to the Prophet, is quickly narrowed to a single individual. The general effect is to highlight the compassionate nature of Muhammad. His action is not held up to be emulated, at least not explicitly. It is simply to be admired and is a part of the collective Muslim memory of the person, Muhammad. As a reminiscence in the third person, it is told simply with no description and no direct speech.

THESIS (AUTHORITATIVE PRONOUNCEMENT)

2. Situation-Action
ʿAbd al-Malik b. ʿAlqama abī ʿAlqama al-Thaqafī reported that a delegation from Thaqīf came to the Messenger of God and presented him with a gift.

Pronouncement-Thesis
He said, "Is this an offering (for the needy) or a gift? With an offering one seeks the pleasure of God, but with a gift one seeks the pleasure of the Messenger."

---

[4] The rhetoricians divided the *chreiai* into three basic classes, the "sayings" *chreiai*, the "action" *chreiai* and the "mixed" *chreiai*, containing both speech and action. Cf. Robbins 1988:11,12.

Commentary

Then he took care of their request, and they questioned him for so long that they had to perform the noon prayer at the time of the midafternoon prayer. (Ṭayālisī, 1336)

This story and the three texts which follow are "sayings" chreiai. Muhammad's speech is a response to the action of the delegation. Thus, the situation is more than simply a statement after something has been seen (Hock and O'Neil:85). Rather, the question and statement are a response to an action that invites a question. Muhammad's response is to introduce a diairetic question (a question that divides the situation into two alternatives). Then Muhammad presents a "thesis," the kind of chreia statement Hermogenes uses to illustrate the elaboration exercise (Hock and O'Neil: 177). After Muhammad's statement, the narrator adds a commentary (Hock and O'Neil: 99-101) that exhibits the positive qualities of the Messenger of God. With this brief story, Al-Thaqafī recalls an incident that occurred during the period of the "delegations," a time when tribesmen from many parts of Arabia came to meet the Prophet and to discuss the terms of their political and economic relationship with him and the community of Muslims. The speaker is the Prophet and the audience is a delegation of leaders or representatives from Thaqīf along with some of Muhammad's Companions. The action which calls forth the pronouncement is one in which we see the authoritative ethos of the speaker. The tribesmen from Thaqīf were already allied with the Muslims by treaty and they had accepted Islam. Their bringing of a gift is an ambiguous gesture, and the pronouncement sets forth the ambiguity without actually making a value judgment, except by implication. First Muhammad asks a rhetorical question, "Is this an offering (for the needy) or a gift?" Either one or the other was in order, but the Muslims needed to keep the two separate. The Prophet-statesman, following the divine revelation which he had received, required of his followers donations for the needy, but any gift to him personally was voluntary, and conceivably would not be offered entirely without self-interest on the part of the giver. Especially would this be the case with the delegations.

After the rhetorical question, the speaker draws upon a Qur'ānic motif (30:38, et al.), "seeking God's pleasure," literally "seeking the face of God," and makes it into an epistrophe, applied to himself as well as to God. The effect of this figure is both to elevate the Prophet in the minds of the hearers and to set him in contrast to God, so that no one should ever make the mistake of attributing to Muhammad a higher dignity than that which God had bestowed upon His Messenger. This pronouncement, then, contains three rhetorical elements: question, thesis, and epistrophe. The conclusion of the story shows that the tribesmen's gift had been for the Prophet, because they sought help and advice from him. In the sense that the pronouncement distinguishes between the motivations for practices in the community in a hortatory way, it may be said to contain deliberative rhetoric, that is, the recommending to the hearers of a certain course of action. This is a much told story, existing in ten or more versions, coming from the Prophet's mature years and involving interaction with his associates, according to some versions, and with his wife, according to others.

3. Situation-Inquiry

Abū Hurayra reported: A man came to the Messenger of God and said, "O Messenger of God, who is most worthy of my companionship?"

Expanded Response

He replied, "Your mother." He asked, "And who, after her?" The reply, "Your mother." He asked, "And then who?" The reply, "Your mother." He asked a fourth time, "And then who?" He replied, "Your father." (Bukhārī, adab, 2)

This example is an expanded response to an inquiry (Hock and O'Neil:87, 101-102). The expansion of the questions and answers occurs through repetition. There is no elaboration of an argument to secure the meaning of the answers. The Prophet defines an exemplary ethos or character in other people; that is, the qualities of mother and father which make them "worthy of companionship." One might ask why the questioner kept on wanting to know who was the most worthy after the mother, but this is a common device in the hadith for conveying the relative importance or gravity of a series of items, such as sins or virtues or persons. Often each repeated question will have a different answer. The rhetorical force of the thrice repeated "Your mother" is to establish maternal respect as a supreme virtue, thus furnishing a deliberative element to the story. The simplicity of this exchange with its monotony and lack of commentary or descriptive detail, and with its use of the word, "companionship," or "friendship" (šaḥāba) creates an atmosphere of lightness, almost of humor, combined with dignity.

4. Situation-Introduction

Abū Ayyūb reported that the Prophet said to him, "O Abū Ayyūb, would you not like for me to suggest to you an offering (ṣadaqa) in which both God and His Messenger take pleasure?" He replied, "O yes!"

Pronouncement-Thesis

The Prophet said, "You should reconcile people who are estranged and bring together those who are separated." (Ṭayālisī: 598)

Here again there is no elaboration of the argument, simply the pronouncement of the thesis. The Prophet's question is stylized. By asking Abū Ayyūb if he would not like to have certain information he assumes the role of teacher and religious counsellor, an ethos which determines much of the rhetorical force of the story. Abū Ayyūb, as an eager follower of Muhammad, replies with a strong affirmative, "O yes!" The tone of his answer adds a note of pathos to the atmosphere. However, the most striking feature is the way in which the sense of ṣadaqa (offering) is broadened in the pronouncement. This concept of offering is common in Islam as a charitable contribution to the poor. The giving of ṣadaqa is one of the basic requirements of the religion. But the recommendation (deliberative) of the Prophet here in the proposition immediately following the introduction is that peacemaking is a form of ṣadaqa. This is not an injunction which can be codified in jurisprudence but a metaphorical identification of one concrete duty (the giving of ṣadaqa) with another (peacemaking). The effect of this metaphor is heightened by the fact that Muhammad does not identify the recipient of the ṣadaqa. God and the Messenger will take pleasure in it, but it is not given to them. A ṣadaqa can literally be given only to people in certain kinds of need. Perhaps the thought is that peacemakers offer a ṣadaqa to those whom they reconcile, but this is not clear. The two halves of the proposition constitute a good example of synonymous parallelism, with the final verbs in each member rhyming.

5. Situation-Statement

ʿAʾisha reported that some people said, "O Messenger of God, here are some people who only recently came out of paganism. They brought us some meat and we do not know whether they pronounced the name of God while slaughtering the animals or not."

Pronouncement-Thesis

He said, "Pronounce the name of God yourselves and eat." (Bukhārī, tawḥīd, 13)

This brief account presents a response to a point of view that has been openly stated (Hock and O'Neil:87). One of the Prophet's wives, ʿAʾisha, is the source of the story. The people do not ask a question explicitly, but their statement implies a desire for the information which Muhammad supplies as a pungent, slightly impatient reaction to the ceremonial punctiliousness of those who hesitated to eat the meat. The Prophet's judgment invalidates the terms of the case as set forth by the speakers. They should go ahead and eat the meat without worrying about whether the neophyte believers who had given it to them had slaughtered according to the law. This is a thesis given in a particular case that can be broadened to apply generally in similar circumstances.

Rationale (Reason)

A chreia may occur "in the manner of an explanation" (Hock and O'Neil:91), that is, with a reason or rationale embedded in it. In the following instance, the statement containing the rationale is a statement by Muhammad that arises out of a specific circumstance (Hock and O'Neil:85).

6. Situation

'Abd Allāh b. 'Umar reported: The Prophet passed by a man who was reproving his brother for being too modest, saying, "You are so modest that it will be harmful to you."

Thesis with Rationale

The Messenger of God said, "Leave him alone, for modesty is a part of faith." (Bukhārī, adab, 77)

The dictum which constitutes the thesis has its rationale contained within it, in a concise expression. The reason given for leaving the modest man alone is, "modesty is a part of faith." This thought is couched in a common syntactical form in which the preposition *min* (literally "from") expresses the relation between the part (modesty) and the whole (faith). The Prophet reproaches the one man for his advocacy of a measured morality, and implicitly commends the other for his morality which is commensurate with its source; that is, faith. In the story the element of pathos (Kennedy 1984:15) is suppressed due to the extreme economy of the narrative. Both praise and blame are intermingled here as the person who criticized the modest man is admonished to "leave him alone." A deliberative element is also evident in the fact that modesty is recommended as a practice of faith.

7. Situation

'Alī reported: The Prophet sent an armed band on campaign, and he appointed a man of the Anṣār as their commander. He ordered them to obey him. The leader became angry with his men and said to them: "Did not the Prophet order you to obey me?" They replied, "Yes." He said, "I have decided that once you have gathered some firewood and built a fire that you should throw yourselves into it." So they gathered the wood and built a fire. And as they considered throwing themselves into it, they looked at each other and said, "We followed the Prophet in order to escape from the Fire. Why should we go into it now?" While they hesitated thus the fire died down and the commander's anger subsided.

Thesis with Rationale

This event was mentioned to the Prophet, and he said, "If they had entered the fire they would never have come out. Obedience is required only in that which is good." (Bukhārī, aḥkām, 4)

This example contains an expanded version of a specific situation (Hock and O'Neil:85, 101-103). The Prophet responds to this situation with a thesis followed by a rationale (Hock and O'Neil:91, 177). The account is unusually artistic, with its negative assessment of the character of the Anṣār, or Medinan natives (epideictic), its evocation of the Prophet's authority as he is told of the event (epideictic), and the parallels of two kinds of obedience, two kinds of fire (hell-fire and physical fire) and two kinds of heat (that of the fire and that of the commander's anger). The thesis is an observation that if the men had followed the commander's order their misguided obedience would not have delivered them from the destruction of the fire. The rationale, "Obedience is required...", gives a broad ethico-political application to the specific case at hand. This statement became one of the watchwords of Islamic political doctrine.

8. Situation

ʿAbd Allāh b. ʿUmar reported: While the Prophet was praying he saw sputum on the wall of the mosque, on the side of the direction for prayer (qibla).

Thesis with Rationale

Angrily he rubbed it off with his hand and said, "When people are at prayer they should not spit in front of them, because God is present there in front of them." (Bukhārī, adab, 75)

In this instance, the Prophet performs an action and makes a statement about something he has seen (Hock and O'Neil:85). His assertion that, "When people are at prayer they should not spit in front of them," is followed by an explanation, "because God is present there in front of them." (Hock and O'Neil: 91). The pathos of the story is seen in the anger of the Prophet-judge. His censure of the act performed in his absence is based, not as modern people might think, on a question of hygiene, but on ceremonial and theological considerations. It is an affront to God, reasons the Prophet, to spit in the direction of His presence. This observation raises the question of a possible contradiction of the belief in divine omnipresence, since the thought is that God occupies the space in front of the worshipers. The problem is resolved when the nature of ritual prayer in Islam is understood. This prayer is a concentrated focus in time, space, and human motivation of a relationship between God and humankind which is all-embracing. So, the divine presence in front of the worshipers is real only because the Almighty is manifest throughout the created world.

Contrary (Argues Against Or Explores Alternatives)

Another method of supporting a thesis in argumentation is to express a contrary (Hock and O'Neil: 177), thus giving a reason against the thesis, or providing an alternative interpretation. When this technique occurs in an abbreviated setting, Theon says the chreia has been composed "in the manner of an enthymeme" (Hock and O'Neil: 91). The point is that there has been a turn of reasoning, and the hearer or reader must deduce the reasons that support the appropriate answer.

> **9. Situation-Thesis**
> Al-Mughīra b. Shuʿba reported that the Messenger of God used to pray until his feet became swollen. People said to him, "O Messenger of God, why do you do that when your former and latter sins have all been forgiven?"
>
> **Contrary**
> The Messenger of God said, "Should I not be a grateful slave?" (Ṭayālisī, 693)

In this account, Muhammad prayed so often and so long that his feet became swollen from the repeated physical gestures, involving, at certain points, sitting upon the feet. The observers censure him mildly ("Why do you do that...?), or show puzzlement. The Prophet's answer goes contrary to their reasoning. The question is based upon a belief that if people multiply acts of piety it is a sign that they are fearful on account of their sins and hopeful that God will forgive them. This motivation does not seem to the observers to be appropriate in the case of the Prophet, for they have learned from the Qurʾān (48:2) that God has forgiven all of Muhammad's former and latter sins. Why, then, they reason, should he pray so much? The prayers meant here are the supererogatory ones, performed at times other than the five daily canonical moments. In reply to their puzzled question Muhammad gives the opposite interpretation to that implied in the query. He emphasizes that the primary response of a person forgiven by God is gratitude, and a primary expression of gratitude is prayer. Comprehensive divine forgiveness evokes extraordinary prayer from the forgiven one, as well as a sense of humility ("grateful slave"). Muhammad is presented in this story as an example of intense devotion to be admired and followed.

> **10. Situation**
> Anas b. Malik reported: As the Prophet and I were going out of the mosque we met a man at the gate. He said, "O Messenger of God, when will be the Hour?" The Prophet said, "How have you prepared for it?"

Contrary

The man appeared to be distressed. Then he said, "O Messenger of God, I have not prepared much for it in the way of fasting, prayer and almsgiving, but I love God and His Messenger."

Thesis

The Prophet said, "You will be with the one you love." (Bukhārī, aḥkām, 10)

There is pathos in this story and the Prophet's ethos as spiritual counsellor is stressed. The more or less groping inquiry at the first ("...when will be the Hour?") leads to an elevation of thought in a few short lines. A negative evaluation of human effort turns into a surprising conclusion of generous promise and approbation. The distressed man's reply to the Prophet's question is at first situated on the level of conventional piety (fasting, prayer, and almsgiving), and he judges himself as lacking. Then he expresses hope that the more spiritual quality of love will not be disregarded. Muhammad's pronouncement raises the discussion to a high spiritual and personal plane. His saying is a promise whose condition (if you love Him) is understood. Conditional promises abound in the hadith, often recommending a certain pattern of action, as here (love for God and his Messenger). Usually the protasis and the apodosis are given fully. In this story the exploration of alternative premises prepares for the striking thesis at the end.

11. Situation

Anas reported: The Prophet saw an old man walking supported by his two sons. He said, "What is wrong with him?" They said, "He has vowed to go on foot to the Kaʿba."

Contrary-Thesis

The Prophet said, "God is not in need of this man's punishing himself." And he told him to ride. (Bukhārī, jazāʾ al-ṣayd, 27)

Here is seen the pathos of an elderly ascetic punishing himself for religious motives. The Prophet's censure involves a theological statement, that a believer's self-inflicted punishment is to no avail with God. As a thesis it contrasts strongly with the misplaced religiosity of the ascetic.

12. Situation

Abū Saʿīd al-Khudrī reported: Some people of the Anṣār begged from the Messenger of God and he gave to them. Then they begged again and he gave, so that when he had given all that he had he said, "Whatever possessions I have I will not withhold them from you,

Alternatives-Thesis

but if you refrain from begging (yasta'fif) God will supply your needs (yu'iffa). If you are satisfied with what you have (yastaghni), God will not cause you to lack (yughni). If you persevere (yaṣbir), God will give you patience (yušabbir). No gift of God is greater than patience." (Abū Dā'ūd, zakāt, 28)

The Prophet is presented as a generous, concerned friend of the poor, but the main point is an exhortation to contentment and patient endurance. This deliberative rhetoric is given force by the pairing of different verb forms from the same root in each of the three elements of the thesis. This manner of expression is identified in Islamic manuals as *taṣrīf* or "variation", the use of derivatives from the same root (von Grunebaum: 118). The thesis contains within it an exploration of alternatives to the course of action announced in the first statement of the Prophet ("Whatever possessions I have I will not withhold them from you").

13. Situation

Ṭalḥa reported, saying, The Messenger of God and I passed by some people in a grove of palm trees. He said, "What are they doing?" Someone said, "They are pollinating the trees. They join the male to the female, and the tree is pollinated."

Contrary, Exploring Alternatives

The Messenger of God said, "I don't think there is any need to do that." The men were informed of what he said, and they gave up the practice. Later the Messenger of God was told about the result of their not pollinating the trees, and he said, "If it is a useful thing to do they should do it. I was only expressing an opinion. Don't bring up to me my personal opinion.

Thesis

On the other hand, if I tell you something that comes from God, then accept that. I will not attribute a lie to God Most Glorious." (Muslim, faḍā'il, 38)

In this story the Prophet, in his mature years, interacts with the common people. The depiction of the Prophet's ignorance of an agricultural practice is true to what we know of his background as a city dweller who had in childhood been introduced to nomadic life, but not to sedentary rural society. As statesman-prophet his authority in Medina is unquestioned. So when he disregards the practice of pollination the peasants obey him, even though they know better. Good sense prevails, however, and the Prophet's contrary reasoning affirms his fallible human nature as it leads up to the pronouncement-thesis at the end of the story. In his mild statement of self-criticism ("I was only expressing an opinion"), or self-justification, perhaps, there is seen a slight element of judicial rhetoric.

14. Situation
Usāma b. Sharīk reported: The Bedouin asked the Messenger of God, "Shall we use medicines?"

Thesis-Rationale
He said, "Yes, O people of God, use medicines. God provides either healing or a remedy for each disease, that is, except one."

Contrary
They said, "O Messenger of God, what is that one?" He said, "Old age."
(Tirmidhī, ṭibb, 2)

The Prophet's answer to the Bedouin's question is epigrammatic, playing upon the alliterative and rhyming qualities of the words *dā'* (disease), *dawā'* (remedy) and *shifā'* (healing). There is a second pronouncement in the story, the one word reply *al-haram* (old age), to the second question. It constitutes an exception to the rule announced in the thesis, providing a contrary element to the argumentation and deepening the import of the story considerably. The interaction, of a light, mildly humorous tone, is between the Prophet and common, inexperienced members of the religious community.

Judgment (Citation of Written Authority, or Maxim)

Many hadith recount instances where the Prophet either approved or disapproved of the behavior of others, or in which he gave a judgment regarding events in the life of the religious community of Islam. So, in texts of this nature we see illustrated the element of judicial argumentation as described by Hermogenes. Often the Prophet's judgments are accompanied by the citation of written authority from the Qur'ān (Hock and O'Neil: 101, 177). Judicial hadith often fit the pattern of a judicial speech as described by Aristotle, in which there is 1) an introduction (proem), 2) a statement giving the facts of the case, 3) proof demonstrating the issue of the case and 4) an epilogue (Mack and Robbins 1989: 3). In a hadith story the proof is usually expressed as a judgment by the Prophet, to whose judicial authority appeal has been made.

15. Introduction-Situation
The father of 'Abd Allāh b. 'Amr b. Rabī'a reported: Once while some of us were traveling the sky became dark and we could not determine the direction for prayer (qibla).

Statement of Case
So we prayed individually in the direction which we supposed to be the right one. When the sky cleared we discovered that some of us had prayed in the wrong direction and others in the right direction.

Thesis-Judgment

We mentioned this to the Messenger of God and he said, "You have all performed your prayer."

Citation of Written Authority

Then was revealed the verse, "Wherever you turn, there will be the face of God" (Qurʾān 2:115). (Ṭayālisī, 1145)

The background of this story is the prescription for ritual prayer in Islam. For the act of worship to be valid, the worshipers must be facing in the right direction (*qibla*), toward Mecca. The seeking of advice from the Prophet emphasizes his ethos as religious leader. His judgment makes clear that, although the correct performance of the prayer is of primary importance to Muslims, honest error does not render the act invalid. The most important fact for the praying community to keep in mind is the omnipresence of God. This truth is stated in the verse from the Qurʾān that is cited as an epilogue.

16. Introduction-Situation

ʿUrwa b. al-Zubayr reported that ʿAbd Allāh b. al-Zubayr related to him that a man of the Anṣār disputed with Zubayr in the presence of the Messenger of God over the irrigation ditches in the Ḥarra which serve to water the date palms.

Statement of Case

The Anṣārī said, "Let the water flow freely." But (Zubayr) refused, and they came quarreling to the Messenger of God.

Thesis-Judgment

The Messenger of God said to Zubayr, "Water your trees, O Zubayr, and then direct the water to your neighbor."

Contrary

The Anṣārī became angry and said, "O Messenger of God, he is your cousin."

Judgment

The Prophet of God's face clouded with anger, and he said, "O Zubayr, water your trees and then dam up the stream until the water rises up to the embankments between the trees."

Citation of Written Authority

Zubayr said, "I think that was the occasion for the revelation of the verse, 'No, by the Lord, they will not believe until they make you a judge between them in their disputes and find no objection to your decisions...'" (Qurʾān 4:65). (Muslim, faḍāʾil, 36)

This story is one of a genre in the hadith called "circumstances of revelation" (asbāb al-nuzūl), in which the Companions of the Prophet recall incidents or circumstances surrounding the revealing of certain passages in the Qurʾān. The circumstances of the story, told with a minimum of detail and in somewhat of an elliptic way, establish an atmosphere of angry tension. Zubayr, the father, and his two sons, who tell the story, were Meccan emigrants to Medina. The Anṣārī was a citizen of Medina. For some time after their emigration to that locality the Prophet and his fellow Meccans had to contend with varying degrees of loyalty on the part of the longtime inhabitants. The rising turbulence of the scene is depicted by the use of two verbal forms from the same root. The first, translated "disputed," implies that the provocation came first from the Anṣārī. Then the reciprocal form of the verb is used, translated, "came quarreling," to signify the mutual embroilment of the two parties. The Anṣārī's request was legitimate since Zubayr was not sharing the water flow as he should have been doing. Muhammad's response is intended to bring reconciliation between the two quarreling men, one of whom is an associate and the other simply one of the local population.

The reader sees the Prophet's ethos of temporal authority. He speaks as a judge, determining the way of justice for both parties. There is good sense in his judgment. Zubayr's trees are nearer to the source of water than those of his adversary. The former is in the process of letting the stream irrigate his trees before sending the water on to the neighbor. The Anṣārī is impatient to get the water right away. Muhammad orders Zubayr to go ahead with his own irrigation, but not to hold up unduly the flow of water. In that way he could oblige the irritated neighbor. But in the next part of the story we see that the Anṣārī is too angry to be mollified. He, like many of his fellow Medinans, is jealous of the Meccans' closeness to the Prophet. He is quick to suspect favoritism and blurts out his suspicion that Zubayr is getting the water first because of his ties of kinship with the Prophet. This is a rare example of the censure of Muhammad by one of his followers. Then Muhammad makes a similarly impulsive response to the Anṣārī's accusation as he quickly revises his order to Zubayr. He tells his friend and cousin to collect a generous measure of water for his trees, taking time to let the level rise. Then he should release it onto the Anṣārī's land. To delay passing the water on to the vindictive neighbor is a way of punishing him. At a calmer moment the deeper significance of the incident becomes clear as the Prophet receives the word which is cited from the Qurʾān as the epilogue to the story. The dramatic interaction between the three characters provides a combination of judicial rhetoric with contrary argument.

CONCLUSION

These few examples serve to introduce the reader to the methods of argumentation in the hadith. While typically representative of the whole literature they are not numerous enough to form the basis for conclusions about the type or types of rhetorical argumentation which are most common. What they do show is that transmitters of hadith used material that corresponds closely in form to the chreiai of Greco-Roman rhetoricians, and that some of the features of argumentation described by Theon and Hermogenes can be seen in the reports handed down from the first generation of Muslims.

WORKS CONSULTED

Sources of the Hadith Texts Cited

Abū Dāʾūd al-Sijistānī
    n.d.   *Sunan Abī Dāʾūd*. Ed. Muḥammad Muḥyī al-Dīn ʿAbd al-Ḥamīd. 4 vols. Cairo: Maṭbaʿat Muṣṭafā Muḥammad.

Al-Bukhārī, Muḥammad b. Ismāʿīl
    n.d.   *Ṣaḥīḥ al-Bukhārī*. 3 vols. Cairo: Dār wa Maṭābiʿ al-Shaʿb.

Muslim b. al-Ḥajjāj
    1955   *Ṣaḥīḥ Muslim*. Ed. Muḥammad Fuʾād ʿAbd al-Bāqī. 5 vols. Cairo: Al-Ḥalabī.

Al-Mubārakfūrī, Muḥammad ʿAbd al-Raḥmān
    1963-1967   *Tuḥfat al-Aḥwadhī bi-Sharḥ Jāmiʿ al-Tirmidhī*. Ed. ʿAbd al-Wahhāb ʿAbd al-Laṭīf and ʿAbd al-Raḥmān Muḥammad ʿUthmān. 10 vols. Al-Madīna al-Munawwara, 1963-1967.

Al-Ṭayālisī, Sulaymān b. Dāʾūd
    1903   *Al-Musnad*. Ed. Abū al-Ḥasan al-Amruhī, et al. Hyderabad: Majlis Dāʾirat al-Maʿārif al-Niẓāmiyya.

English Translations of Hadith Texts

Al-Bukhari
    1979   *Sahih Al-Bukhari*. Trans. Muhammad Muhsin Khan. 9 vols. Fourth revised edition. Chicago: Kazi Publications.

Muslim Ibn al-Ḥajjāj
    1971-75   *Ṣaḥīḥ Muslim*. Trans. ʿAbdul Ḥamīd Ṣiddīqī. Lahore: Sh. Muhammad Ashraf.

Abu Dawud al-Sijistani
    1984   *Sunan abu Dawud*. Trans. Ahmad Hasan. 3 vols. Lahore: Sh. Muhammad Ashraf.

Other Works Cited

Bultmann, Rudolf Karl
    1968   *The History of the Synoptic Tradition*. Trans. John Marsh. New York: Harper & Row.

van Ess, Josef
    1975   *Zwischen Ḥadīth und Theologie: Studien zum Entstehen prädestinatianischer Überlieferung*. Berlin: Walter de Gruyter.

Goldziher, Ignaz
    1971   *Muslim Studies*, Vol. II. Trans. C. R. Barber and S. M. Stern. Chicago: Aldine Publishing Co.

Graham, William A.
    1977   *Divine Word and Prophetic Word in Early Islam: A Reconsideration of the Sources, with Special Reference to the Divine Saying or Ḥadīth Qudsī*. The Hague: Mouton.

von Grunebaum, Gustave E., trans. and ed.
    1950   *A Tenth-Century Document of Arabic Literature Theory and Criticism*. London: University of Chicago Press.

Guillaume, Alfred
    1966   *The Traditions of Islam*. Reprint of 1924 edition. Beirut: Khayat's.

Hock, Ronald F. and O'Neil, Edward N., eds.
    1986   *The Chreia in Ancient Rhetoric. Volume I: The Progymnasmata*. SBLTT 27. Atlanta: Scholars.

Juynboll, G.H.A.
    1983   *Muslim tradition: Studies in chronology, provenance and authorship of early ḥadīth*. Cambridge: University Press.

Kennedy, George A.
    1963   *The Art of Persuasion in Greece*. Princeton: Princeton University Press.
    1984   *New Testament Interpretation Through Rhetorical Criticism*. Chapel Hill and London: University of North Carolina Press.

Mack, Burton L. and Vernon K. Robbins
    1989   *Patterns of Persuasion in the Gospels*. Sonoma, CA: Polebridge.

Powers, David S.
    1986   *Studies in Qurʾān and Ḥadīth: The Formation of the Islamic Law of Inheritance*. Berkeley: University of California Press.

Robbins, Vernon K.
    1988   "The Chreia." Pp. 1-23 in *Greco-Roman Literature and the New Testament*. Ed. David E. Aune. SBLSBS 21. Atlanta: Scholars.

1989 "Plucking Grain on the Sabbath." Pp. 107-141 in *Patterns of Persuasion in the Gospels*. Ed. Burton Mack and Vernon Robbins. Sonoma: Polebridge.

Robson, James
1971 "Ḥadīth" Pp. 23-28 in *The Encyclopaedia of Islam*, Vol. III, New Edition.. Leiden: E. J. Brill.

Schaade, A.
1960 "Balāgha." Pp. 981-983 in *The Encyclopaedia of Islam*, Vol I. New Edition. Leiden: E. J. Brill.

Siddiqī, Muḥammad Zubayr
1961 *Ḥadīth Literature*. Calcutta: Calcutta University.

Speight, R. Marston
1970 *The Musnad of Al-Ṭayālisī: A Study of Islamic Hadith as Oral Literature*. Unpublished doctoral dissertation, Hartford Seminary Foundation.

Wansbrough, John
1978 *The Sectarian Milieu: Content and Composition of Islamic Salvation History*. Oxford: Oxford University Press.

II
EXPANSION AND ELABORATION IN SYNOPTIC STORIES

BIBLICAL SOURCES FOR PRONOUNCEMENT STORIES IN THE GOSPELS

Miriam Dean-Otting
Kenyon College
and
Vernon K. Robbins
Emory University

ABSTRACT

This paper focuses on the selection, modification, and use of ideas, quotations, and stories from the Bible in pronouncement stories. Close attention is paid to the Hebrew and Greek text of the biblical material to see how it acquires the nature of "pronouncements" in New Testament stories. This study has uncovered three kinds of uses of biblical material: 1) abbreviation that modifies the wording of the biblical text in settings of chreia expansion; 2) abbreviation that omits clauses without changing other wording in settings of chreia elaboration; 3) recitation of biblical law and narrative that uses key words from the biblical passage intermingled with words from the discourse of the New Testament story. Biblical materials may serve either as "artistic" or "inartistic" proofs, depending on their function in a story. In the materials examined in this essay, there is a tendency for biblical passages to function as artistic proofs in settings of rhetorical expansion, since abbreviation and adaptation to the discursive context are highly important. In contrast, settings of rhetorical elaboration may accommodate the use of verbatim quotations as inartistic proofs, but they also invite the use of recitations or modified quotations as artistic proofs embedded in argumentative units that can be strengthened by the use of authoritative premises in their discourse.

It is well known that the Hebrew Bible and its Greek translation, the Septuagint, were sources for the writers of the Gospels. If we focus on pronouncement stories alone, we will soon confirm that the Bible,[1] in Hebrew or a Greek version, was a source for parts of these stories, providing ideas, quotations, and stories for the authors of the Gospel narratives. How these ideas, quotations, and stories were selected, modified, and put to use in the Gospel narratives is the focus of this paper. Close attention will be paid to the Hebrew and Greek text of the biblical material to see

---

[1] In using the adjective "biblical" we are referring to text found in the Hebrew Bible or the Septuagint.

how it acquires the nature of "pronouncements" in the New Testament stories.

This study of pronouncement stories in the Gospels has uncovered three kinds of biblical material: 1) abbreviation that modifies the wording of the biblical text in settings of chreia expansion; 2) abbreviation that omits clauses without changing other wording in settings of chreia elaboration; 3) recitation of biblical law and narrative that uses key words from the biblical passage intermingled with words from the discourse of the New Testament story. Other studies in this volume and in other publications have analyzed other aspects of these stories. The purpose here will be simply to analyze the use of biblical ideas, quotations, and stories in New Testament pronouncement stories.

A. Eating with Tax Collectors and Sinners: Matthew 9:10-13/Mark 2:13-17 (cf. Luke 5:27-32):

The Matthean version of a meal with tax collectors (Matt 9:10-13) is a pronouncement story that uses a biblical quotation. As Jesus eats with his disciples, tax collectors and "sinners" also eat with him. Upon seeing this, the Pharisees inquire of the disciples, "Why does your teacher eat with tax collectors and sinners?" Jesus answers in all three synoptic Gospels with: "Those who are well have no need of a physician, but those who are sick .... I came not to call the righteous, but sinners" (Luke adds, "to repentance"). Only the Matthean version inserts between these two sentences a quotation from Hosea 6:6:

> Go and learn what this means, 'Mercy I desire and not sacrifice.'
> (Matt 9:13)

The presence of the biblical quotation in Matthew creates a different form of reasoning than is present in Mark and Luke. To see this more clearly it will help to digress a moment to look at the Markan version. In Mark 2:17, Jesus responds with:

> (a) "Those who are well have no need of a physician, but those who are sick;
> (b) I came not to call the righteous, but sinners."

In the language of Theon, the Markan version is a response to an inquiry (Hock and O'Neil: 85) in the manner of an explanation (Hock and O'Neil: 91). In addition, the response is an argument from analogy (Hermogenes, Mack and O'Neil: 176-77). The first part of the saying establishes an analogy between Jesus' activity and the activity of a physician. Then, the second part of the saying presents an explanation that establishes a metaphorical relation between the well and the righteous, the sick and sinners. In other words, the Markan version argues inductively from the activity of physicians who offer their services to those who are sick, not those who are well.

As we return to the Matthean version, we are aware that the presence of the biblical quotation could be a step in providing "arguments for each part" of the chreia (Theon, Hock and O'Neil: 107). In other words, this brief pronouncement story introduces a number of topics—the well, having need, physicians, the sick, coming, calling, the righteous, and sinners—and the biblical quotation could provide an argument for one or more of these topics. But the Matthean version does not proceed in the manner of a rhetorical elaboration. Rather, the story is an expanded chreia containing an enlargement of the response (Theon, Hock and O'Neil: 101). A type of argumentation available for elaboration, namely a citation of an ancient authority (Hermogenes, Mack and O'Neil: 176-77), has been embedded in the middle of Jesus' response, expanding the argument internally rather than appending an additional argument for a particular part of the chreia in the manner of an elaboration.

Looking more closely at the biblical quotation itself can aid us in understanding how the quotation contributes to the argument in the story. If the quotation occurred in an appended argument, it might be possible that the entire verse as it exists in the LXX would have been quoted:

Διότι ἔλεος θέλω ἢ [or: καὶ οὐ] θυσίαν,
καὶ ἐπίγνωσιν θεοῦ ἢ ὁλοκαυτώματα;

For I desire mercy rather than [or: and not] sacrifice,
and knowledge of God rather than whole burnt offerings.
(Hosea 6:6).

This biblical version contains *parallelismus membrorum* that juxtaposes mercy with knowledge of God and sacrifice with whole burnt offerings. Using the entire verse would introduce elaboration that would break the rhythm of the skillfully crafted speech in the two-part saying. Therefore, the storyteller has used the technique of abbreviation (Theon, Hock and O'Neil: 101), reducing the verse to one brief stich that refers only to "mercy" and "sacrifice." But perhaps not only abbreviation has occurred. The wording of the verse may have been modified, substituting καὶ οὐ for ἢ so it fits into the discourse of the preceding and succeeding sayings. In B, two MSS of the Lucianic recension, and other witnesses, ἢ sets mercy against sacrifice in the first line, and ἢ is repeated in the second line as knowledge of God is set against whole burnt offerings. In the Göttingen text of the LXX, καὶ οὐ appears in the first line and ἢ appears in the second line. It is difficult to know if the καὶ οὐ represents Christian influence on the LXX text from Matthew 9:13 and 12:7 or if the ἢ in the alternate version results from accommodating the first line to the second line, which contains ἤ. If ἤ appeared in both lines in the LXX text, the Matthean version "recites" the verse using some of the same words and some different words (Theon, Hock and O'Neil: 95), producing a quotation "in the manner of a maxim" (Theon, Hock and O'Neil: 89) that functions smoothly in the midst of a maxim and its explanatory clause. If the Matthean version is a verbatim quotation, Matthean discourse has been structured to accommodate the καὶ οὐ with οὐ ... ἀλλ'; καὶ οὐ; οὐ γάρ ... ἀλλά:

> οὐ χρείαν ἔχουσιν οἱ ἰσχύοντες ἰατροῦ ἀλλ' οἱ κακῶς ἔχοντες·
> ἔλεος θέλω καὶ οὐ θυσίαν·
> οὐ γὰρ ἦλθον καλέσαι δικαίους ἀλλὰ ἁμαρτωλούς.
>
> those who are strong have *no* need of a physician but those who are sick,
> I desire mercy and *not* sacrifice,
> for I did *not* come to call the righteous but sinners.

An additional dynamic arises from the statement that introduces the quotation: "Go and learn what this means." This statement functions like the exhortation Hermogenes recommends at the end of an elaboration of a chreia (Mack and O'Neil: 176-77). Thus, the addition of the biblical quotation makes Jesus' response in the Matthean version begin with a thesis chreia and end with an exhortation, like the beginning and ending of an elaboration without the intervening arguments and without the encomium at the outset. This form might be quite natural for an expanded chreia. The opening remark would function like the statement of the chreia and one or more additional statements would form an exhortative conclusion supported by a rationale that summarizes the meaning of the initial statement. In the Matthean version, the opening line of Jesus' response is a chreia statement; the second line introduces an exhortative conclusion; the third line, which is authoritative testimony from the past, rephrases the chreia in terms of mercy and sacrifice; and the final line provides a rationale for the chreia statement and its rephrasing. Here, then, we see a form of chreia expansion that uses techniques that come fully to expression in a chreia elaboration (Hock and O'Neil: 177). The movement from a chreia statement to an exhortative conclusion, and the placement of the rephrasing and the rationale at the end in the context of the exhortation, represents a stage of argumentation through expansion. As long as the rephrasing and the rationale stand at the end, forming a dramatic remark at the end of the episode, the story stays in the environment of chreia expansion. An elaborative context, in contrast, presents the rephrasing and rationale directly after the chreia statement, adds some kind of additional argumentation, and ends with some kind of concluding statement.

The result of Matthew's expansion of the chreia is a chain of reasoning that uses theological assertion grounded in authoritative citation (see Robbins 1985).

Major premise: God wills that [people] perform acts of mercy and not sacrifice.

Unstated minor premise: I came to do what God wills.

Unstated conclusion/major premise: Therefore I came to do [acts of] mercy.

Unstated minor premise: Calling sinners [who like the sick have need] is an [act of] mercy.

Conclusion: Therefore, I call sinners [who have need] and not the righteous.

This chain of reasoning can be clearly stated in the following way:

God wills mercy.

I came to do what God wills.

Therefore, I came to do mercy.

Calling sinners is mercy.

Therefore I call sinners.

This is a deductive (syllogistic), theological chain of reasoning for which the biblical quotation furnishes the major premise (Aristotle, Rhet 1.2.8-22). The Markan version, in contrast, is an inductive and soteriological chain of reasoning based on the widely known acts of healing performed by physicians. In the Matthean version, then, the presence of the biblical quotation makes the reasoning deductive and theological. An abbreviated form of the quotation serves this purpose, rather than the entire verse, which would have imposed the details of the *parallelismus membrorum* onto the skillfully crafted lines of the saying. The Matthean version maintains the form of an expanded chreia, rather than taking the form of a story containing a sequence of argumentation that introduces rhetorical elaboration.

B. PLUCKING GRAIN ON THE SABBATH: LUKE 6:1-5/MARK 2:23-28/MATTHEW 12:1-8

All three synoptic Gospels use wording from the Bible in the story of the disciples' plucking of grain on the sabbath. There are significant differences among the versions of the story, however. Mark 2:23-28 and Luke 6:1-5 are the most similar. Both contain a brief account of the situation which ends with an inquiry by Pharisees (Mark 2:23-24; Luke 6:1-2). In Mark the Pharisees direct their inquiry to Jesus, while in Luke they direct it to the disciples themselves, but in both instances the question is why the disciples do what is unlawful on the sabbath. Since this type of beginning for the story calls for an explanation, one expects an explanatory comment of some kind after an initial response. The issue, then, is how long the response will be. Will it be only a brief statement followed by a brief explanatory remark (Theon, Hock and O'Neil: 87)? Will the response contain some kind of internal expansion (Theon, Hock and O'Neil: 101-103)? Will there be some kind of commentary, objection, or refutation appended to the initial response (Theon, Hock and O'Neil: 101-105)? Or will the response provide arguments for each part of the chreia, perhaps in the form of a complete elaboration (Theon, Hock and O'Neil: 107; Hermogenes, Mack and O'Neil: 177)?

The Lukan version features the shortest response: (a) an argument from example (6:3-4); and (b) an appended maxim (6:5). In Theon's terms, the story is a chreia "in the manner of an example" (Theon, Hock and O'Neil: 91) with an additional comment in the form of an attributed saying (Theon, Hock and O'Neil: 89). Since Jesus' response is a "recitation" of 1 Sam 21:1-7, it is of interest for this investigation to discover which words are repeated from the biblical text. As Jesus narrates how David came to the priest Ahimelech (LXX: Abimelech) when he was hungry and demanded food for himself and the young men who were supposedly with him, seven words stand in common between the recitation in Luke and the LXX version: David, the bread of the presence (οἱ ἄρτοι τῆς προθέσεως), took (ἔλαβεν/λαβών), ate (φάγεται/ἔφαγεν/φαγεῖν), gave (ἔδωκεν), and priest (ὁ ἱερεύς). The key verses are 4 and 6:

> 5 Καὶ ἀπεκρίθη ὁ ἱερεὺς τῷ Δαυὶδ, καὶ εἶπεν, οὐκ εἰσιν ἄρτοι βέβηλοι ὑπὸ τὴν χεῖρά μου, ὅτι ἀλλ' ἢ ἄρτοι ἅγιοί εἰσίν· εἰ πεφυλαγμένα τὰ παιδάριά ἐστιν ἀπὸ γυναικός, καὶ φάγεται.... 7 καὶ ἔδωκεν αὐτῷ Ἀβιμέλεχ ὁ ἱερεὺς τοὺς ἄρτους τῆς προθέσεως, ὅτι οὐκ ἦν ἐκεῖ ἄρτος ὅτι ἀλλ' ἢ ἄρτοι τοῦ προσώπου οἱ ἀφῃρημένοι ἐκ προσώπου κυρίου, παρατεθῆναι ἄρτον θερμὸν ᾗ ἡμέρᾳ ἔλαβεν αὐτούς.

> 4 And the priest answered David, and said, "There are no common loaves under my hand, for there are nothing but holy loaves; if the young men have been kept from women, then they shall eat.... 6 And Abimelech the priest gave him the loaves of the presence, because there was no bread there, but only the loaves of the presence, which had been removed from the presence of the Lord, in order that hot bread should be set on, on the day on which he took them. (1 Sam 21: 4, 6)

In the Lukan version, the recitation uses words or phrases only once, with the exception of "those with him" (οἱ μετ' αὐτοῦ ... τοῖς μετ' αὐτοῦ) in vv. 3-4 and "ate/to eat" (ἔφαγεν ... φαγεῖν) in v. 4. In other words, Jesus' response abbreviates the recitation of the episode as much as possible, except that "took, ate, and gave" looks like a possible eucharistic touch (cf. Luke 9:16-17; 22: 15-16, 19).

After Jesus' response to the Pharisees, the narrator adds the commentary:

And he used to say (ἔλεγεν) to them, "Lord of the sabbath is the Son of man."

The Lukan version of the story is an expanded chreia, since the example has the form of a recitation rather that a quick retort (cf. Chreia 3, Hock and O'Neil: 91). The recitation provides initial closure for the rhetorical situation, however, as it ends with "which it is not lawful to eat, except for the priests only" (v. 4) in response to "why are you doing what is not lawful on the sabbath?" (v. 2). The additional comment, introduced with imperfect tense referring to customary action, has a sharp, maximlike quality. In this version, then, we see a brief recitation of a biblical story as the response and an additional comment that gives the story the abrupt rhetorical closure of a chreia. In this context, again, words from the Bible are a resource, but they function as an "artistic proof," a proof which a narrator has "artificed" for the rhetorical situation. The artistic nature of the proof from example is highly noticeable, in fact, since the story in 1 Sam 21:1-6 does not in and of itself easily fit the occasion of the plucking of the grain. For one, David is not accompanied by several young men as Jesus is; this is just a fiction of the story which David tells Ahimelech in order to receive the bread. Secondly, nowhere does it say in the story in 1 Samuel that the incident with David occurred on the Sabbath (cf. Robbins 1989c: 113-19; Parrott in this volume). The story had to be handled artistically, then, in order for it to speak to this situation.

There are a number of variations between the Markan and Lukan versions of Jesus' response, but we will focus only on those that highlight the use of the Davidic incident as an artistic proof. While the Lukan recitation emphasizes the unlawful eating by David and those with him, the Markan version focuses on the actions of Jesus:

> *he* entered the house of God when Abiathar was highpriest
> and *he* ate the bread of the presence, which it is not lawful to eat, except for the priests,
> and *he* gave it also to those who were with him.
> (Mark 2:26)

This focus on David in the recitation of the incident prepares the way for the syllogistic conclusion:

> The sabbath was made on account of man
> and not man on account of the sabbath.
> So that lord is the Son of man even of the sabbath.
> (Mark 2:27-28)

This final sayings unit simply continues the narration with an imperfect tense (ἔλεγεν), which continues the action in the story (ἤρξαντο ποιεῖν...τίλλοντες, ἔλεγον, λέγει), in contrast to the Lukan version, which shifts from the aorist tense that narrates the story to the imperfect tense, which adds a comment based on customary activity. Thus, the Markan version is an expanded chreia with characteristics related to the Matthean version of Jesus' eating with tax collectors. While Jesus' response in the Matthean story discussed above had the nature of an introduction and conclusion to an elaboration, however, Jesus' expanded response in the Markan version of this story has the nature of an "argument from example" followed by a "rationale" and a "chreia statement" (Hermogenes, Mack and O'Neil: 177). In other words, this expanded form of Jesus' response presents arguments characteristic of an elaboration "in inverted order" (see Parrott's essay in this volume). If the order in the Markan account were reversed, the elaboration would unfold as follows:

Chreia statement: "Lord is the Son of man even of the sabbath."

Rationale: "For the sabbath was made on account of man, not man on account of the sabbath."

Argument from example: "Have you never read what David did ... ?"

The proverbial saying about the sabbath, rather than a quotation from the Bible, provides the major premise for a theological grounding of the argument ("[God] made the sabbath on account of man ..."). The biblical story, in contrast, provides an authoritative example that argues inductively from David's activity to Jesus' activity. To this inductive argumentation is added deductive argumentation which grounds the authority of the Son of man implicitly in the action of God at creation.

In the Markan version, then, the presence of both inductive and deductive argumentation moves Jesus' response toward the environment of rhetorical elaboration. Since the story is an expanded chreia, however, the chreia statement and its rationale stand at the end of the story rather than at the beginning of the response. The result is the presence of argumentative units characteristic of rhetorical elaboration occurring in the opposite order one expects for elaboration. This appears to be characteristic of rhetorical expansion in contrast to rhetorical elaboration.

The Matthean version (Matt 12:1-8) takes the story a number of steps further toward an environment of rhetorical elaboration. First, instead of making an inquiry at the beginning, the Pharisees make a statement to which Jesus responds at length. In this "responsive" situation (Theon, Hock and O'Neil: 87), Jesus presents a sequence of argumentative units to counter the accusation that the disciples are guilty of unlawful action (see Robbins 1989c: 132-39).

The Matthean version exhibits one major feature characteristic of an expanded chreia rather than a chreia elaboration: the rationale and argument from the contrary stand at the end of the response, instead of near the beginning (Mack and O'Neil: 177). This also means there is no exhortative conclusion at the end, since the contrary argument and the rationale stand in its place. More will be said about this below, since the contrary argument is an argument from written authority. But the rest of Jesus' response presents a sequence of arguments characteristic of rhetorical elaboration:

> *Argument from Example:* Have you not read what David did ...?
>
> *Argument from Analogy:* Or have you not read in the law how on the sabbath the priests in the temple profane the sabbath, and are guiltless?
>
> *Argument from Comparison:* I tell you, something greater than the temple is here.
>
> *Argument from the Contrary, with explicit wording from written authority:* And if you had known what this means, "I desire mercy, and not sacrifice," you would not have condemned the guiltless.
>
> *Concluding rationale:* For lord of the sabbath is the Son of man (cf. Robbins, 1989c: 132-33).

Of special interest in this investigation is the use of wording from biblical texts in the argumentation. Only five words stand in common between the Matthean version of the recitation and the LXX version of 1 Sam 21:1-6: David, ate, bread of the presence, priest(s). The Matthean version of the recitation is thus the shortest among the synoptic Gospels (39: Matthew; 40 or 42: Luke; 46: Mark). This version focuses strictly on Jesus' eating of the bread of the presence, without reference to his taking of it or his giving of it to his disciples.

An argument from analogy with the activity of priests on the sabbath follows the argument from example. This argument in Matt 12:5 is based on Numbers 28:9-10 and Lev 24:5-9. One word stands in common among the texts, namely, "the Sabbath" (τῇ ἡμέρᾳ τῶν σαββάτων/τοῖς σάββασιν). The topic of Lev 24:5-9, however, is the preparation, presentation, and eating of the bread of the Presence. The word referring to the priests' "profaning" (βεβηλοῦσιν) of the Sabbath is related to the words in the LXX version of 1 Sam 21:4-5 which refer respectively to "common" loaves (βέβηλοι) and to the "unclean" expedition of David and the young men (βέβηλος). It would appear, then, that language from the text which is the basis for the argument from example is used in the articulation of the argument from analogy. There is no extensive use of wording from the biblical texts about the priests' activity on the Sabbath. In other words, again the Matthean argumentation is artistic, being formulated out of the narrator's discourse rather than from exact words in the "authoritative written testimony."

After the argument from analogy, the Matthean version contains an argument from comparison between Jesus and the temple. Comparison is especially appropriate for summarizing an argument (Aristotle, Rhet 3.19.5-6). Comparison focuses the inductive argumentation for the final statements (Robbins 1989c: 136).

An argument from the contrary follows, with an authoritative citation embedded in the protasis: "I desire mercy, and not sacrifice" (Hosea 6:6). The abbreviation of the verse so that it functions in the manner of a maxim has been discussed in the analysis of the story of Jesus' eating with tax collectors. In that context, the verse contributes to an argument from analogy; in this context, it contributes to an argument from the contrary. The introduction of the verse with the words "If you had known what this means" gives the verse the function of an "inartistic proof" (Aristotle, Rhet 1.2.2, 1.15.1). The context gives the impression that the verse simply has been found and presented in an unaltered form, even though, as discussed above, it may have been modified to function smoothly in the Matthean discourse in that earlier context. If it was modified for that context, then that modification has been maintained as the saying is repeated in this context.

There is one more aspect that attracts attention when one looks at the wording of the biblical texts which served as resources for argumentation in the Matthean version. The omitted parallel stich of Hosea 6:6 refers to "the knowledge of God and whole burnt offerings" and the topic of one of the texts supporting the argument from analogy, namely Num 24:9-10, is the whole burnt offering on the sabbath. Is there an underlying form of reasoning about whole burnt offerings, then, that extends from the analogy to the priests in v. 5 through the argument from the contrary in v. 7? Is the kind of "work" being done by Jesus' disciples, namely the gleaning of grain for food, a direct analogy to the work of priests on the sabbath? The whole burnt offering consists not only of two yearling lambs and a drink offering, but "two tenth parts of fine flour," which, of course, is made from the kind of grain the disciples pick and eat. The passage in Lev 24:5-9 gives further description of the activity with the "two tenth parts of fine flour":

> You shall take fine flour and make of it twelve loaves; each loaf shall be of two tenth parts. And you shall put them in two rows, each row containing six loaves, on the pure table before the Lord. And you shall put on each row pure frankincense and salt; and these things shall be for loaves for a memorial, set forth before the Lord. On the sabbath day they shall be set forth before the Lord continually before the children of Israel, for an everlasting covenant. And they shall be for Aaron and his sons, and they shall eat them in the holy place; for this is their most holy portion of the offerings made to the Lord, a perpetual statute.

How much of the imagery of this passage hovers in the background of the argumentation in the Matthean version of the argument? Is the plucking of the grain and eating of it an intentional subverting of the threshing of the grain, the milling of it into fine flour, and the baking of it into the bread of the Presence? Does the explicit designation of twelve loaves have any relation to the twelve disciples who accompany Jesus (Matt 10:1, 2, 5; 11:1; 14:20; 19:28; 20:17; 26:14, 20, 47, 53)? In contrast to the story in 1 Samuel 21, which makes no reference to the sabbath, the topic of Lev 24:8-9 is the setting forth of the bread of the Presence as a sabbath day offering, and the eating of it by Aaron and his sons. Is it possible that Jesus' speech in the story presents one more way in which Jesus usurps the role of Moses, similar to the manner in which he is the teacher of new commandments on the mountain in Matt 5-7 and is the heir to Moses in the Transfiguration (Matt 17:1-13)? It would appear that the Matthean version has exposed much of the reasoning underlying the selection of the argument from example, in a manner highly analogous to Hermogenes' exposure of the the wide range of reasoning underlying the saying attributed to Isocrates: "The root of education is bitter, but its fruit is sweet" (Hock and O'Neil: 177). Still, the Matthean version exhibits dynamics of an expanded chreia as it presents an argument from the contrary and a rationale as its conclusion. As a matter of special interest for this study, this kind of elaboration in an overall context of chreia expansion exhibits no instance in which words from a biblical context are presented in an unmodified form.

C. ON MARRIAGE AND DIVORCE: MARK 10:1-12
(CF. MATTHEW 19:1-12)

The accounts of Jesus' teaching on marriage and divorce in Mark 10:1-12 and Matt 19:1-12 use three biblical passages in their argumentation. The accounts are highly similar, but there are some notable differences. The Matthean account is a rebuttal dialogue about divorce that ends with a response to the disciples about the expediency of marriage. Thus, the Pharisees ask an initial question (v. 3) and Jesus responds (vv. 4-6), the Pharisees ask a second question (v. 7) and Jesus responds (vv. 8-9), then the disciples ask a question (v. 10) and Jesus responds (vv. 11-12). The Markan account is somewhat different. It also is dialogical, but the initial exchange of questions and responses (vv. 2-4) establishes the situation and Jesus responds at length in vv. 5-9 and summarizes what he has said in vv. 11-12. Thus, the beginning of the Markan version looks like an expanded chreia which has "enlarged upon the questions" (Theon, Hock and O'Neil: 101), and Jesus' long response exhibits signs of rhetorical elaboration. This particular juxtaposition of expansion and elaboration in the Markan version makes it especially interesting for our purposes. For this reason, we will analyze the function of the biblical quotations in the Markan rather than the Matthean version.

Mark 10:1-12 unfolds as follows:

Narrative introduction: And he left there and went into the region of Judea and beyond the Jordan, and crowds gathered to him again; and again, as was his custom, he taught them.

Simple question: And Pharisees came up and in order to test him asked, "Is it lawful for a man to divorce his wife?"

Counter question: He answered them, "What did Moses command you?"

Recitation of a biblical passage: They said, "Moses allowed [a man] to write a certificate of divorce, and to put her away."

Rationale that dismisses the Mosaic law: But Jesus said to them, "For your hardness of heart he wrote you this commandment.

Authoritative citation uses analogy to provide a rationale for a counterproposition: But from the beginning of creation, 'God made them male and female.'

Authoritative citation functions as a counterproposition: For this reason a man shall leave his father and mother [and be joined to his wife], and the two shall become one flesh.

Inference: So they are no longer two but one flesh.

Exhortative conclusion: What therefore God has joined together, let not man put asunder.

Paraphrase of exhortative conclusion in the form of a new law: And in the house the disciples asked him again about this matter. And he said to them, "Whoever divorces his wife and marries another commits adultery against her; and if she divorces her husband and marries another, she commits adultery."

First, the storyteller established the rhetorical situation by applying the skill of expansion that enlarges the question (Theon, Hock and O'Neil: 101). The initial question of the Pharisees is a simple question calling only for a "yes" or "no" answer. Jesus enlarges their question through a question of his own, which requires them to produce a statement to which Jesus needs to respond at length. The first part of the story, then, exhibits an environment of rhetorical expansion. Second, as in the story examined above, a context of expansion calls for the use of biblical materials in abbreviated form. Thus, when the Pharisees respond, they report the Mosaic law in the form of a "recitation" (Theon, Hock and O'Neil: 94-95) that abbreviates the law (Theon, Hock and O'Neil: 100-101). The LXX version of the law in Deut 24:3-6 is as follows:

> And if any one should take a wife, and should dwell with her (ἐὰν δέ τις λάβῃ γυναῖκα, καὶ συνοικήσῃ αὐτῇ), then it shall come to pass if she should not have found favor before him, because he has found some unbecoming thing in her,

that he shall write for her a certificate of divorce (γράψει αὐτῇ βιβλίον ἀποστασίου), and give it into her hands, and he shall send her away (ἐξαποστελεῖ αὐτὴν) from his house. And if she should go away (ἀπελθοῦσα) and be married to another man; and the last husband should hate her, and write for her a certificate of divorce (γραψῇ αὐτῇ βιβλίον ἀποστασίου); and should give it into her hands, and send her away (ἐξαποστελεῖ αὐτὴν) from his house, and the last husband should die, who took her to himself for a wife; the former husband who sent her away (ὁ ἐξαποστείλας) shall not be able to return and take her to himself for a wife, after she has been defiled; because it is an abomination before the Lord your God, and you shall not defile the land, which the Lord your God gives you to inherit.

Rather than responding with this long quotation, the Pharisees simply reply:

ἐπέτρεψεν Μωϋσῆς βιβλίον ἀποστασίου γράψαι καὶ ἀπολῦσαι.

Moses allowed [a husband] to write a certificate of divorce and release her.

This, obviously, is an abbreviated form. But we must notice one other aspect as well. The recitation uses some of the same words in the biblical text and some other words as well (Theon, Hock and O'Neil: 95). Again, as in the first story discussed above, language from other sayings in the context influences the language in the abbreviated version. The Pharisees used ἀπολύειν rather than ἐξαποστέλλειν when they asked their opening question, and they impose this verb on Moses' law when they recite it to Jesus. In other words, the Pharisees' response to Jesus uses the LXX words βιβλίον ἀποστασίου and γράψαι for writing a certificate of divorce, but their recitation substitutes ἀπολύειν for ἐξαποστέλλειν as it refers to sending one's wife away. In the LXX ἀπολύειν is not used to translate the word used in the MT of Deut 24:3 (שִׁלְּחָהּ).[2] In the broader cultural context of the Mediterranean world, however, ἀπολύειν occurs in discourse about divorce (see 1 Esdr 9:36 and Dionysus of Halicarnassus 2.25.7). Such a substitution of language would be natural in a context of rhetorical expansion and abbreviation in a first century Mediterranean text. Abbreviation, then, is a necessary skill in the context of expansion: a storyteller uses abbreviated forms of speech when "enlarging on the questions and responses." As abbreviation occurs, it will be natural for current forms of discourse to replace wording in an antecedent text.

When Jesus responds to the Pharisees' recitation of Moses' law, the context changes from expansion to elaboration (Hermogenes, Mack and O'Neil: 176-77). In other words, instead of simply "enlarging" Jesus' response, the Markan version features Jesus introducing a series of arguments, and these arguments feature a counterproposition, two rationales, two paraphrases, two authoritative citations, and an exhortative conclu-

---

[2] The LXX uses ἐξαποστελεῖ to translate the Hebrew verb in Deut 24:3.

sion. In this context, abbreviation of the quotations occurs by means of careful selection of verbatim wording rather than modification of the biblical wording.

Jesus' response begins in v. 5 by articulating a rationale for dismissing the Mosaic law: Moses gave this law, because of their hardness of heart. This argument clears the way for another law.

Jesus' second statement (v. 6) introduces a rationale for a different law, and this rationale achieves its persuasiveness from two argumentative figures. First, this rationale introduces an argument from analogy: marriage, it argues, is analogous to creation. Second, the phrase "from the beginning of creation" embeds a citation of ancient authority in the argument based on analogy: the reference is to the book of Genesis ("in the beginning he created"). Two quotations from Genesis, then, introduce a rationale and a counterproposition. The rationale uses verbatim language that stands in common between Gen 1:27 and 5:2:

Gen 1:27

καὶ εἶπεν ὁ θεός, ποιήσωμεν ἄνθρωπον
κατ' εἰκόνα ἡμετέραν καὶ καθ' ὁμοίωσιν·
καὶ ἀρχέτωσαν τῶν ἰχθύων τῆς θαλάσσης,
καὶ τῶν πετεινῶν τοῦ οὐρανοῦ, καὶ τῶν
κτηνῶν, καὶ πάσης τῆς γῆς, καὶ πάντων
τῶν ἑρπετῶν τῶν ἑρπόντων ἐπὶ τῆς γῆς.
καὶ ἐποίησεν ὁ θεός τὸν ἄνθρωπον·
κατ' εἰκόνα θεοῦ ἐποίησεν αὐτόν·
ἄρσεν καὶ θῆλυ ἐποίησεν αὐτούς.
καὶ εὐλόγησεν αὐτοὺς ὁ θεός,
λέγων, αὐξάνεσθε καὶ πληθύνεσθε,
καὶ πληρώσατε τὴν γῆν,
καὶ κατακυριεύσατε αὐτῆς.

Gen 5:2

ᾗ ἡμέρα ἐποίησεν θεὸς τὸν Ἀδάμ,
κατ' εἰκόνα θεοῦ ἐποίησεν αὐτόν·
ἄρσεν καὶ θῆλυ ἐποίησεν αὐτούς·
καὶ εὐλόγησεν αὐτούς·
καὶ ἐπωνόμασε τὸ ὄνομα αὐτοῦ Ἀδάμ,
ᾗ ἡμέρᾳ ἐποίησεν αὐτούς.

And God said, Let us make man
according to our image and likeness,
and let them have dominion over the fish
of the sea, and over the flying creatures of
heaven, and over the cattle and all the
earth, and over all the reptiles that creep
on the earth.
And God made man,
according to the image of God he made him,
male and female he made them.
And God blessed them, saying, "Increase
and multiply, and fill the earth and rule
over it.

in the day in which God made Adam,
according to the image of God he made him,
male and female he made them,
and he blessed them;
and he called his name Adam,
in the day in which he made them.

In this instance, abbreviation of the biblical quotation occurs by means of "selection" of a specific clause and "use" of it without modifying the wording. This, then, is an "inartistic proof" (Aristotle, Rhet 1.2.2; 1.15.1). In other words, "male and female he made them" is verbatim wording from the LXX text. Common wording from Gen 1:27 and Gen 5:2 presents an argument "from the beginning of creation" which overrides the limited situation during the time of Moses when people were guided by "hardness of heart."

Jesus' next statement (vv. 7-8a) articulates a counterproposition that supports a new understanding of marriage and divorce. The counterproposition presents verbatim wording from Gen 2:24, another "inartistic proof," perhaps omitting "and shall join to his wife:"[3]

> For this reason a man shall leave his father and mother,
> [and shall join to his wife,]
> and the two shall become one.

Again the biblical wording of the verse remains intact. If abbreviation has occurred, a clause has been omitted without alteration of any of the other wording. The reasoning in the overall argument, however, presupposes the biblical context of the statement:

> And God brought a trance upon Adam, and he slept, and he took one of his ribs, and filled up the flesh against it. And God built up the rib which he took from Adam into a woman, and brought her to Adam. And Adam said, "This now is bone of my bones, and flesh of my flesh; she shall be called woman, because she was taken out of her husband. Therefore, a man shall leave his father and his mother and shall join to his wife, and the two shall be one flesh. (Gen. 2:21-24)

The context provides the reasoning:

> Presupposed premise: Because God made [both] man (male) and woman (female) out of one (Godmade) flesh;
> Conclusion: Therefore, a man shall leave his father and mother [and join to his wife], and the two shall be one flesh.

In Theon's terms, this quotation has been presented "in the manner of an enthymeme" (Hock and O'Neil: 91), since a person must deduce that "God made man and woman out of one flesh." This quotation functions then as an enthymematic counterproposition. After the counterproposition, the time is right to restate the quotations in forms that bring the argument to a conclusion.

---

3 The two earliest manuscripts, ℵ and B, omit this clause.

The first statement on the lips of Jesus after the biblical quotations draws an inference from the counterproposition. In progymnastic discussions of rhetoric, this inference may simply be called "amplification" or "paraphrase," but in more advanced discussions of stasis, the rhetoricians describe this as the important step of drawing the inference (cf. Nadeau: 415).

The next statement is an exhortative conclusion ($παράκλησις$) that performs precisely the function Hermogenes describes for the conclusion to a rhetorical elaboration (Mack and O'Neil: 176-77):

What therefore God has yoked together,
let not a man separate.

Then the conclusion is elaborated by paraphrasing the conclusion in the form of a new law:

Whoever divorces his wife and marries another commits adultery against her; and if she divorces her husband and marries another, she commits adultery.

This story, then, contains a skillful use of inartistic proofs in an environment of rhetorical elaboration designed to provide a rationale and a counterproposition to support a law that does not allow divorce either by a man or by a woman. These are inartistic proofs, because they did not have to be created. They simply were found in ancient written testimony and used without modification. The environment of rhetorical elaboration allows, perhaps invites, the use of verbatim quotation of the biblical verses. The skillful achievement of the argument is to display that the Bible already presented an analogy between marriage and creation (Gen 2:24).

Once again the quotations from the Bible produce deductive theological reasoning:

Major Premise: God created male and female (out of the same flesh and bones);

Unstated premise: Marriage is like God's creation of male and female.

Conclusion: Therefore, a man shall leave his father and mother [and join to a woman] and the two shall become one flesh.

In this instance, then, biblical quotations on the lips of Jesus in the synoptic Gospels present a major premise and a conclusion that counters what is asserted to be the traditional interpretation of marriage and divorce. Verbatim biblical quotations produce deductive and theological reasoning in the service of a new understanding of halakah in Christianity.

D. UNWASHED HANDS: MARK 7:1-13 (CF. MATT 15:1-9)

Mark 7:1-13 contains Jesus' teaching on what defiles a man. When the Pharisees and scribes ask Jesus why his disciples eat with unwashed hands and thus transgress "the tradition of the elders" (Mark 7:5), Jesus responds with a series of arguments in the manner of a rhetorical elaboration. The first unit of Jesus' response includes a quotation from Isaiah 29:13 in the form of a chreia attributed to Isaiah:

And he said to them (ὁ δὲ εἶπεν αὐτοῖς),

Encomium: "How well did Isaiah prophesy (καλῶς ἐπροφήτευσεν 'Ησαΐας) of you hypocrites, as it is written,

Chreia statement:
    'This people honors me with its lips,
      but their heart is at a great distance from me;
      in vain do they worship me,
      teaching as doctrines the ordinances of men.'

Paraphrase: You leave the commandments of God and hold fast the tradition of men."

(Mk 7:6-8)

Jesus' initial comment is an encomium of Isaiah (καλῶς ἐπροφήτευσεν 'Ησαΐας [v. 6]), his second statement is a quotation attributed to Isaiah, and the final statement is a paraphrase of the quotation. This means that Jesus' response begins in a manner directly related to Hermogenes' discussion of the elaboration of a chreia, since first a person should praise the author of the chreia, second a person should state the chreia, and third a person should paraphrase the chreia (Mack and O'Neil: 176-77).

To understand the rhetorical use of the Isaiah quotation in the Markan version, it is necessary to compare the text in Mark with the biblical text. In its biblical context, Isaiah 29:13 is the first part of an oracle attributed to "the Lord" that extends throughout vv. 14-21. In Mark, the selection of the initial verse of the Isaiah passage, and the attribution of it to Isaiah, creates a sayings chreia. The first part of the quotation follows the LXX form which begins simply with "This people," rather than the Hebrew form which begins with "Because (יַעַן כִּי) this people," since the shorter form lends itself more naturally to a self-standing pronouncement. The Markan (and Matthean) passage also abbreviates the biblical verse by omitting "draws near to me with their mouth," giving the saying a succinctness it does not have either in Hebrew or Greek (cf. Theon, Hock and O'Neil: 101). Then, the final clause of the pronouncement follows the LXX rather than the Hebrew. The Hebrew reads:

וַתְּהִי יִרְאָתָם אֹתִי מִצְוַת אֲנָשִׁים מְלֻמָּדָה:
For their fear of me is a learned commandment of men.

The sense is that the people do not worship from true feeling. They do not fear God out of respect for the divine but rather because fear of Deity is a commandment handed down by human beings. The Septuagint and, in turn, the passage in Matthew and Mark, do not emphasize the particular commandment to fear God, but focus on human versus divine commandments:

LXX: μάτην δὲ σέβονταί με, διδάσκοντες ἐντάλματα ἀνθρώπων καὶ διδασκαλίας.

NT: μάτην δὲ σέβονταί με, διδάσκοντες διδασκαλίας ἐντάλματα ἀνθρώπων.

In vain do they worship me, teaching as doctrines the ordinances of men.

In Mark 7:6-8, therefore, Isaiah 29:13 is a chreia attributed to Isaiah which emphasizes that the people teach "human ordinances" as "divine teaching." Selection and abbreviation of the LXX version, attribution to Isaiah, praise of Isaiah, and paraphrase of the quotation make this a unit that admirably fulfills the expectations Hermogenes holds for the beginning of the rhetorical elaboration of a chreia. Again, in this context of rhetorical elaboration, there is no introduction of different wording into the biblical quotation. For this reason, the quotation functions as an inartistic proof. The quotation is abbreviated simply by omitting a clause, and particular wording is achieved through selection of the LXX version. After the quotation, however, a paraphrase of the quotation produces a brief statement in different words—precisely what one has a right to expect from Hermogenes' discussion (Mack and O'Neil: 176-77).

After this initial unit of argumentation, a second elaborated unit occurs. The correlate of praise in an epideictic rhetorical environment is censure (Kennedy: 73-78; Robbins, 1989d: 161-62), and this unit opens with skillful repetition of καλῶς as a statement of censure of the Pharisees and scribes. The unit unfolds as follows:

Censure: And he said to them, "How well do you reject the commandment of God in order to keep your tradition!

Authoritative citations: For Moses said,

'Honor your father and mother';

and

'He who speaks evil of father or mother,

let him surely die';

Contrary: but you say, 'If a man tells his father or his mother, What you would have gained from me is Corban' (that is, given to God) — then you no longer permit him to do anything for his father or mother, thus making void the word of God through your tradition which you hand on. And many such things you do."

(Mark 7:9-13)

Instead of attributing the scriptural quotations to God, as they are in Matt 15:4, the Markan version attributes them to Moses, once again shifting the divine attribution in the biblical texts to an authoritative person in the biblical tradition. The initial quotation is cited in abbreviated form, like the Isaiah quotation, making it a sharply focused statement (cf. Exodus 20:12; Deut 5:16) alongside the second quotation. The full biblical texts are as follows:

Exodus 20:12	Deut 5:16
τίμα τὸν πατέρα σου καὶ τὴν μητέρα σου,	τίμα τὸν πατέρα σου καὶ τὴν μητέρα σου, ὃν τρόπον ἐνετείλατό σοι κύριος ὁ θεός
ἵνα εὖ σοι γένηται, καὶ ἵνα μακροχρόνιος γένῃ ἐπὶ τῆς γῆς τῆς ἀγαθῆς, ἧς κύριος ὁ θεός σου δίδωσίν σοι.	σου, ἵνα εὖ σοι γένηται, καὶ ἵνα μακροχρόνιος γένῃ ἐπὶ τῆς γῆς, ἧς κύριος ὁ θεός σου δίδωσίν σοι.
Honor your father and your mother,	Honor your father and your mother, as the Lord your God commanded you,
that it may be well with you, and that you may live long on the good land, which the Lord your God gives you.	that it may be well with you, and that you may live long on the land, which the Lord your God gives you.

The New Testament quotation is based on the verbatim wording that stands in agreement between the two texts, just as the quotation in the previously discussed story about marriage and divorce used words that stand in exact agreement between Gen 1:27 and 5:2.

The second quotation uses wording from Exodus 21:16 and Lev 20:9:

Exodus 21:16	Lev 20:9
ὁ κακολογῶν πατέρα αὐτοῦ ἢ μητέρα αὐτοῦ, τελευτήσει θανάτῳ.	ἄνθρωπος ἄνθρωπος, ὃς ἂν κακῶς εἴπῃ τὸν πατέρα αὐτοῦ ἢ τὴν μητέρα αὐτοῦ, θανάτῳ θανατούσθω· πατέρα αὐτοῦ ἢ μητέρα αὐτοῦ κακῶς εἶπεν, ἔνοχος ἔσται.
whoever speaks evil of his father or his mother shall surely die.	Every man whoever speaks evil of his father or his mother, let him die in death; has he spoken evil of his father or his mother? he shall be guilty.

In this instance, where the wording varies, the New Testament passage uses wording from the text that stands earliest in the Torah. The New Testament text contains the imperative τελευτάτω rather than the future form τελευτήσει, and the final two words stand in reverse order. Otherwise, the wording agrees verbatim with the LXX of Exodus 21:16.

After the citations, the elaboration contains an argument from the contrary. In the words of Jesus, the Pharisees and scribes do not permit a person to do anything for his father or mother, thus making void the word of God. This brings to a conclusion the theme that the tradition of humans has superseded the commandment of God (vv. 8, 9, 13). The escalation of the language occurs as follows:

v. 8 ἀφέντες τὴν ἐντολήν
      you *leave* the commandment

v. 9 ἀθετεῖτε τὴν ἐντολήν
      you *reject* the commandment

v. 13 ἀκυροῦντες τὸν λόγον
      you make void the word

With each accusation the speaker more sharply reproves those whom he addresses, raising the final pronouncement in v. 13 to a peak of accusation that rises above the previous pronouncements. In Mark 7:1-13, then, an abbreviated biblical quotation serves as a chreia that is first paraphrased, then elaborated through two additional biblical quotations that function as citations from an ancient authority. After this comes an argument from the contrary. There is further elaboration in the unit, but we will not comment further, since Salyer's essay in this volume (namely Salyer's) is devoted to the complete unit.

CONCLUSIONS

On the basis of this survey it can be concluded that the Gospel writers used biblical material in various ways in developing their stories. Biblical narrative contributed ideas, quotations, and stories which served in contexts of the rhetorical expansion of pronouncement stories. In the process, it has become evident that biblical materials may serve either as artistic or inartistic proofs, depending on their function in a story. In the materials we have examined in this essay, there is a tendency for biblical passages to function as artistic proofs in settings of rhetorical expansion, since abbreviation and adaptation to the discursive context is highly important. In contrast, settings of rhetorical elaboration may accommodate the use of verbatim quotations as inartistic proofs, but they also invite the use of recitations or modified quotations as artistic proofs embedded in argumentative units, which can be strengthened by the use of authoritative premises in their discourse.

WORKS CONSULTED

Aristotle
1975   *The "Art" of Rhetoric*. Loeb Classical Library. Cambridge: Harvard University Press.

Biblia Hebraica Stuttgartensia
1966/77   *Biblia Hebraica Stuttgartensia*. Eds. K. Elliger and W. Rudolph. Stuttgart: Deutsche Bibelstiftung.

Hock, Ronald F. and Edward N. O'Neil, eds.
1986   *The Chreia in Ancient Rhetoric. Volume I. The Progymnasmata*. Atlanta: Scholars.

Mack, Burton L. and Edward N. O'Neil
1986   "The Chreia Discussion of Hermogenes of Tarsus: Introduction, Translation and Comments." Pp. 153-81 in Hock and O'Neil.

Mack, Burton L. and Vernon K. Robbins
1989   *Patterns of Persuasion in the Gospels*. Sonoma: Polebridge.

Nadeau, Ray
1964   "Hermogenes' On Stases: A Translation with Introduction and Notes." *Speech Monographs* 31: 361-424.

Robbins, Vernon K.
1985   "Pragmatic Relations as a Criterion for Authentic Sayings." *Foundations & Facets Forum* 1.3: 35-63.
1989a   "Plucking Grain on the Sabbath." Pp. 107-41 in Mack and Robbins.
1989b   "Foxes, Birds, Burials & Furrows." Pp. 69-84 in Mack and Robbins.
1989c   "Plucking Grain on the Sabbath." Pp. 107-41 in Mack and Robbins.
1989d   "Rhetorical Composition & the Beelzebul Controversy." Pp. 161-93 in Mack and Robbins.

Septuaginta
1943   *Septuaginta. Duodecim Prophetae*. Societatis Litterarum Gottingensis, Vol. XIII. Ed. J. Ziegler. Göttingen: Vandenhoeck, 1943.
1962   *Septuaginta*. Ed. A. Rahls. 7th ed. Stuttgart: Württembergische Bibelanstalt.
1977   *Septuaginta. Deuteronomium*. Academia Scientiarum Gottingensis, Vol. III.2. Ed. John. W. Wevers. Götingen: Vandenhoeck, 1977.

CONFLICT AND RHETORIC IN MARK 2:23-28

Rod Parrott
Disciples Seminary Foundation
Claremont, California

ABSTRACT

Mk 2:23-28 begins with actions by Jesus' disciples and continues with an objection by Pharisees. This essay analyzes the text of Mk 2:25-28 as a *chreia* elaboration: 25 is a citation from authority; 26 is an example, 27a is a rationale and 27b is its converse; 28 is the thesis of the elaboration. The change in order from the normal structure of a *chreia* elaboration is due to the conflict in which the Pharisees are seeking to destroy Jesus. The elaboration was employed in the early community to provide self-definition and support.

INTRODUCTION

The story of "the grainfields incident," one of five pronouncement stories in the "Galilean collection" at the beginning of Mark (Dewey 1980: 15), has presented interpreters with two persistent problems. One is to follow the logic or argumentation of the "pronouncement" portion of the passage (vv. 25-28). The other is to determine the meaning of the whole text (vv. 23-28) in the gospel. The first of these two problems alone makes the text interesting, and one could focus solely on the relation between the setting and saying in the story. But we propose to address both problems, examining the text in the context of Greco-Roman rhetoric and offering an illustration of ways other pronouncement stories in the Gospel also may be interpreted. Because the two problems in view correspond to what Vernon Robbins calls the "rhetoric in" and "rhetorical use of" the pronouncement stories (Mack and Robbins: 1-22, 128, 140-41), what follows is organized accordingly.

1. *The Rhetoric in Mk 2:23-28*

Part of the problem of the rhetoric in vv. 25-28 is the indirectness with which it resolves the tension established among the characters in the story (Jesus, his disciples, and the Pharisees). That tension is expressed in v. 24 in a specific charge of sabbath violation (Lane: 115; Dewey 1980: 100), but the succeeding verses provide a multifaceted and diffuse answer. First, there is a quick jibe at the opponents (v. 25a; Lohmeyer: 64), then a precedent-like illustration apparently based on 1 Sam 21:1-6 (vv. 25b-26), followed by a proverb (v. 27) and a christological statement (v. 28)—in the form of an antithetical aphorism (Tannehill 1975: 94)—which relates the story to the preceding controversies (2:1-12, 15-17, 18-20; esp. 2:10; Robbins 1982a: 14; Parrott 1977: 7-8). By the time one reaches the end of the response, one wonders how each of the arguments has spoken to the issue and how they relate to each other. There is uncertainty at two points in particular: 1) the relation of vv. 25-26 to the remainder of the passage; and 2) the way in which v. 28 provides a conclusion to the passage.

The relation of vv. 25-26 to the remainder of the passage is put in question in three different ways. First, the verses address the Sabbath-breaking issue only obliquely. The word "Sabbath" is lacking; the example is of a violation of a different sacred convention (eating the bread of the Presence). Second, the characterization in the example does not correspond directly to that in the setting: the Pharisees accuse a group (the disciples), while the story focuses on a single individual's (David's) actions. Third, the transition from vv. 25-26 to vv. 27-28 (i.e. the formula καὶ λέγει αὐτοῖς [v. 27a]) separates as well as connects the two segments — a disjunction heightened by the reappearance of "Sabbath" language in vv. 27-28 (Dewey 1980: 98; Lohmeyer: 65).

With vv. 25-26 bracketed out for the moment, it would be germane to consider how vv. 27-28 together —or separately— fit with vv. 23-24. But the rhetorical problem involved here is more specific: How is v. 28 a conclusion to the preceding argumentation in the passage? The conjunction ὥστε defines the verse as a result, but it is not clear how it follows from v. 27, if that is the first term of the syllogism. The interpretive key appears to be a second or minor premise which is missing from and assumed by the text. Taking a clue from Quintilian's discussion of the comparison of like or unlike (Institutio Oratoria V.x.73, 86-93), we might propose two different syllogisms as possibilities:

1) The Sabbath was made for human beings.
   (The Son of man is a human being.)
   So the Son of man is lord of the Sabbath.
2) If the Sabbath was made for human beings,
   (and the Son of man is so much greater than mere humans,)
   How much more will the Son of man be lord of the Sabbath.

At the base of each syllogism is the question of whether the "Son of man" is like or unlike "human beings." Depending on how one answers that, one also decides whether or not a Sabbath "made for human beings" means the same as one's being "lord of the Sabbath." In addition to this problem, the conjunction καί places v. 28 in relation to some other statement about the Son of man (in the present setting, 2:10) but does not make clear the basis for the comparison/contrast.

Attempts to handle these two interpretive problems have proceeded largely from the identification of a supposed original ending of the story to the reconstruction of the composition-history of the passage. For a recent example, see Hultgren (1972: 38-43; 1979: 113-15, 139-40). These reconstructions include various understandings of the pre-canonical shape of the tradition. Albertz (1921: 5, 35) argued that most of the material existed in a pre-Markan collection. In this he was followed by W. L. Knox (8-16, 85-92); Klostermann (21); Grundmann (1971: 9); Kümmel (85); Marxsen (130); Cranfield (61); Best (71); Maisch (113); Kuhn (22-23); Dewey (1973: 399; 1980: 42-52); and Perrin and Duling (234). See also the list in Kuhn (22-23, 75). By contrast, Bultmann (349); Schmidt (104); Dibelius (45); and Trocmé (92) doubt the existence of the collection prior to Mark, although the material itself probably antedates the Evangelist. V. Taylor (92) attempts to mediate between these two views by concluding that 2:1-3:6 is based on a collection which the Evangelist himself put together before writing the Gospel.

Three main alternatives result from these investigations. In the first, vv. 25-26 are considered the original answer to the Pharisees' accusation. They answer the charge through a need-argument, suggesting that both the disciples and David had need and were hungry. This basic story-and-word unit is generalized somewhat by the addition of a previously unattached logion on the Sabbath (v. 27) and is put into relationship with other pronouncement stories in a collection by the addition of v. 28 (Bultmann: 16-17; Taylor: 218; Achtemeier: 16; Maisch: 119; Cranfield: 118). The weakness of this solution is that, as we have already noted, vv. 25-26 do not answer the charge of Sabbath violation directly. The second reconstruction is based on v. 27 as the original response to the charge. This originally isolated Sabbath saying (Hultgren 1979: 114) has been given a setting, vv. 23-24 (Bultmann: 11, 18, 46-47; Schweizer: 70; Hultgren 1972: 40-41; 1979: 114). Some time later vv. 25-26 were added to reduce the radicality of the saying by providing a scriptural precedent (Hultgren 1972: 38-43; Kuhn: 73-76; Rordorf: 58; Beare: 91-92; Haenchen: 120; Suhl: 82-84; Dewey 1973: 397; Schweizer: 70-71; Klostermann: 29). Schweizer (71) suggests that vss. 25-26 came into the story about the same time as the original composition. But v. 28 does not presuppose anything specific from vv. 25-26 unless one considers it an extrapolation from the figure of David. As suggested above, v. 27 can stand by itself. The tendency to add such material can be seen by comparing the Matthean parallel (12:1-8). Murmelstein's more radical suggestion (111-20) that an original confrontation over Jesus' messianic claims has been transmuted into a Sabbath controversy has won few, if any, followers. Perhaps v. 28 was added to narrow the scope of the saying and at the same time to connect the story as a whole to a context (Dibelius: 64-65; Bultmann: 16-17; Grundmann 1961: 14; Taylor: 220; Cranfield: 118; Dewey 1973: 401; Käsemann: 39, 101-102). The third alternative takes v. 28 (minus the conjunctions) as the original response/saying. Verse 27 was added to generalize the Son of man's authority to all humankind, and vv. 25-26 were added to shore up both vv. 27 and 28 with a scriptural precedent (Hultgren 1979: 114, n. 65). Among these options, none has won a consensus, although the second reconstruction probably has the most support. In view of this impasse, three of the most recent approaches to the text have sought to read it largely in its canonical rather than pre-canonical form.

The first of these more canonical approaches has been that of Joanna Dewey, who suggests that Mark has given vv. 23-28, along with other passages in the Galilean collection, a particular rhetorical character by incorporating them in a unit with a linear progression and chiastic/concentric pattern (Dewey, 1973: passim; 1980: 65-130). Dewey finds the concentric pattern in a variety of ways. It is visible by noting the basic form of the material:

the narrative (1:45)
    healing story (2:1-12)
        controversy story (2:15-17)
            controversy story (2:18-20)
        controversy story (2:23-28)
    healing story (3:1-6)
the narrative (3:7f)

Or, it may be derived from an analysis of the form of Jesus' answers in each story:

(counter) question (2:1-12)
    proverb/Christological statement (2:15-17)
        counter-question (2:18-20)
    proverb/Christological statement (2:23-28)
(counter) question (3:1-6)

One also could notice that the first and last stories (2:1-12 and 3:1-6) bracket a unit of different controversies in which the opponents take the initiative, and that the outer two stories have much more the flavor of scholastic dialogues than of controversy (cf. Mk 11). Or, one might conceive of the organization of the unit by catch-words: "sin/sinner" connecting 2:1-12 and 15-17; "eating/fasting" connecting 2:15-17 and 18-

20; "eating" connecting 2:18-20 and 23-28; and "what is permitted/on the sabbath" connecting 2:23-28 and 3:1-6. In general, the unit addresses the question, "What is permitted?" (see also 7:1-23; 1 Cor 10:23-11:1).

Besides this chiasmus, Dewey (1980: 104-106) notes a linear development in the hostility towards Jesus, both in the style of relationship of the opponents, as well as in the designations given the opponents; and Rhoads and Michie (51-53) follow Dewey in this analysis. The linear progression serves to establish and advance the opposition between Jesus and other Jewish leaders while the concentric pattern distributes that opposition to Jesus' ministry as a whole (Dewey 1980:116-20).

With respect to the pre-canonical shape of the material, Dewey acknowledges the lack of consensus about the sources and composition of the passage (1980: 229, n. 117) and after discussing the options, adopts the position of H.W. Kuhn: Mark received a series of four stories from the tradition (approximately 2:3-12, 15-17, 18-20, and 23-28 [minus vv. 25-26]) and supplemented them with the material now found in 2:1-2, 13-14, 19 (perhaps!), 21-22, 25-26, and 3:1-6. This latter material came either from elsewhere in the church's tradition or from the Evangelist's own composition (Dewey 1973: 401).

As it now stands the rhetorical structure of vv. 23-28 is itself comprised of three parts (vv. 23-24, 25-26 and 27-28) with "a circular rhythm" and a certain "narrative logic." Hook words such as οὐκ ἔξεστιν, σάββατον, and τί ποιεῖν tie the various parts together, and each part has its particular rhetorical function (Dewey 1980: 94-96). Although she refers only in passing to the opening verses of this story (vv. 23-24), Dewey's comments on vv. 25-28 are more extensive. She acknowledges that the David story (vv. 25-26) does not directly address the issue of Sabbath violation but serves "...first, as a statement that illegal behavior is sometimes appropriate, and second, as an indication that the disciples' behavior is dependent on their relationship to Jesus" (Dewey 1980: 97). Thus the verses give a partial answer to the accusation of v. 24 but primarily shift attention to Jesus as the ultimate authority. Dewey holds vv. 27-28 together on the basis of their proximity and the repetition of key terms in them (Dewey 1980: 98). More importantly, she says they are, with vv. 25-26, "a single (rhetorical) answer" by which Jesus' authority is established vis-à-vis the Sabbath (Dewey, 1980: 98-99). The missing premise about the Son of man is located partially in the text (in 2:10) and partially in the understanding which the reader brings to the text (Dewey 1980: 99-100).

I find Dewey's attempt to discern the Markan pattern of organization, in Mk 2:1-3:6, but especially in 2:23-28, a welcome effort. In my judgment she overstates in her paper the importance of the chiastic pattern at the level of the final redaction but assumes a more reasonable position in her book (Dewey 1980: 116-119). For me, the prominent features of the Markan redaction — seen especially in 2:1-2, 13, 14, 21-22, 25-26, 3:1a,6 — may be a writing over a pre-existing chiasmus with a linear progression. To Dewey's credit, she attempts to account for the material not only in its final form but also in its pre-canonical development.

A second study of the relation between the "setting" and the "pronouncement" was offered by Robert Tannehill almost simultaneously with Dewey's work. Intended as much to classify the pronouncement stories as to understand the rhetoric in them, it focused from a literary-critical perspective on the establishment and resolution of narrative tension (Tannehill 1981). Tannehill's brief excursus in *The Sword of His Mouth* (1975: 152-57) provides a sensitive description of the way in which the settings of the synoptic sayings introduce, maintain, and resolve tension. He notes, for example, that they generate imaginative force (153); that they do not satisfy historical curiosity about the dynamics of the occasion (153); that every story contains tension (154); that in some of the stories there is no resolution (154); and that the stories require that the reader take up some stance vis-á-vis Jesus' word (156-57). Building on that understanding, Tannehill skillfully observes how conflict or tension emerged in the various pronouncement stories in the synoptic Gospels, and on that basis proposes to identify various types of pronouncement stories (1981a).

Tannehill included Mk 2:23-28, along with 2:15-17, 18-22, and 3:1-6 in the category of "objection stories" (1981b: 107), noting that the conflict or tension in the story is established in the "situation" or "setting" by an objection put forward by a second party. To quote him directly:

> In an objection story the responder is already committed to a position through the words or action causing the objection. The resulting challenge creates tension within the story and puts the responder in a difficult situation. However, an impressive response is all the more impressive because it occurs within a situation of difficulty and risk. (1981a: 8)

Related to the objection story is the "testing inquiry." In it,

> ...the question or request usually comes from a hostile or skeptical party. It is designed to put the responder to the test. The responder is placed in a critical situation. There is a sense of risk, for the reputation, influence, and perhaps the safety of the responder are at stake. (1981b: 115)

Tannehill differentiates the testing inquiry from the objection story by a simple criterion:

> Although the responder is also placed in a critical situation when faced with an objection from a hostile party, the testing inquiry differs from the objection

story in that the provoking element is not an objection to something already said or done. (1981b: 115)

In addition to the "objection story" and the "testing inquiry," there are other stories in which the setting establishes no tension. "Correction stories," for example, exhibit the conflict first in the response, and "the response is not provoked by the criticism of the responder," (1981b: 104). "Inquiry stories" present a question or request in the setting, but that question or request is not the source of tension; the responder is not placed in the position of replying to an objection (1981a: 10).

Whether or not one accepts the variety of labels which Tannehill offers, there can be little doubt that his attention to the ways in which tension emerges and is resolved in the pronouncement stories has helped our understanding of them as a whole.

When one turns to the understanding of Mk 2:23-28, however, the results are more ambiguous. It is clear that Tannehill classifies the passage as an objection story because he reads the Pharisees' question in v. 24 as an objection to the disciples' reaping grain on the Sabbath. But how does one know that the Pharisees' question is an objection? Could it not be an inquiry? Is there not a fine line between the two? More importantly, can one decide the question on the basis of the story itself? Certainly there is no explanation in the narrative here, as there is in 2:15c, 18, or especially 7:3-4.

In my judgment, the decision to take v. 24 as an objection rather than an inquiry is made not on the basis of the story, but on the basis of the context. The accumulation of Pharisee/Jesus stories in the Galilean collection (chapters 2 and 3) clearly signals that the Pharisees and Jesus are up to something significant. They do not appear to get along. So we conclude that the question in v. 24 is an objection, and that the Pharisees are critical, misunderstanding, or opposed to Jesus. At this point, Robbins's identification of adversative elements in the passage is a helpful advance (1984/92: 112-113).

In this regard, Tannehill's treatment of Mk 6:1-6 is instructive. He calls it an "objection story," even though he acknowledges that "the questions in 6:2-3 are not clearly negative" (1981b: 108). They receive their negative character from the summary statement, "And they took offense at him." That statement, he says, "clearly indicates that the preceding questions constitute an objection of the townspeople to one of their own claiming or exercising such unusual powers" (108).

To return to Mk 2:23-28, it is clear that the story begins with the disciples' action, to which the Pharisees' response is closely linked. The only clues that the Pharisees object to the disciples' action are 1) the fact that they are named; and 2) the fact that they respond to the action. A tension surely is marked by their response, but it is not clear that this tension is the same as objection. Why the Pharisees respond — and hence whether their response is actually an objection — is hidden in the presuppositions of the story's author. The clearest statement to the reader comes not from the story itself, but from the formulation of 3:1-6, especially 3:6. We will return to the matter of the interplay between the text and its larger narrative setting later.

A wide range of rhetorical techniques, some quite different from those utilized by either Dewey or Tannehill, have recently been applied to the passage by Vernon Robbins. In much of his work in the Pronouncement Stories Work Group of the SBL, Robbins focused on the identification and categorization of the species of rhetoric represented in the stories. In his 1984/92 book he relied primarily on the notions of logical and qualitative progressions to describe the rhetorical shape of the Gospel of Mark. Interestingly, Dewey's suggestion (1980: 95-96) that 2:23-28 is organized by hook words from v. 24 is similar to Robbins's use of logical and qualitative progressions. In the course of Robbins's description, however, he noted how the use of the title, "Son of man," the introduction of the figure of David, and what Robbins calls "aggressive proverbial wisdom" contribute to the movement and development in the gospel (1984/92: 32, 42, 69, n.11, 111-13, 194, n. 20, 199). While both of these studies contribute to our understanding of the rhetorical shape of the gospel and the wide range of rhetoric in the stories, we cannot treat either of them more fully here.

In an early paper for the Pronouncement Stories Work Group, Robbins suggested that the chreia-elaboration model described by the Claremont Chreia Project, and specifically by Burton Mack (Mack and Robbins: 51-52, 56-63), can illuminate the study of pronouncement stories, and indeed the pronouncement story in Mk 2:23-28 as an amplified (i.e. elaborated) chreia (Robbins 1982a: 14). He identified vv. 25-28 as an elaboration consisting of four parts: an example from a written authority (vv. 25-26); a rationale (v. 27a); an argument from the opposite (v. 27b); and an encomiastic epilogue (v. 28; Robbins 1982a: 14).

In more recent work, Robbins reconstructs a basic synoptic chreia from the evidence in the triple tradition, and explores its specific developments in each of the evangelists (Mack and Robbins: 107-141). With respect particularly to Mark, Robbins understands the development (i.e., elaboration) to be away from the original "swerve" expressed in the use of the David Story (vv. 25-26) to a deliberative, enthymeme-like redefinition of Sabbath law (Mack and Robbins: 128-129).

We find this rhetorical analysis intriguing, and want to push it further. We are especially interested in how the elaboration "pattern" fits

Mk 2:23-28 and helps us to understand it. At the outset, however, there seem to be two reasons for hesitation in applying the model to this passage: 1) the variation in order between the elements in the Markan "elaboration" and those in the school elaborations; and 2) the absence of a "thesis" among the elements. Robbins (Mack and Robbins: 109), following Tannehill, asserts that when judicial speech occurs in the pronouncement stories, the introduction and statement of the facts occurs in the narrative and speech of the "setting," with the proof and conclusion in the "response." This places the thesis in the setting, rather than in the response. But we believe the pronouncement story must be seen as two speeches; one an abbreviated accusation; the other a more or less developed defense speech. Hence we expect a thesis in the story's response as well as the setting.

For convenience, Table #1 lists the four Markan elements described by Robbins alongside the parts of the "complete argument" as outlined by Hermogenes (cf. Mack and Robbins: 51-61).

Table #1
Elements of Argumentation in Hermogenes and Mark 2:25-28

Hermogenes	Mark 2:25-28
Encomium/Praise	Citation of Authority
Paraphrase/Chreia (Thesis)	Example
Rationale	Rationale
Converse	Converse/opposite
Analogy	Encomiastic epilogue
Example	
Citation of Authority	
Exhortation	

As the table shows, the two orders are quite different from each other. Such a difference is significant because in rhetorical theory the arrangement of argumentation was considered second in importance only to its contents (Quintilian, Institutio Oratoria 7,pr.2; Perelman and Olbrechts-Tyteca: 357-358), and in the case of the chreia-based elaboration it was specified in detail (Mack and Robbins: 51-57; cf. Rhet ad Her. 2.18.28). Consequently, it is reasonable to wonder whether the Markan passage is really an elaboration, or simply has common rhetorical elements which also happen to occur in the elaboration.

The absence of a thesis weighs even more heavily against the presence of an elaboration. In the school models the chreia-saying becomes the thesis for the speech-like elaboration and stands at its head. It is commonly stated and then restated in a paraphrased fashion before launching into the elaboration which follows (Mack and Robbins: 32,40, 57). Its presence actually enables one to tell the difference between "expansion" and "elaboration."

In Robbins's analysis of the saying in vv. 25-28 this initial thesis is lacking–or is heavily disguised. Robbins surely is correct in identifying the David story in vv. 25-26 as an example cited from authority, a refutation based on precedent (Robbins 1982: 14; Mack and Robbins: 110). And his careful outline of the argumentative force of the example does demonstrate how it presents an antithesis to the Pharisees' charge (Mack and Robbins: 116). But is his explanation enough to allow us to consider the verses the thesis of a chreia-elaboration?

We believe not. Not only is their argumentative force subtle and well-disguised, there is a more obvious thesis: v. 28. While Robbins correctly noted the encomiastic character of v. 28, he mislabeled it "epilogue" (Mack and Robbins: 116). It is not an "epilogue" but is the thesis/conclusion of the present story. Table #2 outlines the analysis as I would state it.

Table #2
Modified Analysis of Mk 2:25-28

Citation of Authority	"Have you never read. . . "
Example	"How David. . . "
Rationale	"The Sabbath was made. . ."
Converse	". . . not man for the Sabbath"
Thesis	"So the Son of man. . . "

Of course this suggestion is not without objections. Two, in particular, deserve attention. The first could be stated thus: if we take the Son of man saying in v. 28 as the thesis of the elaboration, must we not also take it as the original saying of the chreia? To do so, of course, would imply that it comes early in the compositional process. But that would fly in the face of contemporary understandings of the Son of man language. The second objection is more directly focused on the rhetoric of the passage: does the logic or argumentation of the elaboration actually support such a thesis? (In other words, do vv. 25-27 "prove" that the Son of man is [also] lord of the Sabbath?)

To answer the first objection, we might suggest that the elaboration has as its thesis something other than the original chreia-saying. A similar suggestion has been offered by B. Mack with respect to an elaboration in Mk 7. In that passage, according to Mack, the original saying about the inner/outer dichotomy in v. 15 was displaced by the scripture citation of vv. 6-7, and the latter is elaborated (Mack: personal conversation, August,

1985). In our case, one might argue that in an analogous way the Son of man saying in Mk 2:28 has displaced the original chreia-saying.

In that case, one might come up with the following scheme of composition or elaboration: v. 27 was the original chreia-saying. Under the influence of the Markan community's need for self-definition, it subsequently was expanded by: 1) the addition of a setting (vv. 23-24) featuring an adversative relationship between Jesus and "the Pharisees;" and 2) the citation of a "precedent" (vv. 25-26) which not only continued the adversative relationship ("have you never read. . . ?") but also established a continuity of ethos between Jesus and David. This whole configuration is presented, finally (v. 28), as a demonstration of the authority of the Son of man — a figure of significance to Mark's community. Whether the saying in v. 27 is clever enough to be called a "Cynic-type" chreia (to use Mack's terms) remains to be seen. It is aphoristic, and it does respond to the query by citing another "order" (what is permitted/what is created or "made"). It also clearly is "domesticated" (again Mack's term) insofar as it is provided with a scriptural precedent (vv.25-26) and identified with a specific figure accepted within the community of interpretation (v.28; Mack and Robbins: 41-44).

If such a reconstruction is possible, we may continue to view our passage as a chreia-elaboration. But now we must account for the fact that it does not adhere precisely to the school-model. We may do so by applying other tools of rhetorical analysis.

One of those tools which is useful here, and deserves more attention generally, is the definition of the rhetorical situation (Kennedy: 33-38). In calling for this definition of the rhetorical situation to be done even before one identifies the rhetorical species to which the speech belongs, it seems to me that Kennedy offers some methodological assistance to those who would apply rhetorical insights to the gospel materials. Definition of the rhetorical situation can bring the "literary" analysis of Tannehill into relation with Robbins's attention to rhetorical species in such a way that some of the cumbersome categories which have been proposed (see, e.g. Robbins's classification of Mk 2:23-28 as "a juridical defense story with an interrogative setting" (Robbins 1984: 106-107) can be avoided. Such a definition, which George Kennedy says should follow upon the identification of the rhetorical unit in question, means delineating the "persons, events, objects, and relations" in the story (Kennedy: 35; cf. Quintilian, Inst. Orat. IV.i.52). It may seem commonplace and mundane, but it is essential because it enables one to determine the presence or absence of what Kennedy calls the "one overriding rhetorical problem": the hostility or unreceptiveness of the audience (Kennedy: 36). Kennedy says: "This problem is often especially visible at the beginning of a discourse *and conditions the contents of the proem or the beginning of the proof"* (Kennedy: 36; emphasis added).

For Mk 2:23-28, the end of Kennedy's comment is especially important. If hostility or unreceptiveness is present in a given rhetorical situation, we may expect divergence at two points: in the introduction to the speech, or at the beginning of the argumentation. Monroe (161, 216, 429) acknowledges this dual impact when he says that in general there are two rules which govern speeches to hostile audiences: 1) establish some common ground with the audience; and 2) prefer indirect as opposed to direct argumentation. In view of these "rules," —and the clue about the presence of hostility provided in 3:6—we should not be surprised to find that Jesus' "speech" does not follow the conventional order.

But that is to get ahead of ourselves. In the face of hostility, what may we expect the divergence in the introduction to be? The answer, according to Kennedy, is *insinuatio* (the "subtle approach"). He refers for details about it to a discussion in *Rhetorica ad Herennium* (I.vi.9-11, Kennedy: 36). The subject is also discussed by Quintilian when he treats the shape of the exordium (Quintilian, *Institutio Oratoria* IV.1.42-45). For a contemporary discussion, see Monroe (1962), who addresses the problem of the introduction in a paragraph subtitled "Adaptation to personal hostility":

> When your analysis predicts that your audience will be hostile toward you, your first job as a speaker is to try to overcome this attitude. You can hardly accomplish your purpose in speaking without doing so. The method will vary, of course, with the cause of that hostility, and your job will be easier if their respect for you is high. **In any case, try in some way to establish common ground with your audience.** This can often be done by one of the following methods:
> 1. By showing a friendly attitude toward your audience.
> 2. By maintaining an attitude of fairness, modesty, and good humor.
> 3. By pointing out your own agreement with some of their cherished attitudes or beliefs.
> 4. By referring to experiences held in common with them.
> 5. By tactfully complimenting their abilities, accomplishments, or friends.
> 6. By using humor that is in good taste, especially that which is at your own expense. (Monroe: 161, emphasis added)

Monroe repeats this general principle when he treats the first part of a "speech to convince" given to an audience hostile to a given proposal:

> ...since you know there will be hostility toward your proposition or plan of action, you should try, first of all, to conciliate your audience and win a hearing. Approach your proposition indirectly and gradually. Concede whatever you can to your audience's point of view; establish common ground by

emphasizing points of agreement; minimize or explain away differences. Make your listeners feel that you are genuinely interested in achieving the same results they are. (Monroe: 429)

Finally, he makes similar comments with reference to a speech to an audience which does not believe a problem exists (Monroe: 431). In fact, he says that to a hostile audience, even a reference to the subject or problem at the beginning of a speech would be "a slap in the face" (Monroe: 261).

In Ad Herennium, insinuatio is considered appropriate for three situations: 1) when the cause is repugnant to the hearer; 2) when the speaker's opponent already has convinced the audience; and 3) when the hearers are tired (Rhet. ad Her. I.vi.9-vii.11). Specific techniques to be used include agreeing with the audience that some action is repugnant and denying any involvement in it; feigning indecision or astonishment; or provoking laughter (Rhet. ad Her. I.vi.9-vii.11). These and others are used in an attempt to establish rapport with the audience in an indirect fashion (Rhet. ad Her. I.vii.11).

Of course, such an approach ultimately does not inform the mini-speech in Mk 2:25-28 because —unless one considers the "jibe" in v. 25 an "introduction"— it does not have a proem or exordium. Hence it is of more direct relevance to return to the suggestion that in a conflictive situation the rhetoric may modify the "beginning of the proof."

Unfortunately we have not been able to identify with any certainty what the ancient handbooks understood some of those modifications to be. There seem to be several possibilities if one takes the general intention of insinuatio as a starting point.

One is what Quintilian describes as the Socratic method of argumentation with "an adversary," i.e., induction:

> When he had asked a number of questions to which his adversary could only agree, he finally inferred the conclusion of the problem under discussion from its resemblance to the points already conceded. This method is known as induction.... (Quintilian, Inst. Orat. V.xi.3)

Quintilian notes that induction is particularly useful in the interrogation of witnesses, but also may be employed as an argumentative technique in a pre-written speech (Quintilian, Inst. Orat. V.xi.5). What he seems to have in mind by the latter is the introduction of a real or imaginary interlocutor, neither of which we have in Mk 2:23-28. Still, his general endorsement of an indirect approach and his acknowledgement that induction is essentially comparison puts the opening question ("Have you never read...") and example (the David-story) in our passage in a new light. His judgment that such induction/comparison is appropriate both to embellishment and proof (Quintilian V.xi.5) only strengthens the possibility that the "pronouncement" in Mk 2:25-28 has been influenced by "induction."

Perhaps a more promising insight for understanding how the rhetoric of a speech may be modified in the presence of conflict, however, can be gleaned from Quintilian's discussion of altercatio, the give-and-take of forensic debate (Quintilian, Inst. Orat. VI.4.1). Indeed one might even be justified in identifying a pronouncement story such as ours as altercatio.

According to Quintilian, arrangement (dispositio) does not play a significant part in forensic debates (altercatio). Fixed speech types of most kinds are not useful in this setting because of the rapid-fire give and take (Quintilian, Inst. Orat. VI.4.1). Under the pressure of conflict, the rhetor must be able to respond with a variety of arguments and devices, as the occasion demands. These may be used in quite different order from the fixed speech organization.

In induction and altercatio, then, there are two options from the ancient handbooks for explaining the speech-order of Mk 2:25-28. Interestingly, in the speech textbook we cited earlier, Monroe proceeds in much the same way. He confirms that the existence of a hostile situation affects the choice of argumentation and suggests that "the method of implication" is most appropriate for such situations (Monroe: 216). "It is, in fact, almost the only method to use with an audience that is hostile to the point you wish to present." He then outlines the course of such argumentation as follows:

1. Present an analogy or illustration which implies the point you wish to make.
2. Present additional illustrations, instances, figure, and testimony which point inevitably to this conclusion without stating it.
3. Show how these facts lead unavoidably to this conclusion; use explanation if necessary.
4. Definitely state your point as a conclusion. (Monroe: 216)

This outline is remarkably similar to the list of rhetorical elements in Mk 2:25-28, offered in Table #2, above. Although the opening rhetorical question ("Have you never read...?") in v. 25 seems to me to exacerbate the tension and hostility established in vv. 23-24, it is no violation of the remaining verses to say that they proceed indirectly and inductively to the "conclusion" in v. 28. Verses 25-26 present an analogy or illustration; v. 27 presents a maxim used as an explanation; and v. 28 states the conclusion.

2. *The Rhetoric of Mk 2:23-28*

Having examined at some length the relation between the setting and the saying (=speech) in Mk 2:23-28, it is now time to take up some of the observations made in passing about the effect of the context on the rhetoric in the passage. In this phenomenon one meets the very real problem of determining whether the rhetoric in a particular story has been changed in any way by the rhetorical use for which it is employed in the larger context.

In this regard, one expects the larger rhetoric of use to determine the meaning of all smaller constituent rhetorical units. In view of this, see Robbins's defense of the integrity of a given story's rhetoric:

> A pronouncement story has an internal rhetoric that interacts with the rhetorical use of the story by a speaker or writer. The internal rhetoric is not totally subservient to the setting provided outside the story by the speaker or writer. The internal rhetoric stands in a tensive relation to the rhetorical purpose for which it is being employed. (Robbins 1982b: 4; cf. Mack and Robbins: 19)

An adequate demonstration of this interplay calls for attention both to the actual narrative context in which the stories are found and to the social context in which the stories have been constructed or retold.

Two different examples of this approach are available in Robbins's work on Mark. As we have indicated already, in *Jesus the Teacher* Robbins analyzes the gospel in terms of conventional and repetitive progressions which give the gospel its rhetorical structure. In addition to this analysis, however, Robbins also seeks to relate the pronouncement stories to a social context. He asserts that many of them arose out of, reflect, and speak to situations of conflict between the early church and its parent Judaism — if in fact they are not actual reports of Jesus' "run-ins" with religious leaders of his own time. The use of "aggressive proverbial wisdom" in the stories derives from the interplay between the two groups, explained largely from a sociological perspective. On this subject we cite him here at length.

> The aggressive proverbial wisdom in the initial phase of the Markan narrative emerges out of the folklore in early Christianity that celebrated a system of thought and action that deviated from norms established by Jewish leaders...
>
> The identity of the deviant group arises out of antagonism that is directed toward scribes and Pharisees. Therefore Jesus is placed in settings where scribes and Pharisees object to the actions either of him or of his disciples, and Jesus responds with proverbs that appear to be the result of careful reflection and appear to be morally right. (Robbins 1984/92: 113)

Robbins expands on these notions of social formation in his specific treatment of Mk 2:23-28 in chapter 4 of *Patterns of Persuasion in the Gospels*, describing the christological development which the passage achieves as well as its deliberative function in the life of the early Christian community (Mack and Robbins: 128-29).

In contrast to this socio-rhetorical analysis, consider the following general description by Rhoads and Michie of the pronouncement stories in Mark:

> The conflict with the authorities sustains suspense. It is not resolved until the end of the story. On account of his courage and cleverness **in debate** Jesus proves to be superior. Yet the opposition escalates. And Jesus is vulnerable because, as we have seen, he has no authority to dominate people. The suspense builds as to whether they will destroy Jesus, but also whether they will get him on their own terms or his. It is a conflict between the one who thinks the things of God and those who think the things of men—dramatic and hostile, full of tension and trickery. And the resolution, when it comes, is ironic. (Rhoads and Michie: 79, emphasis added)

Clearly this explanation primarily moves on the level of the narrative, and does not seek to account for any actual social dimensions.

Now there can be little doubt that a socio-rhetorical approach is more comprehensive than a purely rhetorical one, and represents a step in the right direction. But more work needs to be done, particularly on the effect of a conflictive context on the pronouncement story. Robbins acknowledges this problem by suggesting a one-to-one correlation between conflict in the social setting and conflict in the narrative, and provides some clues about how a particular species of rhetoric performs when it moves from one rhetorical context to another. He does not, however, study the particular transformation of performance which occurs when a rhetorical unit moves from a relatively congenial to non-congenial situation, or from one to another type of conflictive situation. In view of the suggestions presented in the first section of this paper, some attention needs to be given to this phenomenon.

The same problem arises in the treatment by Rhoads and Michie in a quite different way. In the paragraph cited, the authors assert that in Mark there are two levels to the conflictive encounter between Jesus and other Jewish leaders. The first of these is called "debate." The second, though not named, has aspects of "fight." As we are led to understand it, the story line in the Gospel of Mark focuses on the escalation of the conflict from debate to fight, and particularly on the question of whether Jesus will be destroyed.

But how can one determine if Michie and Rhoads are correct in their description? To answer that question one needs to know what the authors mean by the terms "debate" and "conflict." One needs to know also what they mean by "destroy." Unfortunately, these terms are not defined in the book. It is a weakness for the interpretation of the pronouncement stories generally, and for the Markan stories in particular, that no consistent categories from the sociology of conflict are used in NT exegesis.

That is not because such terms are unavailable. A helpful set may be found in the work of Anatol Rapoport, who defines conflict along a continuum from fights to games to debates (Rapoport). Each of these types or modes is distinguished from the others primarily by the participants' intentions with reference to each other. Where one party seeks to remove or destroy the other, there is fight. Where one party seeks to outwit the other, there is game. Where one party seeks to convince or persuade the other, there is debate (Rapoport: 9-11). This is not the place to enter into the technical discussion about whether debate is to *persuade* or to *convince* (Perelman and Olbrechts-Tyteca: 28).

These conflictual modes are not coterminous with the traditional *species* or purposes of rhetoric, since each of the *species* of rhetoric can function in one or more of the three modes of conflict. Hence "deliberative" rhetoric may be employed not with the intention to convince or persuade, but to destroy. Or "judicial" rhetoric used to outwit or maneuver the opponent. Or "epideixis" may be used to fight (Kennedy: 19-20; Robbins: personal letter, February 19, 1985). But such modes can be used to identify more precisely the kind of conflict present in the rhetorical situation. And the definition of the rhetorical situation is a key to understanding the rhetoric *of* the passage, as well as the rhetoric *in* the passage.

Using these categories, then, we return to the pronouncement story in Mk 2:23-28. Whatever may have been the original setting and purpose of the saying about the Sabbath (our present v. 27), the present pronouncement story does not mean to portray Jesus and the Jewish leaders in "debate" over the proper observance of the Sabbath—contra Bultmann (39-54), Dewey (1980: 15), Rhoads and Michie (79) and others who have argued that the pronouncement stories represent "public debate." They are not seeking to persuade each other (or even a third party?). Rather, the story exhibits aspects of "games" and "fights." In issuing the charge, a verbal joust, the leaders seek to set aside, disarm or even destroy Jesus. This is "fight." Much to the leaders' embarrassment, however, Jesus escapes unscathed, and the final redactor offers encomiastic praise which is akin to game.

This modification of the rhetorical *species* (initially deliberation) in the face of conflict recalls aspects of Mack's discussion of the domestication of Cynic-like chreiai. In bringing this study to a close, we cite him at length:

> They are chreiai in which a $\mu\hat{\eta}\tau\iota\varsigma$-like response masters a situation of challenge, introducing a devastating swerve in the place of expectation that would follow more conventional logic. This is especially true of the so-called controversy stories, and it is also true to some degree of all the pronouncement stories...if they "received" the chreia, they also made judgments as to its rationale and thesis. If they elaborated received chreiai, then, we can

document a stage in the chreia's cultural history. In the case of a chreia with μῆτις-like response, moreover, elaboration should be a wondrous thing to behold. We would be witnessing the attempt to domesticate the enigmatic, to turn the silence at the borders of convention into thesis, or to resolve it in the interest of another λόγος from within the new social formation. (Mack and Robbins: 66-67)

Here Mack clearly uses some of the language of the sociology of conflict (see the references to "conflict" and "dialogue" and "debate") to describe the rhetoric of chreia-elaborations and "controversy stories." We find that usage helpful. And we find his assessment of the rhetoric convincing, even if we believe that the elaboration in Mk 2:23-28 has moved away from domestication: rather than being an elaboration of an original put-off or put-down, it is the development of one, employed in the life of the early community to provide self-definition and support.

WORKS CONSULTED

Achtemeier, P. J.
    1975   *Mark*. Proclamation Commentaries. Philadelphia: Fortress.

Albertz, Martin
    1921   *Die synoptischen Streitgespräche: ein Beitrag zur Formengeschichte des Urchristentums*. Berlin: Trowitzsch & Sohn.

Aune, D. E.
    1982   "Critique of Pronouncement Stories, *Semeia* 20 (1981)." Unpublished paper presented to SBL Pronouncement Story Work Group.

Beare, F. W.
    1962   *The Earliest Records of Jesus*. New York: Abingdon.

Best, E.
    1965   *The Temptation and the Passion: The Markan Soteriology*. SNTSMS 2. Cambridge: Cambridge University Press.

Bultmann, R.
    1963   *The History of the Synoptic Tradition*. Rev. ed. New York: Harper & Row.

Cranfield, C.E.B.
    1972   *The Gospel According to Saint Mark: An Introduction and Commentary*. Cambridge Greek Testament Commentary. Cambridge: Cambridge University Press.

Dewey, Joanna
    1973   "The Literary Structure of the Controversy Stories in Mk 2:1-3:6." *JBL* 92: 394-401.

1980   *Markan Public Debate.* SBLDSS 48. Chico: Scholars.

Dibelius, Martin
1961   *From Tradition to Gospel.* New York: Scribners.

Grundmann, W.
1961   *Die Geschichte Jesu Christi.* 3rd ed. Berlin: Evangelische Verlag.
1971   *Das Evangelium nach Markus.* Theologischer Handkommentar zum Neuen Testament 2. 5. Aufl. Berlin: Evangelische Verlag.

Haenchen, E.
1966   *Der Weg Jesu: Eine Erklärung des Markusevangeliums und der kanonischen Parallelen.* Berlin: Alfred Töpelmann.

Hultgren, A. J.
1972   "The Formation of the Sabbath Pericope in Mark 2:23-28." *JBL* 91: 38-43.
1979   *Jesus and His Adversaries.* Minneapolis: Augsburg.

Käsemann, E.
1964   *Essays on New Testament Themes.* SBT 41. London: S.C.M.

Klostermann, E.
1950   *Das Markusevangelium.* HNT 3. 4. Aufl. Tübingen: Mohr.

Knox, W. L.
1953/57   *The Sources of the Synoptic Gospels.* 2 vols. Cambridge: Cambridge University Press.

Kuhn, H. W.
1971   *Ältere Sammlungen im Markusevangelium.* Göttingen: Vandenhoeck & Ruprecht.

Kümmel, W. G.
1975   *Introduction to the New Testament.* Nashville: Abingdon.

Lane, William
1974   *The Gospel According to Mark.* NICNT. Grand Rapids: William B. Eerdmans.

Lohmeyer, Ernst
1967   *Das Evangelium des Markus.* Meyer 1/2. 17. Aufl. Göttingen: Vandenhoeck & Ruprecht.

Mack, Burton L. and Vernon K. Robbins
1989   *Patterns of Persuasion in the Gospels.* Sonoma: Polebridge.

Maisch, I.
1971   *Die Heilung des Gelahmten: eine exegetischtraditiongeschichtliche Untersuchung zu Mk 2, 1-12.* Stuttgarter Bibel-Studien 52. Stuttgart: K.B.W.

Marxsen, W.
1968   *Introduction to the New Testament: An Approach to Its Problems.* Philadelphia: Fortress.

Monroe, Alan
    1962   *Principles and Types of Speech.* 5th ed. Chicago: Scott, Foresman & Co.

Murmelstein, B.
    1930   "Jesu Gang durch die Saatfelder." *Angelos* 3: 11-120.

Parrott, Rod
    1977   "Sabbath Controversies in Mark: An Analysis." Claremont Graduate School, February 29.

Perelman, C. H. and L. Olbrechts-Tyteca
    1969   *The New Rhetoric: A Treatise on Argumentation.* Notre Dame: University of Notre Dame Press.

Perrin, N. and D. Duling
    1982   *The New Testament: An Introduction.* 2nd. edition. New York: Harcourt Brace Jovanovich.

Rapoport, Anatol
    1960   *Fights, Games and Debates.* Ann Arbor: University of Michigan Press.

Rhoads, D. and D. Michie
    1982   *Mark As Story: An Introduction to the Narrative of a Gospel.* Philadelphia: Fortress.

Robbins, Vernon K.
    1982a   "Identifying and Interpreting Pronouncement Stories in Mark: A Rhetorical Approach." Pacific Coast Region of the SBL, Stanford University, March 26.
    1982b   "Analysis of Pronouncement Stories: A Position Statement." SBL-Claremont Fellowship Lecture, New York, December.
    1984   "A Rhetorical Typology for Classifying and Analyzing Pronouncement Stories." Pp. 93-122 in *1984 SBL Seminar Papers* 23. Ed. K.H. Richards. Chico: Scholars.
    1984/92   *Jesus the Teacher: A Socio-Rhetorical Interpretation of Mark.* Philadelphia: Fortress.

Rordorf, W.
    1986   *Sunday: The History of the Day of Rest and Worship in the Earliest Centuries of the Christian Church.* Philadelphia: Westminster.

Schmidt, K. L.
    1919   *Der Rahmen der Geschichte Jesu: literarkritische Untersuchungen zur ältesten Jesusüberlieferung.* Berlin: Trowitzsch & Sohn.

Schweizer, E.
    1970   *The Good News According to Mark.* Richmond: John Knox.

Tannehill, Robert
    1975   *The Sword of His Mouth.* Philadelphia: Fortress.
    1981a   "Introduction: The Pronouncement Story and Its Types." *Semeia* 20: 1-13.
    1981b   "Varieties of Synoptic Pronouncement Stories." *Semeia* 20: 101-19.

Taylor, V.
  1966   *The Gospel According to St. Mark.* New York: St. Martin's.
Trocme, E.
  1975   *The Formation of the Gospel According to Mark.* Philadelphia: Westminster.

Rhetoric, Purity, and Play
Aspects of Mark 7:1-23

Gregory Salyer
Huntingdon College

ABSTRACT

Three interpretive strategies – rhetoric, social analysis, and deconstruction – are useful in analyzing Mark 7:1-23. The various critical methods can be complementary in offering a meaningful interpretation of a pronouncement story. From a rhetorical point of view 7:6-13 exhibit chreia elaboration of the type discussed by Hermogenes (second level elaboration). Mark 7:14-23 exhibits Theon's elaboration technique of breaking the chreia into parts and providing arguments for each part (first level elaboration). The passage contains epideictic rhetoric concerned primarily with censure of Pharisees and scribes. In the socio-ideological approach to the passage, the essay argues that the Pharisaic purity system was concerned with entrances and exits and the external boundaries of society and the body. Mark's Jesus establishes a new purity system based on the heart or the internal spiritual core of human beings. Jesus and his disciples existed on the margins of the old purity system. Deconstruction takes what has been marginalized and enhances it until the center is shattered and its power dissolved. Jesus exposes the center (the temple coalition) as a margin.

Interpreting pronouncement stories is more and more an exercise in rhetorical criticism.[1] This is entirely appropriate since Bultmann and Dibelius overlooked the influence that ancient rhetorical forms and techniques had on these stories. As an increasing number of essays and books appear that appropriate rhetorical criticism in some fashion, the richness of pronouncement stories and other biblical texts is coming to light. With the emphasis on rhetoric also comes a new sensitivity to the social sphere of biblical stories, where issues of power and ideology come into play. Sociological analyses of stories can open up a text to expose the political underpinnings of religious conflicts as they are represented in texts. The language of politics and power is also being used by more and more biblical scholars who seek to integrate current theories of language and discourse, especially poststructuralism in general and deconstruction in

---

[1] I am indebted to Vernon Robbins, members of the Rhetorical Criticism seminar at Emory University, and the contributors to this volume for critical responses to various versions of this essay.

particular, into their own interpretive exercises. There are ways to describe what is being done with biblical texts such as pronouncement stories other than those I have mentioned, but these three interpretive strategies—rhetoric, social analysis, and deconstruction—are the ones that I will use to analyze Mark 7:1-23. Two observations emerge from this exercise. The first is that various critical methods can be complementary in offering a meaningful interpretation of a pronouncement story. In short, the interdisciplinary approach is a viable one that is underused in the study of biblical texts. The other observation is that pronouncement stories and other biblical texts are richer than we have imagined. They function on multiple levels and in many dimensions. This essay seeks to explore three of the dimensions of Mark 7:1-23 by way of rhetorical analysis, social analysis, and deconstruction.

Rhetorical Analysis

The pronouncement story has been been shown to be a vehicle for sophisticated rhetorical forms of argument. According to Vernon Robbins:

> Pronouncement stories . . . contain rhetorical features that call for rhetorical analysis and interpretation. Many of the situations in them look like settings discussed by the ancient rhetoricians, and much of the action and speech looks like material the rhetoricians considered to be central to rhetorical occasions. (Robbins 1988: 6)

Given this new understanding of the pronouncement story, scholars of gospel literature are seeking to breathe rhetorical life back into this type of story (Mack 1988; Mack and Robbins 1989). Rhetoric was not only the teaching of language and oratory, it was also instruction in the ascertainment and manipulation of speech in particular social settings. Rhetoric was (and is) a pragmatic art requiring an understanding of the social forces at work in a given environment. An awareness that these stories follow a form that was quite common among the ancient rhetoricians has recently come into view and is helping to redefine pronouncement stories. Many of these pronouncement stories are abbreviated chreiai—short statements or actions which are attributed to some character and are apt for the situation or the character of the person. Teachers of rhetoric, like Theon of Alexandria, used these little chreiai as pedagogical devices for their students. One of the exercises found in Theon's *Progymnasmata* instructs students to weave a rhetorical argument from a chreia. The result of some of the chreia exercises such as expansion and elaboration was a story that looked similar to what has come to be called a pronouncement story.

Verses 14-15 have the characteristics of a slightly expanded chreia:

> Again he summoned the crowd and said to them, "Listen to me, everyone, and understand this. Nothing outside a man can make him unclean by going into him, but it is what comes out of man that makes him unclean."

The saying is quite short, it is attributed to Jesus, and it is apt both to the character of Jesus and to the situation in which he finds himself. The disciples in Mark recognize the chreia as a common language form and call it a parable.[2] The chreia functions as a bridge between the two scenes in the story, and it provides the transition from the public character of the first speech to the intimate nature of the second speech. A chreia is, according to Aphthonius, "a concise reminiscence aptly attributed to some character" (Hock and O'Neil: 225). The defining features are the attribution to a particular person and the aptness of the saying. The hellenistic rhetoricians and scholars today disagree on whether the aptness of the saying concerned its attribution to the particular person's character or its relevance to the situation being described (Hock and O'Neil: 23-27). Regardless of the primary referent of the word *aptly*, it should be clear that the chreia is to be distinguished from the maxim or other type of saying. Ancient literature is replete with examples of chreiai such as "Being asked once how far the bounds of Sparta extended, he [Agesilaus] said, with a flourish of his spear, 'As far as this can reach'" (Robbins 1989: 23). The New Testament gospels often depict Jesus uttering a saying in certain situations that call for a chreia:

> Jesus, on seeing someone working on the Sabbath, said to him: 'Man, if you know what you are doing, you are blessed, but if you do not, you are cursed and a transgressor of the law.' (Luke 6:5)

Chreiai can be sayings only, such as if Agesilaus had not flourished his spear but only said "As far as this can reach." If Agesilaus had said nothing but only flourished his spear, it would be an action chreia. The chreia as we have it in Mk. 7:14-15 is a mixed chreia with both saying and action. A chreia can be a spontaneous statement or it can be a response to a question that generates an explanation, such as the chreia in v. 15. According to Theon, chreiai can be modified in various ways including inflexion, abbreviation, and refutation. In Mark 7 the chreia is expanded (another way to modify a chreia), which is done when "we enlarge upon the questions and responses in it, and upon whatever act or experience is in it" (Hock and O'Neil: 101). The chreia uttered by Jesus in v. 15 is a response to the question brought by the Pharisees and scribes in v. 5. The first half of the saying after the introductory exhortation is a statement in itself: "Nothing outside a man can make him unclean by going into him."

---

[2] Bratcher and Nida (231) suggests that παραβολή is used here in the sense of "figure," "illustration," or "riddle."

The second half of the saying is an explanatory addition: "It is what comes out of a man that makes him unclean" (Hock and O'Neil: 87). Without the addition of the exhortation and the explanation, the chreia would have a fully abbreviated form.[3]

The elaboration of a chreia was one of the most common exercises in the rhetorical schools. As Robbins notes in the introduction to this volume, there are two levels of elaboration. The first level is described by Theon as providing arguments "for each part of the chreia, beginning with the first ones, using as many topics as possible" (Hock and O'Neil: 107). Thus a chreia is broken down into its parts and arguments are made for each part. This level of elaboration also contains features of expanded chreiai, such as dialogue that carries the argument forward, changes of scene, and explanation or syllogisms accompanying the chreia. The second level of elaboration is one which attempts to create a complete argument from the chreia. This level is described by Hermogenes. One should begin with a few words of praise followed by the chreia. A rationale then supports the thesis of the chreia as does a statement from the opposite. Statements from analogy, example, and authority provide further support for the chreia. Finally, one should complete the argument with a word of exhortation (Hock and O'Neil: 177; Mack and Robbins: 57-63).

We find the first level of elaboration in vv. 14-23. These verses are still a response to the initial question posed by the Pharisees and scribes. Here we find Theon's elaboration technique of breaking the chreia into parts and providing arguments for each part.

Chreia 7:14-16:
Again he summoned the crowd and said to them, "Listen to me, everyone, and understand this. Nothing outside a man can make him 'unclean' by going into him, but it is what comes out of a man that makes him 'unclean.'"

Scene/Setting Change
Interrogatio 7:17
After he had left the crowd and entered the house, his disciples asked him about this parable. "Are you so dull?" he asked.

Restatement of First Part 7:18
"Don't you see that nothing that enters a man from the outside can make him 'unclean'?

Rationale 7:19a
For it doesn't go into his heart but into his stomach, and then out of his body."

---

[3] We might well reverse the two parts of the chreia and understand "It is what comes out of man that makes him unclean" as the heart of the chreia.

Inference 7:19b

(In saying this, Jesus declared all foods "clean.")

Restatement of Second Part 7:20

He went on: "What comes out of a man is what makes him 'unclean.'

Rationale 7:21-22

For from within, out of men's hearts, come evil thoughts, sexual immorality, theft, murder, adultery, greed, malice, deceit, lewdness, evil eye, slander, arrogance, and folly.

Conclusion 7:23

All these evils come from inside and make a man 'unclean.'"

Characteristics of first-level elaboration are clearly here: restatement, rationale, inference, and summary. This elaboration amplifies the statements in the initial saying, but it does not add significantly new arguments from analogy, example, or ancient written testimony.

Before we show the second level of elaboration in vv. 6-13, we must recognize that there is another chreia present in the passage. The quotation from Isaiah occurs as a chreia on the lips of the Markan Jesus. In second-level elaboration the chreia comes near the beginning, and the argument supports the central thesis of the chreia. The outline below shows that second-level elaboration, the mode of elaboration that Hermogenes displays, occurs in vv. 6-13:

Praise 7:6a

He replied, "Isaiah was right

Chreia 7:6b-7

when he prophesied about you hypocrites, as it is written:
> 'These people honor me with their lips,
> but their hearts are far from me.
> They worship me in vain;
> their teachings are but rules taught by men.'

Paraphrase of Chreia 7:8

You have abandoned the commands of God and are holding to the traditions of men."

Citations of Ancient Authority 7:9-10

And he said to them: "You have a fine way of setting aside the commands of God in order to observe your own traditions! For Moses said, 'Honor your father and mother,' and, 'Anyone who curses his father or mother must be put to death.'

Example 7:11-12

But you say that if a man says to his father or mother: 'Whatever help you might otherwise have received from me is 'Corban' (that is, a gift devoted to God), then you no longer let him do anything for his father or mother.

Paraphrase 7:13

Thus you nullify the word of God by your tradition that you have handed down. And you do many things like that."

Verses 14-15 may be understood in this first argument as a contrary functioning as a counterthesis of the initial charge brought against Jesus and his disciples in v. 5. The chreia in v. 15 then is the pivot on which both of the arguments or types of elaboration turn. The first argument uses Hermogenes' level of elaboration (the second) and a chreia from Isaiah to build a complete argument which is then concluded by a contrary which functions as a counterthesis. The second argument uses Theon's level of elaboration (the first) and divides the pivotal chreia into its parts in order to argue for each part.

The entire passage can now be arranged to show its rhetorical components and two types of elaboration.

Narrative Introduction 7:1-2

The Pharisees and some of the teachers of the law who had come from Jerusalem gathered around Jesus and saw some of his disciples eating food with "unclean"—that is, ceremonially unwashed—hands.

Digression 7:3-4

(The Pharisees and all the Jews do not eat unless they give their hands a ceremonial washing, holding to the tradition of the elders. When they come from the marketplace they do not eat unless they wash. And they observe many other traditions, such as the washing of cups, pitchers and kettles.)

Quaestio (seeking Rationale) 7:5

So the Pharisees and teachers of the law asked Jesus, "Why don't your disciples live according to the tradition of the elders instead of eating their food with 'unclean' hands?"

Argumentatio (functioning as a reply to the Quaestio) 7:6-15
Praise

He replied, "Isaiah was right

Chreia 7:6b-7

when he prophesied about you hypocrites, as it is written:
'These people honor me with their lips,
but their hearts are far from me.
They worship me in vain;
their teachings are but rules taught by men.'

Paraphrase of Chreia 7:8

You have abandoned the commands of God and are holding to the traditions of men."

Citations of Ancient Authority 7:9-10
And he said to them: "You have a fine way of setting aside the commands of God in order to observe your own traditions! For Moses said, 'Honor your father and mother,' and, 'Anyone who curses his father or mother must be put to death.'

Example 7:11-12
But you say that if a man says to his father or mother: 'Whatever help you might otherwise have received from me is 'Corban' (that is, a gift devoted to God), then you no longer let him do anything for his father or mother.

Paraphrase 7:13
Thus you nullify the word of God by your tradition that you have handed down. And you do many things like that."

Contrary as Counterthesis 7:14-16
Again he called the crowd to him and said, "Listen to me, everyone, and understand this. Nothing outside a man can make him 'unclean' by going into him, but, it is what comes out of a man that makes him 'unclean.'"

Scene/Setting Change: Amplification of the Counterthesis
Interrogatio 7:17
After he had left the crowd and entered the house, his disciples asked him about this parable. "Are you so dull?" he asked.

Restatement of First Part of Counterthesis as an Interrogatio 7:18
"Don't you see that nothing that enters a man from the outside can make him 'unclean'?

Rationale 7:19a
For it doesn't go into his heart but into his stomach, and then out of his body."

Inference 7:19b
(In saying this, Jesus declared all foods "clean.")

Restatement of Second Part of Counterthesis 7:20
He went on: "What comes out of a man is what makes him 'unclean.'

Rationale 7:21-22
For from within, out of men's hearts, come evil thoughts, sexual immorality, theft, murder, adultery, greed, malice, deceit, lewdness, evil eye, slander, arrogance, and folly.

Conclusion 7:23
All these evils come from inside and make a man 'unclean.'"

One of the most important things to determine in any speech is its larger goal. What does it do or what does the speaker/writer want it to do? Aristotle divided the goals of a speech into three species—deliberative, epideictic, and judicial (Aristotle *Rhetoric*: I, iii). Deliberative rhetoric is hortatory or dissuasive and is oriented toward the future. It attempts to argue for a particular course of action or stance to be taken and often finds its context in the political assembly. Judicial rhetoric is accusatory or defensive and is oriented toward the past. It is usually found in a courtroom where a legal issue is at hand. Epideictic rhetoric offers praise or blame and is more loosely structured and oriented toward the present. Funeral orators used epideictic rhetoric in their eulogies. It is important to note that the use of one species does not preclude use of the others. Many speeches in antiquity appropriate all three types as does the unit under investigation here. It is also important, however, to determine the overall thrust of the unit since it will indicate the particular goals of the speaker and the speech. While this unit in Mark deftly handles all three species of rhetoric, the primary interest of Jesus and/or Mark appears to be to discredit Pharisees and scribes from Jerusalem. Mark never speaks of Pharisees in isolation in this passage. The scribes (οἱ γραμματεῖς) are mentioned with them in v. 5. In v. 3 it is the Pharisees "and all the Jews." Jesus responds vehemently in verse 6 that his accusers are hypocrites. Were the response not so carefully constructed, it might be tempting to term it a tirade. Jesus is very angry. We will see this in a more detailed way in the explication of the arrangement and the analysis of the movement of the unit. The species of rhetoric involved, moreover, is contingent upon the overall thrust of the passage. In this passage it would be easy to focus on the initial charge by the temple coalition and to interpret the overall rhetoric as judicial. It would be just as easy to focus on the teaching to the disciples and argue for a deliberative thrust to the unit. I will not argue that the elements of judicial and deliberative rhetoric are not to be found in this passage; on the contrary, they are used in a very significant way. The primary motivation in this passage is to invalidate the cultic idea of purity as it has been handed down via the traditions of the elders. To accomplish this goal, Mark has Jesus attack the tradition in verses 6-15. These verses constitute not only the heart but also the bulk of the passage. The passage at hand is thus epideictic rhetoric concerned primarily with censure of Pharisees and scribes.[4] They are to be blamed for erecting a tradition around the law that nullifies the law itself. Bultmann, without using rhetorical terminology, recognized this as the primary emphasis of the passage as well when he observed that: "[t]he point of the story lies in the polemic against the scribes" (Bultmann: 17).

Mark's introduction serves primarily to explain the subject of the issue at hand. He sets up the argument in a way that provides Jesus a venue for his initial response. Mark uses the term "tradition of the elders" in verse 3 and mentions "other traditions" in verse 5. In order to see how this provides an opening for the speech of Jesus it is necessary to look at how

---

[4] See Mack and Robbins (161-93) on the intricacies of negative epideictic rhetoric.

Jesus repeats the phrase in verses 8, 9, and 13 by setting it in contrast to the "commandment of God":

παράδοσιν τῶν ἀνθρώπων (the tradition of men)	vs. 8	ἐντολὴν τοῦ θεοῦ (the commandment of God)
παράδοσιν ὑμῶν (your tradition)	vs. 9	ἐντολὴν τοῦ θεοῦ (the commandment of God)
παραδόσει ὑμῶν (your tradition)	vs. 13	λόγον τοῦ θεοῦ (the word of God)

By introducing the idea of tradition and by making it the central issue of the debate, Mark provides Jesus with the basis for challenging the purity system of the Pharisees, which is the foundation from which they attack Jesus. Moreover, he has biased the reader implicitly by linking the Pharisees to tradition, which allows Jesus to contrast this to the more powerful authority—the commandment of God.

Another phrase that appears in the introduction and is picked up by Jesus is found in verse 4. Mark states that the Pharisees "observe many other traditions." The point here is that the issue of unclean hands is only a synecdoche for the larger problem of the power of tradition. In Jesus' refutation he repeats the introduction's implicit charge by saying in verse 13 "and you do many things like that." The issue is not the particular incident in question; rather, it is the entire body of tradition that has grown up around the law. Even the Pharisees imply that this is the issue, by asking why Jesus' disciples do not "live according to the tradition of the elders" (περιπατοῦσιν κατὰ τὴν παράδοσιν τῶν πρεσβυτέρων).

Mark's attribution of this practice to "all the Jews" has a parallel in the *Epistle of Aristeas*.[5] It seems to be a common usage, therefore, when explaining Jewish customs to Gentiles (Lane: 243). This formula would work nicely for Mark if he were writing to a gentile audience who was under pressure to conform to Jewish purity norms. Thus while it may have been common to refer to Jewish customs in this way, it may also be very deliberate on the part of Mark the polemicist. Finally, the small note that the Pharisees and teachers "gathered around Jesus" brings the entire scene into tight focus. Everyone is standing close enough to hear, and this creates a situation (or a rhetorical problem).

---

[5] "And as is the custom of all the Jews, they washed their hands in the sea and prayed to God and then devoted themselves to reading the particular passage [upon which they were engaged], and I put the question to them, Why it was that they washed their hands before they prayed? And they explained that it was a token that they had done no evil . . ." *Epistle of Aristeas* 1:17-22 in Barrett (214).

The quaestio (v. 5) appears in the form of an accusation from the Pharisees. It should be noted that Mark need not have any interest in representing the Pharisees with any historical accuracy. They are here to serve as rhetorical players for Jesus and should not be considered a faithful representation. Mark's Pharisees may be a Christian set-up designed to make Jesus look good, not unlike Plato's various sophists who engage Socrates so unsuccessfully.[6]

The Pharisees question Jesus without offering any sort of rationale such as would be characteristic of ancient rhetoric. While Mark may have no interest in having them give a fine rhetorical rationale for their accusation, it is plausible that one may not be needed. The purity system that requires handwashing is their proof. They stand within it and are representatives of the temple's cultic system. We will see just how strong the idea of purity was at the time of this incident when the social dynamics of the situation are analyzed below. For now we can say that the Pharisees speak from a position of power.

The question which is posed by the Pharisees carries with it heavy judicial implications, but these are pre-trial deliberations. Jesus may appear as a lawbreaker who should be found guilty of violating the purity code. In that sense the quaestio has judicial force. After all, laws are in a very real sense lines or "fences" that are there to prevent "transgression" or crossing of boundaries. For this reason it would be difficult for Jesus to go directly to the thesis in verse 15. He must first answer and defend himself before the crowd; he must destroy the impression made by the charge that his disciples are behaving as outsiders. Aristotle comments:

> The speaker who is replying should first address himself to his adversary's speech in the way of refutation...especially if the adverse arguments have gained applause; for the mind rejects a speech, against which it is prepossessed, just as it rejects a man, supposing the adversary to have made a good impression. It is necessary, then, to make room in the hearer's mind for the coming argument. This room will exist, if you remove the obstacles. Hence

---

[6] However, Roger Booth argues that this characterization is entirely probable if we understand the interrogators to be members of the *haberim*, a subgroup of the Pharisees:

> We conclude that the Pharisaic question is credible in the time of Jesus on the basis that the Pharisees concerned were *haberim* who did handwash before *hullin*, and were urging Jesus and his disciples to adopt the supererogatory handwashing which they themselves practised, i.e. to become *haberim*. It was an exhortation to undertake a higher standard of piety, addressed to Jesus as a religious leader. In this sense, the question could be elaborated—"Why do your disciples (since you, their Teacher, 'are true, and teach the way of God truthfully') not wash their hands before they eat and observe the same standard of purity as we pietists do?" (Booth: 202).

you should begin by combating the adverse arguments—all of them, or the chief, or the plausible, or those which are easy to refute—and then establish your own arguments. (Aristotle *Rhetoric* III. xvii)

The attention of everyone is commanded by the first statement of Jesus (v. 6) as he sets up the quotation from Isaiah 29:13. As is appropriate to an elaborated chreia argument, Jesus begins with brief words of praise, "Isaiah was right." The affirmation of Isaiah then quickly turns to censure of the Pharisees. This prominent prophet in Jewish history is doubtless a representative of the "tradition," and Jesus calls him forth as a personal witness to confirm that the Pharisees are out of favor with God. Seizing the advantage, Jesus frames the quotation in a way that has Isaiah speaking of this very moment or at least of these very people who are bringing the charge against Jesus. Isaiah prophesied about *"you hypocrites* as it is written." Jesus embeds a citation of authority in the chreia of Isaiah to immediately and profoundly shatter the initial impression made by the charge of the Pharisees. He cites a prominent person from Scripture and points the explicit accusation directly at his accusers. What does scripture have to say about the accusers?—they are hypocrites and, as we shall see, are on the fringes of God's purity system. Burton Mack explains the rhetorical significance of this initial move:

> The chreia response is a well-chosen prophecy, a text that requires elaboration. The procedure is perfect. Instead of Jesus expounding upon his own saying, he will develop a thesis taken from a chreia of a well-known author just as a student of rhetoric would have done. The choice is devastating, because it is taken from the opponents' own tradition, but can be used against them. Rhetors would have called this "invention," or finding a text just right for the purpose. In this case two sets of contrastive images are combined in a single saying that will allow both the original chreia and the new chreia elaboration to be combined. One set is the lips/heart contrast. The other is the contrast between the worship of God and the precepts of men. Both will be elaborated thematically and intertwined. (Mack: 191)

The paraphrase of the Isaiah chreia in v. 8 appears as a countercharge that works from the initial set-up in Mark's introduction, where we are introduced to the idea that it is the tradition that is the larger issue in this case. The argumentatio functions to show what the real facts of the case are (the tradition versus the commandment) and to imply that the moral character of the Pharisees is in question. In this particular case the moral character of the accusers is in great jeopardy, since the Pharisees are understood to be breakers of the law of God, by virtue of their letting go of the commandments in order to follow the tradition. The guardians of the law are themselves law breakers. Jesus' countercharge rhetorically levels the structure of the Pharisees' system.

The remainder of the speech in vv. 9-13 shows how the Pharisees have let go of the commandments in favor of the tradition. In proving that the Pharisees have set aside the commandments of God, the oppositional tactic first found in the introduction is used to set tradition against commandment. The argument presents the opposition in terms of the commands of God versus "your own traditions." Verse 9 continues the implication of the paraphrase in verse 8 and introduces the citation of ancient authority in verse 10. More importantly, perhaps, with the argument in verse 9 Jesus has moved from the defensive to the offensive. This is a frontal attack which will be bolstered by verses 10-12 so that the conclusion can be emphatically stated in verse 13.

As a prophet, Isaiah is a felicitous source for a chreia; as the torah-giver, Moses provides evidence from authoritative written testimonies. When Jesus does cite Moses, the citation functions as an exemplary instance of how the Pharisees set aside the commands of God. Thus, this is an instance both of argument from example and of argument from citation of authority, since the authority of Moses is certainly exerting an influence in the argument. The tradition of the Corban will be played off of the citation as a contrary example. Citations set up the contrary example, and the opposition is between what "Moses said" and what "you say." In citing Moses, Jesus is appealing to the highest human legal authority—the one who received the very law of God and gave it to the people of Israel. The fifth commandment is cited as a synecdoche for the law of God, the ultimate written authority. One must honor her father and mother or be put to death.

Of the rhetorical devices that have been noted to this point, we must now add that of a chiasm. A chiasm works on the principle of placing the most important idea of a group of ideas in the center of the unit with the other ideas being balanced above and below the central idea. For example:

A   You are my son
B   Today I have become your father
B' I will be to him a father
A' and He will be my son (Hebrews 1:5)

The central idea is father in the B phrases which is balanced by the idea of sonship in the A phrases. In our unit in Mark, the central idea is the commandment versus the tradition, and the balancing idea is honor.

A   These people *honor* me with their lips, but their hearts are far from me. They worship me in vain; their teachings are but rules taught by men.
B   You have let go of the *commands of God* and are holding to the *traditions of men.*

B' And he said to them: You have a fine way of setting aside the *commands of God* in order to observe your own *traditions*!
A' For Moses said, "*Honor* your father and mother."

The Pharisees and scribes, on the other hand, say that if a man says to his parents that any future assistance he may render to them is Corban, or a gift devoted to God, then he is released from performing the duty required by the fifth commandment. Therefore, the law (the fifth commandment) has been nullified by the tradition (of Corban). Jesus was referring to a particular formula which was commonly used by Jews before and during the Christian era. The idea behind the Corban was to set aside something for sacred use, thereby prohibiting it from being used in its normal way. It came to be that the object did not have to be offered to God, but was considered Corban if it had been set aside as if it were an offering. Should a son proclaim something Corban, the effect was the legal exclusion of the parents from ever owning or benefitting from the object. Moreover, the scribes rarely allowed the vow to be retracted should the person change his mind about declaring the object Corban. It appears that Jesus was not using hyperbole when he claimed that the Pharisees did not allow a person to do "anything" for his parents under these circumstances. Not only could our hypothetical son not lend financial assistance to his parents, the prohibitions sometimes extended to helping the parents perform religious duties or providing for their care in sickness (Lane: 251). We have in the Corban, therefore, a perfect example to sustain the thesis of verse 9. The example also relates nicely to the written judgment.

The paraphrase sums up the argument from example and essentially restates the argument of the citations. The paraphrase also is oriented more toward the present since it sets up an example of Pharisaic and scribal practice. It introduces us to the fact that the tradition has been "handed down," and thus has a history. It also informs us that other examples of the nullification of the law by the tradition could be called forth if necessary. "And you do many things like that" is a phrase that connects with the introduction, where Mark tells us that "they observe many other traditions." This comment subtly indicts Pharisaic-scribal ideology in general rather than simply one of its tenets. The issue of the commandment versus the tradition is sustained and amplified consistently in the initial reply of Jesus. Mark's introduction first raises the issue, and the speech of Jesus manipulates the tension within it, using oppositional tactics and a chiasm. Mark has taken us behind the cultic fence, as it were, in order to expose the false assumptions on which the purity tradition had been built.

Jesus ends the first part of his speech with his own chreia, which is marked by his call to the audience.7 The effect of this calling is analogous to an attorney finishing his cross examination and turning to the jury to speak. Jesus has discredited the Pharisees and is now ready to summarize the argumentatio in a saying that the audience will remember. This is a statement of the contrary in the form of a counterthesis. Stating the contrary as a counterthesis shows the dynamics of chreia expansion. Rather than the deliberative elaboration of Hermogenes, we see an elaboration that carries the drama of the story forward like an expanded chreia. Thus we have a unit that merges techniques of chreia expansion with techniques of chreia elaboration.

Jesus reiterates the initial charge of uncleanness first by denying that uncleanness comes from "out there" and then by stating that real uncleanness comes from "in here"—that is, within ourselves. The saying implies that the outside fence of tradition is not the object of concern; rather, concern should be shown toward the inside where breaking the law of God finds it provenance. This is what makes a man unclean.

> The boundaries of collective identity, which the kosher diet and other aspects of the purity code were originally instituted to maintain, are now redrawn in essentially moral terms, as indicated by the vice list....In this teaching the purity code is ethicized and universalized, and the justification for social segregation is subverted. (Myers: 220)

The shift in scene from the crowd to the house is significant in that the speech of Jesus is no longer public but private. In his public speech, Jesus was perceived to be outside the purity system of the Pharisees. In order to counter that perception, Jesus had to reverse the outside/inside structure by switching the ruling concept from cultic tradition to moral law. Under a moral purity system, the Pharisees are outside and Jesus and his disciples are inside. Once the group enters the house, they are all insiders. This entails a shift in the rhetorical dynamics of the situation. No longer is Jesus refuting an accusation. He is now teaching those who follow him about the new purity system that is to replace the old one.

Even though he is among his own followers, Jesus continues to react with impatience. When the disciples ask about the meaning of the "parable," Jesus responds by asking them "Are you so dull?" Thus another separation has taken place. Jesus is not on the defensive as he was before, but now he is exasperated with those whom he has just defended. The interaction of Jesus and his disciples illustrates aspects of chreia

---

7 This saying also has a parallel outside the tradition in the Gospel of Thomas 14:3: "For what goes into your mouth will not defile you, but that which issues from your mouth—it is that which will defile you."

expansion as these questions serve to carry the story forward. Jesus explains the new purity system and its rationale very carefully by using a device called an enthymeme. An enthymeme is a logical syllogism with one of the premises suppressed. For example, "Blessed are the poor in spirit, for theirs is the kingdom of heaven" is an enthymeme that is based on the syllogism "All who obtain the kingdom of heaven are blessed; the poor in spirit will obtain the kingdom of heaven; therefore, the poor in spirit are blessed." An enthymeme usually states the conclusion first and uses a "for" (ὅτι) clause at the end (Kennedy: 49; Robbins 1985: 39-56).

Jesus uses two enthymemes in this speech—one positive and one negative. They are based on two syllogisms. The first syllogism would be on the order of "What does not go into the heart is not unclean; things entering the body do not go into the heart but into the stomach; therefore, nothing coming from outside a man makes him unclean." The second enthymeme is based on a similar syllogism but approaches the issue from the positive side. "Uncleanness is evil thinking, immorality, etc; evil thinking, immorality, etc. come from men's hearts; therefore, what comes out of a man's heart makes him unclean." One syllogism is the contrary of the other. If this sounds to us redundant and simplistic, it should be remembered that Jesus is in a teaching setting and has already implied that the disciples are dull. Jesus must unpack the final argument for the disciples, and he must do it very carefully to those who are so dull. The two approaches to the enthymemes also play out the diaresis in the counterthesis in v. 15. Verse 19 provides the rationale for the first part (nothing coming from outside can make a man unclean), while vv. 21-22 provide the rationale for the second part (what comes out of a man makes him unclean).

The reiteration of the first part of v. 15 (restatement of the first part of the counterthesis) helps to clarify and supplement the initial paraphrase in v. 8 (Mack and Robbins: 179-182). First Jesus tells them what the new purity system is not. Nothing coming in from outside can defile (v. 18). The reason for this is given in v. 19; namely, what comes in does not stay inside but passes out into the sewer. Even for the purity system of the Pharisees, feces were not unclean (Neyrey 1988: 86). Booth calls this the "medical" argument and states that the idea that food was clean because it passes through into excrement was a hellenistic rather than a Palestinian concept. If this is so, then Myers is right to point out that Mark not only uses this argument to make the account intelligible to a gentile audience, but he feels free to use it because he rejects the symbolic code of the Pharisees (Myers: 220).

Jesus uses word play in explaining his statement by once again setting up two oppositional terms—heart and belly—which happen to rhyme in

Greek. Heart is καρδίαν and belly is κοιλίαν, so Jesus says in verse 19: "οὐκ εἰσπορεύεται αὐτοῦ εἰς τὴν καρδίαν ἀλλ' εἰς τὴν κοιλίαν" or "it does not go into his kardian but his koilian." This device would surely have been noticed by hearers of the Greek tongue or readers of the Greek language.

The inference in v. 19b is of course Mark's and is designed to insure that the reader draws the right conclusions from this statement of Jesus. We might have expected this to be an explanation of the chreia, but perhaps, given the change of scene, Mark felt it more appropriate to insert it in the teaching setting with the disciples. Mark is no doubt trying to insure that Jesus is not misinterpreted here (Mack and Robbins: 115-17). The inference has an almost doctrinal tone and indicates exactly where Mark or an early Christian scribe stands regarding one of the most divisive issues in the early church.[8] We have observed Mark helping the argument along before when in verses 3-4 he explains to us that Pharisaic handwashing is a cultic issue rather than an hygienic one. These asides from Mark point strongly to the presence of a gentile audience in Mark's mind. Myers, following Booth, argues that "The Pharisaic objection to 'unwashed hands' may in this case be an allusion to the fact that the disciples are assumed to be contaminated *because they have already been eating with gentiles and sharing their unclean foods* (Myers: 219; Booth: 120). We know from Paul's experiences recounted in Galatians and Acts that certain members of the Jerusalem church were pressuring gentile converts to abide by at least some form of the purity code. Mark makes it clear that for his gentile audience this code has been abolished. Moreover, he wants his Jewish audience to know that the tradition that has been erected to guard them from uncleanness has in fact exploited them.

> By conflating the issues of table fellowship and (implicitly in his criticism of *korban*) the political economy of the temple, Mark demonstrates his consciousness of the central ideological underpinnings of oppression in the symbolic system. This story serves not only to legitimize the community's practice of integration with gentiles, who otherwise would have been excluded by the rules of ritual purity, but also serves to persuade poorer Jews that the very purity system that purports to "protect" their ethnic/national identity is the system that exploits them. Against the dominant group boundaries Mark offers a countervision in which a new, morally defined community upholds the radical demands of scriptural tradition, which condemns profiteering and defends the welfare of the weakest members of society. (Myers: 222-23)

It is not enough to discredit the old purity system. Another must take its place, and the statement in v. 20 is its new creed. This is also a reiteration of the last part of the counterthesis in v. 15. "What comes out of a man" is defined in vv. 21-22. Thus there can be no confusion about the

---

[8] See Romans 14 and Acts 15 for example.

nature of this new purity system. "Uncleanness" is a moral rather than a legal or cultic term. The shift creates a problem of sorts, however, since the moral status of individuals cannot always be determined. Whether someone eats with clean hands or not is in some sense verifiable, but what is in the heart is not. This problem is resolved by the vice list in vv. 21-22. Anyone who evinced the qualities on this list was morally unclean.

The rationale for the statement that what comes out of a man makes him unclean is given in terms of a list of vices found in vv. 21-22. Jerome Neyrey has shown that these vices are based roughly on the ten commandments.[9] Adding or changing words of the conclusion is another characteristic of paraphrase and, by extension, elaboration. The foundation of the new purity code is thus the law rather than the tradition. The conclusion in verse 23 rephrases the positive part of the counterthesis that is being argued after verse 20 and summarizes the short argument.

Social Analysis

Social analysis of a pronouncement story such as Mark 7:1-23 can be seen as a function of rhetorical analysis. George Kennedy has developed a methodology for rhetorical criticism that includes a step that he calls determining the rhetorical situation. The rhetorical situation may be said to be roughly comparable to the *Sitz im Leben* of form and redaction criticism. According to Kennedy, the rhetorical situation arises out of certain psychosocial conditions that open up the possibilities for speech. He cites Lloyd F. Bitzer's definition of the rhetorical situation as:

> a complex of persons, events, objects, and relations presenting an actual or potential exigence which can be completely or partially removed if discourse, introduced into the situation, can so constrain human decision or action as to bring about the significant modification of the exigence. (Bitzer in Kennedy: 34)

Exigence here is the psychosocial pressure for an individual to come to speech in order to remove or modify that very pressure. The goal in constructing the rhetorical situation is to identify audience expectations and presuppositions and to observe how the speaker manipulates these factors to reverse the pressure put on him and to move toward the particular rhetorical goal.

The rhetorical situation of Mark 7:1-23 appears on the surface to be quite simple—something on the order that Jesus does not do what the Pharisees expect all good Jews to do (he never does in Mark), and that

---

[9] Neyrey (1986: 120): kill=murder; adultery=fornication, adultery, licentiousness; steal=theft; false witness=envy, slander; defraud=covetousness; honor father and mother=Mark 7:9-13.

Jesus becomes angry first at the Pharisees and scribes for forcing their purity norms upon him and his disciples and then at the disciples for not understanding his reasoning. While this account is only superficially accurate, as we shall see, it does provide a clue toward the reconstruction of the rhetorical situation in terms of a conflict between the ideas of purity as understood by Jesus and the Pharisees.

The issue that prompts the challenge from the Pharisees and the speech of Jesus is that the disciples of Jesus were eating with unwashed hands—or at least their hands were not washed according to the Pharisaic tradition. In other words, the disciples were not conforming to the purity system of the Pharisees. The idea of purity in the New Testament has received much critical attention lately and has been informed in a very influential way by the observations of British cultural anthropologist Mary T. Douglas in her work *Purity and Danger*. She understands purity and pollution in a broader, more systematic, way than we are usually familiar with. It is perhaps helpful to understand her concept of purity in terms of its opposite—that is, dirt or pollution. Dirt is appropriate in some situations or places but not in others. For example, when we take our automobile for repairs, the dirt and grease on the mechanic's hands are a positive sign that she is doing her job. She is working with the parts of the engine that we are not willing or able to engage. However, when the mechanic is eating her lunch or (better) is at our house for dinner, the grime is inappropriate for the situation, and it should be removed. This is a rather mild example, however, when we compare the severe implications of the purity code in Jesus' time. More analogous to our society might be an instance where dog was served at a formal dinner party. If even thinking of this example affects us emotionally, then we begin to have some idea of how strong was the purity code Jesus was fighting to reform.

> It (dirt) implies two conditions: a set of ordered relations and a contravention of that order. Dirt, then, is never a unique isolated event. Where there is dirt there is a system. Dirt is the by-product of a systematic ordering and classification of matter, in so far as ordering involves rejecting inappropriate elements. (Douglas: 35)

Purity then means a process of ordering executed in the social arena that draws boundaries on what is acceptable under certain conditions. Thus the concept of purity denotes much more than specific laws about what is clean or unclean (although it does not lose this meaning in the process); rather, it refers to the symbolic systems that culture appropriates in mediating the experience of individuals and in ordering the ideas and values of a culture (Douglas: 34-39). While it is not the purpose of this essay to fully explicate the implications of Douglas's work on our understanding of the Bible, her contribution toward the reconstruction of the rhetorical situation in our unit is invaluable. It is helpful then to recount some of her observations on the biblical sense of purity in conjunction with Jerome Neyrey's specific observations of how these ideas are embodied in Mark's gospel (Neyrey 1986: 91-128).

An understanding of purity may be traced back to the creation story where God sets creation itself in a particular order. Birds were made for the air, fish for the sea, and man and other creatures for the land. Moreover, these were made whole and without blemish. The temple system in Israel was based on this idea of initial order so that it could prescribe what animals may be offered, who may offer them, when and where they may be offered, as well as who could participate in the ritual. For example, the offering must only be whole animals without defect offered by a whole priest who himself is "clean" (Neyrey 1986: 94).

There were clearly defined maps in the Judaism of Jesus' day that offered one an understanding of the places, persons and things that were pure and their internal purity ranking. Jerome Neyrey lists several of these important maps based on the Mishna and Tosefta (Neyrey 1986: 95-99). For example, there are ten degrees of holiness:

Map of Places

1. The *land of Israel* is holier than any other land
2. The *walled cities* (of the land of Israel) are still more holy
3. *Within the walls* (of Jerusalem) is still more holy
4. The *Temple Mount* is still more holy
5. The *Rampart* is still more holy
6. The *Court of Women* is still more holy
7. The *Court of the Israelites* is still more holy
8. The *Court of the Priests* is still more holy
9. *Between the porch and the Altar* is still more holy
10. The *sanctuary* is still more holy
    The *Holy of Holies* is still more holy...(*m. Kelim* 1.6-9)

Map of persons:

1. Priests
2. Levites
3. Israelites
4. Converts
5. Freed slaves

6. Disqualified priests
   (illegitimate children of priests)
7. *Netins* (temple slaves)
8. *Mamzers* (bastards)
9. Eunuchs
10. Those with damaged testicles
11. Those without a penis (*t. Meg* 2.7)

Map of impurities

1. There are things which convey uncleanness by contact (e.g. a dead creeping thing, semen)...
2. They are exceeded by carrion...
3. They are exceeded by him that has connexion with a menstruant...
4. They are exceeded by the issue of him that has a flux, by his spittle, his semen, and his urine...
5. They are exceeded by (the uncleanness of) what is ridden upon (by him that has a flux)...
6. (The uncleanness of) that is ridden upon (by him that has a flux) by what he lies upon...
7. (The uncleanness of) what he lies upon is exceeded by the uncleanness of him that has a flux. (*m. Kelim* 1.3)

These lists are explicit references to the boundaries of purity as set by the temple coalition in Jewish culture at the time. There is a place for everything and everything should be in that place. Moreover, it is easy to observe that there is a rippling effect at work here where the temple and its affiliates are at the center of power and are able to exert pressure outward to those farther away from the center. According to Douglas, such a strong purity system will always be concerned about these outer perimeters so as to keep what is "out there" from getting "in here." She also notes that with nearly every purity system a form emerges that can be understood in terms of external boundaries, margins, and internal structures. The external boundaries are the lines which separate Jews from non-Jews and find their manifestation in such prohibitions as a kosher diet, circumcision, and observance of the Sabbath. These lines separate "us" from "them." In every such attempt at separation, however, there are people and things that fall on the lines rather than on one side of them. People falling in these margins included lepers, the blind, the lame etc. who are fully Israelites but are not whole. Their incompleteness entailed that they were only marginally "in" the society. Again, this is based on the idea that in the creation all were created whole so that someone less than whole did not quite fall within the lines. This emphasis on the creation norm extended to regulations regarding the offerings that prohibited offering an out of place animal (for example, sea creatures that do not have scales such as shellfish). A bird that walks on the ground instead of flying is unclean because it is out of place. Even among those within the group, there were gradations that internally ranked people and things according to the purity boundaries. Neyrey offers the following list based on incidents from the New Testament:

1. Dead Israelites:
    concern over Jesus' dead body (John 19:31);
2. Morally unclean Israelites:
    tax collectors & sinners (Luke 15:1-2; Matt 9:10-13);
3. Bodily unclean Israelites:
    lepers (Mark 1:40-45; Luke 17:11-14),
    poor, lame, maimed, blind (Luke 14:13; see Lev 21:18-21);
4. Unobservant Israelites:
    Peter and John (Acts 4:13),
    Jesus (John 7:15, 49);
5. Observant Israelites:
    the rich young man (Mark 23:50-51),
    Joseph of Arimathea (Luke 2:25-38);
6. Pharisees (Mark 7:3-5; Luke 18:11-12);
7. Scribes and Priests (Luke 10:31-32);
8. Chief Priests (John 18:28; Heb 7:18-28).
             (Neyrey 1986: 101)

The structure of society then may be indicated in terms of purity distinctions and gradations by the following diagram:

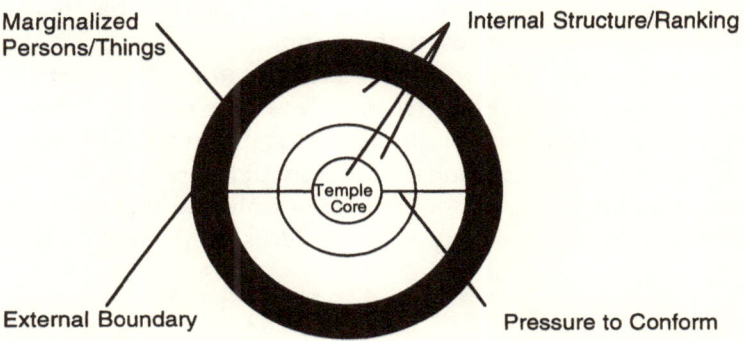

The temple in all of its aspects provides the rationale for the structure, and is, at the same time, the thing which is to be guarded by an elaborate system of fences. Neyrey offers this observation:

> It is not surprising, then, that a group like the Pharisees built a "fence" around its life. To keep the core clean and pure, one extended the boundary around that core, put a fence on the perimeter, and guarded that outer "fence." Hence the chief rule was "Make a fence around the Law" (*m. Aboth* 1.1). And if a fence was appropriate around the Law as a whole, it was appropriate around individual aspects of the Law. Hence a proliferation of fences might be expected:
>
> > "The tradition is a fence around the Law;
> > tithes are a fence around riches;
> > vows are a fence around abstinence;
> > a fence around wisdom is silence." (*m. Aboth* 3.14)
> > (Neyrey 1986: 102)

One of the most important and most frequently appropriated symbols that is operative in purity systems is that of the human body. Society and the body share a macrocosm-microcosm relationship. Just as the society must guard and protect its entrances, exits, and boundaries, so too must one protect his body so as to keep the impure "out there" from getting "in here." Control of the body is an expression of social control. Hence the importance of clothing in the Jewish tradition, which again goes back to the creation story where the realization of sin and nudity are synchronous. Nudity is impurity since it leaves the body open to penetration. The nude body has no fence. Similarly, the orifices of the body become increasingly important since these are its entrances and exits. Accordingly, there was a great concern with the genitals, anus, mouth, nose, eyes, and ears. Finally, the surface of the body is to be protected, since this is equivalent to the outer boundaries. The concern with the ritual washing of hands that is at issue in our unit is a function of a concern for the surface (hands) and the mouth, since what is touched by the hands may enter the body through the mouth.

We can now discuss the rhetorical situation at hand in Mark 7:1-23. The Pharisees and scribes, as representatives of the temple coalition, are putting pressure on Jesus and his disciples to conform to the purity norms that emanate from the controlling group. It should be noted that Jesus and his disciples are lower in rank on the purity scale and that the Pharisees and scribes come ἀπὸ Ἱεροσολύμων (from Jerusalem)—that is, from the source of power.[10] According to Mark 6:53 this debate takes place at Gennesaret in Galilee.

Though the temple itself was a number of miles away, its influence extended to Galilee and beyond.

> ... [A]lthough the Temple was far away, Temple persons and food were not. The priests in Galilee would officiate in the Temple according to their course (Sukkah 5:6-8), and some of the local people would accompany them (Bikkurim 3:2); further, many Galileans probably made the pilgrimage to Jerusalem for the three Feasts. (Booth: 155)

Thus the Pharisees' only function in this situation need be to point out when certain lines were crossed and when the system was therefore in danger. The pressure to conform is implicit in the culture. This is one reason why there is no rationale given for the Pharisees' charge—one is not needed. The lack of a proof does not in any way vitiate the charge against the disciples. They have broken the purity laws and know the consequences of that transgression. Jesus and his followers have a low ranking in the internal structure anyway. Such a transgression threatens to push them beyond the borders and out of society altogether; that is, they may become unclean themselves. Jesus and his disciples have crossed the lines by allowing unclean things to cross their personal body boundaries. This creates a need for discourse. Jesus must do something, and each of the audiences has some expectation of what this will be. The Pharisees count on the purity system itself to insure that they have scored rhetorically against Jesus. All that remains from their point of view is the acknowledgment that Jesus has been discredited. Their confidence in their position is indicated by the lack of any specific statement on just why the action of the disciples was wrong. They only see that the tradition is not being followed. Their charge, rather, is in the form of a rhetorical question that can have no answer in their eyes and has the effect of saying "Why do you do this? Do you not realize what you have done?".

From a social and ideological point of view, the problem for Jesus in Mark 7 is that the temple coalition has power to put pressure on the outer boundaries of society. That is to say that the particular purity system of the temple was the dominant system in place at the time. To cross its boundaries was to be threatened to be pushed farther out toward the fringes or even excluded from society at large. Mark's Jesus must not be perceived to be an outsider, for then he will lose any authority that remains. It seems important to have Jesus persuade those inside society,

---

[10] It is interesting to speculate that, if Mark was written after the destruction of the temple, the pressure that the temple coalition puts on Jesus might generate not from a sense of power but a sense of desperation as they struggle to secure the fences.

although there is less concern about those at the center. In order to speak authoritatively and minister to those on the margins, Mark's Jesus must remain in society. At the same time, he must dissociate himself from the current purity system since, within its own purview, Jesus is a victim of the centrifugal force emanating from the temple. Jesus has just crossed one of society's major purity lines by allowing his disciples to eat with unclean hands. There is, then, no turning back; he must challenge the system itself and establish his own authority above that of the temple coalition. How Mark's Jesus can make this challenge and maintain his own ethos as a valid member of society is the rhetorical problem which he must overcome.

The particular citation of Isaiah's chreia is carefully chosen, for it introduces the idea of a new purity system[11] to be established by Jesus that has at its core the heart rather than the lips. It is helpful here to recall the insights of Douglas and Neyrey on the body as the symbol of purity. The Pharisaic purity system was concerned with entrances and exits and with the external boundaries of society and the body. In the Isaiah chreia the word "lips" is balanced against the word "heart" to set in contrast the two systems. God is not concerned with the external boundaries in his purity system (such as lips, hands, and other bodily details); rather, he is concerned only with the heart or the inner being. Jesus explicates this idea in the second elaboration in vv. 17-23. Moreover, the Isaiah citation connects this inadequate purity system—one that distances its participants from God—to the handing down of tradition by men. Thus each time the tradition is handed over, it is a further step away from the core. With each new fence around the law, the law itself becomes smaller on the horizon, and those who control the borders are far from the center. Thus in one master stroke, Mark's Jesus has reversed the pressure upon him and his disciples and has shown the Pharisees and scribes themselves to be on the fringes of, if not completely outside, God's society. They are therefore "unclean" themselves since "their hearts are far from me."

The Corban is cited in the argument from example as only a particular instance. The Pharisees and scribes do many other things like this so that they have not only sinned once but do it continually. Even worse, they continue to pass down this tradition of disrespect for the law to generations of their followers. We have already seen that the Corban tradition is one that could indeed be used in the way Mark's Jesus indicates.

---

[11] It could be successfully argued that Jesus is re-establishing the old purity system as it was intended by God. Certainly Jesus considers himself to be doing just that, and thus it is essential to his argument. I use the term new to reflect the perception of the audience to whom this was surely new when compared to the Pharisaic system.

Josephus, in recounting Pilate's surreptitious infiltration and eventual massacre of a crowd of Jews, informs us that the crowd had gathered there because Pilate had appropriated money from Corban gifts to build an aqueduct (Josephus, *The Wars of the Jews* II.ix.4). This gives us an insight into just how explosive people could be when the purity structure was threatened or outrightly violated. It is not surprising, then, that when Mark's Jesus is challenged, he responds with anger. The purity code, even in our own society, provokes deep emotional responses.

Jerome Neyrey has shown that this new purity system of Jesus is based on the heart or the internal spiritual core of human beings, and it is verifiable just as the old one was. Instead of the tradition as its base, it has the law. It is verifiable by the list of vices in verses 21 and 22 which, as we saw earlier, can be shown to correspond quite closely to the Ten Commandments. A person who exhibits these evils is unclean and outside in a very real sense (and in the most important sense). The followers of Jesus are now inside and are able to put pressure (in a different way of course; that is, in a polemical way) upon those outside. Neyrey sets out the comparison between the two systems in the following way:

Pharisees et al.	*Jesus & His Followers*
1. Purity rules are extended to 613 laws, the tradition of "fence" around the Law.	1. Purity rules are concentrated in the core law, the Ten Commandments.
2. Purity concerns focus on the washing of hands, cups, pots, vessels—external & surface areas.	2. Purity concerns are focussed on the heart—interior & core areas.
3. Purity rules prevent uncleanness from entering.	3. Purity rules guard against uncleanness which is within from coming out.
4. Purity resides in specific external actions relating to hands and mouths.	4. Purity resides in a person's interior, in faith & right confession of Jesus.
5. Purity rules are particularistic, separating Israel from its unclean neighbor.	5. Purity rules are inclusive, allowing Gentiles and the unclean to enter God's kingdom.

(Neyrey 1986: 116)

Having examined the passage in terms of rhetoric and the socio-ideological spheres that were in existence, what can be said about what the narrator of this passage has achieved? First of all, Mark has Jesus make a clear indictment of the Pharisees and scribes. This indictment is accomplished by establishing a division between the cultic laws of purity and ethical principles of action. The larger audience of Mark probably already knew and accepted this division and thus read the passage not in terms of a deliberative appeal but as an epideictic censure of the cultic laws as they were interpreted by the temple coalition. The first argument moves within the sphere of the ideology of the tradition. Jesus exposes the fences built around the law as the protective layers of a politically powerful coterie whose allegiance is not to the commandments but to the tradition which protects and empowers them. The second argument of Jesus offers the disciples and Mark's Christian readers an affirmation of the new center of purity—the human heart. The heart is the new locus of meaning and has its own code of sorts. The vice list functions as a social litmus test for a pure individual: "All these evils come from inside and make a man unclean." Purity has nothing to do with things outside, but exists or does not exist in the human heart. These important arguments are executed deftly by the use of two separate chreiai. The first chreia from Isaiah is used to effect the indictment of the Pharisees and set the stage for a redefinition of purity. The second chreia serves to complete and refine this redefinition. First Mark's Jesus uses the chreia attributed to Isaiah; then he enacts his own chreia in a teaching setting.

The Rhetoric of Deconstruction

The unit in Mark 7 has been analyzed using ancient rhetorical categories and praxis and socio-anthropological notions of purity, and these analyses have helped to show new dimensions of the situation and argument of the unit. If we continue to think about what Jesus or Mark has accomplished and how it was effected, another theoretical lens—that of current deconstructive practice—can bring the passage into focus. The rhetorical tactics used by Jesus are remarkably similar to those used by deconstructive interpreters of literary and philosophical texts. It is interesting to see how Jesus deconstructs the argument of the Pharisees and how deconstruction can describe the new purity norms that Jesus inaugurates or resurrects. Deconstruction, then, can offer a new way of understanding the rhetorical and social aspects of the situation described in Mark 7.

Before deconstruction is invoked to help interpret Mark 7, it will be useful to think further about what we stand to gain with this exercise. Deconstruction is a synchronic practice that refuses to bow to history or any other objective presence as a constraint on its performance. Thus Derrida can claim that writing existed before the letter, in the system of differences found in every culture, and Derrida's disciples can subject any text from any period in history to a deconstructive interpretation. Scholars of the Bible and religion have typically been slow to accept such an intrusion into their field of study. The recent issues of some of the field's major journals, however, show that deconstruction has indeed entered the arena and has been met with a genuine attempt to integrate it into critical practice.[12] Rhetoric and deconstruction have much to offer and much in common. Both are highly sensitive to language and the social constructs in which language operates. Deconstruction has a place in rhetorical readings if only by virtue of the fact that it is one of the potent rhetorical strategies in existence at this time. As Gary Phillips notes in his introduction to a *Semeia* volume on poststructuralism: "One consequence of the poststructuralist posture to be drawn from these essays is the recognition that whatever else 'historical description' is, it is fundamentally rhetorical [in] nature . . ." (Phillips: 4). I will not claim that Jesus was an early deconstructionist, just as I will not claim that Derrida is a prophet. What I do hope to show is that current rhetorical practices such as deconstruction can offer a way to make sense of what is happening in a story. If the sense that is made of a story resonates in the reader's culture, then that story comes alive in new ways.

In the social analysis of Mark 7 we saw that Jesus and his disciples existed on the margins of the purity system. One of the primary functions of deconstruction is to take what has been marginalized and enhance it until the center is shattered and its power dissolved. The edges of the page, what is left unsaid, are like the edges of society, those who are disempowered and unheard. The center is the center of control and power. It provides structure and constrains meaning.

> The function of [the] center [is] not only to orient, balance and organize the structure—one cannot in fact conceive of an unorganized structure—but above all to make sure that the organizing principle of the structure [will] limit what we might call the *play* of the structure. . . . And even today the notion of a structure lacking any center represents the unthinkable itself. (Derrida: 278-79)

The temple coalition invoked the power of the center to censure the actions of Jesus and his disciples. We have already seen how Mark's Jesus is a marginal person and is disempowered from a social standpoint. Jesus, however, works the argument to expose the center (the temple coalition) as a margin. What the Pharisees excluded, namely the commandments of God, returns to haunt them as the absolute presence of the tradition begins to dissolve. By recreating the center in the individual heart instead of the tradition, Jesus has effectively decentered the tradition of the elders. The new center has no foundational presence but is dispersed among

---

[12] See for example *Semeia* 51 and *Journal of the American Academy of Religion* LVIII (Winter 1990). There were of course scholars such as John Dominic Crossan and Robert Detweiler who confronted the problems and promises of deconstruction early on.

individual believers. Such an amorphous and ambiguous center borders, as Derrida says, on the unthinkable.

Jesus does not offer a positive display of alternatives to the traditions of the elders. He lists, instead, the things that truly defile. Thus the entire unit stays within the arena of censure by establishing and maintaining a negative attitude toward both ceremonial purity laws and evil acts. Purity is defined by what it is not; or to put it a better way, purity is defined by absence. The center of power, the constraint on social behavior, is no longer defined by the tradition but by the commandment. We recall that Neyrey shows that each of the vices has an analog to one of the ten commandments. The commandments, however, are not presented as abstract entities but as registers of human behavior. The new center, the new source of power and meaning, is the human heart. Jesus is not proclaiming a new solipsistic mysticism, however, since the vice list offers a set of social signifiers of individual states of purity under the new norm.

The absence of any positive list of behaviors may indicate that absence itself is a spiritual quality of Jesus and his kingdom in Mark. We are familiar with other "absences" in the Gospel of Mark such as the messianic secret and the empty tomb. Ultimately Jesus himself is absent after experiencing the absence of the father while on the cross. This quality of absence is reflected in the texture of the language in the Gospel. Secretiveness, abrupt endings or no endings, and metaphoric reversals such as "one gains by losing" are the stuff of which the Gospel of Mark is made. By leaving the definition of purity undefined or by defining it in terms of its absence, Jesus displays a hermeneutics of suspicion regarding language and its ability to carry the weight of the message he has come to bring.

We saw that in the unit in chapter 7 Jesus often used word play to articulate the difference between the understanding of purity by the Pharisees and his own. Play, in the sense of game and in the sense of movement with regard to meaning, is a term that deconstructionists have adopted to describe what they do. If the foundations of western rationality have been cut away, and truth and history become social constructions subject to social change as deconstructionists claim, then interpretation itself must be seen as play. Play involves the recognition that language is unreliable and slippery, that it never stands still. Even a cursory glance at the words of Jesus in Mark can show that Jesus is playful with the language he wields. His use of parables is another example, as are his metaphorical inversions, which were mentioned above. We saw this in detail in the explication of the argument in Mark 7 where tradition is set against commandment in creative ways and connected to the lips/heart contrast and the belly/heart contrast. As Derrida notes, structure attempts to limit play. The Pharisees are represented as emissaries of structure as opposed to play, and therefore are sensitive to issues of power, language, and behavior. Jesus, on the other hand, does not seem to take language too seriously and frequently uses it against itself in good deconstructive fashion as a way to subvert power and commonly held assumptions about behavior.

This brief rehearsal of Jesus' performance in terms supplied by deconstruction is an attempt to sketch out a new vision of Jesus and Mark, one that sees them as rhetoricians and one that uses the rhetorical and interpretive strategy of deconstruction as a framework. All three types of analysis that I have employed in this paper are ideologically motivated to show the richness of interpreting pronouncement stories from a variety of perspectives and positions. Too often interpretations of biblical texts seek to nail down the particular text to an historical moment or meaning. We are beginning to see that such an exercise is like attempting to nail smoke or water. The biblical text refuses to be pinned or backed into a corner, and any interpretive closure that is effected is transitory at best. The types of analysis used here (and there are many more) attempt to do the opposite—to open up texts, to affirm their conventional use of language, their social dimension, their invitation to play.

WORKS CONSULTED

Barrett, C.K.
    1961   *The New Testament Background: Selected Documents.* New York: Harper & Row.

Bitzer, Lloyd F.
    1968   "The Rhetorical Situation." *Philosophy and Rhetoric* 1: 1-14.

Booth, Roger P.
    1986   *Jesus and the Laws of Purity: Tradition History and Legal History in Mark 7.* Journal for the Study of the New Testament Supplement Series 13. Sheffield, England: JSOT Press.

Bratcher, Robert G. and Eugene A. Nida
    1961   *A Translator's Handbook on The Gospel of Mark.* London: United Bible Society.

Bultmann, Rudolph
    1963   *History of the Synoptic Tradition.* Trans. John Marsh. New York: Harper & Row.

Crossan, John Dominic
    1986   *Sayings Parallels: A Workbook for the Jesus Tradition.* Foundations and Facets: New Testament. Philadelphia: Fortress.

Derrida, Jacques
    1978   *Writing and Difference.* Trans. Alan Bass. Chicago: University of Chicago Press.

Douglas, Mary T.
    1966   *Purity and Danger: An Analysis of the Concepts of Pollution and Taboo.* London: Routledge & Kegan Paul.

Hock, Ronald F. and Edward O'Neil, eds.
    1986   *The Chreia in Ancient Rhetoric: Volume I. The Progymnasmata.* Atlanta: Scholars.

Jebb, Sir Richard Claverhouse
    1909   *The Rhetoric of Aristotle.* Ed. John Edwin Sandys. Cambridge: University Press.

Kennedy, George A.
    1984   *New Testament Interpretation Through Rhetorical Criticism.* Chapel Hill: The University of North Carolina Press.

Kinneavy, James
    1987   *Rhetorical Origins of the Christian Faith: An Inquiry.* New York and Oxford: Oxford University Press.

Lane, William L.
    1974   *The Gospel According to Mark.* NICNT. Grand Rapids: Eerdmans.

Mack, Burton L.
    1988   *A Myth of Innocence.* Philadelphia: Fortress.

Mack, Burton L. and Vernon K. Robbins
    1989   *Patterns of Persuasion in the Gospels.* Sonoma, CA: Polebridge.

Malina, Bruce J.
    1988   "A Conflict Approach to Mark 7." *Foundations & Facets Forum* 4.3: 3-30.

Myers, Ched
    1988   *Binding the Strong Man: The Political Reading of Mark's Story of Jesus.* Maryknoll, New York: Orbis.

Neyrey, Jerome
    1986   "The Idea of Purity in Mark's Gospel." *Semeia* 35: 91-128.
    1988a   "A Symbolic Approach to Mark 7." *Foundations & Facets Forum* 4.3: 63-91.
    1988b   "Unclean, Common, Polluted, and Taboo: A Short Reading Guide." *Foundations & Facets Forum* 4.4: 72-82.

Phillips, Gary A.
    1990   "Editor's Introduction." *Semeia* 51:1-5.

Räisänen, Heikki
    1982   "Jesus and the Food Laws: Reflections on Mark 7.15." *Journal for the Study of the New Testament* 16: 79-100.

Robbins, Vernon K.
    1985   "Pragmatic Relations as a Criterion for Authentic Sayings." *Foundations & Facets Forum* 1.3: 35-63.
    1988   "Pronouncement Stories from a Rhetorical Perspective." *Foundations & Facets Forum* 4.2: 1-31.
    1989   *Ancient Quotes & Anecdotes: From Crib to Crypt.* Sonoma, CA: Polebridge.

Ronen, Yochanan
    1981   "Mark 7:1-23—'Traditions of the Elders.'" *Immanuel* 12 (Spring) 44-54.

Tannehill, Robert C., ed.
    1981   *Pronouncement Stories. Semeia* 20.

Whiston, William
    1979   *The Works of Flavius Josephus.* Grand Rapids: Baker Book House.

A Socio-Rhetorical Analysis of Simon of Cyrene: Mark 15:21 and Its Parallels

Brian K. Blount
Princeton Theological Seminary

ABSTRACT

This study investigates the Simon of Cyrene traditions in the synoptic Gospels (Mark 15:21; Matthew 27:32; Luke 23:26) from the point of view of the recitation of the "narrative" (διήγημα) in Theon's *Progymnasmata*. Blount argues that individually recited stories take on new meanings which may be distinct from their separate meanings when they are cast as smaller pieces in the makeup of a larger, single story. The Simon material itself is epideictic rhetoric: in Matthew and Mark the readers are encouraged to praise and admire Simon's actions; in Luke the narrative is part of a context that focuses on Jesus and censures the Jewish community which does not respond positively to his claims.

Introduction

In this study, we explore the three units in the synoptic Gospels that feature Simon of Cyrene (Mark 15:21; Matthew 27:32; Luke 23:26). The category of "narrative" (διήγημα) in abbreviated form best describes the structural design of the units. In the *Progymnasmata*, Theon defines the narrative as "...an explanatory account of matters which have occurred or as if they have occurred" (Butts: 291). While Cicero agrees by using approximately the same descriptive terminology (Butts: 362), Quintilian makes a helpful addition. He not only describes the form, but includes in his definition a statement of the narrative's function: "The narrative is an exposition, useful for persuasion, of that which either has been done or is supposed to have been done" (Butts: 362). Though the persuasive powers of narrative are most clearly defined when the form functions within the context of a speech, we believe a similar purpose can be ascertained for the Simon pericope in each of its three gospel environments.

Theon provides helpful direction. At the elementary level of rhetorical study there exists the exercise which he describes as recitation (Butts: 219-21). Such recitation involves a reciprocal interactive exercise between *grammateus* and student. The *grammateus* rehearses a particular text. It is the student's task to write a recitation of the stated material both in words of the *grammateus* and in words of his own choosing. Theon introduced this process when discussing the chreia, but he determined that it was no less valuable a tool when working with narrative materials. One must clearly understand, however, the different interpretive nuances involved when the literary venue is altered. The recitation process, when involved with the narrative forms, should be more straightforward than with the chreia. The form of the recited text must bear a clear technical similarity to the text originally submitted by the *grammateus*. For example, while its meaning remains relatively constant, the chreia may be structurally expanded or abbreviated in the recitation process. In the narrative process, however, not only the meaning, but the construction of the form must remain similar to the structural parameters of the original.[1] "With fables, however, the interpretation must be simpler, naturally suitable, and where possible free from artifice and clear" (Butts: 261).

Inherent in the process of such recitation is reorientation. When the form of a story changes, there are also subtle changes in meaning, especially if part of the recitation process is not only internal, but external as well. That is to say, individually recited stories take on new meanings which may be distinct from their separate meanings when they are cast as smaller pieces in the makeup of a larger, single story.

As Theon understands it then, when a redactor alters his source material there is much more occurring than a mere revision of an earlier document. Reinterpretation is taking place. The material is performed anew, and the novel performance suggests a different literary and, in this case, theological emphasis. In the light of such an understanding, it becomes the task of the serious student to investigate how, given the use of grammar, style, and narrative structure, the author has performed his Simon material.

The persuasive strategy of the material can be more adequately understood when we understand its rhetorical classification. Rather than directing a future course of action (a deliberative function) or judging the legality of a past one (a judicial function), the Simon passage encourages the reading audience to praise the actions of its central character (an epideictic function). It is through such celebration that the readers are encouraged to imitate the actions which are highlighted, and to agree with the censures that are levied. Vernon Robbins notes that epideictic rhetoric:

---

[1] While Theon does allow for "expansion" and "abbreviation" within the fable and narrative, the process is strictly governed. The process is regularly allowed only for speeches, or chreia-like material, within a narrative format. Any such changes in the narrative structure itself must either add or delete information about some fact already present within the narrative.

is commonly known as the oratory of praise and censure, and it treats members of the audience as spectators or observers rather than judges. The goal is to confirm already held values rather than to call forth a decision about the legality of a past action or the expediency of a future action. (Mack and Robbins: 161)

It will be our contention that the Markan and Matthean passages present Simon as the central character and highlight his actions as worthy of praise and imitation. The Lukan passage, on the other hand, focuses on Jesus as the primary player, and it censures the Jewish community which does not respond positively to his claims and office of authority through the use of highly negative epideictic language. Indeed, the expression is so negative that judicial language arises as well. This is not an unusual phenomenon, since "the negative use of epideictic rhetoric easily creates a judicial situation" (Mack and Robbins: 160). The persuasive epideictic purpose of the material, however, remains unchanged. The Lukan passage attempts to confirm negative values that the church holds towards the recalcitrant, and therefore hostile, segment of the Jewish community. The Markan and Matthean passages praise, and therefore recommend, the valued concept of discipleship.

The Markan Version

Internal Rhetoric

While Jesus is highlighted throughout the gospel of Mark, in 15:21 it is Simon, not he, who is mentioned by name. It is Simon with whom the narrator is preoccupied, and it is Simon who performs the critical action in the text. Jesus, now, is a passive and silent player. In this literary microcosm the Jesus material performs the function of framing the Simon material. The narrative doublet which Mark presents in the repetition of ἵνα clauses in 15:20b and 15:21b establishes the concept of crucifixion by focusing on the σταυρός terminology. Each of those clauses concludes with a pronomial reference to Jesus. Emphasis on Jesus' crucifixion surrounds and therefore highlights material which is singularly concerned with Simon. What role, the reader then asks, is the Simon unit playing in this situation?

A helpful place to begin is with both the word use and the figurative concept of σταυρός. Mark uses it in this verse and only twice more in the passion narrative in 15:30, 32. The only time Mark uses it outside of the passion is in 8:34, where Jesus uses the noun in a description of discipleship. There the verb ἀκολουθεῖν picks up the motif of discipleship explicitly (Donaldson: 74). Mark appears not only to be narrating Jesus' ordeal with the cross in chapter 15, but to be relating that ordeal to a theme of discipleship which he has clearly placed in chapter 8. However, at the point where Jesus would himself function as the disciple, Simon steps in and bears the cross for him. By having Simon perform in such a manner, it appears that Mark is as much creating an epideictic image of discipleship worthy of praise, and therefore imitation, as he is narrating history.

> Consequently, historical detail which has been handed down began to "speak" to the church and became for the hearers a picture of the discipleship to which they were called. (Schweizer 1970: 343)

Information from classical instructors of rhetoric is invaluable at this point in our study. Theon notes that a narrative should have three necessary qualities. It should be concise, clear, and plausible (Butts: 297). Plausibility is necessary so that the material can fulfill its persuasive purpose. Mark maintains the plausibility of Simon carrying the cross by placing this scene after the scourging. So weakened, Jesus predictably needs help bearing his cross.

Conciseness, too, warrants mention here. A logical criticism of our discipleship interpretation would be that if Mark had intended such emphasis on discipleship he would have explicitly mentioned it in the text. Classical authors, however, disagree. For them, a properly concise narrative relates key concepts in such a way that the audience is compelled to search for them and thereby participate in the actual creation of the very theme the author has had in mind all along. Cicero states that a story is concise if "the story is told in such a way that at times something which has not been mentioned can be gathered from what has been said" (Cic. De Inv. 1.20.28; Butts: 370). Hermogenes and Theon quite agree, so that James Butts declares:

> Thus συνυπακούεσθαι is the process of supplying content or specific words which have not been explicitly mentioned on the basis of what has been mentioned. And Theon's advice is that writing a narrative in such a way that it requires your reader to supply the content on these words contributes to the conciseness of that narrative. (Butts: 375)

Conciseness very capably explains why discipleship, which is so clearly mentioned in connection with "to take up his cross" in 8:34, is only subtly implied in 15:21.

Rhetoric Within Formal Literary Structure

It is now appropriate that we focus on the literary plotting of the chapter as a whole. The rhetoric external to 15:21 enhances this critical theme of modeled discipleship. Our suggestion for a rhetorical structure of the chapter hinges on the verb σταυρόω and the concept "King of the

Jews." As did Matera (34ff), we suggest that Mark is using here in chapter 15 his stylistic concept of bracketing material with key terms. Robbins is of special help because he senses the significant impact of the verb "to crucify" as a bracketing element early in the chapter (Robbins 1992: 1167). Verses 1-15, which he labels "Selection of Prisoner to be Humiliated and Crucified," are concluded when Pilate delivers Jesus to be crucified. Because the verb is placed in the climactic position at the end of the scene it provides not only closure, but also thematic transition into the next section.

> This response leads to the final item in the closing sentence where he hands him over "to be crucified" (Mk 15,15). The scene closes, then, with two completed actions, Pilate's release of Barabbas and Pilate's handing over of Jesus. (Robbins 1992: 1167)

The kingship theme is also on prominent display in this section, as "Pilate identifies Jesus near the beginning, middle, and end as 'the King of the Jews' (Mk 15:2, 9, 12)" (Robbins 1992: 1167). It is important to note, however, that the kingship theme is portrayed ironically by Mark. While the spectators and Romans use it in a derogatory manner, Mark suggests that it is the key to realizing the hope immanent in such a tragic situation.

> According to the Markan version, the kingdom of God occurs in and through the sequence of the ironic death of Jesus as "King of the Jews" followed by the empty tomb which points to his appearance in the future. (Robbins 1992: 1182)

We are, of course, especially concerned with the second section because it includes Simon of Cyrene. Robbins correctly identifies this section as moving from verse 16 through verse 24. The δέ in verse 16 inaugurates a succession of verses connected by the καί parataxis until another section begins with δέ in verse 25. The language of crucifixion and "King of the Jews" links this scene with what precedes it. The climax comes in verse 24 where once again the verb "to crucify" is highlighted.

The third rhetorical section, verses 25 to 32, is bracketed into a unit by the climactic use of "to crucify with" in verse 32. Once again the theme "King of the Jews" and the language of crucifixion provide a sense of thematic unity between the units. Mark's use of the verb "crucify" now ends. Other signals are necessary in our further determination of sectional units.

Though they never use the specific vocabulary in describing the death of Jesus, verses 33-39, the fourth section, maintain the central themes of crucifixion and kingship. The key symbol is the centurion. "The centurion who was placed in front of Jesus represents those to whom Jesus was delivered for crucifixion and those who have mocked him as 'King of the Jews'" (Robbins 1992: 1170-71).

The chapter concludes with the final section, verses 40-46. The continuity this time is provided through the women who view the crucifixion and now witness his place of burial. There is as well another, perhaps even more significant, connecting link. Pilate, the character who in verses 1-15 hands over this "King of the Jews" becomes, as he was in that first scene, the major player. In fact, his role is so integral to these two scenes that Robbins accurately senses that his character has been used in a manner similar to that of the concept "to crucify." Mark has used him to bracket the material in chapter 15 into a programmatic unit:

> The analysis begins with Mk 15:1 and ends with Mk 15,46. Pilate's function as the overseer of the selection and deliverance of Jesus to the soldiers (15,15) and the one who grants Jesus' corpse to Joseph of Arimathea (15,45) establishes the opening and closure of this unit. (Robbins 1992: 1164)

Conclusions: Simon as a Representation of Discipleship

We have, then, established that Mark 15 is a rhetorical unit with specified thematic links, developed narrative scenes, and visible literary boundaries. Particularly, we have shown that the Simon pericope is internally concerned with the theme of discipleship. Externally, the passage is concerned with the themes of crucifixion and kingship. Crucifixion is thus structurally envisioned as the road, the path of discipleship in its highest degree. Jesus walks that road; Simon anticipates it by carrying the cross. The theme of kingship represents an ironic victory over this treacherous path. It is then the true end of discipleship, that which lies beyond the cross. It is the ultimate positive which is to encourage later disciples to imitate Simon always, and Jesus when necessary.

The rhetorical design of verses 16-24 proves quite illustrative. First, as we have previously stated, verse 21 centers thematically on Simon as the central character. Verses 16-20 and verses 22-24 center on Jesus. Jesus, though not mentioned by name in v. 21, is the common character who programmatically makes the three a single unit. The καί parataxis makes the unifying effort grammatically complete.

Understanding this sense of compilation clarifies Mark's external strategy for the Simon pericope. The Simon piece becomes the narrative median between two illustrative Jesus materials. Robbins writes: "The opening, middle, and closure of the scene occur through a progression which links 'leading away' [15:16] and 'leading out' [15:20] with 'crucifying' [15:24]" (Robbins 1992: 1167). Verses 16-20 demonstrate Jesus being led away and then led out. Verses 22-24 detail the crucifixion. Why, then, since the flow is so natural, does Mark interrupt it at the halfway point with a piece about another character who has had no narrative introduction?

The apparently logical question is in reality flawed. Indeed, Simon of Cyrene has not been introduced as a character. However, the character role he plays has been a central thematic construct throughout the gospel: Simon is important because he is a functional representative of correct Markan "discipleship."

> Finally, as the author emphasizes the disciples' failure he also points to a different possibility through very brief references to contrasting figures. These figures include...Simon of Cyrene, who must "take up" Jesus' cross (15:21)....These are figures who replace the disciples in the roles which they fail to fill. They appear in such brief flashes that they do not allow the reader to shift his attention from Jesus and the disciples and become deeply involved with these other characters. But they do point the way which contrasts with the disciples' failure. (Tannehill: 152)

Mark, then, allows Simon to play a key discipleship role without allowing the focus on Jesus to lapse. And to appreciate fully how this role has rhetorically developed, one must understand the purpose for which Mark was writing. Tannehill is again very helpful.

> The decision of the author to write a gospel...rests on the assumption that there are essential similarities between the situation of these disciples and the sentiment of the early church, so that, in telling a story about the past, the author can also speak to his present. (Tannehill: 141)

Social Analysis of Markan Discipleship

If indeed the rhetorical arrangement of past narrative scenes is guided by present historical concerns, it becomes imperative that we understand Mark's social situation if we are to ascertain his literary strategy. Generally dated in the second half of the decade 60-70 C.E. Mark's gospel is considered to be located within a crisis atmosphere for the Christian community. While Lane feels that the crisis is specifically the situation of the church at Rome, Mann extends the scope, hypothesizing that both hostilities in Rome and Palestine provided the background for the gospel. The key recognition, however, endures beyond the differences about specifics. Christian believers were being physically and emotionally accosted, and Mark wrote with this reality in mind. He projected Christian faith into a context of suffering which exhibited a similarity with the situation faced by Jesus himself. They are taunted. They are physically abused. Many are even crucified.

> In crucial statements on discipleship brought together by Mark, Jesus had made it clear that what he demanded was a radical abandonment of life in response to a call to martyrdom (ch. 8:34-38). He had spoken of cross bearing, which Tacitus affirms was a literal reality for Mark's readers in Rome. (Lane: 16)

Simon is important because he provides the illustrative example of a "disciple" doing as Jesus commanded in chapter 8. He "takes up" Jesus' cross. He becomes a positive example for Christians caught up in a situation where they too might be called upon literally to bear Jesus' cross. As Simon was caught in the middle, so are they. As Simon was compelled by higher authorities and had no choice, so will they be compelled. For a believer there is no choice: to affirm Jesus will be to risk the reality of the cross.

The believer, we feel, is caught up with Jesus through Simon. Jesus initiates the confrontation. By following him, the believer is compelled to be a part of it. Simon is forced to live the reality of discipleship which Jesus explained in chapter 8. He is forced to lose authority over his life; he is compelled to take up the cross. And as Jesus dies, so is there the potential of death for anyone carrying the cross. But while the theme of kingship moved towards hope of resurrection for Jesus, for the Christian caught up in imitating him, it provides the hope of the Parousia. The Christian then is not only caught up with Simon on the way to the cross, but because of the thematic and structural parallel of kingship, he or she is caught up as well with Jesus' hope of renewed life. But only positive discipleship brings forth this connotation, the kind of discipleship demonstrated by Simon.

Mark's community is at the midpoint between suffering in imitation of Jesus and possible imitative death, just as Simon is at the midpoint between Jesus' suffering and death. And as the hope of Jesus' resurrection was ironically bound up in the theme of his kingship, so is the hope of the parousia bound up within the positive theme of discipleship. "He who loses his life for my sake will find it." Simon is the positive representation of such a disciple, and as such he is a model worthy of imitation in the Markan community. This is his strategic rhetorical importance.

Mark, then, has not simply transmitted a passion story; he has edited and stylized the material with a strategic rhetorical purpose in mind. The entire section highlights, we believe, Jesus as the central character who is presented positively fulfilling the most demanding rigors of the discipleship to which he has enjoined others. In this regard, he is worthy of praise and, as one obedient to the authority and planning of God, imitation as well. Jesus, however, does more than the audience could rightfully entertain as possible for everyone. The Simon passage, therefore, becomes vital to the hermeneutic. Simon is a sort of "every-human" who participates in a discipleship centered on God's divine plan. Everyone cannot function as Jesus. Everyone can, however, function like Simon.

SIMON AS OUTSIDER: A HERMENEUTICS OF INCLUSIVE DISCIPLESHIP

Martin Dibelius believed that the character traits noted for Simon are insignificant as far as Markan rhetorical and theological strategy are concerned. His sentiments, largely echoed by most of the scholarly community, note that while Simon is important as the one who carried the cross, his person and his ethnography are incidental details incorporated only to suggest historical accuracy.

> We observe that in Mark xiv, 51 and xv, 21, two quite insignificant persons are introduced into the narrative, the unnamed young man who flees leaving his garment in the hands of the bailiffs, and Simon of Cyrene who carries the cross of Jesus and who is described as the "father of Alexander and Rufus." In both cases the persons are characterized by features of minor significance. (Dibelius: 182)

It is our contention, however, that Simon's ethnography is of key interest to Mark's rhetorical and theological strategy. As he figures in this critical juncture in the narrative, Simon is not only the one who carries the cross, but the one who, as we have demonstrated, represents the picture of discipleship. The timing is critical: Simon acts the part of disciple at the very moment that Jesus' actual disciples have abandoned not only that role, but Jesus himself.

Each of the two character traits assigned to Simon is important, and it would be helpful if we were to consider them in turn. The first establishes that he is a native of Cyrene. As there was a Jewish colony established there by Ptolemy I Soter and acknowledged by Luke (see Acts 2:10, 6:9, 13:1), one cannot be certain whether Simon was Jew or Gentile. However, such considerations, which can be answered only doubtfully at best given the textual evidence, are not our concern. We are interested instead with what the text explicitly gives us. What we note is that someone from Cyrene, a north African, Libyan colony, is a geographical outsider. Indeed, Frank Snowden, building upon evidence drawn from studies by F. Cumont, notes that the personification for a person from Cyrene also designated unique ethnic distinctions:

> a head (part of a statue) of approximately the same period from the vicinity of Rome, described as the idealized portrait of a young quadroon or mulatto from Cyrene, has been regarded as a personification of Libya. (Snowden: 182)

The African orientation, whether or not its racial connotation is accepted, cannot be denied geographically. Simon is rhetorically marked as an outsider.

This emphasis is strengthened when Mark next states that Simon was coming in from the fields. Ched Myers notes that with this terminology Mark is maintaining an ironic presentation. In 11:8 we are directed to the text which describes those who greet Jesus upon his entrance into Jerusalem as ones who cut straw "from the fields" to line his way.

> Now [15:21] Mark reproduces the scene in a negative image: Jesus exits Jerusalem in a Roman procession, accompanied (under duress) by a single rural dweller. This functions in two ways. It provides ironic closure to the Jerusalem narrative. And it reminds us once more of the spatial (geopolitical) tension between city/country and center/periphery, which Mark exploits to the end. (Myers: 385)

It is the acute spatial tension which interests us here. Simon is again marked as an outsider, this time in terms of the Jerusalem-Jesus proceedings. That is to say, he is not one who was from the beginning part of the Jesus story, nor has he been in Jerusalem during the proceedings of the day. And yet his contribution is central to the Markan theme of discipleship; he becomes the ultimate insider. He successfully performs the functions of the true disciple. The message to the Markan readership is quite explicit.

> But Mark is warning his readers, If you think you understand, if you think of yourself as an insider, beware, you may not be. If these insiders, the disciples, could find themselves on the outside, so could the readers. (Johnson: 156)

The warning is however also a promise; outsiders can, by their imitative behavior, become insiders. Simon's personal character traits represent an inclusive strategy of discipleship at one of the most critical moments in the Jesus narrative. The possibilities for discipleship extend beyond the geographical, ethnic, and time boundaries of the gospel story itself. Discipleship is an all-encompassing concept, and through the imagery set forth by Simon anyone is welcomed powerfully into its imitative embrace.

In their own ironic way personal character traits therefore end up becoming insignificant in the Markan story. Simon's ethnography is relegated to a secondary position only because of Simon's behavior. It is cross-bearing which Mark focuses on; however, it is only by using someone so clearly different from others in the story that Mark can so powerfully suggest that behavior is more important than heritage. He has used character traits in such a way as to make their use as elements of limitation and exclusion in the community of future disciples untenable.

The Matthean Version

Rhetorical Focus: The Simon Pericope as Narrative Heading

Whereas in Mark the Simon pericope exists structurally at a midpoint in the story, in the Matthean account it opens a new narrative episode. One immediately notices, for example, that verses 27:31b and 27:32b no longer have the same rhetorical affinity as that portrayed in their Markan parallels. The double ἵνα pattern is broken so that the reader no longer senses a thematic parallel between the two verses. Likewise, the pronomial relationship between the two verses has changed. Rather than using the Jesus reference, αὐτόν, as an inclusio to encircle the Simon material, as Mark has done, Matthew concludes verse 31 with a verb and returns to Jesus only after the reference to Simon has been concluded. The result is that Simon rhetorically stands on his own.

Further justification for this view that Matthew uses the Simon material to initiate a narrative sequence is evinced by the very design of verse 32. A temporal participle is chosen in place of the paratactic καί construction favored by Mark. This is of major significance because of the way in which Matthew externally designs his story in relationship to his Markan source.

Externally, the markers which delineated the chapter divisions in Mark have been retained. The verb, "to crucify," is on prominent display, as is the term "King of the Jews." Also, as in Mark, in Matthew the material that concludes the chapter provides an inclusio. Pilate, the character who opened the proceedings, is now conspicuously present at the close. He remains the bracket which makes the material a complete whole.

Externally, then, if one were, for a moment, to disregard the unique Matthean material, the structural design of the Matthean piece is remarkably similar to that in Mark 15.

Matthew 27	Mark 15
vv. 1-26	vv. 1-15
vv. 27-36	vv. 16-24
vv. 37-44	vv. 25-32
vv. 45-54	vv. 33-39
vv. 55-60	vv. 40-46

It is critical, however, that the reader recognize how Matthew initiates each of his narrative scenes. Rather than combining them rhetorically as Mark does with the καί parataxis, Matthew initiates new units by eliminating the parataxis exactly at the point where the scenes divide. This observation retains a further significance because, internally, Matthew often follows the parataxis format quite conspicuously. Consider 27: 27-36. We have already discussed how Mark initiates the καί parataxis with the δέ in 27:16 and carries the pattern through until 27:25. Matthew opts for τότε in 27:27 (parallel Mk. 15:16), but then matches the Markan parataxis in verses 28 through 31. However, instead of continuing the pattern in 27:32, Matthew opts for the temporal participle and then picks up the parataxis pattern again in 27:33. The resulting rhetorical effect is the establishment of a separate unit, initiated by the Simon material, which moves from 27:32-37.

Following these observations, a more nuanced breakdown of Matthew 27 would then be as follows.

Matthew 27
vv. 1-26
vv. 27-31
vv. 32-37
vv. 38-44
vv. 45-54
vv. 55-60

Rhetorical Emphasis: Discipleship

The unique rhetorical perspective suggests that Matthew has a slightly different use in mind for the Simon characterization. And yet, as we have noted, rhetorical similarities do remain. If the external rhetoric in Mark is preoccupied with discipleship through the themes of crucifixion and kingship, then so, too, is it in Matthew. Simon's role is once again compared to Jesus' role: he imitates God's ultimate disciple. Once again, however, the mimicry is incomplete. What he begins, Jesus finishes. Simon bears a cross; Jesus dies on it. It is human struggling that follows in the best way possible the awesome footsteps of Jesus.

The concept of discipleship is further developed in the Matthean story in the same way that Mark developed it. The internal drama of the Simon unit is described in the language of a cross-bearing discipleship which has been given the same sense of textual historicity. Because the critical language in Mt 27:32 matches exactly that in Mt 16:24, just as Mark's cross-bearing language concerning Simon matched that in his 8:34, there can be no doubt that Matthew is also presenting Simon as the active exemplar of one of Jesus' earlier calls of discipleship. As in Mark, Simon is linguistically presented in Matthew as doing exactly what Jesus asks of his true follower in the very verbal manner in which Jesus asked it.

Rhetorical Innovation: Suffering and Participative Discipleship

Matthew 27, like Mark 15, is therefore concerned with the theme of discipleship. The structural similarities assure both an internal and external thematic consistency. However, we have also noted that there are several rhetorical changes. It is in these changes, and the story additions which surround them, that Matthew's unique rhetorical perspective can be adduced. We contend that new plot elements have been added for the express purpose of introducing epideictic sub-plots, which, when considered together, create one single epideictic presentation of discipleship that is subtly, yet critically, distinct from that demonstrated in Mark.

The most obvious place to begin is with 27:3-10. By adding the story of Judas' demise, Matthew has made a substantive literary change. Schweizer is of particular assistance here even though he begins with a misstep. In his epideictic study of Judas he seeks illumination through the character of Peter rather than Simon of Cyrene.

> The fate of Judas in his remorse stands in harsh contrast to that of Peter in his remorse, of which we have just heard. Perhaps Matthew's purpose is even to suggest that the man who wants to make amends on his own even to the point of executing his own sentence will not find salvation, whereas the man who can only break down and weep, expecting nothing more of himself and his efforts but recalling only what his Lord had said, remains within the realm of salvation. (Schweizer 1975: 505)

We have shown, however, that, like Mark, Matthew has provided a thematic unit in this chapter on the crucifixion. Rhetorically then, the Peter material is alien to its immediate structural scope. Other than Jesus, the only figure with whom Judas can be contrasted is Simon of Cyrene. While Judas, the treacherous figure, is destroyed, Simon goes the expected way of true discipleship. In these two the community is given its choices for imitative behavior. The subtle irony is that suffering lies ahead despite the road one chooses. While Judas's is described adequately enough, Simon's is figuratively portrayed through the very language of "bearing the cross." The critical difference is that Simon suffers with Jesus, not against him. As a result, the kingship, to which Jesus ironically holds title, is held out as a promise. These are the true epideictic options available to the community through the Judas subplot.

Schweizer is of more assistance when he discusses the fulfillment perspective which is latent in this text. Key elements of the story are found thematically in significant Hebrew Bible texts. The notations are striking: Psalm 109:18—may his days be few; Numbers 5:22—the curse soaks into the body like water; Psalm 69:25—their place become as a desolation; Zechariah 11:12—blood money of 30 silver coins (Schweizer 1975: 503-504). Indeed, the themes are so strong that Schweizer proclaims with conviction that "the entire story, in all its essentials, is a product of the Old Testament read as prophecy..." (Schweizer 1975: 504).

But to what end? Schweizer correctly suggests the epideictic one: "Matthew's final use here of his accustomed formula of the fulfillment of Scripture shows how important this episode is to him, obviously because it serves to warn the disciple of Jesus about the judgment he faces if he does not remain a faithful follower" (Schweizer 1975: 504). Schweizer is correct only to a degree. Because he is concentrating on the subplot, he sees only partially. Certainly the material is aimed for the edification of the Christian community; the structural similarity with Mark has already assured that. It is just as certainly a warning about discipleship. However, a key element has been suggested and too easily dismissed: fulfillment. It is, we believe, the bridge which connects the historical event and the community directed epideictic. It is the piece which ties this Judas story in with the other narrative additions which Matthew has made to the Markan outline. Therefore, to dismiss it prematurely is to perceive only a piece, and a small piece at that, of what Matthew is interested in modeling before his community. The epideictic subplot suggests a larger, more vital epideictic whole.

The direction towards which this fulfillment theme is moving is anticipated by the next Matthean additions to the Markan structure. In verses 12 and 14 there is a stress on Jesus' silence before his accusers and tormentors. Schweizer is correct in stating that here Matthew has in mind the theme of the Suffering Servant who fulfills God's plans by innocently struggling on behalf of others. Judas, who would have interrupted those plans, has gone as was told of one acting in such a negative capacity. The one who would abort God's plans of salvation has been removed; the stage is set for the plan to move forward. Jesus takes his place in the manner predicted in the scriptures of the Old Testament. "His addition and stress on Jesus' silence is also deliberate. He was probably thinking of the example of the suffering servant of God in Isaiah 53:7" (Schweizer 1975: 507). Key here are two elements. One, Jesus is seen as innocent. Two, as one who suffers on behalf of others, his role is understood vicariously.

The transition to the brief scene about the governor's wife is now understood to be a smooth one. Jesus is once again perceived as an innocent victim. The conviction that God is moving forward with the realization of his will is clear. The sense is that the elements must somehow be related. Jesus, it seems certain, is suffering vicariously for the sins of others, at the direction and behest of God.

> The omen of the governor's wife heightens the grotesqueness of the decision against Jesus Christ and for Jesus Barabbas. The expression "in a dream" is typical of the infancy narratives (1:20; 2:12, 13, 19, 22). As in those, Matthew

probably sees here God's personal intervention in behalf of Jesus. (Schweizer 1975: 508)

The sense that Jesus is innocent of the charges against him is heightened with the decision which allows Barabbas his freedom. After initiating the chapter with his own unique designation that "all" the crowd (v. 1) was responsible for what happened to Jesus, and not just the chief priests and scribes, Matthew asserts with verse 18 that it was not only the leadership but the populace as a whole which desired Jesus to be handed over instead of Barabbas. The reason is envy, not guilt. By verse 23 the crowd is so rabid that they declare responsibility for Jesus' blood. Here is where Matthew shifts the focus. Attention to culpability now moves permanently away from Jesus and begins its process of settling on the Jews.

But of course, before the story is allowed to play itself out, another diversion takes place. In a master stroke of stagemanship, Pilate attempts to divest himself of all responsibility. Although it is unlikely that Pilate would have historically used this predominately Jewish ritual in a way which would have demonstrated his impotence against the demands of his subject populace, it is clear that Matthew's intent is to absolve the Romans and blame the Jews (Schweizer 1975: 508-509). But Schweizer recognizes, as should we, that more is taking place here. Epideictic has resurfaced through the innocence of Jesus and the guilt of the Jewish community. Once again there is a lesson to be learned.

> Now, however, the people of God's own covenant call on him to bring judgment down upon them, so terrible is their blindness....The only thing that makes the verse defensible is Matthew's repeated warning to the Christian community not to go the same way. As his interpolated account of the fate of Judas has shown, he takes quite seriously the possibility that the Christian community, too, could fall victim to God's judgment. (Schweizer 1975: 509)

Simon remains the critical human model. Once again he is the alternate version for the community. He is what Judas and the Jews are not; one who responds appropriately to the sometimes harsh plans of Jesus' God.

The end result of the Matthean interpolations is a higher view of suffering than that found in the Markan account. The themes of innocence guarantee that he did not suffer on his own behalf. The epideictic image is one which involves all of these themes, not one of them in isolation. It is the image of suffering as fulfillment.

Schweizer correctly notes that unlike Mark, Matthew, even in the crucifixion story proper, reveals glimpses of the victory God has achieved through the suffering of Jesus. The earthquake, the open graves, and the dead walking about signal the end of death's power and the permanent interruption of human behavior.

> Thus the question posed by Matthew's account is not whether these bizarre events are credible or not, but whether we can follow the evangelist in seeing as he does the death of Jesus as the epochal event from which to date a change in our way of living, seeing the final power of love over death. (Schweizer 1975: 517)

Therein lies the key to understanding Matthew's rhetorical perspective, for this is the ultimate reason for his structural emendations. The only positive image in the chapter, other than Jesus, whose death is the epochal event, is Simon. He is an example of the change in the way of living necessary to complete the journey which Jesus has begun: suffering on behalf of others. So Jesus' suffering in Matthew is not so much simply a model as it is a call for correct response. First, the wrong responses are shown, from a tragically wayward disciple to the people of God's own covenant. Then the correct response is shown: Simon. His response leads to suffering, but it is a suffering cloaked in positives, made endurable by the anticipation of an inbreaking of God's power which conquers even death.

> Yet it is safe to say that the suffering following of Christ by the disciples is a reply to the suffering of Jesus. Thus the judgment asks about confirmation through testing: whether they have answered the Son of Man who gave himself up entirely for others with a complete dedication of life and imitation in suffering. (Schweizer 1975: 102)

It is then more than a mere imitation. There is an indication that this imitation responds to and fulfills what Jesus had done through his suffering. The key is not so much that they act like Jesus, but that they, by suffering innocently themselves, act for the same reasons he acted. In other words, rather than merely doing what Jesus did, they participate in the process he began. Simon is not so much central because he encourages doing what Jesus did, but because he participates in the fulfillment process in which Jesus too was a part, albeit a greater one. It is what one should call the difference between the imitative discipleship that is found in Mark and a participative discipleship. One suffers not simply because Jesus suffered, one carries the cross not simply because Jesus carried it, but for the reasons that Jesus carried it. One is acting not just like him, but with him.

> The cross as the way of costly love and faithful obedience was the final act in doing what Jesus had been doing all through his ministry; he `came not to be served but to serve, and to give his life as a ransom for many' (xx. 28), in this verse the consistency between the death and the ministry is clearly expressed. And this lets us see how Jesus could ask others to take up their crosses; the spirit of his life and death must be reflected by his followers in active, costly love. (Filson: 38)

Through the image of Simon and the larger context, Matthew is suggesting that one must not only carry the cross as Jesus carried it, but must respond to why Jesus carried it, to participate in the process of why he carried it. He creates this picture by juxtaposing the separate epideictic images against one another. Jesus is, of course, the model, the image of innocent suffering. The negative examples represent the negative potential in the Christian community itself. God's design is rejected; destructive and well deserved suffering immediately follow. Simon, in helping Jesus, follows God's design and thereby participates in that salvific design instead of acting against it. The theme of discipleship is that by imitating, one participates in God's plan of salvation. Simon's crossbearing allows Jesus' suffering to bear fruit. The community's discipleship should do the same. As the disciple suffers he works for himself and for others, because he participates in the process of a salvation which Jesus' suffering created.

Conclusions: Ethnography

Matthew includes only one character trait for Simon in his presentation of the cross-bearing scene. However, his particular use of the material maintains, and even heightens, the ethnographical considerations for inclusivity. Instead of pairing the city of origin with the name Simon, Matthew posits the formulation "a man of Cyrene," before introducing his name. The rhetorical emphasis settles not on the name Simon, but on the fact that the image of participatory discipleship is established by a man from the outside, a man from Cyrene.

Such a recognition is valuable when dealing with a Gospel noted for its disdain towards outsiders.

> But it was also a community that was forced to work out its particular identity—perhaps as the lost sheep of the house of Israel—in confrontation with a developing Pharisaic Judaism and that so thoroughly appropriated the symbols of Judaism to itself that it called those outside the messianic community, simply, Gentiles (18:17). (Johnson: 192)

And yet Matthew has been careful in the latter part of the gospel to indicate a more universal concern into which the Simon material fits quite comfortably. In 24:14, Jesus promises that the gospel is to be preached before all nations, and in 25:32, all nations are gathered before God in judgment. The emphasis on Simon as an outsider disciple not only fits well within this pattern, but is particularly highlighted when in 28:19 the risen Jesus commands that the eleven make disciples of all nations. The command has already been demonstrated as a powerful possibility in the Cyrenian who does what no other disciple would; he bears Jesus' cross.

Social Analysis

Unlike Mark, Matthew is concerned not so much with the troubles of persecution as with the development of a community of believers. It is no longer enough to mandate imitation; instruction is also pertinent.

> Matthew is the Gospel of the church; not only is it the only Gospel to use the term "church," *ekklesia* (16:18; 18:17) but both its contents and structure indicate an interest in providing clear and coherent guidance to a community of believers. (Johnson: 172)

Mark explained that Simon must be imitated. Matthew explains why. The difference for a community would be critical. The impetus to follow resides no longer solely in the hope of a kingdom beyond the present struggle, but it exists as well in the present mandate for discipleship. Jesus suffered and died that others might have the opportunity to make a decision for life. To participate with Jesus in that process means that the church, too, struggles with an immediate purpose. As it recalls Jesus' act, as its disciples, like Simon, initiate their own positive response to Jesus' call for a change of life, so does it energize a similar decision for life in those who witness its endeavors. It participates with Jesus, it suffers like Jesus, like Simon, not for its own sins, but for the furthering of Jesus' own cause of salvation which was initiated by God. By following Jesus, the church no longer merely copies Simon's behavior, but, like Simon, it becomes a part of Jesus' behavior. Just as Simon's act allowed Jesus' role as one sacrificed for others to be carried to its fruition, so too does the church's imitation of Simon allow Jesus' salvific function to become potent in its later historical reality.

THE LUKAN VERSION

Rhetorical Innovation: Jesus as Protagonist

In Matthew and Mark, the Simon pericope is a form of abbreviated composition. In each case the author establishes the scene and then moves narratively onto another. The Simon story becomes an abbreviated unit with settings on either side which establish its rhetorical meaning. Luke prefers a broader story design. Instead of bridging or heading other narrative units, the Simon pericope flows forth into a unique story all its own. The process is most accurately described as elaboration.

The initial signs of rhetorical elaboration in the Lukan account appear in the grammatical presentation. Where Mark and Matthew needed a verse and a half, Luke opts for a single descriptive verse. In this verse Luke reduces the grammatical emphasis on the concept "to crucify" by choosing to disregard the ἵνα clauses and the verb altogether. The rhetorical result is a relaxation of the emphasis on discipleship evident in the other synoptics. The motif is not eliminated however. Luke continues the discipleship motif with the terminology of carrying the cross "behind" Jesus. Luke's use of ὄπισθεν in 23:26 rather than ὀπίσω is part of a unique feature of discipleship: they "lay" the cross "on" Simon, rather than as in Mark, "compel him...to carry it" (Soards: 226). However, something else also is present: emphasis on the character Jesus. Unlike Matthew and Mark, Luke refers to Jesus by name in the verse about Simon. In fact, Jesus' name occupies the climactic position at the close of the verse. The staging prepares the reader for the prominent position Jesus will play throughout the passage which flows from 23:26 to 31. The rhetorical effect is that, while Simon remains an important epideictic figure, he functions as a participant in a larger Jesus story rather than as a central character in his own story.

Lukan Discourse

Luke's narrative employs a compact sequence of καί...δέ...καί to connect Jesus and the other characters who populate the scene. The first καί sets the narrative context for Simon in 23:26. After noting "and they led him (Jesus) away," Luke alone concludes with the comment that Simon carried the cross behind Jesus. Then immediately after this, verse 27 describes the people and women. Instead of focusing on Jesus and Simon alone, Luke has created a scene with two brief acts that function as an encomiastic *prooimion* to Jesus' response. Description (ἔκφρασις) of the lamentation in the great crowd that follows in his processional wake establishes Jesus as a positive figure and brings the weight of rhetorical approval upon his character.[2]

Verses 28-31 make up the saying section. Jesus' statements to the women closely parallel the epideictic category which Menander Rhetor categorizes as consolatory speech:

> The speaker of a consolatory speech himself also laments the fallen and raises the misfortune to great significance, amplifying the emotion as best he can in his speech by means of the topics we have explained in connection with the monody....It is not in bad taste to philosophize in this context on human nature generally, how the divine power has condemned men.... (Russell and Wilson: 161-163)

The interpretative focus begins with the material topic, "and of women who bewailed and lamented him" in verse 27. Amplification of this dirge begins with the proposition in verse 28 where Jesus presents a form of

---

[2] For comparative material see discussion of *prooimion* in Mack-Robbins: 108.

counter statement. Mourning is appropriate; Jesus, however, is not its proper focus.

The formal material topic, then, emerges with verse 28. It is a counter to the funeral thesis already established in the narrative of verse 27. The topic itself, it should be stressed, remains constant: the weeping and mourning over a funeral situation. It is the focus of that weeping which verse 28 challenges. The parameters of the topic are thus established. This redirected mourning becomes the subject of the extended material which follows in verses 29-31.

The key to an accurate understanding of the material is therefore verse 28. Here lies the saying which the evangelist has apparently attached to the narrative of verse 27 for epideictic reasons. However, verse 28 does not fully explain the situation. More information is necessary. The method of adding such material is admirably highlighted in the rhetorical patterns of the Graeco-Roman world. A careful reading establishes parallels whereby a short, pithy saying such as verse 28 is elaborated into an expanded statement. A study of one such rhetorical example will illustrate that Luke has followed the pattern almost exactly.

Theon first cites the chreia. Our parallel, too, establishes a funeral-mourning motif.

> Epameinondas, as he was dying childless, said to his friends: "I have left two daughters—the victory at Leuctra and the one at Mantineia." (Robbins 1988b: 10)

The chreia is subsequently expanded.

> Epameinondas, the Theban general, was of course a good man even in time of peace, but when war broke out between his country and the Lacedaemonians, he performed many brilliant deeds of courage. As a Boeotarch at Leuctra, he triumphed over the enemy, but while campaigning and fighting for his country, he died at Mantineia. While he was dying of his wounds and his friends were particularly grief-stricken that he was dying childless, he smiled and said: "Stop grieving friends, for I have left you two immortal daughters: two victories of our country over the Lacedaemonians, the one at Leuctra, who is the older, and the younger, who has just been born to me at Mantineia." (Robbins 1988b: 10)

The chreia here is elaborated with narrative prior to the critical speech. The narrative effectively established a positive ethos for the central character and gives a more detailed setting for the statement itself. One also notes that here, too, the grief is redirected. Epameinondas, like Jesus, demands that the people cease weeping for him and redirect their concern. Joy is the proper motif, for he has not died childless but has left two quite visible daughters in the form of his battlefield victories.

A close inspection of the Lukan material indicates a quite powerful parallel. If verse 28 is the central focus of the piece, it can now be established that what has taken place is a chreia elaboration. The evangelist has given a narrative setting to the material. The narrative has been attached to the saying.

Such a possibility quite admirably allows for Dibelius's conception that Luke is composing a scene based on ancient martyr accounts. The martyr is presented positively, with a procession trailing in his wake. These martyrs, he instructs, often win the unprejudiced, and even opponents, to his side. While such a conversion does not take place in this piece, Jesus is ultimately viewed as righteous.

> But the multitude which in the soteriological presentation defiantly takes the responsibility upon itself and thus brings the curse upon the Jewish people, here strikes its breast and goes home, frightened by the martyr's blameless suffering. (Dibelius: 203)

Luke, then, in Dibelius' opinion, is not depending on a source but acting as a creative writer: "All this rests upon a unified conception and therefore cannot be traced back to a source but to the only `author' among the Synoptics" (Dibelius: 203). In other words, Luke is elaborating.

While Marion Soards disagrees that the ancient martyr concept can explain all that takes place in this passage, because the "daughters" are a specific referent without parallel, he agrees that verses 27 and 28 are the author's own creative enterprise. For him "Luke composed the scene on the road to the cross in order to heighten the image of Jesus in his version of the Passion narrative" (Soards: 241). He, too, thereby allows for a process of an author's elaboration. Jerome Neyrey also agrees that Luke has created the critical elements of this passage himself (Neyrey: 84). It is therefore quite likely that the narrative of verse 27 is part of the scene elaboration for the chreia in verse 28.

The function of this narrative element of elaboration would be the same as that witnessed in the Epameinondas episode. The positive ethos which the material establishes for Jesus prepares for the redirection of grief. The narrative of verse 27 therefore functions not alone, but as the encomiastic *prooimion* of the chreia. It establishes Jesus as a positive figure and brings the weight of rhetorical approval upon his character. This is achieved by noting the manner in which his death is lamented and the large number of people who follow in the processional wake. Although the reason behind Jesus' redirection is different, the parallelism of form is striking.

This parallelism continues in the grammatical construction of verse 28: "In this form we find efficient periodic construction containing one participial clause with the finite verb ἔλεγε to introduce the saying"

(Robbins 1988b: 10). Vernon Robbins is describing the Epameinondas chreia discussed by Theon.³ This is the compact form which paves the way for later elaboration. Luke's verse 28 has the same form of efficient periodic construction. It begins clearly with a participial clause which is anchored by στραφείς. Then participial construction is immediately followed by the finite verb εἶπεν, which introduces the saying "Daughters of Jerusalem, weep..." Verse 29 then expands the chreia through the concluding proverb in verse 31. Luke's program and structure of elaboration proves to be quite similar to that discussed by Theon.

The Lukan elaboration form, however, is not the paratactic construction which Robbins notes as the general construction of most gospel pronouncement stories (Robbins 1988b: 10). Instead of using δέ or καί to connect the sentences, Luke has used ὅτι twice and τότε once. This produces rhetorical elaboration rather than mere textual expansion: "In the context of the New Testament, the writer's material topics become his propositions; these he then amplifies or works out in the body of his work" (Kennedy: 20).

The epideictic chreia begins with an enthymeme: verse 28 provides a proposition, and verse 29 the rationale. Vernon Robbins states that "...the rationale for the proposition creates an enthymeme, which is the strongest way to begin a speech" (Robbins 1988b: 19). He has drawn such an observation from authors like Aristotle. "Now all orators produce belief by employing as proofs either examples or enthymemes and nothing else..." (Aristotle: 19). We are aided in seeing the remaining structure when we turn to the *Rhetorica Ad Herennium. Ad Herennium* 2.18.28 states that a complete argument may contain five elements. They are as follows:

1. Proposition: "...we set forth summarily what we intend to prove."
2. Rationale: "...sets forth the causal basis for the proposition..."
3. Proof of Reason: "...corroborates, by means of additional arguments, the briefly presented reason..."
4. Embellishment: "...in order to adorn and enrich the argument..."
5. Resume: "...a brief conclusion, drawing together the parts of the argument" (Ad Herennium: 109).

The *Ad Herennium* further instructs that while a complete argument must contain a proposition, reason, and proof of the reason; an embellishment and/or resume may be left out. I propose that the chreia elaboration in verses 28-31 omits an embellishment. It contains:

1. Proposition: v. 28. Daughters, weep for yourselves.

---

³ The Greek text of both the brief and the expanded *chreia* can be found in Hock-O'Neil: 100-103.

2. Rationale: v. 29 Because the days are coming when...
3. Proof: v. 30. They will say to the mountains...
4. Resume: v. 31.

The rationale after the proposition is strengthened with the analogy of mothers who are barren. The proof is bolstered with the language from Hosea 10:8 that provides authoritative censure from the past which will be confirmed in the future. The statement of censure at the end draws the argument together and provides its closure.[4]

A careful textual observation now yields one final piece of analytic evidence. In verse 28, Jesus is clearly addressing the Daughters of Jerusalem, who are a figurative device for the city and its people as a whole. Yet the climactic negatives of verse 29 and following return to the "they" referred to in verse 26. Luke 23:13 tells us who "they" are: the chief priests, the leaders, and the people. The people who are responsible for Jesus' death receive the invective. It is they who are responsible for the widespread destruction that will ultimately engulf all of Israel. Perhaps to one's surprise the "daughters" do not escape the wrath to come. Evidently, they are implicated because they follow the leadership in its rejection of Jesus' claims to Messiahship, and thus they reject God's plan of salvation.

The negative epideictic language of the chreia elaboration, then, introduces a judicially tinged presentation of the people of Jerusalem, and this language no doubt confirmed the value judgment in the community of Luke's time concerning the divine reason behind the destruction of Jerusalem. The argument presents an overall syllogism as follows:

A. v. 31. Because of their intransigence the people of Jerusalem are culpable for Jesus' death.
B. vv. 29,30. Destructive judgment is approaching.
C. v. 28. Therefore, Daughters of Jerusalem, weep for yourselves.

Luke 23:26-31 then is epideictic rhetoric. The juxtaposition of these apparently disparate materials ultimately provides the key to understanding them. The Simon narrative provides a positive image of one who appropriately responds to Jesus as Messiah. The cross-bearing image of discipleship does not stand alone as it does in Mark but is tied to Jesus as a proper response. Verse 28 and its elaboration then present a negative image of the recalcitrant people of Jerusalem who give an improper response to Jesus as Messiah.

---

[4] Neyrey believes that the Daughters of Jerusalem are a figurative device for the city and its people as a whole (Neyrey: 76; cf. Is. 37:22; Zeph. 3:14; Zech 9:9).

This is where the ultimate program of the persuasive argument concludes: Simon evokes a positive image because he follows; the people of Jerusalem evoke a negative image because they remain recalcitrant. The Daughters who represent the people of Jerusalem are drawn into the destruction because they follow the lead of the Jerusalem officials. The argument is complete only when both accounts are kept together. Simon is a character of praise; the people of Jerusalem are characters of invective. But on a deeper level the invective becomes censure. Censure is the ultimate goal, because the readership is ultimately Christian. The unit highlights Christian discipleship. The Christian community is urged to be like Simon. But an additional ingredient is now added: inappropriate behavior, recalcitrance rather than discipleship, will meet with a negative, even punishing divine response. The consequent reference to God's judgment against Jerusalem confirms the values held in the Lukan community that decisions for or against Christian discipleship were not to be taken lightly: "...with this procedure the reader sees what is not good character. The perpetuation of images of anti-character is a primary means of building and maintaining character" (Mack and Robbins: 192).

The Lukan Strategy of Inclusion

Luke maintains the two character traits used so efficiently by Mark. However, in the Lukan framework, with its emphasis on universalism, the connotations of inclusivity so subtly implied in the second gospel are now fully visible as part of a larger, quite obvious strategy. A statement made by Clarice Martin regarding the Ethiopian Eunuch has powerful implications here as well.

> We would argue that the story of a black African Gentile from what would be perceived as a "distant nation" to the south of the empire is consistent with the Lucan emphasis on "universalism," a recurrent motif in both Luke and Acts, and one that is well known. The declaration that the salvation accomplished in Christ is not ethnocentric—but is available to both Jew and Greek, is already heard at the beginning of the Third Gospel ("all flesh shall see the salvation of God," Lk 3:6) with the universal scope of the Christian kerygma. (Martin: 114)

While some of the specific references to "Gentile" and to "the south" may not apply directly to Simon, there are obviously notable parallels between the eunuch and Simon. Robbins notes specifically that Cyrene, in the geographical social location of the Lukan narrative world, marks the outer western boundary. In a narrative whose primary geographical space lies between Jerusalem and Rome, Cyrene, like Ethiopia, is a distant and foreign signification. Yet persons from even this distant location are included within the membership of Jesus followers.

> In sum, the implied author has in view people from as far south and west as Ethiopia and Cyrenaica, as far east as Arabia, Elam, Media, and Parthia, as far north as the southern coast of the Euxine Sea and the northern coastal region of the Aegean Sea, and as far west as Rome. Every kind of person living in this area, including many women, become fully-constituted members of Christianity. (Robbins 1991: 138)

In three separate Acts accounts, — 2:10; 6:9; and 13:1 — Cyrene, specifically, is represented as "included" within the Lukan faith perspective. Simon's designation as a foreigner from Cyrene therefore fits neatly within a pattern of inclusion which Luke-Acts has demonstrated towards its farthest western region.

This inclusive image is heightened by the role which Simon plays in the text. Robbins notes the process of surprise inclusion as it revolves around the signification "Samaritan." In Luke 9:52 the Samaritans appear as the first unwelcome foreigners. Yet Jesus, in 10:29-37, soon represents a Samaritan as a model neighbor, and in 17:18 demonstrates that of the ten cleansed lepers, only the Samaritan gave appropriate praise. The signification "Samaritan" is notable, therefore, not only because of the foreign quality, but as well because this foreign symbol responds appropriately to Jesus' activities, whereas the audience which is expected to be responsive, namely the Jewish community, does not (cf. Robbins 1991:327).

This element of surprise is further heightened with Simon. Here, with the assistance of the chreia elaboration, the outsider imagery continues an obvious and striking contrast with the Jewish community. Further, the foreigner not only contrasts with the people of Jerusalem who respond inappropiately in the chreia elaboration, but also contextually with those who have deserted Jesus; Simon carries the burden which the disciples had been directed to lift. The element of censure directed at the Christian community now becomes quite explicit. "Foreign" is a concept which deals more with an improper response to Jesus and a lack of proper discipleship activity than with nationality. Outsiders may become insiders by following Simon's image, and insiders may well be in reality outsiders because they have rejected that image.

J.P.V.D. Balsdon notes that it was part of Roman ideology to grant full citizenship to people of various ethnic groups simply for showing allegiance to Rome. This practice was acutely different from that of the Greeks who wanted instead to maintain a distinction between themselves and barbarians and were therefore unwilling to grant citizenship unless persons learned the Greek language and participated in the gymnasium. Robbins suggests helpfully that Simon of Cyrene is only one facet in Luke's overall strategy to imitate the inclusive strategy of the Romans. Who Simon is, therefore, is just as important to the image of discipleship

Luke is developing as what he does. Discipleship, as Luke demonstrates it, knows no ethnographical bounds.

WORKS CITED

Aristotle
    1926   *The Art of Rhetoric*. Cambridge: Harvard University Press.

Balsdon, J.P.V.D.
    1979   *Romans and Aliens*. Chapel Hill: University of North Carolina Press.

Bultmann, Rudolf
    1963   *The History of the Synoptic Tradition*. New York: Harper and Row.

Butts, James
    1987   *The "Progymnasmata" of Theon*. Ann Arbor, Michigan: Dissertation Information Service.

Caird, G.B.
    1963   *The Gospel of St. Luke*. New York: Penguin Books.

Cartlidge, David R. and David L. Duncan
    1980   *Documents for the Study of the Gospels*. Philadelphia: Fortress.

Cicero
    1954   *Ad Herennium*. Cambridge: Harvard University Press.
    1949   *De Inventione*. Cambridge: Harvard University Press.

Cranfield, C.E.B.
    1959   *The Gospel According to Saint Mark*. London: Cambridge University Press.

Danker, Frederick W.
    1988   *Jesus and the New Age*. Philadelphia: Fortress.

Dibelius, Martin
    1965   *From Tradition To Gospel*. New York: Charles Scribner's Sons.

Donaldson, James
    1975   "Called To Follow." *Biblical Theology Bulletin*. 5: 67-77.

Fenton, J.C.
    1963   *Saint Matthew*. Baltimore: Pelican Books.

Fitzmeyer, Joseph A.
    1985   *The Gospel According To Luke*. Garden City, New York: Doubleday and Company.

Hill, David
    1972   *The Gospel of Matthew*. London: Oliphants.

Hock, Ronald F. and Edward N. O'Neil, eds.
    1986   *The Chreia in Ancient Rhetoric.* Atlanta: Scholars.

Jeremias, Joachim
    1966   *The Eucharistic Words of Jesus.* Philadelphia: Fortress.

Johnson, Luke
    1986   *The Writings of the New Testament.* Philadelphia: Fortress.

Johnson, Sherman
    1960   *Commentary on the Gospel According to St. Mark.* London: Adam and Charles Black.

Kennedy, George A.
    1984   *New Testament Interpretation Through Rhetorical Criticism.* Chapel Hill: University of North Carolina Press.

Koester, Helmut
    1982   *Introduction To The New Testament.* New York: Walter De Gruyter.

Mack, Burton and Robbins, Vernon K.
    1989   *Patterns of Persuasion in the Gospels.* Sonoma, CA: Polebridge.

Mahoney, Aidan
    1966   "A New Look at The Third Hour of Mk 15,25." *Catholic Biblical Quarterly* 28: 292-99.

Martin, Clarice J.
    1989   "A Chamberlain's Journey and the Challenge of Interpretation for Liberation." *Semeia* 47: 105-127.

Matera, Frank J.
    1982.   *The Kingship of Jesus.* Chico: Scholars.

McNeile, Alan Hugh
    1915   *The Gospel According to St. Matthew.* London: MacMillan and Co., Limited.

Meier, John P.
    1979   *The Vision of Matthew.* New York: Paulist Press.

Myers, Ched
    1988   *Binding the Strong Man: A Political Reading of Mark's Story of Jesus.* Maryknoll, New York: Orbis Books.

Neirynck, F.
    1971   "Duality in Mark." *Ephemerides Theologicae Lovaniensis* 47: 394-463.
    1972   "Duplicate Expressions in the Gospel of Mark." *Ephemerides Theologicae Lovaniensis* 48: 150-209.

Neyrey, Jerome H.
    1983   "Jesus' Address to the Women of Jerusalem—A Prophetic Judgment Oracle." *New Testament Studies* 29: 74-86.

Nineham, D.E.
   1963   *The Gospel of St. Mark.* New York: Penguin Books.

Peacock, Heber F.
   1978   "Discipleship in the Gospel of Mark." *Review and Expositor* 75: 555-564.

Plummer, Alfred
   1906   *Gospel According to S. Luke.* Edinburg: T & T Clark.

Quintilian
   1920   *The Institutio Oratoria.* Cambridge: Harvard University Press.

Rice, George E.
   1981   "The Role of the Populace in the Passion Narrative of Luke in Codex Bezae." *Andrews University Seminary Studies* 19: 147-53.

Robbins, Vernon K.
   1988a   "The Crucifixion and the Speech of Jesus." *Forum* 4.1:33-46.
   1988b   "Pronouncement Stories From a Rhetorical Perspective." *Forum* 4,2: 3-32.
   1991   "The Social Location of the Implied Author of Luke-Acts." Pp. 305-332 in *The World of Luke-Acts.* Ed. J. H. Neyrey. Sonoma, CA: Polebridge.
   1992   "The Reversed Contextualization of Psalm 22 in the Markan Crucifixion: A Socio-Rhetorical Analysis." Pp. 1161-1183 in *The Four Gospels 1992. Festschrift Frans Neirynck*, vol. 2. Ed. F. Van Segbroeck, C. M. Tuckett, G. Van Belle, J. Verheyden. BETL 100. Leuven: Leuven University Press.

Russell, D.A. and N.G. Wilson, eds.
   1981   *Menander Rhetor.* Oxford: Clarendon.

Schweizer, Eduard
   1970   *The Good News According To Mark.* Atlanta: John Knox.
   1975   *The Good News According To Matthew.* Atlanta: John Knox.

Snowden, Frank M.
   1970   *Blacks in Antiquity: Ethiopians in the Greco-Roman Experience.* Cambridge, Mass: Belknap Press.

Soards, Marion L.
   1987   "Tradition, Composition, and Theology in Jesus' Speech to the "Daughters of Jerusalem.'" *Biblica* 68:221-244.

Taylor, Vincent
   1926   *Behind The Third Gospel.* London: Oxford Press.
   1957   *The Cross of Christ.* London: MacMillan.
   1972   *The Passion Narrative of St. Luke.* London: Cambridge University Press.

III
LITERARY AND SOCIAL STUDIES OF PRONOUNCEMENT

THE STORY OF ZACCHAEUS AS RHETORIC: LUKE 19:1-10

Robert C. Tannehill
Methodist Theological School in Ohio

ABSTRACT

The rhetoric of Luke 19:1-10 includes attracting the reader's attention to Zacchaeus and his quest by making him an interesting individual character. Two quests are taking place at the same time: Zacchaeus, although he is rich, finds the salvation he seeks, and Jesus finds the lost person he has come to seek. Both perspectives on the story serve to defend Zacchaeus's right to share in the salvation promised the children of Abraham. The crowd twice functions as a blocking force in the narrative. The article explains the logic of the two enthymemes in vv. 9-10 and how vv. 8-10 work together as a response to the crowd.

The whole of Luke 19:1-10 is rhetorical in that it is designed to persuade readers to view Zacchaeus and Jesus in particular ways and thereby take certain attitudes toward life. The rhetorical dimension is pervasive in language, including narrative. Not only the direct speech of persons can be analyzed for its rhetorical effect. The descriptions of characters, settings, and actions in narrative also have a rhetorical function. The study of narrative rhetoric (on this see the work of Booth) should embrace more than a concern with how characters speak, for everything that the narrator tells us can be evaluated for its rhetorical significance. To do this well, we must draw on the resources of both ancient and modern rhetoric.

The story of Zacchaeus in Luke 19:1-10 has a number of strongly Lukan features (cf. Loewe, O'Hanlon) and has an important function in the larger Lukan narrative (cf. Tannehill 1986: 107-9, 111-12, 122-25). These are matters on which the reader should consult the literature just cited.

Luke 19:1-10 is a pronouncement story in which Jesus' final words rhetorically dominate. For a pronouncement story, however, the narrative gives an unusual amount of attention to another person, Zacchaeus. He is presented as an individual, not merely a character type. We are told his name, one of his physical characteristics (he is short), and an unusual action is narrated (he climbs into a sycamore tree), even though none of this information is strictly necessary for Jesus' final pronouncement.[1] This expansion of narrative detail has a function in the rhetoric of the story. Attention is directed to Zacchaeus as an individual, who begins to stand out as a subject of interest in his own right. Those who become interested in Zacchaeus as an individual will be interested in what happens to him. When he seeks for something, readers are likely to become interested in whether he will find what he seeks and even hope that he will find it, if it is a worthy goal. When Zacchaeus becomes the focus of attention, readers tend to look at events from his viewpoint and to sympathize with his goals. Descriptive detail tends to awaken our interest, and a quest for a worthy goal by a highlighted character tends to awaken our sympathy.

Two important identifying terms are added to Zacchaeus's name in v. 2. We are told that he was a "chief toll collector" and that he was "rich." The impact of this information is likely to be ambiguous, if one is guided by the values affirmed in Luke's Gospel. On the one hand, the toll collectors have been portrayed as responsive to the preaching of John and Jesus, and Jesus has welcomed their company (5:27-32, 7:29, 15:1-2). Not long before the story of Zacchaeus, Jesus told a parable in which a toll collector received God's approval (18:9-14). But Zacchaeus is a *chief* toll collector and is rich. This information may well raise questions about Zacchaeus, for the rich have not been favorably portrayed in Luke. Jesus pronounced a woe upon the rich (6:24), and since Luke 12 the rich have been presented as fools (12:16-21), callous (16:19-31), and incapable of responding to Jesus' call (18:18-23). Thus the indication that Zacchaeus is rich complicates the story and produces uncertainty in expectations. Readers cannot be sure whether this story will follow the pattern of previous stories about toll collectors or whether Zacchaeus will be presented in the manner of other rich men. The importance of Zacchaeus's wealth to the story is indicated by the sentence structure of v. 2. It would have been easy for the narrator to say that Zacchaeus was a rich toll collector. Instead, Zacchaeus's wealth is noted as a separate item and is thereby emphasized (καὶ αὐτὸς ἦν ἀρχιτελώνης καὶ αὐτὸς πλούσιος).[2] Furthermore, he is a *chief* toll collector, one in a position to make big profits.[3]

---

[1] Compare the following *chreia*: "Damon the gymnastic teacher whose feet were deformed, when his shoes had been stolen, said: 'May they fit the thief'." (Quoted from Hock and O'Neil: 310.) Here an individual physical characteristic is noted, but it is essential for an understanding of the pronouncement.

[2] The phrase καὶ αὐτός will be repeated by Jesus in v. 9 in another important identification of Zacchaeus.

[3] Schottroff and Stegemann (17-18) point out that the toll collectors of the synoptic tradition, the people like Levi (Luke 5:27) who actually sat at the toll booths, were underlings. Far from getting rich, they were likely to be people who could find no other work than this thankless task.

The fact that Zacchaeus is rich is important to the plot, which deals with the question left dangling by 18:18-27: whether and how a rich man can be saved. The possible negative effect of Zacchaeus's riches, in light of previous descriptions of rich men in Luke, is balanced by strong indications of Zacchaeus's eagerness to see Jesus and responsiveness to him. When the crowd prevents him from seeing Jesus, he runs ahead (rather than walking) and climbs into a tree (probably an undignified thing for an adult to do). When Jesus says, "Hurry and get down ($\sigma\pi\epsilon\acute{\upsilon}\sigma\alpha\varsigma\ \kappa\alpha\tau\acute{\alpha}\beta\eta\theta\iota$)," Zacchaeus does exactly that ($\sigma\pi\epsilon\acute{\upsilon}\sigma\alpha\varsigma\ \kappa\alpha\tau\acute{\epsilon}\beta\eta$), and he welcomes Jesus to his home "rejoicing." Then v. 8 presents his wholehearted response to the new situation created by Jesus.

Zacchaeus's announcement that he is giving half of his goods to the poor may seem like a halfhearted response when we compare it with 18:22. There Jesus commanded a rich man to sell all and give it to the poor. However, Zacchaeus's statement in 19:8 indicates that he has two important obligations: He, like other rich people, must care for the needs of the poor with his wealth, but he must also restore fourfold what he has gained by false use of his office. The second obligation concerns a different group, since the poor are not likely to be moving goods that would be subject to Zacchaeus's toll. Zacchaeus's wealth is simply divided in half to meet these two obligations. Thus the reference to "half" is not meant as a limit on the distribution of wealth, permitting Zacchaeus to keep the rest, but simply recognizes that he must also compensate those from whom he has extorted wealth. Of course we cannot know how much Zacchaeus owes in compensation, but nothing is said about keeping a portion for himself. Thus it is a mistake to assume that Zacchaeus is trying to strike a bargain, offering less than Jesus demanded of the rich man in 18:22. Rather, 19:8 is intended to be an enthusiastic announcement of a new life that will be devoted to the needs of others.[4]

Zacchaeus's announcement is an act of repentance. Fitzmyer (1220-21, 1225) objects to this view, instead interpreting the present tense verbs in v. 8 as expressing customary action (what Zacchaeus has been doing all along) rather than a decision made at that moment (which must be carried out in the future). This view is not required by the present tense verbs and fits neither the immediate context nor the general Lukan perspective. If v. 8 does not announce a new way of life, the reference in v. 9 to "salvation" coming "today" does not follow from it, since there is no indication in v. 8 of anything new happening "today." Fitzmyer's view makes the sequence of thought unnecessarily difficult. Furthermore, 5:29-32, which is closely

---

[4] Compare Pilgrim: 98-102, 132-34. Pilgrim believes that 19:1-10 stands in tension with passages that call for total surrender of possessions, since it indicates that all of one's possessions need not be surrendered.

related to 19:1-10—indeed, it is another example of the same type-scene (see Tannehill 1986: 170-71; on type-scenes see Alter: 47-62) —makes clear that Jesus came to call toll collectors and other sinners "to repentance" (unique to Luke). The important theme of "salvation" which reappears in 19:9-10 is closely related to repentance and release of sins in Luke-Acts (see especially Luke 1:77; Acts 2:21, 38, 40; 5:31). The announcement in v. 8 indicates the repentance of a man who amassed wealth through disregarding the needs and rights of others.[5]

While the reference to Zacchaeus as "rich" may have made the outcome of this scene somewhat uncertain, the portrayal of Zacchaeus's eagerness to see Jesus and responsiveness to him when they do meet suggests a favorable outcome for Zacchaeus. That is strongly confirmed when Jesus announces in v. 9 that "today salvation has come for this house." This announcement controls evaluation of Zacchaeus and the events of this scene, unless the reader is prepared to reject Luke as a whole. For eighteen chapters Jesus has been presented as one who is fulfilling God's purpose in word and deed, which creates a heavy presumption that Jesus' judgment is true in this case also. The authority with which Jesus is endowed in Luke as a whole is a major factor in the rhetoric of each scene in which he appears, for a figure of such authority tends to persuade readers to view events as he does.

This is certainly true when those events are closely tied to Jesus' divinely ordained mission, as in the Zacchaeus story. There is a hint of this in v. 5 when Jesus says, "Today I must stay in your house." Granted, there is no explanation here of why Jesus "must" stay with Zacchaeus, but the repeated use of δεῖ in connection with Jesus' divinely ordained path, which not only includes suffering and death (9:22; 17:25; 24:7, 26) but also other aspects of his mission (2:49, 4:43, 13:16, Acts 3:21), suggests that the necessity derives from Jesus' mission. This is confirmed by Luke 19:10, for Jesus' final statement in the scene relates his encounter with Zacchaeus to Jesus' mission "to seek and to save the lost." Jesus must stay with Zacchaeus in order to fulfill that mission.

Early in the narrative of Jesus' ministry, Luke's Gospel presents a similar scene. There as here Jesus' association with a toll collector produces grumbling from critics, and Jesus responds with a statement of what he has "come" to do, i.e., a statement about his fundamental mission. In 5:32 he says, "I have not come to call the righteous but sinners to repentance." In 19:10 he says, "The Son of man came to seek and to save the lost." These statements in similar scenes, occurring early and late in the narrative of Jesus' mission to the outcasts, bracket Jesus' ministry

---

[5] Hamm provides further argument for this view of v. 8.

and interpret it as a whole. The latter statement reminds readers of the former and of the intervening instances of Jesus' ministry to the outcasts in Luke. The reference to "the lost" in 19:10 especially recalls Luke 15, where a similar situation arose (critics grumbling at Jesus' association with toll collectors and sinners) and Jesus responded with parables about the finding of the lost. Thus the general statement about Jesus' mission in 19:10 functions as a summary of the previous narrative. It also underscores the importance of Jesus' encounter with Zacchaeus, which becomes an outstanding example of Jesus fulfilling his central mission.

In the Zacchaeus scene two quests are taking place at the same time. In the end Jesus says that he "came to seek (ζητῆσαι)... the lost," but the main sequence of action in the scene begins with the statement that Zacchaeus "was seeking (ἐζήτει) to see Jesus" (v. 3). The scene is enriched by this dual perspective. It can be understood as an example of Jesus seeking the lost. But it can also be understood as a successful quest by Zacchaeus, who happily finds more than he expected. Zacchaeus's successful quest is placed within the context of Jesus' quest for the lost.

Zacchaeus's quest can be understood as the thread that unifies the story. Tension enters the scene as Zacchaeus seeks to see Jesus and is unable. Tension relaxes and the scene ends when Zacchaeus receives what he needs. This is an example of a type of pronouncement story that I have called a "quest story." Quest stories are structured around a person's quest; they give the quester a prominent role alongside Jesus, and do not end without reporting the success or failure of the quest (an indication of the quest's importance in the scene).[6] Such quest stories are especially characteristic of Luke (cf. Tannehill 1986: 111-127). There is subtlety to the narration of Zacchaeus's quest. It is presented in a limited way at first (Zacchaeus "was seeking to see Jesus, who he was"). This could simply indicate curiosity, but the end of the scene suggests that Zacchaeus comes to a deeper perception of who Jesus is: he is "Lord" (v. 8) and source of salvation (vv. 9-10).[7] The realization repeatedly overshoots expectations. At first Zacchaeus simply wants to see Jesus, but surprisingly Jesus decides to stay at his house. And Jesus not only stays at Zacchaeus's house, but brings salvation to those who are there.[8] The eagerness with

---

[6] On the definition of the quest story see Tannehill 1981: 9.

[7] See O'Toole: 111-16. O'Toole understands the Zacchaeus story as a successful quest to see who Jesus is.

[8] Note the similarity between the two statements of Jesus in v. 5 (σήμερον γὰρ ἐν τῷ οἴκῳ σου) and v. 9 (σήμερον σωτηρία τῷ οἴκῳ τούτῳ). The reference to salvation in the second statement indicates an important progression that deepens the meaning of Jesus' stay in Zacchaeus's house. After Zacchaeus's announcement in v. 8, Jesus can show that his stay with this man was more than a temporary association that left life unchanged.

which Zacchaeus responds to Jesus shows that his real need and desire were deeper than watching Jesus' procession. Consciously or unconsciously he was seeking the salvation that Jesus could bring. Thus the real object of Zacchaeus's quest is gradually disclosed as we learn what he finds through Jesus.

In this quest the crowd functions as a blocking force. This is clearest in v. 7 when "all" grumble at Jesus' decision to stay with Zacchaeus, because he is a "sinner." A negative reaction is a standard element in the stories of Jesus' association with toll collectors and sinners. Even the key word "grumble" (γογγύζω or διαγογγύζω) is repeated (5:30, 15:2). However, in these previous scenes the Pharisees and scribes grumbled at Jesus' association with tax collectors and sinners; in 19:7 "all" grumble. This shift is an indication of another problem that this scene addresses. It is concerned not only with the question of whether a rich man can find salvation through Jesus but also with the relationship of Zacchaeus to the Jewish community. The community rejects Zacchaeus as a sinner, but Jesus intervenes on his behalf, reminding the people of a fact that they have ignored, that "he also is a son of Abraham" (v. 9). This is a relevant remark because Zacchaeus's rights as a Jew, including his right to share in the promises to Abraham and his seed, are being denied. In this conflict between the Jewish community and the outcast, Jesus insists that Zacchaeus must be reinstated as a Jew.

The conflict appears in the contrasting responses of Zacchaeus and the crowd when Jesus announces that he will stay with Zacchaeus. Zacchaeus rejoices at Jesus' proposal (v. 6), but the crowd grumbles (v. 7). The rest of the story is a response to the crowd's objection. In light of the crowd's unfriendly attitude toward Zacchaeus in v. 7, his problem with the crowd in v. 3 may not be as innocent as commonly assumed. In this story the crowd twice acts as a blocking force separating Zacchaeus from Jesus, showing the importance of the issue of Zacchaeus's standing in the community. The open opposition in v. 7 suggests that negative attitudes toward Zacchaeus may also be a factor in v. 3. People might allow a respected member of the community to come to the front in order to see, but they would not do this for Zacchaeus. Zacchaeus's short stature reinforces his helplessness with respect to the crowd, and his position up in a tree symbolizes his isolation from it. When the crowd objects to Jesus' association with Zacchaeus, it is seeking to maintain this isolation. The objection heightens the tension in the story. A strong answer from an authoritative source is necessary in order to persuade readers and hearers that a new attitude toward Zacchaeus is appropriate.

At first glance, however, the response to the objection may seem rather fragmented and unclear. First Zacchaeus makes a statement, not to the crowd but "to the Lord." If this statement does not contribute to a convincing response to v. 7, it will weaken that response by introducing a competing issue. When Jesus speaks, he addresses not the crowd but Zacchaeus. To be sure, some interpreters, noting that Jesus goes on to speak of Zacchaeus in the third person, would like to translate πρὸς αὐτόν as "about him" rather than "to him," but the use of πρὸς following a verb of speaking to indicate the one addressed is so common in Luke as to make the alternative translation very unlikely. Jesus makes a basic assertion followed by two supporting statements that seem to have little to do with each other, and it may not be clear how the first of these supports the assertion. Thus vv. 8-10 pose a series of questions: why the crowd is not addressed directly, how the declaration of salvation in v. 9 is supported by the following statements, and whether the three verses fit together to present a strong answer to the objection.

We should note first that v. 9, although it rather awkwardly presents Jesus addressing Zacchaeus while referring to him as "he," accurately reflects the fact that Jesus' statement has a double function in the structure of the story. This is a quest story that directs our attention to the successful or unsuccessful outcome of Zacchaeus's quest. The tension of this quest is resolved when Jesus states in v. 9 that this quest has been successful. This concerns Zacchaeus's fate and is properly addressed to Zacchaeus. But the crowd's objection must also be addressed if Zacchaeus's salvation is to be accepted as appropriate. Jesus speaks to the crowd's objection in the brief supporting statements after the announcement of salvation.

Since the story is centrally concerned with Zacchaeus's quest, it is appropriate for Jesus to address him at the climax. However, we can also understand why the narrator would be tempted to modulate into a statement about Zacchaeus in response to the crowd. Furthermore, some comments of ancient rhetoricians may help us to judge the rhetorical appropriateness of the result. In a paper presented to the SBL Work Group on Pronouncement Story (and now included in this volume), Rod Parrott applied some observations of George A. Kennedy to the pronouncement story in Mark 2:23-28. Kennedy points out that ancient rhetoricians recognized that the speaker's usual approach must be modified when faced with a hostile or unreceptive audience. "Classical rhetoricians developed a technique of approaching a difficult rhetorical problem indirectly, known as *insinuatio*" (Kennedy: 36).[9] The crowd is a hostile audience in the Zacchaeus scene, for it not only denounces Zacchaeus as a sinner but also criticizes Jesus for association with him.

---

9 *Insinuatio* is discussed by *Rhetorica ad Herennium* I.vi.9-11 and by Quintilian, *Institutio Oratoria* IV.i.42-50.

The problem is to speak to the issue without alienating this audience still further. The approach taken fits the hostile situation. Neither Zacchaeus nor Jesus speaks to the crowd directly nor directly challenges its opinion. Indeed, Zacchaeus and Jesus appear to ignore the crowd's objection, speaking only of Zacchaeus's new situation. But indirectly their statements do speak to the objection. It is difficult to continue to apply the term "sinner" to one who is giving away his wealth to the poor and compensating fourfold those he has injured. This is a changed man who must now be viewed differently. If so, Jesus' declaration of salvation does not seem ridiculous. Furthermore, the people who hope to share in God's salvation as children of Abraham cannot easily reject a repentant man who shares that heritage.

The discussions of ancient rhetoric may help us in another way. The declaration of salvation in v. 9 is followed by two supporting reasons. Thus it is argumentative. Indeed, it has the form of an enthymeme. Enthymeme is the rhetorical form of deductive proof. As Kennedy (16) points out, "An enthymeme commonly takes the form of a statement and a supporting reason." Furthermore, "Behind any enthymeme stands a logical syllogism." However, in speeches part of the logical chain is omitted because, it is assumed, some premises are obvious and the audience will automatically supply them. It is a rhetorical fault to clutter the speech with the obvious.

While vv. 9-10 apparently present arguments, their force may not be clear to modern readers. Two supporting reasons are given, but they do not seem to be related. And the missing premises of the argument may not be obvious to us. Supplying them, of course, does not necessarily mean that modern people will be convinced by the argument, for assumptions may appear that many will find debatable. But supplying them would at least help us to recognize what made sense to the narrator of Luke. Since what is not stated is assumed to be obvious, unstated premises should be among the basic assumptions of the narrator and the anticipated readers. We will be on the safest ground if we can supply the missing premises from the work that we are studying or the cultural context from which it comes.

Jesus supports his assertion that today salvation has come to Zacchaeus with a double rationale. The logic behind the second rationale (v. 10) is not really obscure. A fuller argument would go like this: The Son of man (Jesus) came to seek and save the lost; Zacchaeus is one of the lost; therefore, Jesus came to seek and save Zacchaeus (and this task has now been fulfilled, bringing Zacchaeus salvation).[10] This argument would be

---

[10] This is a valid syllogism only if Jesus came to seek and save *all* the lost. Aristotle notes, however, that most propositions in enthymemes will be usually true rather

most convincing to someone who shares the Lukan vision of Jesus' work, in which Jesus' saving mission to the oppressed and excluded has a central place (cf. Tannehill 1986: 60-68, 103-139). Thus we might say that Luke's larger narrative serves to establish the premise in 19:10, which, in turn, summarizes a major theme of that narrative.

The logic behind the first rationale may be less clear, but again missing parts can be supplied from the rest of Luke-Acts. I would suggest that the logic moves as follows: God has promised salvation to the children of Abraham; Zacchaeus is a child of Abraham; therefore, God has promised salvation to Zacchaeus (and this promise has now been fulfilled through Jesus).[11] Supporting the declaration of salvation by the rationale "for he also is a son of Abraham" presupposes a first premise that connects salvation with the children of Abraham. The narrator's acceptance of such a premise can be supported from parts of Luke-Acts in which authoritative interpreters emphasize God's saving purpose for Israel (see Luke 1:54-55, 68-79; Acts 2:39; 3:25-26; 13:23, 26, 32-33). These passages show how seriously Luke-Acts takes the promise to the Jewish people. This promise is not weakened by the invitation to Gentiles to share in God's salvation. Even awareness that the fulfillment of this promise will encounter rejection does not weaken the narrator's conviction that the promise rightly belongs to those who are "sons of the prophets and of the covenant which God covenanted with our fathers" (Acts 3:25), the "sons of the family of Abraham" (Acts 13:26; cf. 13:32-33).[12]

Thus attention to the way that logic functions in rhetoric helps us to see that vv. 8-10 are not such a confused response to the challenge in v. 7 as they might appear. The indirectness of these remarks has a rhetorical value in responding to a hostile audience, and the argument, though very compact, raises three significant points which together undermine the critics' charge: Zacchaeus is a new man who can't be dismissed as a sinner; he, too, is a member of the people to whom most of the scriptural

---

than necessarily true. Cf. *The "Art" of Rhetoric* I.ii.1357a. Arguments with such propositions are used to create a presumption of truth. If detractors wish to exclude Zacchaeus from those sought by Jesus, they would be expected to state a reason.

[11] Again, this is a valid syllogism only if the promise is to *all* the children of Abraham. While some might not accept this, detractors would be expected to give reasons why Zacchaeus, specifically, should be excluded. The preceding statement in v. 8 undercuts the most obvious reason that might be advanced by emphasizing that Zacchaeus is no longer the kind of man that he was.

[12] On the tension in Acts between this promise and Jewish rejection, see Tannehill 1988; on the significance of Jewish rejection in Luke-Acts as a whole, see Tannehill 1985. My comments about the promise to the Jewish people touch on the controversial issue of the Lukan attitude toward the Jews. The following works provide a sampling of the recent debate: Brawley, Tyson, Sanders.

promises are directed; and Jesus was sent to bring salvation to the lost, i.e., to just such a person as Zacchaeus.

The story of Zacchaeus combines important Lukan themes: repentance, the responsibility of the rich for the poor, salvation as a present possibility through Jesus' ministry, Jesus' mission of seeking and saving the lost. In particular, it concerns the possibility of a rich man repenting and finding salvation in spite of a past life of oppression. This story continues to be told frequently in church schools, for it is one of the scenes in which a minor character in the gospels stands out as an interesting individual. The interest that Zacchaeus attracts has a rhetorical effect: readers and hearers become involved in his quest, which is stated in a minimal way in v. 3 but deepens in significance. The crowd's rejection of Zacchaeus and resistance to Jesus' association with him are strongly expressed, and the most pointed rhetoric of the story is found in vv. 8-10, in which statements by Zacchaeus and Jesus combine to form an indirect response to the crowd's objection. It may seem surprising that the author of Luke would be concerned with the crowd's acceptance of Zacchaeus as a Jew, but this is one of many signs that salvation for the Jewish people is a continuing concern in Luke-Acts.

WORKS CONSULTED

Alter, Robert
    1981   *The Art of Biblical Narrative*. New York: Basic Books.

Aristotle
    1959   *The "Art" of Rhetoric*. With a translation by John Henry Freese. LCL. Cambridge: Harvard University Press.

Booth, Wayne C.
    1983   *The Rhetoric of Fiction*. 2nd. ed. Chicago: University of Chicago Press.

Brawley, Robert L.
    1987   *Luke-Acts and the Jews: Conflict, Apology, and Conciliation*. Society of Biblical Literature Monograph Series. Atlanta: Scholars.

[Cicero]
    1954   *Ad C. Herennium de ratione dicendi*. With a translation by Harry Caplan. LCL. Cambridge: Harvard University Press.

Fitzmyer, Joseph A.
    1985   *The Gospel According to Luke X-XXIV*. Garden City, NY: Doubleday & Co.

Hamm, Dennis
    1988   "Luke 19:8 Once Again: Does Zacchaeus Defend or Resolve?" *Journal of Biblical Literature* 107: 431-37.

Hock, Ronald F., and Edward N. O'Neil
 1986   *The Chreia in Ancient Rhetoric*. Volume I. The *Progymnasmata*. Atlanta: Scholars.

Kennedy, George A.
 1984   *New Testament Interpretation through Rhetorical Criticism*. Chapel Hill: University of North Carolina Press.

Loewe, William P.
 1974   "Towards an Interpretation of Lk 19:1-10." *Catholic Biblical Quarterly* 36: 321-31.

O'Hanlon, John
 1981   "The Story of Zacchaeus and the Lukan Ethic." *Journal for the Study of the New Testament* 12: 2-26.

O'Toole, Robert F.
 1991   "The Literary Form of Luke 19:1-10." *Journal of Biblical Literature* 110:107-16.

Parrott, Rod
 1985   "Rhetoric in the Sociology of Conflict: An Examination of Mark 2:23-28." Unpublished paper presented to the Work Group on Pronouncement Story at the annual meeting of the Society of Biblical Literature.

Pilgrim, Walter E.
 1981   *Good News to the Poor: Wealth and Poverty in Luke-Acts*. Minneapolis: Augsburg.

Quintilian
 1960   *Institutio Oratoria*. Volume II. With a translation by H. E. Butler. LCL. Cambridge: Harvard University Press.

Sanders, Jack T.
 1987   *The Jews in Luke-Acts*. Philadelphia: Fortress.

Schottroff, Luise, & Wolfgang Stegemann
 1981   *Jesus von Nazareth: Hoffnung der Armen*. 2nd ed. Urban-Taschenbücher. Stuttgart: Verlag W. Kohlhammer.

Tannehill, Robert C.
 1981   "Introduction: The Pronouncement Story and Its Types." *Semeia* 20: 1-13.
 1985   "Israel in Luke-Acts: A Tragic Story." *Journal of Biblical Literature* 104: 69-85.
 1986   *The Narrative Unity of Luke-Acts: A Literary Interpretation*. Volume I. The Gospel according to Luke. Philadelphia: Fortress.
 1988   "Rejection by Jews and Turning to Gentiles: The Pattern of Paul's Mission in Acts." Pp. 83-101, 150-52 in *Luke-Acts and the Jewish People: Eight Critical Perspectives*. Ed. Joseph B. Tyson. Minneapolis: Augsburg.

Tyson, Joseph B., ed.
 1988   *Luke-Acts and the Jewish People: Eight Critical Perspectives*. Minneapolis: Augsburg.

HOSPITALITY AND CHARACTERIZATION IN LUKE 11:37–54: A SOCIO-NARRATOLOGICAL APPROACH

David B. Gowler
Chowan College

ABSTRACT

This essay features a socio-narratological analysis of an elaborated chreia (Luke 11:37–54). A socio-narratological approach integrates insights into characterization by literary critics and knowledge about cultural scripts among cultural anthropologists. From the perspective of socio-narratological criticism, a cultural context of hospitality creates the reading environment for evaluating the characters in this pericope. The meal setting in the Pharisee's home implies that the Pharisees were continuing to test Jesus as a stranger, a person who, by definition, was a possible danger to their community. The agonistic setting of this episode is part of a larger narrative strategy that clarifies the disputes between Jesus and his opponents throughout Luke. To demonstrate Jesus' role as a prominent, the narrator portrays Jesus freely ignoring Pharisaical purity concerns such as handwashing. In Luke's narrative world, this disregard contradicts the scribes' and Pharisees' entire *Weltanshauung*, and they quickly respond to Jesus' indifference toward their socially-shared view of reality. The narrator creatively utilizes this rejection of the cultural expectations of hospitality (which includes honor and purity concerns) to illustrate Jesus' new system of purity, honor, and virtue that replaces the purity system of the scribes and Pharisees.

[Augustus] hardly ever refused hospitality; and having been entertained to a very frugal, and, so to speak, everyday dinner, he just whispered in his host's ear, as he was saying good-by after the poor and ill-appointed meal: "I didn't think that I was so close a friend of yours."

– Macrobius
Saturnalia 2.4.13
(Robbins, 1989: 46 [#109)]

When the host who was entertaining him . . . served up asparagus dressed with myrrh instead of olive oil, [Julius] Caesar ate of it without ado, and rebuked his friends when they showed displeasure. "Surely," said he, "it were enough not to eat what you don't like; but he who finds fault with ill-breeding like this is ill-bred himself."

– Plutarch
Caesar 17.9-10
(Robbins, 1989: 101 [#296])

While [Jesus] was speaking, a Pharisee asked him to dine with him; so he went in and sat at table. The Pharisee was astonished to see that he did not first wash before dinner. And the Lord said to him, "Now you Pharisees cleanse the outside of the cup, but inside you are filled with rapacity and the evil of covetousness. You fools! Did not the one who made the outside make the inside also? So give for alms those things that are within; and see, everything will be clean for you."

–Luke 11:37–39

INTRODUCTION

The articles in this volume investigate the rhetoric of pronouncement, and most of them use rhetorical discussions of the *chreia* as a means of sharpening the analysis. This study brings insights concerning chreiai, characterization, and hospitality together to interpret the meal scene in Luke 11:37–54. People of the first century had a fascination with, and fear of, the power of words to form character (Mack and Robbins: 43). Therefore, characterization is one of the primary goals of chreiai. Both speech and action characterize; they help to create a character, project that character's ἦθος (Robbins 1988b:10–13), and they can support or critique the accepted cultural views of virtue (ἀρετή; Mack and Robbins: 43, 63). In Luke 11:37–54, powerful words and exhibition of attributes of character occur in a cultural context of hospitality. The challenge will be to describe the dynamics of the social situation in a manner that gives fresh insight into characterization in this literary context.

The use of discussions of the chreia as a way into an analysis of Luke 11:37–54 calls for an understanding of chreia elaboration. A chreia, broadly defined, is "a concise statement or action which is attributed with aptness to some specified [person] or something analogous to a [person]" (Theon, *Progymnasmata*, 201,18–20, Hock and O'Neil: 82–83, cf. Robbins 1989:xi). The term "concise" has led many New Testament scholars away from the study of the chreia in Mediterranean literature and rhetorical treatises. But chreiai did not only exist in abbreviated form; chreiai were commonly expanded and elaborated (Robbins, 1988b: 10). An expansion amplifies the situation and/or response internally. An elaboration does more than just amplify the story; it is a form of argumentation that serves to question the actions and responses of the persons involved. For a typical expansion, see Theon (*Progymnasmata*; Hock and O'Neil: 101–102) and for a typical elaboration ('ἐργασία), see Hermogenes (*Progymnasmata* 7,10–8,14, cf. Mack and Robbins:31–67). First, then, we must turn to an analysis of Luke 11:37–54 as a rhetorical elaboration that uses chreia-like speech to advance its agenda.

LUKE 11:37-54 AS AN ELABORATED CHREIA

Luke 11:37-54 is a rhetorical elaboration—that is, it does not end with a single, pointed rejoinder but contains a complex set of sayings. A close inspection of the meal scene reveals a chreia/pronouncement story (vss. 38-41) in the passage (see Aune, 1987:122). Many have discussed the possible relationships between Luke 11:37-54 and Mark 7, Mark 12:38-40, Matthew 23, and the Q source (e.g., Bultmann: 113-114; Crossan: 171-174; Marshall: 491-493; cf. Ellis: 170). For the issue at hand, it is important to acknowledge that the Lukan narrative achieves its rhetorical goal through elaboration of a chreia. Burton Mack aptly illustrated Luke's skill in rhetorical composition in the elaboration of a meal-scene *chreia* and the resulting effects on the characterization of Jesus (Mack and Robbins: 85-106). Mack argued that the original story behind Luke 7:36-50, Mark 14:3-9, Matt. 26:6-13, and John 12:1-8, was a chreia. He believed that the *chreia* was expanded in two different ways during the process of transmission, and the expansions followed the standard pattern of *chreia* elaboration as learned in the elementary rhetorical exercises by which people learned to read/write/speak Greek.

As Mack noted in his discussion of Luke 7:36-50, the *chreia* has three major components: setting, challenge, and response. Vernon Robbins noticed that the challenge and response found in such stories are vehicles for transmitting the $\mathring{\eta}\theta os$ of the main character and for achieving the rhetorical goal of the story. Every pronouncement story, therefore, contains at least some epideictic influence, because the display of the main character's $\mathring{\eta}\theta os$ is the foremost duty of a pronouncement story (1984b:94-97).

For a full discussion of the rhetoric involved in the elaboration of a *chreia* into a meal-scene narrative concerning Jesus and the Pharisees, I invite the reader to see Mack's analysis. That rhetorical garden is well-tended. His study primarily delineated the rhetorical form, the parallels to the elaboration exercises found in the elementary progymnasmata (rhetorical handbooks), and gave a description of the component parts. Mack's discussion left the function of the rhetorical manipulation basically open ended (Mack and Robbins: 104-105). My purpose is a different one. This essay will take that rhetorical discovery at least one step further: Description will take a back seat to function. Luke's rhetoric in 11:37-54 aims toward a characterization of Jesus—as well as that of his opponents—and it achieves that aim in a social framework.

The elaborated *chreia* unfolds in the following manner:

(a) The narrator creates the specific setting in verses 37-38: Jesus implicitly challenges the Pharisees' purity system, and the host Pharisee implicitly (counter)challenges Jesus by being astonished that Jesus "did not first wash before dinner." The Pharisee's unspoken astonishment forcefully brings into question both the identity of Jesus and the decision that the characters and the reader necessarily must make about him.

(b) Verses 39–41 contain Jesus' three-part response to the unspoken challenge. First, Jesus censures the Pharisees, adopting the mode of epideictic rhetoric: ". . . inside you are full of rapacity and wickedness" (11:39). Second, in verse 40, Jesus authoritatively pronounces judgment against them in the form of an *interrogatio*, the strongest form of an assertion: "You fools! Did not [God] . . . make the inside also?" Third, in what appears to be a contrary, Jesus exhorts the Pharisees to "give for alms those things that are within" (11:41). This exhortation moves the *chreia* beyond epideictic censure to deliberative rhetoric, because Jesus gives the Pharisees advice for future actions. As Kennedy noted, exhortation can be epideictic, if it seeks to inculcate belief without action. If the exhortation encourages the recipient to a particular course of action, it is deliberative (146). Jesus' use of deliberative rhetoric (the advice to give alms) seeks to argue that such action is in their inherent self interest, since the Pharisees seek after purity ("and see, everything is clean for you"). Jesus' response to the challenge, then, speaks against the resistance and tries to bring about a change in attitude. The rhetoric of the narrative is asking the reader to affirm or reaffirm a similar shift in attitude (Tannehill 1980:53; 1981:111–113).

(c) Luke 11:42–52 provides a dialogical elaboration of the chreia. Three sayings of censure (woes) on the Lukan Pharisees initiate the elaboration. Jesus utilizes two arguments from example in verses 42–43: (1) ". . . you tithe mint and rue and herbs of all kinds, and neglect justice and the love of God" (11:42); and (2) ". . . you love to have the seat of honor in the synagogues and to be greeted with respect in the market places" (11:43). These examples exemplify the proposition of the *chreia* (that the Pharisees are "fools" who in practice deny the sovereignty of God), and they bring this theme to a specific focus: the Pharisees' pride leads to self-aggrandizement. Jesus' third censure uses an argument from analogy: the Pharisees are like "unmarked graves" (11:44). This apt comparison elaborates the principle that the Pharisees impart impurity to unsuspecting victims just as a hidden grave imparts impurity to those persons, unaware of its presence, who walk over it (11:44).

The objection raised by "one of the lawyers" (11:45) allows the narrative to elaborate the lawyers' actions and responses to Jesus. The lawyer protests that by rebuking the Pharisees, Jesus also reproaches the lawyers. Jesus' response to the lawyer follows the three-fold pattern of censure that he directed against the Pharisees in 11:42–44, but the elaboration differs substantially. The first woe is a generalized censure against the lawyers who "load people with burdens hard to bear" but do not touch the burdens themselves (11:46). The second censure is an enthymematic argument (11:47-48). This syllogism concludes that the lawyers witness and approve of the deeds of their ancestors (i.e., killing the prophets). The narrative then utilizes a citation from an ancient authority (the Wisdom of God, 11:49-51) to elaborate the second woe and further its theme: "the blood of all the prophets ... will be charged against this generation." The third censure against the lawyers (11:52) provides the concluding summary to the elaborated chreia: The lawyers have taken away the key of knowledge, they did not enter (Wisdom's house?; cf. Prov. 9:1) themselves, and they hindered others from entering. The voice of the narrator returns in Luke 11:53-54 to provide the transition in spatial setting and to note the Pharisees' and lawyers' heightened opposition to Jesus. In Luke 12:1 the narrator completes this transition by clarifying the shift in temporal setting as well. The Pharisees and lawyers have tested the honor and authority of Jesus, and Jesus emerges triumphant.

In outline form, therefore, the structure of the elaborated *chreia* is:

Chreia component: Setting
Rhetorical function: *Narratio*
 Luke 11:37: A Pharisee asks Jesus to dine

Chreia component: Challenge, Question
Rhetorical function: *Quaestio*
 Luke 11:38: Jesus does not wash before dinner, and the Pharisee is astonished

Chreia component: Response
Rhetorical function: *Argumentatio*
 Luke 11:39-41: Jesus, as Lord, rebukes the Pharisees in toto
  11:39: Censure – Pharisees cleanse outside, but inside they are full of rapacity
  11:40: Judgment (interrogatio) – Pharisees are fools; God made the inside also
  11:41: Exhortation – Give alms, and everything is clean

(Dialogical elaboration of the chreia through censure [11:42-52])
 Luke 11:42-44: Jesus levels three woes on Pharisees
  11:42: Argument from example – tithe but neglect justice and love of God
  11:43: Argument from example – love seat of honor in synagogues and greetings of respect
  11:44: Argument from analogy – Pharisees are like unmarked graves

Chreia component: Counter-challenge, Question
Rhetorical function: *Quaestio*
 Luke 11:45: Interlocution by a lawyer – "You reproach us also"

Chreia component: Response
Rhetorical function: *Argumentatio*

    Luke 11:46–52:   Jesus levels three woes on lawyers
        11:46:   Generalized Censure – load people with burdens and do not touch them
        11:47–48:   Enthymematic argument with example – You consent to your ancestors' killing of the prophets
        11:49–51:   Citation from ancient authority (with amplification) – the Wisdom of God says "the blood of all the prophets . . . will be charged against this generation"
        11:52:   Concluding summary – Lawyers took away the key of knowledge
    Luke 11:53–54:   Narrative conclusion – Pharisees respond by "lying in wait for him, to catch him at something he might say"

This rhetorical analysis helps to substantiate the thesis that Luke 11:37–54 primarily concerns the $\hat{\eta}\theta o\varsigma$ of Jesus, and that the passage helps to delineate the characters ($\hat{\eta}\theta\eta$) of his opponents as well (the Pharisees and the lawyers/scribes). A specific rhetorical classification of the scene is even more corroborative. The story is a self-defense against the astonishment of the Pharisee. At first the story evokes the context of a judicial defense for Jesus' not washing before dinner. But Jesus offers no legal rationale or declaration of innocence; the legal action is not as important as the question of his authority and reputation. The narrative touches on judicial issues but quickly moves to other concerns. Jesus also uses deliberative rhetoric to instruct the Pharisees. But epideictic rhetoric is also present, since epideictic rhetoric often turns on matters of honor (e.g., the grounds for praise or blame; see Mack 1990:34). The raconteur skillfully narrates this encounter in order to enhance Jesus' person, authority, and honor, as well as to diminish the authority and honor of his opponents. The narrative is a deliberative self-defense placed in a setting of censure (cf. Robbins 1984b:109–111). Jesus, as the authoritative Lord (11:39), has the final words of censure, correction, and prophetic insight.

CHARACTERIZATION AND HOSPITALITY IN LUKE

While the analysis thus far exhibits the nature of the rhetorical argumentation that produces a positive portrayal of Jesus and a negative portrayal of Pharisees and lawyers in Luke 11:37-54, it is possible to probe much deeper into the dynamics of characterization in Luke (see e.g., Gowler 1989; 1991; cf. Darr 1987; 1992). The generation of a character in the reader's experience of a narrative is a dynamic process of creation (Docherty). Characters emerge as *doppelgängers*, ghostly doubles of living persons who during the dynamic process of reading come to exist in the consciousness of the reader. The text generates the characters, but a reader must apprehend them; texts signify characters but do not prescribe them. *Character*, in other words, is a metaphor, a "bright chimera" the reader creates through interaction with the signposts in the narrative (Wilson). Different texts play with diverse levels of ambiguity, but, as Thomas Docherty noted, a plot-centered narrative—such as the Gospel of Luke—heightens the narrator's authority and attempts to place strong limits on a reader's subjectivity (Docherty: 54, 88). The reader interacts with the text, and may even "play with the details" and "mingle with the characters," but the text lays down the outline of the story (Flaubert: 109).

So narratives give guidelines to readers for how they are to interpret the characters. Initially, a character may be a *blanc sémantique*, a gap in the reader's understanding that prompts him or her to read further (Docherty: 47). As the reader and text dialogue during the reading process, together they will confirm, fill in, or develop that "empty space" of the character. Perhaps this dialogue will even leave the initial impressions of a character permanently ambiguous. The critical reader (cf. Fowler: 27–31), however, may outline the process of character-creating in the following way (Gowler 1989:54–62; 1991:55–75; cf. Rimmon-Kenan: 59–70; Alter: 116–130). Scales of descending reliability and explicitness play an important role in character evaluation. *Direct definition*—the overt naming of someone's qualities—is the most explicit form of characterization, but an interpreter needs to apply a descending scale of reliability to evaluate it. Reliability is the measure of the extent to which a speaker can be trusted, and direct definition varies in importance with the level of authority inherent in the voice that is speaking. The Gospel of Luke contains three voices of absolute authority for the reader: (1) the unrestricted, reliable narrator; (2) Jesus; and (3) the voice from heaven. Other characters have varying degrees of reliability, and the reader—if she or he follows the wishes of the narrator—evaluates them according to their congruence with the statements of the more reliable voices. The words of Jesus' opponents, of course, carry the least weight, and the narrator expects the reader to consider those characters to have the least reliable voices in the narrative.

Direct definition guides the reader directly and clearly. The only question is how much the interpreter should trust the direct definition. *Indirect presentation*, on the other hand, displays or exemplifies traits or qualities of the characters, leaving the reader to make the appropriate inferences. Therefore, both the reliability and the explicitness of the characterization may vary. The importance of these references also varies with the order of presentation, the number of the reported incidents, or any other technique the narrator chooses to utilize (see Gowler 1989:54–62; 1991:61–75).

A structured approach to characterization may appear reductionistic. When a critic rips characters from text and context, character analysis is woefully inadequate. The critic cannot explain everything; the reader has to dialogue with the narrative *in the sequence in which it is encountered*. Later scenes often cause a reevaluation of earlier ones, so the critical reader must strike a balance: a sequential, cumulative reading must be informed by an appreciation of the rhetorical strategy of the narrative as a whole.

An important element of allowing the text to speak for itself is the recognition of the various cultural scripts inherent in every narrative. These cultural scripts vary from age to age and culture to culture, but every text is a socially symbolic act and assumes certain cultural norms. For example, how can a critical reader evaluate an epithet about a character if she or he does not understand the cultural implications of the terms used in the direct definition? Cultural scripts are just as important for evaluating indirect presentation of characters. Actions and speech of characters in a narrative could imply vastly different things, depending on the cultural context. Therefore, a knowledge of these culturally-specific scripts is essential for a more informed reading of a narrative. The most important cultural context for the passage at hand is the law of hospitality.

Julian Pitt-Rivers noted that hospitality is founded on ambivalence (see Pitt-Rivers: 12–30; cf. Malina 1986b:181–187). When a person outside a community is invited to feast or lodge with the host, that person temporarily undergoes a change from *stranger*—an unknown and therefore possibly dangerous person—to *guest*. The stranger's worth is often tested in this situation, but the extension of hospitality, although it does not eliminate conflict, places any conflict in abeyance and prohibits its expression. The avoidance of disrespect then becomes paramount. The guest's "worth," however, is often gauged in this atmosphere of apparent hospitality. Many times, the important question is: Can the guest subscribe to the cultural rules expected of a guest in the host's home? The host and his community will evaluate the guest by the extent to which his behavior conforms to cultural expectations of the host/guest relationship (16). The connections to Luke 11:37–54 are obvious. Jesus is not a member of the Lukan Pharisees' voluntary community, and they want Jesus to conform to their standards of conduct (see Luke 11:38 in particular). The Pharisees are testing the worth of this possibly dangerous stranger, and they evaluate his behavior in light of their cultural expectations.

The host gives precedence to a person who is a guest in the host's home for the first time over habitual guests with whom a greater familiarity exists. The treatment of any person, though, depends on that person's social status, and the whole community gains honor when one in its community hosts a guest of high status. Individually, the host gains honor through the number and quality of guests. The host also gains honor when he shows honor to a superior person; he loses honor, however, by neglecting to show honor to a person who deserves honor. The host, in turn, expects the guests to show honor to him. The host and guest must never be seen as equal as they act out their roles of the hospitality relationship, because any presumption of equality invites the rivalry that is supposed to be dormant. If the meal proceeds according to protocol, the stranger becomes a guest by the formality of the host's offering of food. This high degree of intimacy invokes the sacred and involves an exchange of honor (Pitt-Rivers:12–30).[1]

The guest has but one obligation: to respect the host. Hospitality involves—with rare exceptions—the subordination of the guest. The host's attitude to the guest—or visa versa—often reproduces the collective attitude one has to the social or cultural group the other represents (Herzfeld: 75–89). Here the Lukan story takes its decisive turn. Character traits Luke has attributed both to Jesus and to the Pharisees prior to this point in the narrative reappear in the host's response to Jesus' neglect of purity regulation and Jesus' condemnations of the Pharisees and lawyers.

As suggested above, expectations of the host and guests may vary. For example, some cultures require that the guest compliment the host for the meal. In other cultures, however, the host might interpret this compliment as an insult: the host would assume that such a compliment impolitely presupposes even the possibility that the gracious host could have served a bad meal to the guest. Laws of hospitality declare that certain behaviors, though, are universally in bad form. A guest could violate the law of hospitality by: (1) insulting the host by any show of hostility or rivalry; (2) usurping the role of the host by taking precedence over the host; (3) refusing the food and drink offered by the host. A host, on the other hand, could infringe the law of hospitality by: (1) insulting the guest or by showing any hostility or rivalry; (2) failing to protect the honor of a guest; (3) failing to show concern for his guests' needs or wishes. As Pitt-Rivers noted, "Failure to offer the best is to denigrate the guest" (27–28). Any infringement upon the law of hospitality eliminates the reciprocal relationship of giving honor to each other. An affront or insult entitles the

---

[1] As Michael Herzfeld noted, the term hospitality allows a "more precisely calibrated" analysis than does the more general term honor (1987:75–89). Herzfeld also appropriately noted the various problems associated with the current concept of the "unity of the Mediterranean." A more careful analysis of these cultures needs to be made—utilizing ancient literature—so that scholars from Western industrialized nations will take a less patronizing view of Mediterranean cultures. See also João de Pinal-Cabral (1989:399–406).

slighted person to abandon the role of guest or host and to attempt to maintain honor. The resolution of this combat—which reflects the ambivalence that underlies the law of hospitality—may end in one of two ways: it may lead to the incorporation of the guest as an accepted friend or to the rejection of the guest as an enemy of the host (29–30).

Luke 11:37–54 may belong to the *genus litterarium* of the hellenistic symposium. Some objections have been raised against this hypothesis, but the Lukan meal scenes between Jesus and the Pharisees quite possibly could be adaptations from the symposium genre (see Aune 1978:69–70; Steele 1981, 1984). David Aune noted that the symposium was both a social custom and a *loosely* (emphasis mine) structured literary form that was ordinarily an independent piece of work (1987:122). Steele noted, however, that Luke's Gospel is quite capable of modifying various hellenistic "genres" (Steele's word; 1984:386–387). Whatever the case, Greco-Roman cultural conventions had influenced the Jewish meal, as they had many other areas of Jewish life.

Yet most recent work in this area (e.g., Steele's analysis) concentrates upon the *structure* of the Lukan meal scenes and whether or not they can be called symposia. Of more importance, however, is the function of this type scene in the narrative of Luke. What function do the meal scenes perform, and—more central to this study—what effects do they have upon the portrayal of the characters? For example, Steele claimed that having Pharisees as the hosts of Jesus meant that the Pharisees are placed in a favorable light (1981:174). Yet Denaux noted that the hosts in the symposium genre were ridiculed, and he even claimed that "Le fait que dans les symposia de Luc, les Pharisiens jouent presque toujours le rôle d'hôtes, révéle en quelque sorte indirectement son jugement défavorable sur eux" (262; cf. Carroll: 610–611). Denaux's claim that the hosts were always ridiculed is an exaggeration, but there is a more fundamental difference between the meal scenes in Luke and Plato's *Symposium*, for example. Jesus is undergoing—as a stranger—a time of testing while he is dining with the Pharisees. Mutual rejection will ensue. The time of testing, as described by Pitt-Rivers, does not really occur in Plato's *Symposium*, and that difference from Luke 11:37–54 is crucial.

In Luke 11:37–54, the host's response to Jesus represents the Lukan Pharisees' typical response to Jesus' neglect of purity regulations. In turn, Jesus' condemnations of the Pharisees and lawyers are indicative of his attitude (in Luke) to their misplaced priorities. Jesus' blatant disregard of the laws of hospitality creates a potential problem for the reader. In a culture that prizes hospitality, where guests must avoid disrespect to their host, why should the reader admire Jesus, when he acts in this socially objectionable way? The critical reader finds the answer in the narrator's rhetorical strategy. In other words, a hermeneutical circle appears. First, a knowledge of the law of hospitality clarifies many issues concerning the portrayal of characters in this elaborated chreia. Second, the narrator's ideology, the way he relates this particular story, his portrayal of the characters, and his overall narrative strategy persuasively condition the readers' perspective of Jesus' violation of these enculturated hospitality laws. When readers come to agree with the narrator's ideological (conceptual) point of view, they can actually look favorably on Jesus' rejection and reconfiguration of their cultural expectations of hospitality and the interrelated systems of honor and purity. In sum, the narrator paradoxically uses Jesus' apparently shameful actions to enhance Jesus' stature in the eyes of the reader (narratee).

One way that the narrator achieves this fundamental reversal in readers' cultural expectations is the way he portrays the characters in Luke 11:37–54. It is not feasible to present a full account of the characters' roles up to this point in the narrative, but a brief synopsis will set the stage for an informed analysis of this pericope. All of the characters in the Gospel of Luke direct one's attention to the main character, Jesus (cf. Shuler: 103). A critical reader evaluates other characters in the narrative according to their response to Jesus, because, as characters, they set off, contrast with, dramatize, and engage the main character (cf. Culpepper: 103). Without question, Jesus dominates the narrative of Luke. Beginning with Luke 4:1, he is the center of interest, at the center of all exchanges, and, until the passion narrative, in charge as the main actor. The issue at hand in the early chapters of the Gospel is the identity of Jesus. Direct definition clearly identifies Jesus from the beginning: Jesus is "Lord" (1:43, 76), the "Son of the Most High" (1:32), the "Son of God" (1:35), the "Christ" (2:26–32), and various other positive evaluations (e.g., 2:40, 46–47, 49, 52; 3:15–17). These statements are made by reliable characters: Simeon, for example, is "righteous and devout . . . and the Holy Spirit was upon him" (2:25). Such initial information has a critical influence on the reader's process of perception. The attitudes imbued in the early stages of the narrative encourage the reader to interpret the rest of the narrative in that light, unless the later narrative causes a reprocessing of that initial information (i.e., the *primacy effect*; cf. Sternberg 1978:102–104). The characterization of Jesus, however, is primarily achieved through indirect presentation, which also is quite effective (e.g., Luke 2:41–51), and God, the ultimate voice of authority in the narrative world, confirms this initial positive impression: the voice from heaven declares that Jesus was "my beloved son" with whom God was well pleased (3:22). The entire narrative reinforces this positive portrayal of Jesus. Thus when Jesus performs some actions that seem shameful, the narrator implicitly declares that those actions are actually honorable (e.g., Jesus' violation of hospitality laws). Different actions are judged honorable according to the overall standing of the person performing those actions. Honor depends on one's perception and ideological point of view. Therefore evaluations of moral worth are mutable and underscore the reversal of values the narrator seeks to inculcate in the reader. For members of Jesus' group, his deviant actions are honorable, simply because he as *Lord* (11:39) performs them.

The Pharisees and lawyers in the Lukan narrative serve as legitimation devices *via negativa* for Jesus. The conflicts between Jesus and the Pharisees and lawyers play a crucial role in their characterizations. When the narrative implicitly and explicitly contrasts Jesus' teachings, authority, and person with those of the Pharisees and lawyers, all the portrayals become clearer. Because of his victories in verbal contests with various religious leaders, Jesus gains honor and confirms his authority and stature.

The Pharisees who appear in Luke 11:37-54 are not a blank slate. The narrative has already generated quite a pejorative picture of them. They initially appear, almost unannounced, in response to the rising fame of Jesus (5:17). Since the narrator associates the Pharisees with the teachers of the law, the reader should recognize that the honor Jesus was receiving from the people (e.g., 4:37; 5:15) impinged upon the honor of the Pharisees. Jesus was acting outside his social role, and the Pharisees come to defend their status as brokers of God's blessings (see below). A series of five controversies depicts an evolution of Pharisaic hostility to Jesus that culminates with the Pharisees deliberating an ambiguous course of action against Jesus (6:11). The next appearance of the Pharisees includes an authoritative pronouncement by the narrator that the Pharisees and lawyers reject the purpose of God for themselves (7:30). The narrator then concretely illustrates his overt evaluations of "all the people and the tax collectors" as opposed to "the Pharisees and the lawyers" (7:29-30) by the differing responses to Jesus by the "sinful woman" and Simon the Pharisee (7:36-50). This first meal scene where a Pharisee acts as host for Jesus symbolizes Jesus' defamiliarization of societal norms by receiving sinners (see Resseguie 1984:307-322; 1991). The so-called righteous persons object to his actions. The conflict between Jesus and the Pharisees then escalates the next time Jesus dines in a Pharisee's home (Luke 11:37-54).

Lawyers also appear in this pericope. The Pharisees' connection to the lawyers in Luke-Acts remains partly ambiguous. No voice in the narrative clearly defines the terms *scribe*, *lawyer*, and *teacher of the law*. Teacher of the law is to a certain extent self-descriptive, but the reader encounters no precise description of authority in the narrative. The references to teachers of the law and scribes in Luke 5:17 and 5:21, however, suggest that they are one and the same. In addition, the references to lawyers and scribes in Luke 11:45 and 11:53 imply that the scribes are the same as lawyers. Sometimes the narrative connects scribes/lawyers with the Pharisees (e.g., 5:21; 6:7; 11:53; 15:2), and twice the narrator calls them scribes of the Pharisees (5:30 [with textual variants]; Acts 23:9). Yet in other places the narrative associates them with the elders (e.g., 9:22) and chief priests (e.g., 9:22; 19:47; 20:1; 22:2; 23:10). The narrator only permits one possible positive depiction of the scribes (20:39) but mitigates even that minimal reference (20:40, 45–47). In the passion narrative the chief priests become the persecutors, and the scribes, elders, and others support them. Yet the narrator appears to separate the Pharisees from the chief priests; the scribes are the only possible connection between them. The narrative depicts some connection between at least some scribes and Pharisees, but—for reasons the book of Acts will make clear—the narrator assiduously avoids connecting the Pharisees to the death of Jesus. The pericopes in the narrative prior to Luke 11:37–54 provide evidence for this reading. The narrative connects the Pharisees to the scribes/lawyers/teachers of the law in several pericopes where conflicts with Jesus arise (Luke 5:17, 21, 30; 6:7; 7:30), but when Jesus predicts his upcoming death, the Pharisees disappear from the formula, and the scribes are conspicuously present (Luke 9:22). The lawyers (scribes) are the only possible link between the Pharisees and the people responsible for Jesus' death (*pace* Moessner 1988:21–46; 1989:192–207, 212, 229; cf. Jack T. Sanders:3–23, 84–131).

A Socio-Narratological Reading of Luke 11:37–54

With these insights into chreia elaboration, characterization, and hospitality, let us turn to a socio-narratological reading of Luke 11:37–54. Jesus accepts a Pharisee's invitation to dinner. The narrator thus links this scene to Luke 7:36–50 as well as to the more immediate context (with the phrase ἐν δὲ τῷ λαλῆσαι; cf. Esler:119; Tannehill 1986:180–182; Garrett: 93–105). The reader immediately notes similarities between Luke 7:36–50 and Luke 11:37–54: a Pharisee invites Jesus to dinner; Jesus accepts; complications arise; and Jesus responds to the Pharisee's unspoken thoughts. The reader also will perceive variations between the two scenes: the provocation is not as great, but the rebuke by Jesus is much stronger—woes on all Pharisees carry more power and vehemence than a parable against one Pharisee. The various parallels between Luke 11:37–54 and other Pharisaic meal scenes are important because a reader evaluates characters not only by their performance in this story, but also by all of their performances as the narrative proceeds. The repetition and variation of sundry words and themes in the three meals that Jesus shares with the Pharisees in Luke (7:36–50; 11:37–54; 14:1–24) generate a powerful rhetorical effect. As Janice Capel Anderson noted:

> The similarities between episodes are important in their own right. They engage the implied reader's memory and at times emphasize an aspect of characterization or an element of the plot, etc. However, the similarities are also important because they cause variations to stand out in relief. The implied reader must account for the variations . . . . Further, the overall arrangement of these episodes will shape his or her reading. The order in which the events appear is important (72–73).

A discussion of the effect of these similarities and variations on the reader, though, must await analysis of the characterization in the scene itself.

Narratio and Quaestio: The Setting and the Challenge (Luke 11:37–38)

Verse 37 represents both a spatial and temporal shift in setting. Jesus was speaking to the crowds, and a Pharisee invited him to dine. Jesus enters the Pharisee's house and sits at his table. The speed of the narration then slows for the conflict; the delay of the exposition is brief but effective: Jesus did not wash before dinner, and the Pharisee was astonished.

The reader immediately encounters several cultural scripts. The law of hospitality demands that guests show honor to the host and that the host respect the guests, at the very least by avoiding any show of hostility. Unlike Luke 7:36–50, the narrator notes no overt slight of Jesus by the host. The host invites Jesus to dinner, and Jesus does not wash his hands. When the Pharisee reacts with astonishment, Jesus unleashes a verbal attack against not only the host, but against all Pharisees. As Bourdieu noted, an "accomplished man" must always be on the alert, ready to take up the slightest perceived challenge. Yet Bourdieu went on to note that a lack of moderation on the part of a participant should be met with disapproval (199–200). Therefore, cultural expectations of readers in this environment should actually be offended; Jesus' actions would be shameful for at least two reasons: (1) He did not conform to his host's purity regulations; (2) His attack on the Pharisees goes beyond what his host's subsequent response ("astonishment") calls for. Because Jesus is a guest in the Pharisee's home, this show of hostility nullifies any possible positive ramifications of sitting down to dine together. The infringement of the hospitality code destroys the social roles of host and guest; incorporation from guest to friend does not occur; and Jesus, the Pharisees, and the lawyers all revert to a hostile relationship. They are no longer host and guest; they are enemies (cf. Pitt-Rivers: 27–30).

The invitation the Pharisee extended to Jesus was supposed to suspend any overt hostility, although a time of testing could ensue. Since the process of subordination often involves the assumption that guests subscribe to the cultural expectations of the host, the host Pharisee was thus astonished at Jesus' failure to follow the Pharisee's purity rules (11:38). Jesus' failure to wash before dinner not only was a possible rejection of hospitality codes, but it also was tantamount to a rejection of the Pharisee's social order and the values that order mediates (see Malina 1988a:12; Moxnes 1988:105; Smith 1985:151–156). Because purity rules tend to replicate one another, the whole system may seem threatened when someone disregards even one aspect of it. The concern for clean hands is a symbol of concern for a strong overall system of purity.[2] The Lukan Pharisees would naturally conclude that Jesus purposely rejected the God-given ordered system that structured their lives (see Neyrey 1988:79, 83; 1991b:271–304). As Pitt-Rivers noted, the stance that the host takes to the guest represents his group's collective attitude to the guest and to the group that guest represents (77). Thus this Pharisee's astonishment at Jesus' actions is illustrative of the Pharisees' general sentiment about Jesus—at least to this point in the Lukan narrative. The rationale for Jesus' rejection of their purity system is a concern for the inner, core values of God's law. Jesus declares that pollution does not result from unwashed hands—the outer surface of the body—but the sins that come from inside a person, such as rapacity and the evil of covetousness (vss. 39–41).

A clarification is in order. People tend to label (directly define) a person who acts outside his or her social role in one of two ways: as a deviant or prominent. A *deviant* is a person whom others perceive as acting outside his or her social role to such an extent that they define him or her in a new, negative way. Many places throughout the narrative of Luke, mostly in indirect ways, the Pharisees attempt to categorize Jesus as a deviant. A *prominent*, on the other hand, is a person whom others see as also acting outside his or her social role, but whom they redefine that person in a positive way. The narrator of Luke categorizes Jesus in this positive way. Jesus' role as prominent also, according to the narrator, makes him a *limit breaker*, that is, someone who can transcend the socially-defined limits in a given culture in some socially accepted—by some, at least—way (see Malina 1986a:143–154; Neyrey 1986:91–128; and Malina and Neyrey 1988:40). Jesus' actions were shameful from the Pharisees' point of view, but he preempts that negative labelling process and

---

[2] I should note that handwashing is not a biblical requirement. See the discussion in E. P. Sanders: 203–204, 228–231. I wish to thank Professor Sanders for making an earlier version of this work available to me for a previous project. See also Neyrey, 1991a:361–387. Neyrey claimed that the Pharisees' table behavior embodies and confirms their view of a distinctive Israel, even as it affirms their particular role and status (384).

actually reverses it: Jesus condemns the condemners. Jesus' response indicates that he expected to be labelled a deviant. Yet according to the information supplied thus far to the reader, Jesus' activity was quite honorable. Jesus is a deviant only in the eyes of the Pharisees and the lawyers/scribes, because his behavior jeopardizes their interests and social standing (Malina and Neyrey 1991a:100–110; 1991b:47–49). In the narrative of Luke, those persons who label Jesus as a deviant are unreliable characters who themselves lose honor; those who label Jesus as a prominent are usually more reliable characters. Recognition by demons and the use of irony are two exceptions. Most often a strict correlation exists between reliability and acquired honor.

Honor, in the broadest sense of the word, is compliance with the traditional patterns of behavior. Thus honor, in this sense, is nearly identical to "goodness" or "virtue." A man of honor is simply a good or virtuous man, with honor being attained and maintained by conformity to prevailing cultural norms. Yet honor also requires more than this passive acceptance of societal norms. Honor also depends on the achievement of superiority and distinction (see Abou-Zeid:258). The honor rating that the narrator and others ascribe to Jesus, though, goes well beyond these customary standards. Jesus, according to the narrator, is a prominent and a limit breaker who can transcend the prevailing cultural norms. Therefore, Jesus' actions dictate a new pattern of behavior based on his own authority as God's representative (or *broker*, see below). The narrator's strategy is to convince or confirm readers' affirmations of the essential correctness of Jesus' words and actions.

The extent of Jesus' ascribed honor is well-established. The narrator, God, and other reliable characters label Jesus with titles of the utmost honor and position (e.g., 1:32–35, 76; 2:11, 26–32; 3:22). All of these direct definitions ascribing honor to Jesus are spoken by characters who are both reliable and honorable. These labels applied to Jesus greatly overshadow the negative epithets that characters who are both unreliable and dishonorable apply to him (e.g., by this "faithless and perverse generation" [9:41]). The narrative leads the reader to accept Jesus' evaluation of this "evil generation" (11:29) and to reject any negative labels applied to Jesus by his opponents (Gowler 1989:58). The crucial test is whether or not other characters—such as the Pharisees—accept Jesus' authority as *limit-breaker, broker* (see below), and, finally, *Lord*. In this instance the Pharisees do not (11:53–54).

The agonistic honor and shame setting of Luke 11:37–54 is evident. Previously, after a series of five honor and shame contests between Jesus and the Pharisees, the narrator noted that the Pharisees and scribes were discussing "what they might do to Jesus" (Luke 6:11). Later the narrator notes that the Pharisees "lie in wait" for Jesus in order to "catch him in something he might say" (11:53). The narrator in Luke 11:38, though, does not report any verbal protest from the Pharisee over what he would perceive to be Jesus' implicit challenge of the Pharisees' purity system (i.e., Jesus' neglect of washing before the meal). The result seems to be that the Pharisee does not really question Jesus directly. He offers an indirect affront to Jesus' honor, not the more serious direct affront (see Pitt-Rivers: 27–28). The person who is challenged ambiguously may choose to ignore the affront, but here Jesus responds to the unspoken question about his behavior. Jesus' reaction to the host Pharisee's astonishment openly initiates an honor and shame contest: he unleashes a verbal barrage against all Pharisees (11:39–44). Jesus' response to the Pharisee's silent astonishment, of course, makes the debate public. A lawyer will later attempt to respond to his challenge (11:45), but Jesus foils that attempt (11:46–52). Jesus reigns supreme in the duel fought according to honor and shame rules. In the eyes of the reader, Jesus gains honor, and the Pharisees and lawyers lose honor. The critical reader perceives the status reversal inherent in this characterization of the Pharisees. The process of defamiliarization of norms—a recurrent literary device in Luke—continues. The narrator thus successfully defends what appears to be indefensible: Jesus' allegedly shameful actions. The so-called religious authorities—who should have a high honor rating—lose honor to Jesus. But by the time the reader of Luke has progressed thus far in the narrative, the association of a Pharisee with negative traits has become quite familiar.

Once the reader understands that the lawyers and Pharisees have lost honor to Jesus, their response is seen as quite appropriate: They press Jesus hard, provoke him, lie in wait for him, and try to catch him in a verbal blunder (11:53–54). All such activities—and any sense of setting a trap, testing, spying on, and so forth—are indications of this honor/shame framework (see Malina and Neyrey 1991b:50–52). The readers are aware that the suspense is building and therefore can anticipate the action in the next meal scene with Pharisees (14:1–24), where the narrator initially comments that they "were watching him" (14:1).

The focus upon Jesus is also clearer because the critical reader understands that he is acting as a broker of God's blessings. The cultural idiom of patron-client relationships is intrinsically linked to the basic conceptions of cosmic order (see Eisenstadt and Roniger: 206). Note, for example, the analogies used to illustrate God's person and behavior—Lord (1:15), Savior (1:47), Most High (1:76), Father (3:49), Lord of heaven and earth (3:49). The use of such titles points to another analogy that is implicit in the narrative: God as patron. The kinship terminology of

Father, as used by Jesus, signifies such a patron-client relationship (but cf. the warning of Davis:148). In fact, Jesus is the mediator *par excellence* of God's blessings: God delivered "all things" to Jesus, and Jesus has the sole power to reveal God (10:22). Jesus is the mediator, or *broker*, of God's blessings because he has strategic contact with God the patron. The critical reader, who is familiar with the patron-client relations inherent in Luke's narrative world, recognizes that Jesus' conflicts with the Pharisees are competitions for the role as brokers of the heavenly patron's favors (see Malina 1988b:11-13).

Argumentatio: The Response (Luke 11:39-44)

The growing conflict in Luke 11:37-54 now reaches a fever pitch, and the direct definition of characters appropriately increases. Direct definition identifies character traits, highlights them, and embeds them in the readers' minds. The narrator, for example, refers to Jesus as "the Lord" (11:39). This label has been utilized by the narrator before (e.g., 7:13, 19; 10:1) as well as by various characters (e.g., 5:8, 12; 6:5), and its use here underscores the authority of Jesus. The presence of this direct definition by the narrator in verse 39 reinforces the reliability and authority of Jesus' direct definition and indirect presentation of the Pharisees and lawyers in verses 39-52. Jesus' roles as an honored *broker*, *prominent*, and *limit breaker* are therefore reemphasized for the reader's benefit as well.

The narrative sets Jesus' words concerning the Pharisees in the context of a mixture of direct definition and indirect presentation that the critical reader analyzes in conjunction with one another. The host Pharisee is astonished that Jesus did not wash. The narrator's observation concerning the Pharisee draws attention to his feelings about Jesus and clarifies the differing ideological points of view between Jesus and the Pharisees as a whole (see also Luke 13:14; 14:1; 16:14; cf. Resseguie 1982:41-47; Uspensky; and Lanser). The *Lord* then replies to the Pharisee's unspoken thoughts with a string of rebukes. There is enough of a connection between handwashing and cleansing the outside of the cup that the reader is not bewildered—the connection lies in the fact that the exteriors were being cleansed but the internal situations were being ignored (cf. Neusner: 486-495)—but the vehemence of Jesus' attack is surprising. The first two sentences of Jesus' speech contain direct definitions of the Pharisees that are most damaging: ". . . inside you are full of rapacity (ἁρπαγή) and the evil of covetousness (πονηρία). You fools!" (11:39-40). Ἁρπαγή signifies taking something by violence and greed and is best translated as *rapacity* (Bauer: 108). The narrator later reinforces Jesus' direct definition of the Pharisees by his own direct definition in Luke 16:14: the Pharisees are "lovers of money." Two of the three highest voices of authority, then, accuse the Pharisees of rapacity or avarice, and that trait clings to them like barnacles throughout the entire narrative of Luke. That is why Jack T. Sanders's argument that Luke "slanders" the Pharisees in Luke 16:14 "without any justification" is incorrect. Sanders also maintained that Luke 16:14 provided "no real information" about Luke's portrayal of the Pharisees (199). The converse is actually the case. This narrative aside, as well as Jesus' statement in Luke 11:39, is of utmost importance because it is a direct, explicit comment made by a voice of the utmost authority and reliability. The "slander" of Luke 16:14 is closely intertwined with the entire characterization of the Pharisees in the Gospel and must rank as one of the most important depictions of the Pharisees in Luke. On the other hand, Halvor Moxnes tended to overstress the importance of Luke 16:14 (1988). The interpreter should evaluate this verse in the context of the overall rhetorical plan of the Gospel. Yet Moxnes was exactly correct when he stated, "Their 'love of money' is part of a consistent pattern of social behavior that Luke attributes to the Pharisees" (147). Both of these direct definitions, as well as the many indirect presentations that illustrate the Pharisees' love of money (e.g., 16:19–31), create not only an ideological distance between Jesus and the Pharisees, but also—since Jesus is the hero of the story—a distance between the reader and the Pharisees. Such polemical language also functions literarily to provide an antithesis to the description of the ideal philosopher or teacher, and the term φιλαργυρία is a term commonly used in hellenistic literature in polemics against various philosophers (see Moxnes 1988:4–9; Brawley 1978:68; 1987:86). In addition, πονηρία (Luke 11:39) can mean simply *wickedness* in a moral sense, but used in conjunction with ἁρπαγή it means moral worthlessness as a result of avarice (cf. Rom. 1:29; Mark 7:22). The narrative once again emphasizes the Pharisees' desire for material possessions. What, however, does the Pharisees' association with greed mean in cultural terms?

Interpersonal social interaction in the narrative of Luke occurs on a continuum of *reciprocity* ranging from those exchanges based on altruism to those based on self-interest. There are three main categories of reciprocal exchanges:

1) Generalized reciprocity – An open sharing founded on altruism, which focuses completely on the needs of the other person. Assistance is given without a specific obligation to return the favor (e.g., family relationships).

2) Balanced reciprocity – An exchange based on the common interests of the two parties. Social norms judge the gifts to be

equivalent; there is a symmetrical *quid-pro-quo* agreement (e.g., exchange of goods or services).

3) Negative reciprocity – An exchange of pure self-interest in which one party attempts to receive from another without giving anything in return (e.g., lying, cheating, or theft). Such behavior is acceptable in an agonistic society when one is dealing with strangers. No ongoing social relationship occurs (Malina 1986a:101–104; Neyrey 1991a:372).

Character portrayal of the Pharisees in Luke 11:37–44 associates them with negative reciprocity. Rapacity drives their speech and actions, and Jesus' command to give alms calls for a radical shift in their perspective. No longer are the Pharisees to operate in the mode of exchange that involves negative reciprocity; Jesus requires them to participate in almsgiving—*vertical generalized reciprocity*—a redistribution from the advantaged to the disadvantaged that expects nothing in return (Moxnes 1988:127–138). Luke 11:11–12 gave an example of generalized reciprocity in a familial setting, and Luke 14:21–23 is an example of generalized reciprocity in a meal setting. Since God—the referent in both cases—showers humankind with vertical generalized reciprocity, humankind should follow God's lead in their relationships with each other (Neyrey 1991a:385). Jesus makes this point in the third and final Pharisaic meal scene, where he advises the Pharisees not to engage merely in balanced reciprocity (14:12–14). The Pharisees, it is assumed, invite friends, brothers, kinsmen, and rich neighbors to their feasts (14:12). Jesus advises them instead to invite the poor, maimed, lame, and blind (vertical generalized reciprocity). Luke 16:14 will add another building block in this portrayal of the Pharisees, because lovers of money do not operate from Jesus' perspective of vertical generalized reciprocity. The redistribution of goods from the elite to the non-elite does not take place, and the image of the Pharisees as recalcitrant idolaters who worship material possessions remains.

The next direct definition, *fool* (11:40), besides being an explosive term in an honor and shame contest, is the equivalent of being *a denier of God*, that is, someone "who contemptuously disrupts fellowship between God and [humankind]" (Bertram: 225). Jesus, one of the highest voices of authority in the narrative, labels the Pharisees as fools. Interaction with the Pharisees and lawyers invested Jesus with acquired honor, and the narrator, another authoritative voice in the narrative, attributed to him the highest ascribed honor possible: Lord (11:39). Therefore, since Jesus *the Lord* labels the Pharisees *fools*, this appellation is of momentous importance. The accusation not only shames them, but labels them as moral failures who disregard their social responsibilities (Malina, 1981:50). No description could be more provocative (Danker:239). Such labels are social weapons, and they function as a device to effect social distance between the accuser and the accused. The fact that Jesus labels the Pharisees as *fools* once again creates an ideological distance between the reader and the Pharisees as well. The narrator's objective is for the reader to identify with the ideology of Jesus, not that of his foolish opponents. The additional fact that the Pharisee is shocked at Jesus' behavior ironically demonstrates that Jesus' conduct is honorable, because it is an honorable thing to be at odds with such "morally reprehensible" persons (see Malina and Neyrey 1991a:109).

The effect of these direct definitions on the reader can hardly be overstressed. Jesus confirms the narrator's analysis of the Pharisees (7:29–30). As noted above, two of the three voices of utmost authority in the narrative of Luke condemn the Pharisees. The third voice of authority, the voice from heaven, indirectly condemns them if they do not "listen to him" (9:35). The stress again appears to be on the identity of Jesus—the Lord—as well as on the responses to him, and the Pharisees thus far have refused to recognize him (cf. Edwards: 62). Direct definition of one character by another always is an indirect presentation of the first character. Thus not only does Jesus' reliable and authoritative voice condemn the Pharisees, the narrative leads the reader to identify Jesus as their opponent. Jesus stands for the opposite of what he condemns in the Pharisees, and his superiority to them is also evident in his lecturing both the guests and the host. The Pharisees and lawyers considered themselves to be brokers of God's blessings to the people, but Jesus proves them to be inferior brokers of God, the patron of Israel. Yet even after this shocking denunciation Jesus offers hope for escape: repentance (11:41). If the Pharisees overcome their rapacity, they will be accepted; if they give alms, everything will become clean.³ Apparently, only vertical generalized reciprocity can break the connection between unrighteousness and the desire for material possessions (Moxnes 1988:145–146).

Jesus then utters a series of three woes against the Pharisees (11:42–44). The negative implications of these woes are substantial. First the Pharisees tithe mint, rue, and every herb—which they should do (11:42)—but they have neglected the more important things: justice and the love of God. The Pharisees' love of money (11:39; cf. 16:14) and their love of

---

³ See Marshall: 495. It is interesting to note that the Pharisees and the lawyers had not been baptized by John the Baptist and that here Jesus refuses their baptism (ἐβαπτίσθη, 11:38; cf. 7:29–30; noted by McMahan: 177). See also the discussion by Moxnes (1988:109–126). The conjunction of ἁρπαγῆς and πονηρίας makes the link between 11:37–44 and 16:14 even closer than Moxnes stated.

honor (11:43) prevent them from loving God and God's justice. The second woe against the Pharisees characterizes them through indirect presentation. Jesus' judgment of their actions—they love the seat of honor in the synagogues and being greeted with respect in the agoras—clearly portrays them as being greedy for social prominence. The grasping after such honors is an essential part of their greediness; honor is a polysemous concept that includes aspects of wealth and status (Gilmore 1982:175-205; cf. Campbell: 145). The seat of honor in the synagogue is, of course, a place of prominence, as is sitting at the head table at dinner. To be greeted first by another person is a sign of respect that acknowledges the honor of another (Windisch: 498). These failings tie into the Pharisees' abuse of social relationships, especially being indifferent to the plight of the poor. Later Lukan pericopes will confirm this hypothesis (see the conclusion below, as well as Easton: 189; Büchsel: 941-942; Marshall: 497-499; and Moxnes 1988:109-126). The Pharisees' greediness for social honors also explains more fully why Jesus' public rebuke to them was so strong. Persons who grasp after honor indiscreetly often are reprimanded publicly so that their pretensions to superiority may be illuminated and effectively eliminated (see Bourdieu: 191-241). Jesus emphatically declares that religious matters should not be used to enhance one's status in society.

Jesus' third woe leaves out "Pharisees" in the "Woe to you" formula, but the intended addressees are still clearly the Pharisees. This final woe against the Pharisees contains a great amount of irony: the Pharisees are like unmarked graves over which people walk unknowingly (11:44). The implication is that those persons become unclean because of their contact with a gravesite. The Pharisees hide their true evil nature and lead unwitting persons astray. The pericope thus begins in 11:38 with the Pharisees' zealous concern for purity rules—the concern for tithing mentioned in the first woe (11:42) also played a part in the Pharisees' purity rule system—and ends with Jesus comparing them to unmarked graves that impart impurity to others. The irony lies in the fact that the Pharisees were so concerned about purity, but they themselves cause uncleanness among those who come into contact with them. The Pharisees who lust after honor, purity, and possessions will lose all of those things (cf. Luke 14:7-24). As Jesus notes in Luke 16:15, such people are "an abomination ($\beta\delta\acute{\epsilon}\lambda\upsilon\gamma\mu\alpha$) in the sight of God." Any person or thing that is abhorrent in the sight of God is something that violates God's system of purity and thus is unclean. The social and economic behavior of the Pharisees has rendered them unclean before God, even with their zealous regard for purity rules (Moxnes 1988:148).

Quaestio and Argumentatio: Challenge and Response (Luke 11:45–54)

One of the lawyers concludes that Jesus was reproaching them also. Jesus evidently concurs, because he immediately launches into three woes against the lawyers (11:45–52). The lawyer, still mindful of the law of hospitality, addresses Jesus politely as "Teacher." Note the contrast between the narrator's labelling of Jesus as *Lord* (11:39) and the lawyer's use of *teacher* (11:45). Although *teacher* is a term of respect, it still is deficient in the eyes of the narrator. The lawyer does not (cannot?) recognize Jesus as Lord, the response the narrator sees as normative. The lawyer objects, as is to be expected in an honor and shame society, that Jesus has insulted (ὑβρίζω) the lawyers also by his three woes upon the Pharisees. Thus the lawyer is in the classic position of defending the honor of his own voluntary social group, the scribes, against the verbal, public affront by Jesus against the Pharisees. The use of the term ὑβρίζω makes this connection even clearer; the lawyer must respond to the public insult.

The fact that a lawyer responds to the challenge Jesus offers to the Pharisees does not necessitate that the lawyers are also Pharisees. An inhabitant of the same village is obliged to defend another community member from an affront by a stranger. So the lawyer, according to cultural standards, would be obligated to respond to Jesus, even if the lawyer were a member of a rival group (which he is not). At the same time, it is a disgrace for several men to challenge one man. Therefore, instead of all the lawyers and Pharisees entering the fray, a single lawyer responds to Jesus, and he still uses a title of respect. Both the Pharisees and lawyers are seeking to maintain their honor. *It is up to Jesus and the narrator to unmask them for the reader.* Thus the narrative makes some connection between the Pharisees and the scribes, but the lawyer's response to Jesus also necessitates some social distinction: he must clarify that in denouncing the Pharisees Jesus dishonors lawyers *also*. Indirect presentation portrays the lawyers as distinct in some way.

Jesus' first woe against the lawyers, uttered in response to the lawyer's remonstrance (11:46), is an echo of the first woe against the Pharisees (11:42). The lawyers load people down with burdens (i.e., minute stipulations derived from Mosaic law), but "do not touch the burdens with one of [their] fingers" (11:46). The implication seems to be not that the lawyers neglect to follow their own prescriptions, but that those prescriptions are an inordinate burden upon others, and the lawyers do not care enough to help them (cf. Moxnes 1988:105–126; Fitzmyer: 945–951; Danker: 241). The second woe, however, takes a much harsher tone than any of the woes against the Pharisees. This second woe against the lawyers—like the third woe against the Pharisees—does not label them directly, but the intended addressees are quite clearly the lawyers. The lawyers "build the tombs of the prophets" (more evidence of only "external piety?") and thus consent to their ancestors' killing the prophets. The effect of this woe is devastating. The lawyers assent to the killing of the prophets, and, as the reader knows, "this generation," specifically the elders, chief priests, and scribes/lawyers, will reject and even kill the "Son of man" (9:22). Fresh in the reader's experience is the crucial reference to "this generation" in Luke 11:29–32. "This generation" will be condemned, because they did not believe in the one who was greater than Solomon and greater than Jonah. The "this generation" of Luke 11:51—which includes the lawyers—will also be responsible for killing prophets and apostles—and Jesus. The narrative later validates this specific accusation of being responsible for Jesus' death (e.g., Luke 19:47; 22:2; 23:10). The reader, though, already expects the connection between the scribes/lawyers and Jesus' death after reading the prophecy in Luke 9:22.

One final question concerning this woe remains: Are the Pharisees implicated by Jesus' accusation against the scribes about killing prophets, apostles, and Jesus? The Pharisees, of course, are often connected with the scribes, but the connection to the Pharisees is not strong enough to blame them also for the death of Jesus. The narrative always keeps the Pharisees separated from any threat to Jesus' life.[4] But the reader will not be (fully) aware of that fact until after reading all of Luke and Acts. The accusation is only directed against the scribes/lawyers (cf. Luke 9:22), but readers are also aware of some connections between the Pharisees and the scribes (e.g., 5:30; 11:45; 20:46). So the narrative heightens the readers' suspicions of the Pharisees—especially after Luke 11:53–54—but readers must wait for the unfolding drama of the narrative before they can render a more complete estimate of the Pharisees' complicity in the death of Jesus. The final conclusion from the Lukan narrator's point of view is that the Pharisees are not responsible for Jesus' death.

The third and final woe against the lawyers reflects the same type of immense irony found in the final woe against the Pharisees. The Pharisees who strive after purity, actually are unmarked graves who are impure and who impart impurity to others. And the lawyers/scribes/teachers of the law, who are so concerned about the knowledge of the law, have "taken away the key of knowledge." They themselves "did not enter" and

---

[4] The Pharisees' absence in the Passion narrative is striking. After Luke 19:39, where Jesus is nearing Jerusalem, the Pharisees disappear from the scene. As merely a matter of interest, I should note that the other Gospels depict a diminished role for the Pharisees, but their complete absence in the passion narrative of Luke is unique (cf. Mark 12:12–18; Matt. 21:45; 22:15, 34–41; 23:1–39; 27:62; John 18:3). The narrator of Acts also tries to avoid blaming the Pharisees directly for the death of Jesus and the later persecution of the church.

actually "hindered those who were entering" (11:52). This ignorance is intimately connected to the fact that the lawyers did not listen to the "Wisdom of God" (11:49).

Thus Jesus offers a devastating attack against Pharisees and lawyers in general, in effect authoritatively confirming the narrator's comment concerning them (7:30). Pharisees, because of their misplaced concern for purity, exploit people. Lawyers, because of their utter lack of knowledge concerning the Wisdom of God, lead people astray. The result is, as Moxnes noted: "Consequently, their claim to leadership is illegitimate" (1988:112). The result of Jesus' attack upon these two groups leads to a higher level of opposition to Jesus. The verb ἤρξαντο (11:53) and the adverb δεινῶς used in conjunction with ἐνέχω indicate the beginning of this heightened opposition that will continue through the narrative (Tannehill 1986:181; Moessner 1988:21–46; 1989:197, 216, 221). The raising of hostility is now a consistent pattern. Since a successive reading of any narrative involves consistency-building, anticipation, and retrospection, the reader now anticipates a higher plane of conflict and through retrospection can follow the crescendo of discord (see Resseguie, 1984:307–324).

One of the primary traits of the Lukan Pharisees, hypocrisy, provides the connecting link to the following pericope. The narrator noted the shift in spatial setting in 11:53 but does not clarify the change in temporal setting until 12:1. The myriads that "trampled on one another" amplify the situation encountered by the reader in 11:29: the opposition of the Pharisees and scribes greatly contrasts with the many thousands who come out to see Jesus. Thus far, Jesus has apparently found favor among the people. Jesus then warns the disciples to "beware of the yeast of the Pharisees." *Yeast*, of course, has a permeating influence whether for good or for evil, but the warning of Jesus (προσέχετε ἑαυτοῖς) includes the explanatory comment, ἥτις ἐστὶν ὑπόκρισις. Once again, the Pharisees serve as an example of what to avoid. What, then, are the failings of the Pharisees to be avoided? The rest of the narrative will expound several deficiencies apparent in Luke 11:37–54, which will serve as a helpful summary:

First, the Pharisees improperly interpret the Law (11:38, 42). In Luke 14:1, they watch Jesus to see if he would heal a man on the sabbath. They also continue to murmur against Jesus receiving sinners and eating with them (15:2). The dichotomy presented in Luke 7:29–30 is still quite evident: Luke 16:14–18 critiques the Pharisees, and here Jesus as a *prominent* can expound the law. The Pharisees, in their zeal for the law, ironically are opposing the purpose of God (7:30), whereas Jesus is fulfilling God's will.

Second, the Pharisees are rapacious and filled with avarice (11:39). What Luke 14:12–14 only implicitly demonstrates, Luke 16:14 makes explicit: the Pharisees are lovers of money (cf. 11:39–43). The narrator clearly establishes a principal trait of the Pharisees: they are primarily concerned with material goods. The parable of the Rich Man and Lazarus continues this theme. The rich man reflects φιλάργυροι, which, in turn, reflects the Pharisees. The Pharisees who lust for honor, purity, possessions, and social prominence will lose all of those things (16:14–31). Those persons, like the Pharisees who "serve . . . wealth" (16:11–14), become repugnant and unclean before God (βδέλυγμα; 16:15). The Pharisees are recalcitrant idolaters who worship material possessions, and their lack of concern for human beings correlates with their concern for wealth, a point made excruciatingly clear by the following parable. It seems that God's commandment to love one's neighbor is not compatible with striving after unrighteous mammon (Derrett: 80–82).

Third, since the Pharisees are filled with self-righteous pride, they love to exalt themselves over others (11:43). In Luke 14:1–14, Jesus again chastises the social elite for seeking after honor. The narrator explains that Jesus observed how the guests scrambled for "places of honor" (14:7). Thus the narrative again closely identifies the Pharisees with the desire for self-glorification. The suggestion that their tendency to self-advertisement has eternal consequences (ἔσχατον, 14:9–10; cf 14:11, 14) increases their negative rating even more. The narrative intimately connects such self-aggrandizement to a love of possessions and a disregard for the poor, as Jesus' words and parable illustrate (14:7–24). Instead, Jesus expects the Pharisees to participate in vertical generalized reciprocity, a redistribution from the advantaged to the disadvantaged. In Luke 16:14–15 the voices of both Jesus and the narrator once again connect the Pharisees' greed with their grasping after honor. After the narrator declares that the Pharisees were "lovers of money," Jesus' remark about the Pharisees' greed for public honor is almost an apodosis to the narrator's protasis about their love of money. The Pharisees' greed and lust for prominence intertwine even more closely because these two direct definitions come from two of the highest authorities in the narrative: Jesus and the narrator.

Thus when the narrator notes that Jesus told the parable of the Pharisee and the Toll Collector "to some who trusted in themselves that they were righteous and despised others" (18:9), the reader knows who is included in that description. This narrative aside has become a metonymical reference to the Pharisees (cf. 5:30; 6:6–11; 7:36–50; 11:37–12:1; 15:2; 16:15), and the alternating pattern of audiences from the disciples to the Pharisees in this section of the narrative also strongly suggests that the Pharisees are the audience here (see Johnson: 108;

Moessner 1989:212–214). The Pharisee of Jesus' parable can label "others" as extortioners (ἅρπαγες; 18:11), but the reader may manage a rueful smile at the Pharisee's pious words since Jesus has already declared that the Pharisees actually were the ones "full of extortion" (ἁρπαγῆς; 11:39). Thus the Pharisee's words in 18:11 are almost completely vacuous. Just as Luke 11:42–44 made the implicit connection between righteousness and pride (cf. 16:15), Luke 18:14 makes the same point. The exalted will be humbled, and the humbled will be exalted. Thus more of the Pharisees' failings coalesce: Tithing and fasting had set this Pharisee apart from others (18:11–12), but his lack of humble contrition set him apart from God. The Pharisees keep striving after honor, but become dishonorable; they continue to strive after purity, but paradoxically remain impure (cf. 11:42–44; see Moxnes 1988:125).

Fourth, the Pharisees have a deficient view of who Jesus is (11:38). Even Luke 13:31–35, which many commentators view as positive to the Pharisees (e.g., J. T. Sanders: 192; Brawley 1978:154; Fitzmyer: 1030; Tannehill 1986:178; Rese: 209–215; Arndt: 333–334; Tyson 1986:316–319; Schweizer: 229; Ziesler: 156), reveals this deficient perspective of the Pharisees. The reader cannot glean from the narrative itself whether the Pharisees *intended* to help Jesus, but their critical misunderstanding of Jesus is quite clear. The important point of this pericope is not whether the Pharisees have good or bad motives for warning Jesus; the overriding concern of the narrator is that the Pharisees have once again misunderstood the role and identity of Jesus. Even if the Pharisees have the best of intentions—and Luke 11:53–54 suggests otherwise—they do not understand that a prophet *must* suffer and die. Once again the Pharisees have fallen short (see Tiede: 71–72).

Luke 14:1–24 reinforces the Pharisees' opposition to Jesus: they continue to *watch him* (cf. 6:7; 11:54; 14:2). This watching becomes murmuring once again (15:2), and then develops into scorn (16:14): They scoff at Jesus (ἐξεμυκτήριζον; literally "turned up their noses"). They not only reject Jesus' message, they reject *him* (Johnson: 141). Jesus then notes that whatever is exalted among human beings is an abomination (βδέλυγμα) before God (16:15). Thus the converse of Luke 7:30 is now also true. In 7:30, the Pharisees rejected the purpose of God for themselves; now God does the rejecting. The Pharisees have not really obeyed the law or prophets, and, worst of all, they are opposing Jesus. They cannot even recognize that the kingdom of God is in their midst (17:20), even after the ten lepers were cleansed by Jesus (17:11–19; cf. 10:8–12; 11:20), and they continue in their errors (18:9–14).

Therefore, in the Gospel of Luke, the Pharisees are paradigmatic secondary characters whom the critical reader evaluates on the basis of

their response to Jesus and his message. They are narrative foils—
chameleons in reverse—who set off, contrast with, and dramatize Jesus,
and they represent those who do not adequately recognize Jesus' identity
or respond correctly to his message. The Pharisees in Luke, then, become
almost antitypes of Jesus and the disciples (Moxnes 1988:305). Jesus tries
to leave the door open to them ("give alms," Luke 11:41), but the
Pharisees ultimately reject his message.

Yet the portrait radically changes in Acts, a fact that I have delineated
elsewhere (Gowler 1991:274-317).[5] The Pharisees, in Luke and Acts, exist
in four subgroups that span the spectrum of responses to Jesus. Tensions
appear in the portraits in Luke and Acts because the Pharisees cannot be
forced into one simple category. Some reject Jesus completely (e.g., Luke
7:30; 16:14); others accept him totally (e.g., Acts 26:5). Others bridge the
chasm between those two positions (e.g., Acts 5:34-39; 15:5; 23:9). The
Pharisees play almost an intermediary role in Luke and Acts, and
therefore the critical reader does not lump them together with the other
Jewish leaders. The reader makes comparisons and contrasts, of course,
because the Pharisees are part of the Jewish leadership, but the narrative
leads the reader to distinguish the Pharisees' portrayal from the
characterization of the Jewish leadership as a whole. Even without the
evidence gleaned from Acts, Luke is singular among the Gospels for its
separation of the Pharisees from the other Jewish leaders. The separation
is not complete, but it is crucial.

Unfortunately, the portrait of the scribes (lawyers, teachers of the law)
is even more murky. One of the reasons for this vague portrayal is that
they are less important in the narrative than are the Pharisees. They are
plot functionaries who perform at least two purposes in Luke and Acts.
The scribes are regularly affiliated with the elders and chief priests who
plot the death of Jesus (9:22; 20:1, 19; 22:2, 66; 23:10; Acts 4:5-12; cf. 6:12).
Scribes are also sometimes connected to the Pharisees (5:21, 30; 6:7; 11:53;
15:2; Acts 23:9) in order to highlight the Pharisees' deficient view of the
law and the resulting flawed purity system. Yet the scribes are never
associated *at the same time* with the Pharisees on the one hand and the
chief priests and elders on the other (see J. T. Sanders: 20-21; cf. Tyson
1978:147-148).

---

[5] This difference, in a sequel that continues the same story line, should not be
surprising. Other ancient literature manifests similar changes; sometimes even a
protagonist in a completely unified narrative changes (abruptly) or develops. The
main character in Sophocles's *Antigone*, for example, changes dramatically, with very
little warning given to the audience (see Gowler 1991:94-103).

CONCLUSION: CULTURAL CODES AND THE NARRATOR'S STRATEGY

The narrator of Luke uses many characterization strategies, some of which become more intelligible when viewed through a cultural-anthropological lens and a literary-critical framework. Literarily, the technique is a straightforward reversal of expectations. The narrator expects the narratee to bring to the text a certain repertoire of knowledge, which may be literary, cultural, historical, and so on. In Luke 11:37–54 and many other places (e.g., Luke 7:36–50), the narrator places familiar elements into unfamiliar territory and expects the narratee to reassemble those elements into new configurations. The narrator seeks to make the familiar seem strange, that is, to defamiliarize norms. The critic's job, then, is to analyze what norms, conventions, and values are dismantled by the text and to ask why the text does so (see Resseguie 1991:138). In this instance, the narrator creatively rejects the cultural expectations of hospitality (which include honor and purity concerns) to illustrate the new system of purity, honor, and virtue that replaces the purity system of the scribes and Pharisees.

This literary strategy, therefore, reveals a most interesting cultural strategy: The narrator uses the apparently shameful action of violating hospitality codes—Jesus' berating of the host and other guests—to enhance Jesus' stature in the eyes of the reader. The Jewish cultural setting of Luke's narrative world actually enculturated a disposition to regard such offenses against the social order as exceptionally deviant. Jesus' actions are clearly shameful according to societal standards. One prime example of this social indifference is that Jesus acts outside of his inherited social role, something that the elite of Luke's narrative world define as shameful (Malina and Neyrey 1991:27). But the narrative declares—through the honorific titles attributed to Jesus, for example—that his activities are actually honorable. For the narrator, Jesus' deviant actions are honorable, simply because he as *Lord* performs them. The goal of the narrator's strategy is to inculcate this ideological point of view in the readers.

So in one sense, the narrator portrays Jesus as shattering cultural expectations and rejecting certain social responsibilities (e.g., see also Luke 9:59–60). To illustrate what is occurring culturally, it is helpful to compare the cultural implications of the actions of the Lukan Jesus with the cultural dynamics found in various stories about the Cynics:

> The "shamelessness" with which the Cynics attacked convention was celebrated in stories and pithy sayings, especially of Diogenes. In a society where honor and shame were the constant sanctions for guarding acceptable behavior, some of the actions attributed to Diogenes were so outrageous that

Cynicism might seem determined to undermine the whole social order (Meeks:54–55).

It is not surprising that some Jews (in Acts) accuse Christians of "turning the world upside down" (17:6). The narratives of Luke and Acts portray Jesus and his followers as seeking to transform their entire social order. Diogenes—respected by some; ridiculed by others—rejected his society's purity system and other norms, but offered little or nothing to replace them. Jesus' words and actions in Luke reflect a more serious situation. The Lukan Jesus offers a new system by which to live, a reordering of priorities. In addition, the narrator's claim that Jesus is Lord necessitates a higher level of ideological pressure on the reader that is not found in stories about Diogenes.

I submit that Luke 11:37–54 is a confrontation not only between Jesus and the scribes and Pharisees, but also between Jesus' revolutionary understanding of purity/virtue and the purity system of the specifically Jewish culture of the Lukan scribes and Pharisees. This clash takes place in the reflective context of hospitality, which graphically illustrates societal norms of purity and honor that Jesus seeks to transform. Note how the narrator defends the purity of Jesus, even when Jesus crosses the Pharisees' purity/impurity boundaries. In fact, Jesus remains a figure of unsurpassed holiness: holy in pedigree (e.g., 1:5–6, 27; 2:4; 3:23, 31–32), observances (e.g., 2:21–24, 41; 4:16, 33; 19:45–47), and evaluations by reliable characters (e.g., 1:35; 2:11, 25–32, 38; 3:22). Therefore, the narrator sincerely classifies Jesus as an insider, although a reforming insider (Neyrey 1991:289–291). To further this point, the narrator portrays Jesus as not only unaffected by contact with impurity, but Jesus actually imparts purity and wholeness to the impure. As a limit breaker Jesus possesses the authority to cross boundaries of purity/impurity, and he can also invest others with that power to cross purity boundaries. For example, the exhortation to give alms implies Jesus' belief that such vertical generalized reciprocity would generate purity. Ironically, according to the scribes and Pharisees' purity regulations, if you offer alms from the inside of an impure vessel, then the alms you give become impure. The result is that you transfer impurity to the receiver of the alms. Yet Jesus proclaims that giving alms has the same effect as ritually cleansing that impure vessel. In other words, Jesus transposes the question of ritual purity into the wider spectrum of moral behavior. He interiorizes the purity code, and in that context can declare that true purity/virtue is antithetical to rapacity and the other vices of the scribes and Pharisees (see Salo: 121–122). Jesus and his followers, obeying the dictates of God and the Holy Spirit, initiate a modified purity system based on a new set of inner values (Neyrey 1991:294).

Persons of social prominence, notably the scribes and Pharisees, reject Jesus' interiorized purity system and designate Jesus as a *deviant*. The portrayal of Jesus in Luke, however, exhibits Jesus as in fact a *limit-breaker* and a *prominent*. In Luke 11:37–54, those persons who have prominence in society dictate the terms of the encounter in a hospitality framework of testing a stranger, but the narrator vividly portrays the Pharisees and scribes being bested by Jesus. They fail in their roles as brokers because they actually block access to God, instead of facilitating it. They are the true deviants, according to the narrator. The reader who identifies with the narrator's ideological point of view will also identify with Jesus, the hero of the story. Thus, because of the narrative's characterization of Jesus and his opponents, when Jesus defies cultural expectations, even one so dear as the law of hospitality, the reader happily goes along.

Perhaps I can illustrate this cultural dynamic with the quotes listed at the beginning of this article. Note how the chreiai concerning Augustus (Macrobius, *Saturnalia* 2.4.13) and Julius Caesar (Plutarch, *Caesar* 17.9–10; see also Suetonius, *Lives* 1.53.1) support and reinforce cultural expectations of hospitality. Even the cultural maverick Diogenes, who graphically violated cultural norms in almost every area of life, demands to be treated with honor and respect in the setting of hospitality (see Diogenes Laertius, *Lives* 6.34; 6.46). Those persons who disregard hospitality laws must either suffer rebuke as deviants (e.g., Plutarch, *Caesar* 17.9–10), or, because of their roles as prominents, transcend those cultural expectations. Both of these latter things occur in Luke's narrative: Jesus rebukes Simon the Pharisee because Simon neglects to honor Jesus appropriately (Luke 7:36–50), and Jesus himself can violate hospitality laws because of his status as a prominent (Luke 11:37–54; 14:1–24).

Other cultural codes reinforce this image of Jesus as a limit breaker and prominent. For example, Jesus' verbal lances easily win the honor/shame debate. A more important aspect of this verbal jousting, however, is the content of that debate. The crucial element is that the Lukan Jesus modifies the purity system to include what could be called a *virtue code*. Jesus challenges a specific cultural code of Jewish society (i.e., purity) and responds with a virtue code (i.e., a purity code based on inner virtue). In Jesus' new purity/virtue system, actions are laudable because of the internal motivations behind them: justice and the love of God (cf. Luke 10:25–37). In other words, Jesus appeals to these higher virtues (and condemns moral vices) that are more significant in the cultural contexts of the greater Mediterranean area.

These concerns about inner moral virtues and vices are prevalent in much ancient literature, both Jewish and Greco-Roman. Plutarch, for example, noted that a change in external lifestyle does not relieve the soul of its anxieties (*A Tranquil Life*, 466c). In addition, pride and avarice, the vices that the Lukan Jesus denounces in the Pharisees, are universally condemned in ancient literature. The discussion of Dio Chrysostrom, for example, is especially interesting. Dio claimed that "roughly speaking," there were three prevailing types of lives which the majority adopt: (1) luxurious and self-indulgent; (2) acquisitive and avaricious; (3) one that loves honor and glory, deluding itself into believing that it is enamored of some noble ideal (*Discourses*, 4.83–84). Dio later notes that "very often two or all of them get hold of the same individual" (4.133). Dio's answer to these problems comes through "heavenly instruction," where one, especially a king, should actively work to achieve virtue. Dio defines virtue as concern and service for others, not being a "slave of glory" (see 4.29; 4.42; 4.60–100, especially 4.89–90).

It is very clear that these higher virtues were intimately connected to the honor/shame framework of the ancient world. For example, the concept of honor, implicit in hospitality relationships, is to a large extent based on the cardinal virtues as defined by Aristotle and other Greek and Roman writers. In fact, Julio Caro Baroja claimed that the ideas of honor and shame were "furnished by the classical world" (83). Baroja overstates his case but correctly demonstrates the powerful influence that moral virtues (and vices) had on the cultural concepts of honor/shame and purity (note, for example, Dio Chrysostom's comments about πονερία, ἀρετή, and "rites of purification" in *Discourses* 4.89–90). This concept of ἀρετή greatly influenced Diaspora Judaism, especially in its relationship to the hellenistic world. Ἀρετή and δικαιοσύνη, for example, become almost synonymous in some Jewish literature (e.g., Wis. 8:7; see Bauernfeind:458).

The comparison of the cultural dynamics of Luke 11:37–54 with other Jewish and Greco-Roman narratives is not merely an exercise in literary or anthropological acumen. Its importance lies in the fact that the Lukan narrative was written in a cultural milieu in which such conversations were taking place, and Luke naturally takes part in that dialogical social discourse (see Bakhtin: 259–422). The reader of Luke therefore produces meaning, but only by participating in a complex of socially constructed practices with which the text inherently interacts (see McLaughlin:6). More specifically, in Luke 11:37–54, Jesus utilizes these higher moral virtues of justice and the love of God to redefine the Jewish concept of purity (in Luke), that is, to transform one form of the Jewish purity system into another more acceptable to the broader hellenistic cultures.

In sum, the implications of this article lead to a three-fold closing plea. First, narrative critics must recognize the inherent nature of the various social, cultural, political, ideological, and economic codes in these narratives and should begin to take their literary importance more seriously.

Many literary critics, for example, realize that literary study can be "the servant of cultural understanding" (Greenblatt: 227). Second, those scholars who analyze the cultural environments of these texts must take them more seriously as narratives. Both literary criticism and social-scientific approaches have much to learn from one another and ought to utilize each other's invaluable contributions. As Stephen Greenblatt correctly stated:

> Eventually, a full cultural analysis will need to push beyond the boundaries of the text, to establish links between the text and values, institutions, and practices elsewhere in the culture. But these links cannot be a substitute for close reading. Cultural analysis has much to learn from scrupulous formal analysis of literary texts because those texts are not merely cultural by virtue of reference to the world beyond themselves; they are cultural by virtue of social values and contexts that they themselves successfully absorbed (226–227).

Finally, both literary analysis and cultural analysis also should continue to explore other ancient narratives, both Jewish and Greco-Roman, in order to learn more about first-century literary and cultural conventions. A critical reader ought to be more aware of the numerous and diverse webs of signification in any narrative. Socio-narratological criticism provides an interdisciplinary approach that weaves these various narrative and cultural threads together. Only a merger of narrative-critical, anthropological, and other approaches can facilitate the profound stylistic, artistic, and ideological perspicacity that we need for dialogue with these texts. The texts themselves inherently request that dialogue.

WORKS CONSULTED

Abou-Zeid, Ahmed
    1966   "Honour and Shame Among the Bedouins of Egypt." Pp. 243–260 in *Honour and Shame: The Values of Mediterranean Society*. Ed. J. G. Peristiany. Chicago: University of Chicago Press.

Alter, Robert
    1981   *The Art of Biblical Narrative*. New York: Basic Books.

Anderson, Janice Capel
    1985   "Double and Triple Stories, the Implied Reader, and Redundancy in Matthew." *Semeia* 31:71–89.

Arndt, William F.
    1956   *Luke*. St. Louis: Concordia Publishing House.

Aune, David E.
- 1978 "Septum sapientium convivium." Pp. 51–105 in *Plutarch's Ethical Writings and Early Christian Literature*. Ed. Hans Dieter Betz. Leiden: E. J. Brill.
- 1987 *The New Testament in its Literary Environment*. Philadelphia: Westminster.

Bakhtin, Mikhail
- 1981 *The Dialogic Imagination*. Austin: University of Texas Press.

Baroja, Julio Caro
- 1966 "Honour and Shame: A Historical Account of Several Conflicts." Pp. 79–138 in *Honour and Shame: The Values of Mediterranean Society*. Ed. J. G. Peristiany. Chicago: University of Chicago Press.

Bauer, Walter
- 1979 *A Greek-English Lexicon of the New Testament and Other Early Christian Literature*. 2nd ed. Chicago: University of Chicago Press.

Bauernfeind, Otto
- 1964 "ἀρετή." Pp. 457–461 in *TDNT*. Vol 1. Grand Rapids: Eerdmans.

Bertram, Georg
- 1974 "ἄφρων." Pp. 220–235 in *TDNT*. Vol 9. Grand Rapids: Eerdmans.

Bourdieu, Pierre
- 1966 "The Sentiment of Honour in Kabyle Society." Pp. 191–242 in *Honour and Shame: The Values of Mediterranean Society*. Ed. J. G. Peristiany. Chicago: University of Chicago Press.

Brawley, Robert L.
- 1978 "The Pharisees in Luke-Acts: Luke's Address to the Jews and His Irenic Purpose." Ph.D. dissertation, Princeton Theological Seminary.
- 1988 *Luke-Acts and the Jews: Conflict, Apology, and Conciliation*. Atlanta: Scholars.

Büchsel, Friedrich
- 1965 "κρίσις." Pp. 941–942 in *TDNT*. Vol. 3. Grand Rapids: Eerdmans.

Bultmann, Rudolf
- 1963 *The History of the Synoptic Tradition*. Trans. J. Marsh. New York: Harper.

Carroll, John T.
- 1988 "Luke's Portrayal of the Pharisees." *CBQ* 50:604–621.

Crossan, John Dominic
- 1983 *In Fragments: The Aphorisms of Jesus*. San Francisco: Harper & Row.

Culpepper, R. Alan
- 1983 *Anatomy of the Fourth Gospel: A Study in Literary Design*. Philadelphia: Fortress.

Danker, Frederick W.
- 1988 *Jesus and the New Age*. Philadelphia: Fortress.

Darr, John A.
1987 "'Glorified in the Presence of Kings': A Literary-Critical Study of Herod the Tetrarch in Luke-Acts." Ph.D. dissertation, Vanderbilt University.
1992 *On Building Character: The Reader and the Rhetoric of Characterization in Luke-Acts*. Louisville: Westminster/John Knox.

Davis, John
1977 *The People of the Mediterranean: An Essay In Comparative Social Anthropology*. London: Routledge and Kegan Paul.

Denaux, A.
1973 "L'hypocrisie des Pharisiens et le dessein de Dieu: Analyse de Lc., XIII, 31–33." Pp. 245–285 in *L'Évangile de Luc: Problèmes littéraires et théologiques*. Ed. F. Neirynck. Gembloux: J. Duculot.

Docherty, Thomas
1983 *Reading (Absent) Character: Towards a Theory of Characterization in Fiction*. New York: Oxford University Press.

Easton, B. S.
1926 *The Gospel According to St. Luke*. New York: Charles Scribner's Sons.

Edwards, O. C., Jr.
1981 *Luke's Story of Jesus*. Philadelphia: Fortress.

Eisenstadt, S. N. and L. Roniger
1984 *Patrons, Clients, and Friends*. Cambridge: Cambridge University Press.

Ellis, E. Earle
1981 *The Gospel of Luke*. The Century Bible, 2nd ed. Grand Rapids: Eerdmans.

Esler, Philip
1987 *Community and Gospel in Luke-Acts: The Social and Political Motivations of Lucan Theology*. Cambridge: Cambridge University Press.

Fitzmyer, Joseph A.
1981/5 *The Gospel According to Luke*. The Anchor Bible, 28 & 28A. Garden City: Doubleday.

Flaubert, Gustave
1857 *Madame Bovary*. Trans. Eleanor Marx-Aveling. Rpt. 1968. New York: Franklin Watts.

Fowler, Robert M.
1991 *Let the Reader Understand: Reader-Response Criticism and the Gospel of Mark*. Minneapolis: Augsburg Fortress.

Garrett, Susan
1989 *The Demise of the Devil: Magic and the Demonic in Luke's Writings*. Minneapolis: Augsburg Fortress.

Gilmore, David
1982 "Anthropology of the Mediterranean Area." *Annual Review of Anthropology* 11:175–205.

Gowler, David B.
   1989   "Characterization in Luke: A Socio-Narratological Approach." *BTB* 19:54–62.
   1991   *Host, Guest, Enemy, and Friend: Portraits of the Pharisees in Luke and Acts.* New York: Peter Lang.

Greenblatt, Stephen
   1990   "Culture." Pp. 225–232 in *Critical Terms for Literary Study*. Ed. Frank Lentricchia and Thomas McLaughlin. Chicago: University of Chicago Press.

Herzfeld, Michael
   1987   "'As in Your Own House': Hospitality, Ethnography, and the Stereotype of Mediterranean Society." Pp. 75–89 in *Honor and Shame and the Unity of the Mediterranean*. Ed. David D. Gilmore. Washington, D.C.: American Anthropological Society.

Hock, Ronald F. and Edward N. O'Neil
   1986   *The Chreia in Ancient Rhetoric. Volume I. The Progymnasmata.* Atlanta: Scholars.

Johnson, Luke T.
   1977   *The Literary Function of Possessions in Luke-Acts.* SBLDS 39. Missoula: Scholars.

Kennedy, George A.
   1984   *New Testament Interpretation through Rhetorical Criticism.* Chapel Hill and London: University of North Carolina Press.

Lanser, Susan
   1981   *The Narrative Act: Point of View in Prose Fiction.* Princeton: Princeton University Press.

Mack, Burton L.
   1990   *Rhetoric and the New Testament.* Minneapolis: Augsburg Fortress.

Mack, Burton L. and Vernon K. Robbins
   1989   *Patterns of Persuasion in the Gospels.* Sonoma, CA: Polebridge.

McLaughlin, Thomas
   1990   "Introduction." Pp. 1–8 in *Critical Terms for Literary Study*. Ed. Frank Lentricchia and Thomas McLaughlin. Chicago: University of Chicago Press. .

McMahan, Craig
   1987   "Meals as Type-Scenes in the Gospel of Luke." Ph.D. dissertation, The Southern Baptist Theological Seminary.

Malina, Bruce J.
   1981   *The New Testament World: Insights from Cultural Anthropology.* Atlanta: John Knox.
   1986a   *Christian Origins and Cultural Anthropology: Practical Models for Biblical Interpretation.* Atlanta: John Knox.

1986b   "The Received View and What It Cannot Do: III John and Hospitality." *Semeia* 35:171–194.
1988a   "A Conflict Approach to Mark 7:1-23." *Forum* 4/3:3–30.
1988b   "Patron and Client: The Analogy Behind Synoptic Theology." *Forum* 4/1:2–32.

Malina, Bruce and Jerome Neyrey
- 1988   *Calling Jesus Names: The Social Value of Labels in Matthew*. Sonoma, CA: Polebridge.
- 1991a   "Conflict in Luke-Acts: Labelling and Deviance Theory." Pp. 97–122 in *The Social World of Luke-Acts*. Ed. Jerome H. Neyrey. Peabody, MS: Hendrickson.
- 1991b   "Honor and Shame in Luke-Acts: Pivotal Values of the Mediterranean World." Pp. 25–65 in *The Social World of Luke-Acts*. Ed. Jerome H. Neyrey. Peabody, MS: Hendrickson.

Marshall, I. Howard
- 1978   *Commentary on Luke*. Grand Rapids: Eerdmans.

Meeks, Wayne A.
- 1986   *The Moral World of the First Christians*. Philadelphia: Westminster.

Moessner, David P.
- 1988   "The Leaven of the Pharisees." *JSNT* 34:21–46.
- 1989   *Lord of the Banquet*. Minneapolis: Augsburg Fortress.

Moxnes, Halvor
- 1986/7   "Meals and the New Community in Luke." *Svensk exegetisk årsbok* 51/52:158–167.
- 1988   *The Economy of the Kingdom: Social Conflict and Economic Relations in Luke's Gospel*. Philadelphia: Fortress.

Neusner, Jacob
- 1976   "'`First Cleanse the Inside': The `Halakhic' Background of a Controversy Saying." *NTS* 22:486–495.

Neyrey, Jerome
- 1986   "The Idea of Purity in Mark's Gospel." *Semeia* 35:91–128.
- 1988   "A Symbolic Approach to Mark 7." *Forum* 4/3:63–91.
- 1991a   "Ceremonies in Luke-Acts: The Case of Meals and Table-Fellowship." Pp. 361–387 in *The Social World of Luke-Acts*. Ed. Jerome H. Neyrey. Peabody, MS: Hendrickson.
- 1991b   "The Symbolic Universe of Luke-Acts: `They Turn the World Upside Down.'" Pp. 271–304 in *The Social World of Luke-Acts*. Ed. Jerome H. Neyrey. Peabody, MS: Hendrickson.

Pinal-Cabral, João de
- 1989   "The Mediterranean as a Category of Regional Comparison: A Critical View." *Current Anthropology* 30:399–406.

Pitt-Rivers, Julian
    1968   "The Stranger, the Guest and the Hostile Host: Introduction to the Study of the Laws of Hospitality." Pp. 13–30 in *Contributions to Mediterranean Sociology*. Ed. J. G. Peristiany. Paris: Mouton.

Rese, Martin
    1975   "Einige Überlegungen zu Lukas XIII, 31–33." In *Jésus aux origines de la christologie*. Ed. Jacques Dupont. Leuven: Leuven University Press.

Resseguie, James
    1982   "Point of View in the Central Section of Luke (9:51–19:44)." *JES* 25/1:41–47.
    1984   "Reader Response Criticism and the Synoptic Gospels." *JAAR* 52:307–324.
    1991   "Automatization and Defamiliarization in Luke 7:36–50." *Journal of Literature & Theology* 5:137–150.

Rimmon-Kenan, Shlomith
    1983   *Narrative Fiction: Contemporary Poetics*. New York: Methuen & Co.

Robbins, Vernon K.
    1984/92   *Jesus the Teacher: A Socio-Rhetorical Interpretation of Mark*. Philadelphia: Fortress.
    1984b   "A Rhetorical Typology for Classifying and Analyzing Pronouncement Stories." Pp. 93–122 in SBLSP. Ed. Kent Richards. Chico, CA: Scholars.
    1988a   "The Chreia." Pp. 1–23 in *Greco-Roman Literature and the New Testament*. Ed. David E. Aune. Atlanta: Scholars.
    1988b   "Pronouncement Stories from a Rhetorical Perspective." *Forum* 4/2:3–32.
    1989   *Ancient Quotes and Anecdotes*. Sonoma, CA: Polebridge.

Salo, Kalervo
    1991   "Luke's Treatment of the Law: A Redaction-Critical Investigation." Helsinki: Suomalainen Tiedeakatemia.

Sanders, E. P.
    1990   *Jewish Law from Jesus to the Mishnah: 5 Studies*. Philadelphia: Trinity International.

Sanders, Jack T.
    1987   *The Jews in Luke-Acts*. Philadelphia: Fortress.

Schweizer, Eduard
    1984   *The Good News According to Luke*. Trans. David Green. Atlanta: John Knox.

Shuler, Philip
    1982   *A Genre for the Gospels*. Philadelphia: Fortress.

Smith, David
    1985   "Jesus and the Pharisees in Socio-Anthropological Perspective." *Trinity Journal* 6ns:151–166.

Steele, E. Springs
    1981   "Jesus' Table Fellowship with Pharisees: An Editorial Analysis of Luke 7:36–50, 11:37–54, and 14:1–24." Ph.D. dissertation, University of Notre Dame.
    1984   "Luke 11:37–54: A Modified Hellenistic Symposium?" *JBL* 103:379–394.

Sternberg, Meir
    1978   *Expositional Modes and Temporal Ordering in Fiction*. Baltimore: Johns Hopkins University Press.

Tannehill, Robert
    1980   "Synoptic Pronouncement Stories: Form and Function." Pp. 51–56 in *SBL 1980 Seminar Papers*. Ed. Paul Achtemeier. Chico, CA: Scholars.
    1981   "Varieties of Synoptic Pronouncement Stories." *Semeia* 20:101–119.
    1986   *The Narrative Unity of Luke-Acts*. Philadelphia: Fortress.

Tiede, David L.
    1980   *Prophecy and History in Luke-Acts*. Philadelphia: Fortress.

Tyson, Joseph
    1978   "The Opposition to Jesus in the Gospel of Luke." *PRS* 5:144–150.
    1986   *The Death of Jesus in Luke-Acts*. Columbia, SC: University of South Carolina Press.

Uspensky, Boris
    1973   *A Poetics of Composition: The Structure of the Artistic Text and Typology of a Compositional Form*. Trans. Valentina Zavarin and Susan Wittig. Berkeley: University of California Press.

Wilson, Rawdon
    1979   "The Bright Chimera: Character as a Literary Term." *Critical Inquiry* 5:725–749.

Windisch, Hans
    1964   "ἀσπάζομαι." Pp. 496–502 in *TDNT*. Vol. 1. Grand Rapids: Eerdmans.

Ziesler, J. A.
    1978   "Luke and the Pharisees." *NTS* 25:146–157.

Cursing Fig Trees and Robbers' Dens
Pronouncement Stories Within Social-Systemic Perspective
Mark 11:12-25 and Parallels

Douglas E. Oakman
Pacific Lutheran University

ABSTRACT

This essay argues that within its originating social system, the early Jesus tradition maintained a fairly consistent focus: The "what" of its pronouncements had to do with interest in the emergence of a new material order, symbolized under the umbrella concept "kingdom of God." The "why" of Jesus tradition pronouncements was given by institutions of the old order that blocked the coming of the kingdom.

Recent social science approaches to the New Testament, continuing and deepening older conceptions of historical and form criticism, have stressed that texts require social context for interpretation. These approaches have argued that grasping the meaning of biblical texts requires an understanding of the social system or world in which they originated (Malina, 1981; Elliott, 1986; Neyrey, 1991). The present essay explores the social dynamics behind pronouncement within the early Jesus tradition and proposes a cluster of interrelated interpretations for the Cursing of the Fig Tree/Cleansing of the Temple stories that depend upon an understanding of the social system encompassing Jesus and much of the Jesus tradition up until Mark's time.[1] The reader is urged to appreciate the importance of the social system for understanding crucial dimensions of the two stories. The "selectivity" of the tradition regarding what kind of saying would be associated with a situation, especially while the tradition was in Palestine, was governed to a significant degree by the experienced social system of the tradition's originating society (the cases

---

[1] In this essay, "Jesus" is often used interchangeably with "early Jesus tradition" without prejudice to deciding the historical questions. Likewise, "redaction" may imply "composition" without prejudice to tradition critical decisions. "Jesus tradition" and "tradition" can also be used synonymously.

of Q, Mark, early Johannine tradition).[2] As the tradition moved away from the society of origin (Matthew [in part], Luke, Johannine redactor[s]), the stories could be reworked, condensed, or even eliminated.

In each instance, a literary analysis of the texts is an essential preliminary for understanding pronouncement in social-systemic perspective. In this analysis, some sense needs to be gained of the formal structure of the units, as well as of the relation between tradition and composition or redaction. Important questions for the present essay are: Are pronouncement stories purely arbitrary creations at the stage of composition? Are they arbitrarily reformulated within early tradition? Or can some understanding of the shaping and meaning of pronouncements be gained by attention to social system? Does social system play a significant role in what pronouncements are made, and why?

THE FIG TREE EPISODE AND APPENDIX

Mark 11:12-14 and Matthew 21:18-19 constitute the only Jesus traditions about the Cursing of the Fig Tree. There is a similarity between these two stories and Luke's parable about a fig tree (Luke 13:6-9). Elsewhere, fig leaves are known to herald summer's arrival (Mark 13:28). Nathaniel is marked as an Israelite by reference to a fig tree (John 1:48). Fig trees were long associated with peace and safety in Israelite tradition.[3]

In Mark, furthermore, the Cursing episode receives an Appendix (20-25) which adds a series of sayings of Jesus in response to the withered fig tree. Matthew retains the Marcan Appendix as an *immediate* response of disciples and Jesus to the immediate withering of the fig tree. The withering is only implied in Mark and separated from the Cursing by the Temple "Cleansing." Moreover, Matthew's version of the Appendix contains only three of Mark's four sayings. Matthew has the fourth saying in the Sermon on the Mount (Matt 6:14-15).

An analysis of the structure of the Fig Tree episode reveals a root similarity between the Marcan and Matthean versions. In each case, the main verbs (indicative mood, aorist tense) trace out a first-order structure

---

[2] The metaphors of "selectivity" and "resonance" (used at various points of this essay) are borrowed from the realm of radio reception. Resonance is the property in tuning circuits that allows a radio to receive a station at a precise frequency; the circuits oscillate, are resonant, at that frequency only. A receiver with high selectivity can separate and clearly distinguish stations close together on the broadcast spectrum. High selectivity implies a pickiness with respect to what is received. It is argued in this paper that the early Jesus tradition analogously was resonant to certain concerns and was picky about what it passed on. Later stages of the tradition proved resonant and selective in other ways in response to new social settings.

[3] Micah 4:4; Zechariah 3:10; 1 Macc 14:12; see Hunzinger, 1971: 752.

and likely delineate the common tradition. Around this first-order structure, subordinate clauses make clear a second-order structure, far more influenced by redaction. When these two orders of the structure are seen, the unique aspects of each redaction stand out.

The primary-order structure becomes clear from the following table of the main Greek verbs:

	Mark 11		Matthew 21
12	ἐπείνασεν	18	ἐπείνασεν
13	ἦλθεν	19	ἦλθεν
	οὐδὲν εὗρεν		οὐδὲν εὗρεν
	(οὐκ ἦν)		(—)
14	εἶπεν		λέγει
	(ἤκουον [disciples subj.])		ἐξηράνθη [tree subject]

The basic skeleton outlined by the main Greek verbs is striking: Jesus hungered, came, found nothing, said (Matt: says). This structure seems anchored in the tradition, especially when it is noted that in the Lukan near-parallel, a similar structure inheres in the Fig Tree Parable: The owner of the vineyard came (seeking fruit on the fig tree), he did not find, he said.

At the end of the Cursing pericope, the divergence is equally striking in suggesting redactional influences. Mark has the disciples listening to Jesus. This is a theme consistent with the Marcan redaction (e.g. Mark 4:3, 9; 9:7). Matthew, by contrast, emphasizes the immediate effect of Jesus' word of curse: The fig tree dries up! Elsewhere in Matthew, the immediate effect of Jesus' word is also brought out (e.g., Matt 8:13; 9:22).

It is likely, as Bultmann thought (1963: 218), that Matthew preserves the more original *form* of the Cursing story (while being selective about details). As the analysis shows, the traditional story ends with a pronouncement, the curse by Jesus. Since both Matthew and Mark have the Appendix, although in different configurations, Cursing - Appendix belonged together in the tradition. The Appendix, therefore, represents a development of the pronouncement that happened at a stage of the tradition prior to Mark.

The secondary-order differentiates quite distinctly the Marcan and Matthean redactions of this tradition. Three aspects are especially striking. First of all, Matthew 21:18a stresses the goal of Jesus' movement toward the πόλις (Jerusalem), while Mark notes (11:12) Jesus' departure out of the village Bethany. These characterizations localize the stories quite differently (especially in terms of the social system).

Secondly, the object of Jesus' sight in Matthew (v. 19) is the fig tree by the road; Mark's object (v. 13 ἔχουσαν φύλλα) is a fig tree in leaf. The motive for Jesus' approach to the fig tree is explained better by the Marcan tradition.

Thirdly, what Jesus says in each case is different. Matthew's version stresses the eternity of the curse. The emphatic οὐ μηκέτι ("never ever") is reinforced by the proximity of εἰς τὸν αἰῶνα ("forever") to the subjunctive verb. Mark's version does not say "never...forever"; rather, by keeping μηκέτι together with εἰς τὸν αἰῶνα, Mark stresses the validity of the curse only during the present "aeon" (consonant with Mark's consistent apocalyptic outlook on his times). Mark's weaker optative mood verb ("may no one eat"), suggests also that Mark did not understand the curse in as binding a manner as Matthew (consider Matt 18:18—unique to that gospel).

A final consideration relates to the well-known difficulty in Mark's Cursing story, v. 13b "for it was not the time for figs." This gloss disrupts the first-order structure completely and betrays its redactional origin. Furthermore, the word-order of the sentence is absolutely crucial for understanding its Marcan sense. A variant reading for this sentence attempted to move the adverb and verb to the sentence's beginning and to place καιρός together with σύκων.[4] The undoubtedly more difficult word order in the Nestle-Aland[26] text says something peculiarly Marcan when observed. The word καιρός, translated "time" or "season" here, appears five times in Mark, more than in any other New Testament writing. Mark 1:15 effectively marks this word as a synonym for "kingdom of God." Mark 10:10 contrasts the present καιρός with the future age. Similarly, Mark 13:33 refers to the return of the Son of man at an indefinite καιρός. The usage in Mark 12:2 seems to return to the mundane referent of harvest time. These usages should alert us to the importance for Mark of the present declaration. What this importance is can only be brought out by reference to the social system.

The Appendix, briefly, consists of a response by the disciples to what has happened to the fig tree. Jesus, in turn, responds to the disciples in the form of three (Matt)/four (Mark) sayings. In Mark, the catch-words "faith/believe" have contributed to the linking of the first three sayings, while "prayer" has led to the fourth addition. In Matthew's form of the tradition, the Appendix followed the Cursing immediately; Mark then is responsible for separating Appendix from Cursing and probably for linking the fourth saying (as its absence in Matthew suggests). Whether

---

[4] The described changes are present in A, C (second corrector), numerous other Greek manuscripts, and some versions.

there is a more compelling reason for the linkage of these sayings—in tradition or redaction—remains to be seen.

Cursing Fig Trees

As Figure 1 illustrates, when leaves were visible on a fig tree, fruit was normally present.[5] Jesus could reasonably expect to find fruit in various stages of ripeness on the tree. Viewed in this light, the statement of Mark 11:13b is utter foolishness *as a botanical statement*.[6] It is not necessarily foolishness as a social statement. This insight will need further exploration in a moment.

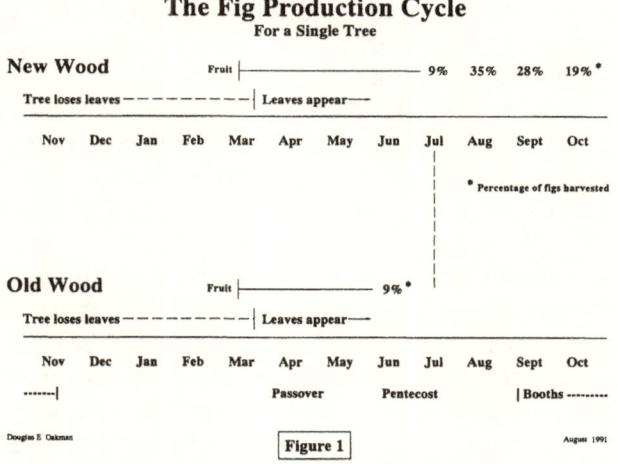

Figure 1

Because of the imagined botanical difficulties, the dating of the Cursing episode has long been discussed. Is this event to be associated with Jesus' entry into Jerusalem during the Feast of Tabernacles in the fall (Nineham 1963: 293)? In this case, Jesus would be seeking fruit roughly in the period September to October, before the leaves drop off for the winter (November). The fruit on the new wood, representing the major part of the fig harvest for the year, would be available at this time. Jewish peasants did not pick all of the fruit at once, since it was not all ripe at once (Hamel 1990: 10).

---

[5] Figure 1 was developed especially with the help of Childers: 489-496; Trevor 1962; and Hunzinger 1971. The chart represents the fig production per average year from one tree. The new wood produces in the fall the majority of the year's crop (roughly 90%). The old wood produces the early figs. Included for reference are the chief Greek and Hebrew words for these fruits and the major Jewish festivals.

[6] It has been suggested that Jesus held up unreasonable expectations for fruit based upon conditions in Galilee: Near Genesareth, fig trees bear ten months of the year (Jos. *War* 3.519; Billerbeck 1922: 857). This interpretive option seems unlikely, however, because in either locale leaves normally appear with the maturing figs.

The other dating option is to place the Cursing episode in the spring before Passover. Here the leaves would be just on the tree (appearing at the end of March). The early fruit, ready by late-May, would hardly be ripe, although some fruit from the previous season might be on the tree. Mark's comment has often been taken to imply such a date, if ὁ καιρός ("the season") means the late-summer fig harvest. Otherwise, Mark's comment can be referred to the June harvest of the early figs (on old wood).

In view of the previous assertion that the presence of leaves made it reasonable to expect fruit, a different line of inquiry seems warranted. The dating discussion, while important, overlooks a yet more important question: The question is not, *When* did Jesus not find fruit? but *Why* did Jesus not find fruit? Considering this story in the light of the social system, several interlocking answers emerge.

The Augustan Age and the Principate are frequently thought to have ushered in an era of peace and prosperity. It is true that Augustus brought to a conclusion the disastrous and disruptive civil strife (especially in the eastern provinces) of the late Republic. The *Pax Augusta* also encouraged commerce.[7]

Yet many citizens and subjects of the early Empire did not share in this prosperity and commerce. This is a social fact that must not be forgotten. The Herodian period in Palestine is illustrative of this fact. Herod the Great, by any standard, was a brutal dictator who established a police state, bled his subjects nearly to death through taxation, and established monuments to a prosperity shared only by the wealthy and powerful.[8]

Yet the social problem was not just the problem of a political regime that once gotten rid of would allow things to return to a more equitable arrangement. What emerged in Herodian Palestine was a systemic problem, which undoubtedly got its start earlier in the Hellenistic Period (Hengel 1974). Figure 2 outlines the general features of the social matrix in which the Jesus tradition took shape.[9] The features of most importance

---

[7] Koester has a useful summary in 1982: 322-336. See also Jeremias 1969: 31ff.

[8] Josephus on Herod in general: *AJ* 16.154. Police state: *AJ* 15.291, 295. Heavy taxation: *War* 2.84ff. Herod's building programs are well known, especially the expansion of the Temple complex that began in 20 BCE. See also Horsley and Hanson 1985: 66.

[9] The model has been developed with the help of modern comparative treatments of agrarian societies, especially that of Lenski, 1966. The vertical dimension of the model represents the relative power of various groups. The groups and institutional relationships are described more closely in the text. For a similar approach to the society of early Roman Palestine, see Saldarini, 1988.

A previous version of this model was presented in a paper delivered at the Social Sciences and New Testament Interpretation Section of the Society of Biblical Literature, New Orleans, 1990.

here are the consolidation of judicial power in the hands of the landlord-commercial class and their religious legitimation through alignment with (or identity as) those who controlled the Jerusalem Temple, the use of debt to enlarge landed estates, and the shift to cash cropping and tenancy agriculture.

The Judaean oligarchy in the early first century, ascendant over all Jews in Palestine, was comprised primarily of three groups, traditionally labelled by their religious views as Sadducees: The priestly upper crust (high priests and high priest) comprised of four major families (Boethus, Kathros, Hanin [Annas], and Phabi); village and town lay nobility tracing their lineage back to important families in Israel's past (elders); and the recorders and administrators of the system (scribes).[10] Members of the Herodian family and their adherents also played a part in the elite picture.

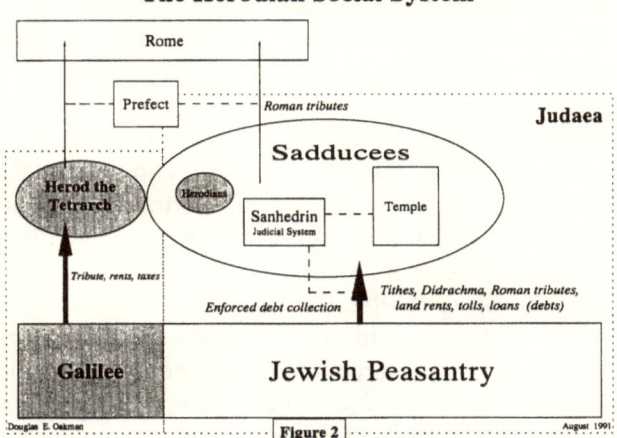

Figure 2

Palestinian Judaism at this time took the ancestral law traced back to Moses very seriously, although there were disagreements about what belonged to that law and how to interpret it. The supreme court of the land, the Sanhedrin, ultimately decided how especially the civil aspects of law were to be interpreted. Before 70 CE when the Temple was destroyed, this body was controlled by the previously described Judaean elite. The court rigorously backed creditors. A first century legal ruling attributed to Hillel reveals this quite clearly:

> [A loan secured by] a *prozbul* is not cancelled [by the Seventh Year].... This is the formula of the *prozbul*: 'I affirm to you, such-a-one and such-a-one, the judges in such-a-place, that, touching any debt due me, I will collect it whensoever I will.' (M. Sheb. 9:3-4; Danby, 51)

---

[10] The New Testament Gospels, especially Mark, know the Jewish elite triad, e.g. Mark 11:27. On the four major families, see T. Menahoth 13:21.

By placing debt contracts with the courts, the creditor could circumvent traditional Jewish law (e.g. Deut 15:2). Jacob Neusner sees as the effect of the *prozbul* the making of debt "a perpetual burden."[11]

Debt contracts enforced through court proceedings enlarged the estates of creditors. Their control of the Temple and of "sacred" debt records also contributed to growing agrarian problems. M. Shek. 1:3 relates that those unable to pay the Temple tax had to make pledges. Under such debt burdens, peasants lost their patrimonial land and became tenants on that same land (which now belonged to the creditor). Some peasants fought back as bandits. Hobsbawm's notion of social banditry is helpful in understanding the aspirations for justice of these groups (Horsley and Hanson 1985: 48). Agrarian factors played a significant role in the Jewish War at the end of this period (Kreissig 1969; Goodman 1982). These bitter changes can only be traced in the historical record with difficulty. Residents of the Judaean village of Bethar celebrated the downfall of the system in 70 CE, because patrimonial land was stolen from them through fraudulent contracts (Midrash Lam. R. 2.5 19; Applebaum 1977: 371).

Landlords of growing Palestinian estates understandably shifted their agricultural priorities from purely subsistence concerns to sharing in the commercial bonanza of the early Augustan period. Cash crops and other commercial agricultural investments would have grown in importance. Chief among commercial crops were wheat (primarily in local trade) and the grape and the olive (better for long distance trade because more portable as wine or oil). Nakdimon ben Gorion, Kalba Sabbua, and Ben Zizit Hakeset were remembered long after 70 CE as wholesalers who could supply the food needs of Jerusalem for ten years (Midrash Lam. R. 1; Applebaum 1976: 659, 687). Eleazar ben Harsum later controlled merchant ships, "but his family and his large estates go back to the pre-70 period" (Applebaum 1976: 689). These and similar merchants, who also controlled significant amounts of Palestinian land, would have played a significant role in determining agricultural production. While exact patterns are not known, there are indicators in the scanty historical record that crops of greater commercial significance were displacing subsistence crops in the pre-70 period. T. Menahoth 8:3 indicates that wine and grain were privileged in Judaea. Olives were cultivated everywhere (Jeremias 1969:45-46). M. Shekelim 7:4 attests to much livestock in the vicinity of Jerusalem that was used for sacrifices. According to Applebaum (1976: 651):

---

[11] Neusner 1973: 16. See also Applebaum 1976: 662. The difficulties of applying rabbinic traditions to the period before 70 CE are notorious. The approach in this essay is to accept only those that seem appropriate to the late-Second Temple epoch.

Although it belongs to the third century, R. Johanan's advice, 'Let your holdings be divided into three parts, a third grain, a third olives, and a third vines [b. Baba Metzia 107a],' would certainly have been accepted also in the first.

Fig cultivation was consequently of much less importance, since it was ordinarily a subsistence staple. Figs, for instance, remained a part of the marriage contract provisions for Jewish women (M. Ket. 5:8). Josephus (*War* 3:519) calls the fig the "royal fruit" along with the grape, but this is in reference to Galilee. While fig and vine figure prominently in the older Israelite tradition, Sirach already drops mention of the fig when mentioning olive and vine (Sirach 24:13-17). As Luke 13 clearly shows, keeping a fig tree bearing required a sizeable amount of care and labor. To the Palestinian Jew, the care required had become proverbial: "He who tends a fig tree will eat its fruit" (Proverbs 27:18). Commerce in figs was likely to be a purely local affair.[12] Early figs were offered as first-fruits at the Temple. Bethany and Bethphage were renowned for these (Avi-Yonah, 1977: 192). It is likely that fig orchards near Jerusalem belonged to estates of the oligarchy. Bethany may in fact have meant "house of Hino" or "house of Hanan," rather than "house of unripe figs" (Billerbeck 1922: 855-56). The Temple utilized fig wood for sacrifices, but significantly olive wood and the vine were not permitted (M. Tam. 2:3; Jeremias 1969: 50).

Luke 13, therefore, implies that a dramatic shift to tenancy agriculture was underway in early first century CE Palestine, and such a transition meant a shift away from subsistence agriculture to other crops; especially olives, grapes, and wheat; or to herding. Whether through neglect or through loss to specialized production, Judaean, and perhaps also Galilean, peasants were deprived of one of their staple crops. A rabbinic tradition implies that bearing fig trees were jealously watched by their owners.[13]

From this viewpoint, Jesus visits a fig tree that has gone to wood because of intention or neglect. The fig tree's barrenness again testifies to the shift in the agricultural priorities of the elites. By cursing the fig tree, Jesus in effect curses the social system that has led to its neglect. Understanding that fig trees might supply so much wood for the sacrificial fires, the Q word of John the Baptist (Luke 3:9) holds ominous overtones for the Temple elite!

If the fig tree were not neglected, Mark implies by, "for it was not the season for figs," that figs under ordinary circumstances could be expected from this tree. When the Jerusalem elite took all figs to the storehouse or

---

[12] Jeremias 1969: 46. Expensive figs were available in Jerusalem (M. Maas. 2:5).

[13] Y. Taan. 4.4; Hamel reproduces this text in translation and has a useful discussion. John 1:48 has important significance if it corroborates this fact.

to the local market, their policies resulted in an "artificial famine" of such staples.[14] Consequently, nothing was left for the peasant family or hungry passerby (consider the gleaning of Mark 2:23-28). Queen Helena had to provide Jerusalem with dried figs during the famine in the late forties CE (Jos. AJ 20.51; Jeremias 1969: 129). The elite storehouse was in permanent competition with peasant subsistence. Jesus' curse, typical of Galileans,[15] was occasioned by more than just the lack of figs on a fig tree.

Will the tree be barren forever? Answering this question depends upon how εἰς τὸν αἰῶνα is interpreted. Could this phrase anticipate Jesus' word at the Last Supper: "I will no longer drink of the fruit of the vineyard until that day when I drink it new in the kingdom of God" (Mark 14:25)? For Mark, the curse is effective in this aeon, not in the next. The fig tree will no longer benefit its self-aggrandizing owners. In the new aeon coming, they are out of business. At that καιρός, figs will be freely available for human consumption.

For Jesus, the grace of the kingdom of God is especially a material grace (Luke 12:22-32 = Q). The conclusion of the Cursing narrative brings this point out strongly. When Peter sees the withered fig tree (Mark 11:21), Jesus reminds him of God's faithfulness. While πίστις in Mark usually means the subjective faith of the disciple, in 11:22 another linguistic option is possible. Most versions translate v. 22b, "Have faith in God" (objective genitive stressing the act of the disciples' belief). The imperative verb form is ambiguous here; ἔχετε can also be indicative. The verse can equally well be translated, "You have God's pledge."[16] This reading would strengthen the foregoing interpretation. This much is probably Marcan redaction, for it recalls Jesus' previous statement that what is not possible for human beings is possible for God (Mark 10:27).

Is the referent of "this mountain" (11:23) in Mark's mind the Mount of Olives with its specialized arboriculture, or the Temple mount? In either case, Jesus' curse extends to the site of specialized production and the place of its sanctification/legitimation. God, in contrast to the current elite, is a faithful patron (vv. 23-24).[17] The new distributive order of God, which Jesus calls God's βασιλεία ("kingdom"), will provide adequate

---

[14] Note that the Jesus tradition knows this mentality: Matt 24:45. On famines, see MacMullen 1966: 249-254; Jeremias 1969: 140ff; Hamel 1990: 44ff.

[15] Galileans were renowned for their swearing: M. Ned. 5:5 and B. Ned. 48a. Mark documents this elsewhere: Mark 8:12, εἰ δοθήσεται, is strong enough to be translated, "I'll be damned if (a sign is given)." See further Klausner 1925: 231; Freyne 1980: 277; Goodman 1983: 99-100.

[16] On this meaning of the word πίστις see Moulton-Milligan 1980: 515; Acts 17:31.

[17] Malina (1988) investigates and explains this analogy in a very helpful way.

subsistence to the hungry and dishonored.[18] The final word of Jesus, which echoes the fifth petition of the Lord's Prayer, enjoins the need for debt forgiveness.[19] Clearly Mark is responsible for placing the saying about debts/transgressions here. The current dishonorable order derives from indebtedness. It can only be effaced by radical means, as the Temple Cleansing will show. Debt exploitation, which is unworthy of God's βασιλεία, shall not be found among Jesus' disciples. The total effect of these sayings in Mark's Appendix to the Fig Tree episode is to elucidate the significance of the curse and point to its antidote in God's gracious patronage.

THE TEMPLE EPISODE

The so-called Cleansing of the Temple appears in all four canonical gospels. These are the only accounts of the Cleansing in the Jesus tradition. One recent commentator on this passage has called into question the traditional label "Cleansing" for this reported action of Jesus. E. P. Sanders thinks that Jesus' activity is best understood as a prophetic action to symbolize the Temple's destruction (1985: 75). Craig A. Evans, however, has recently argued against Sanders and for the traditional Cleansing understanding (Evans 1989). For the purposes of the following analysis, Cleansing, Incident, and Action will be used interchangeably without prejudicing a final conclusion about the significance of Jesus' deed.

The synoptic evangelists report the incident at the end of Jesus' ministry (Mark 11:15-19 and par.), while John places it early in his gospel narrative (John 2:13-17). Both versions agree on proximity in time to Passover.

The basic structure of the story is Action-Saying. Mark brings this out in v. 17 with ἐδίδασκεν καὶ ἔλεγεν ("he was teaching and he said"). For Mark, Jesus' teaching often involves action (e.g. 1:27 in response to an exorcism).

A comparison of the Marcan and Johannine accounts of the Temple action of Jesus shows that the tradition agrees on several things: Both

---

[18] As Malina 1981: 84-85 points out, injustice and deprivation are also experienced here in terms of dishonor.

[19] The Aramaic word for debt, ḥôbāh, can also mean sin. See Oakman 1985: 72 or 1986: 153. Matthew 5:23, parallel to this saying in Mark, also has an economic implication: Do not give a gift to God until you have satisfied your [material] obligation to your neighbor. This also reflects Jesus' negative attitude regarding the *Corban* dedications, Mark 7:11. On ἔχειν τι κατά τινος ("to have something against someone") as a legal phrase frequently implying court proceedings against debtors, see Moulton-Milligan 1980: 322, s.v. κατά I. (2) and 544, s.v. πρός (3) (c). Matthew 6:23-26 confirms this connection.

versions agree that the action of Jesus focused upon buying and selling in the Temple (John: sacrificial animals, Mark: unspecified merchandise), upon the activities of the money-changers (Mark: κολλυβίσται, John: κερματίσται/κολλυβίσται), and upon the sale of doves. Mark diverges from John in alone reporting that Jesus prevented anyone from carrying vessels (σκεῦα) through the Temple; perhaps the Court of Gentiles is meant, since commercial activity is known to have taken place there (Eppstein 1964; Jeremias 1969; Evans 1989).

Luke has only a severely truncated version of the action (19:45b). This action leads to a "judgment" that the Temple is a house of prayer.[20] Vss. 47-48 extend the unit in narrative fashion to show that the Jerusalem leadership seeks a way to kill Jesus.

Matthew's version also condenses the Marcan account. However, Matthew does not see an immediate controversy with the Jerusalem leadership (as do the other three versions); rather, the blind and the lame come to Jesus to be healed. It is this healing activity and the praise of Jesus by the healed that leads to the controversy (v. 16).

Since the synoptic and Johannine versions of what Jesus said in conjunction with the Temple incident are remarkably divergent, pronouncement seems arbitrarily selected. In Mark, Jesus quotes from Isaiah 56:7 and Jeremiah 7:11. This dual quotation technique is familiar in Mark (e.g. 1:2-3, 11). Matthew and Luke, with some minor variations, follow Mark's quotations. John (2:16) diverges, however, with an allusion to Zechariah 14:21.

Cursing Robbers' Dens

The question of arbitrariness can only be decided when the meaning of these pronouncements is evaluated. Is Jesus thought to be pointing to the need for the Temple's purification or signifying the need for its removal? The cleansing view would imply a great degree of concern by Jesus for the purity of the Temple as a religious institution. Often in the past, interpreters have thus opposed "bloody sacrifice" (implied: impure, fleshly religion) with "prayer" (implied: pure, spiritual religion). Besides the fact that this view imposes a dualism unlikely in Jesus' (admittedly hellenized) Jewish context and an anachronistic assessment of what constitutes vital religion, it fails to take into account the role of the Temple in the wider social system.[21]

---

[20] On the notion of a "judgment," or legal decision, see Mack and Robbins 1989: 28-29.

[21] See Evans's appropriate remarks (1989: 257) about inappropriate Christian assessments of the Temple cultus.

What is important to note, therefore, in both the Marcan and Johannine versions of this incident is the emphasis upon buying/selling (Mark: of sacrificial animals?)—money-changers, sellers of doves. The implications of this confluence need to be explored. The ordinary person of the time became religiously indebted to God for various reasons—through life-events, personal actions, or vows. The Temple as a religious system existed to alleviate these debts incurred to God.[22] Even if people did not perceive a debt, the system operated so as to indebt them anyway. This is especially noticeable in the case of the Temple tax. Temple scribes recorded people's indebtedness, as previously noted. These debts had real economic repercussions upon most Jews of the time.[23] Debts had to be expunged in ways acceptable to the official interpreters of the sacred traditions. Animals offered had to be ritually acceptable to the priests. Coins of payment had to be of requisite Tyrian currency (M. Bekh. 8:7). The buying and selling, as well as the money-changers, supplied these needs. The people who controlled the Temple trafficked in goods that the Temple system mandated. Oil and livestock were central to this activity; so was the use and exchange of money. Jesus' action calls all of this into question. His action focuses attention on the visible mechanisms of the Temple and the power of Temple elite.

The sayings connected with Jesus' action explicate its social-systemic implications. While John's and Mark's pronouncements differ in specifics, they agree at least in a fundamental respect. Both sayings bring out the meaning of Jesus' action within the agrarian context of Judaea. Commerce, as Polanyi long ago noted, disrupts local agrarian economies. For this reason, medieval European aristocracies were careful to keep local agrarian economies insulated, especially from long-distance commerce.[24] The Judaean oligarchy, during the early first century, had not done this. One reason for this was that the Temple was an international focus of commerce at the time, especially for the Diaspora. In addition, the Judaean elite themselves engaged in commerce.[25] The second part of Mark's saying—"den of robbers"—brings out the destabilizing effects of long-distance commerce in agrarian societies. This is a reverse social banditry practiced by the elite. "House of trade" is roughly translated in

---

[22] I am indebted to Belo for this insight (1981: 38ff).

[23] Priests were exempt: M. Shek. 1:3.

[24] Polanyi 1944: 64: "An increasingly strict separation of local trade from export trade was the reaction of [medieval] urban life to the threat of mobile capital to disintegrate the institutions of the town."

[25] Kreissig 1969 emphasizes this. Case of Baba b. Buta: Y. Yom Tob 2.61c, cited in Haenchen 1984: 182. See critical comments in Applebaum 1976: 662.

peasant terms by "den of robbers"; Jesus expresses the view of the countryside and its exploited people.[26]

What, then, can be implied by "house of prayer"? Haenchen, despite noting that Isaiah 56 does not oppose prayer and sacrifice, takes the cleansing episode to signify (for John at least) the end of the Jewish cult.[27] Mark and Jesus may not have so understood this event. For the real problem with the Temple system, which Jesus' action exposes and opposes, is that ordinary people are for the most part deprived of their own offerings. Jesus opposes the Temple system as a system of exploitative redistribution for the benefit of the few. What would "prayer" imply in place of *this* system?

The answer to this question is suggested by a slight agreement between Mark's and John's versions of the incident. Mark: "*My house* shall be called a house of prayer." John: "Do not make *my father's house* a house of trade." The image of the Temple as God's house, familiar from the Old Testament, implies by extension God's household. A house of prayer, then, suggests a household in which petition to the householder results in the meaningful satisfaction of needs—material as well as spiritual. Jesus envisions, under the image of kingdom of God or household of God, a storehouse of blessing rather than a cave of curse. The $\beta\alpha\sigma\iota\lambda\epsilon\acute{\iota}\alpha$ Jesus proclaims opens the storehouse of God's patronage (Luke 12:31 = Q; Mark 10:30). The continuation of Mark's tradition with the Fig Tree revisited brings this idea out further in the sayings catena. Jesus condemns the social system of the Herodian Temple, without necessarily envisioning the end of sacrifice. Yet the sacrificial system will be one that no longer prolongs indebtedness; all will share in it as at Passover (Deut 16:11-12).

Conclusions

The foregoing literary and social analyses have suggested the need for further exploration of pronouncement within a social-systemic perspective. The analyses urge moving beyond purely religious or theological inquiries into these episodes, since only in modern individualist existence are religious dimensions of life neatly insulated from other dimensions. A social-systemic analysis insists on keeping the "literal" or "mundane" situation in view, together with the Jewish context that shaped the Jesus tradition, and on conceptualizing the social system of Roman Palestine to shed light on otherwise puzzling episodes.

---

[26] A view also argued, on different grounds, by G. Theissen 1976.
[27] 1984: 187b; cf. 186: "'House of prayer' is thus not being contrasted here [in Isaiah] with sacrifices."

Furthermore, modern literary approaches to the gospels that proceed without reference to the real context of Jesus traditions will miss significant meanings in those traditions. Elizabeth Struthers Malbon rightly acknowledges in her recent discussion of Marcan characterizations of Jesus' opponents that "a literary approach to Mark ... is bounded by our understanding of its probable historical context" (1989: 274). Malbon's otherwise excellent literary discussion still does not plumb the depths of agrarian anger that led Mark's Jesus to refer to the Jerusalem elite as bandits.

Even recent treatments that one might expect to explore or to make deeper reference to the political-economic connotations in the texts only do so in part. Both Fernando Belo and Ched Myers read the Cursing of the Fig Tree as an acted parable (with little or no meaning in itself) prefiguring the Temple's and Temple elite's doom (Belo 1981: 180; Myers 1988: 299). Belo and Myers manifest the general modern exegetical tendency to take the Cursing of the Fig Tree as a figurative action, which reflects negatively upon the religious/moral quality of Judaean society. Why precisely *this* figure is used is not explained. Herman Waetjen comes closest to articulating the argument laid out in the foregoing paragraphs (1989: 182):

> It is [the temple] episode which makes the seemingly senseless act of cursing the fig tree intelligible, while at the same time its far-reaching significance is obviated by it. The two incidents are interdependent.... Like the fig tree, the temple is intended to serve the needs of human beings. But while a fig tree can produce fruit only in its season, the temple as an institution that mediates divine-human relationships cannot be, indeed must not be, regulated by the cycles of nature.... The cursing of the fig tree symbolizes the condemnation of the temple institution which, as the central systemic structure of Judaism, has been regulating the religious, political, economic, and social life of the Jewish people.

The strength of the argument in the present essay is that it makes sense out of *both* Cursings and shows how the two episodes are bound together by the social system. Each pronouncement episode examined has a significant tie to first century, Palestinian social realities. Since the originating social system did not appreciably change over the period when the Jesus tradition was being formed and integrated into, say, Mark's conception, it is quite possible to make some judgments about how the traditions reflect/react to that system. The system itself can be modeled with available historical evidence and conceptual tools offered by comparative social studies.

It has been suggested by some that the Fig Tree Incident really is a parable like Luke 13 that has been historicized (Taylor 1966: 459; Harrington 1990: 620). Although it is difficult to see why such a parable should have been historicized, especially given the destructive nature of Jesus' action, it can now be appreciated that such a transformation at an earlier stage would not have happened arbitrarily. Since Luke's and John's compositions drop the Cursing, tradition later moved away from an account requiring a specific social setting for its comprehension. The tendency was to forget the story, not to create it.

Similarly, even though there are historical difficulties in saying precisely whether Jesus cleansed the Temple, and what he might have said on such an occasion, the incident can hardly have been concocted wholesale by the tradition. Such an arbitrary invention would be difficult to understand at the hands of a later, apparently Temple-loyal Christian movement (Acts 2:46). The criterion of dissimilarity, therefore, suggests "authenticity" at some level for both pronouncement stories. Social-systemic considerations urge resonance in both accounts with wider social concerns as the source of this authenticity. These concerns helped the early Jesus communities in Palestine to understand and to preserve Jesus' pronouncements quite selectively. Variability within the tradition is seen to have been controlled to an important extent by the experienced social system.

Within that social system, the early Jesus tradition maintained a fairly consistent focus: The "what" of its pronouncements, and related prophetic actions, had to do with interest in the emergence of a new material order, symbolized under the umbrella concept "kingdom of God." The "why" of Jesus tradition pronouncements was given by institutions of the old order that blocked the coming of the kingdom. A fair amount of cursing was necessary to bring in the new order of blessing.[28]

WORKS CONSULTED

Applebaum, Shimon
    1976   "Economic Life in Palestine." Pp. 631-700 in *The Jewish People in the First Century*. Compendia Rerum Iudaicarum ad Novum Testamentum, 2. Eds. S. Safrai and M. Stern. Amsterdam: Van Gorcum.
    1977   "Judaea as a Roman Province; the Countryside as a Political and Economic Factor." Pp. 355-396 in *Aufstieg und Niedergang der römischen Welt*,

---

[28] I am grateful for having received perceptive critique on earlier drafts of this paper from John J. Pilch, Paul O. Ingram, Patricia O'Connell Killen, and James F. Sennett. These colleagues helped me immensely in formulating the argument. Vernon K. Robbins has graciously encouraged me at several crucial stages. Of course, the faults of the paper remain mine alone.

8. Eds. H. Temporini and W. Haase. Berlin, New York: Walter de Gruyter.

Avi-Yonah, Michael
1977 *The Holy Land: From the Persian to the Arab Conquests (536 B.C. - A.D. 640)*. Grand Rapids: Baker.

Barrett, C. K.
1978 *The Gospel According to St. John*. 2d ed. Philadelphia: Westminster.

Belo, Fernando
1981 *A Materialist Reading of the Gospel of Mark*. Maryknoll: Orbis.

Billerbeck, Paul
1922 *Kommentar zum Neuen Testament aus Talmud und Midrasch*, 1. Munich: Beck'sche.

Bultmann, Rudolf
1963 *History of the Synoptic Tradition*. Rev. ed. Trans. J. Marsh. New York: Harper and Row.

Childers, Norman F.
N.D. *Modern Fruit Science: Orchard and Small Fruit Culture*. Horticultural Publications. New Brunswick, NJ: Rutgers University Press.

Cranfield, C. E. B.
1959 *The Gospel According to Saint Mark*. Cambridge: Cambridge University Press.

Danby, Herbert
1933 *The Mishnah: Translated from the Hebrew with Introduction and Brief Explanatory Notes*. Oxford: Oxford University Press.

Elliott, John H., ed.
1986 *Social-Scientific Criticism of the New Testament and Its Social World*. Semeia 35.

Eppstein, Victor
1964 "The Historicity of the Gospel Account of the Cleansing of the Temple." *ZNW* 55: 42-58.

Evans, Craig
1989 "Jesus' Action in the Temple: Cleansing or Portent of Destruction?" *CBQ* 51: 237-270.

Freyne, Sean
1980 *Galilee From Alexander the Great to Hadrian: 323 B.C.E. to 135 C.E.* University of Notre Dame Center for the Study of Judaism and Christianity in Antiquity, 5. Wilmington: Michael Glazier.

Goodman, Martin
1982 "The First Jewish Revolt: Social Conflict and the Problem of Debt." *JJS* 33: 417-427.

1983 *State and Society in Roman Galilee: A.D. 132-212.* Totowa, NJ: Rowman & Allanheld.

Haenchen, Ernst
1984 *John 1: A Commentary on the Gospel of John, Chapters 1-6.* Hermeneia—A Critical and Historical Commentary on the Bible. Philadelphia: Fortress.

Hamel, Gildas
1990 *Poverty and Charity in Roman Palestine, First Three Centuries C.E.* Berkeley, University of California Press.

Hamilton, N.
1964 "Temple Cleansing and Temple Bank." *JBL* 83: 365-372.

Harrington, Daniel
1990 "Mark." Pp. 596-629 in *The New Jerome Biblical Commentary.* Eds. R. Brown, J. Fitzmyer, and R. Murphy. Englewood Cliffs: Prentice-Hall.

Hengel, Martin
1974 *Judaism and Hellenism.* 2 vols. Trans. John Bowden. Philadelphia: Fortress.

Hiers, R.
1971 "Purification of the Temple: Preparation for the Kingdom of God." *JBL* 90: 82-90.

Horsley, Richard and John S. Hanson
1985 *Bandits, Prophets, and Messiahs.* San Francisco: Harper & Row.

Hunzinger, Claus-Hunno
1971 "συκῆ, ktl." Pp. 751-759 in *Theological Dictionary of the New Testament,* 7. Eds. G. Kittel and G. Friedrich. Trans. G. W. Bromiley. Grand Rapids: Eerdmans.

Jeremias, Joachim
1969 *Jerusalem in the Time of Jesus.* Trans. F. H. and C. H. Cave. Philadelphia: Fortress.

Klausner, Joseph
1925 *Jesus of Nazareth: His Life, Times, and Teaching.* Trans. H. Danby. New York: Macmillan.

Koester, Helmut
1982 *History, Culture, and Religion of the Hellenistic Age. Introduction to the New Testament,* 1. Philadelphia: Fortress.

Kreissig, Heinz
1969 "Die Landwirtschaftliche Situation in Palästina vor dem judäischen Krieg." *Acta Antiqua* 17: 223-254.

Mack, Burton and Vernon Robbins
1989 *Patterns of Persuasion in the Gospels.* Sonoma: Polebridge.

MacMullen, Ramsay
1966 *Enemies of the Roman Order: Treason, Unrest, and Alienation in the Empire.* Cambridge: Harvard University Press.

Malbon, Elizabeth Struthers
- 1989 "The Jewish Leaders in the Gospel of Mark: A Literary Study of Marcan Characterization." *JBL* 108: 259-281.

Malina, Bruce
- 1981 *The New Testament World: Insights from Cultural Anthropology.* Atlanta: John Knox.
- 1988 "Patron and Client: The Analogy Behind Synoptic Theology." *Foundations and Facets Forum* 4: 2-32.

Moulton, J. H. and G. Milligan.
- 1980 *The Vocabulary of the Greek New Testament.* Reprint ed. Grand Rapids: Eerdmans.

Myers, Ched
- 1988 *Binding the Strong Man.* Maryknoll: Orbis.

Neusner, Jacob
- 1973 *From Politics to Piety: The Emergence of Pharisaic Judaism.* Englewood Cliffs: Prentice-Hall.

Neyrey, Jerome, ed.
- 1991 *The Social World of Luke-Acts: Models for Interpretation.* Peabody, MA: Hendrickson Publishers.

Nineham, Dennis
- 1963 *St. Mark.* The Pelican New Testament Commentaries. New York: Penguin Books.

Oakman, Douglas E.
- 1985 "Jesus and Agrarian Palestine: The Factor of Debt." Pp. 57-73 in *SBL Seminar Papers*, 24. Ed. K. Richards. Chico: Scholars.
- 1986 *Jesus and the Economic Questions of His Day.* Lewiston, NY: The Edwin Mellen Press.

Polanyi, Karl
- 1944 *The Great Transformation.* Boston: Beacon.

Saldarini, Anthony
- 1988 *Pharisees, Scribes, and Sadducees: A Sociological Approach.* Wilmington: Michael Glazier.

Sanders, E. P.
- 1985 *Jesus and Judaism.* Philadelphia: Fortress.

Taylor, Vincent
- 1966 *The Gospel According to St. Mark.* 2nd ed. Thornapple Commentaries. Grand Rapids: Baker.

Telford, William R.
- 1980 *The Barren Temple and the Withered Tree.* JSNT Supplementary Series, 1. Sheffield: JSOT Press.

Theissen, Gerd
　　1976　　"Die Tempelweissagung Jesu: Prophetie im Spannungsfeld von Stadt und Land." *Theologische Zeitschrift* 32: 144-158.

Trevor, J. C.
　　1962　　"Fig Tree, Fig." P. 267 in *The Interpreter's Dictionary of the Bible*, 2. Ed. G. Buttrick. Nashville: Abingdon.

Waetjen, Herman
　　1989　　*A Reordering of Power: A Socio-Political Reading of Mark's Gospel.* Philadelphia: Fortress.

IV
RESPONSES

A Response
The Chinese Box: Method within Method

Bernard Brandon Scott
Phillips Graduate Seminary

The essay by Andersen and Robbins, "Paradigms in Homer, Pindar, the Tragedians, and the New Testament," corrects a mistake introduced into New Testament studies by Martin Dibelius. Dibelius had confused the paradigm with the pronouncement story or chreia. Dibelius had assumed that the real context for early Christian sayings was the sermon. "Of course we must not forget one thing. When these reports were gathered into a Gospel, then what had hitherto been the 'material' of a preacher now became reading matter for Christians" (Dibelius 1934: 42). Robbins previously had demonstrated this confusion in Dibelius (Mack and Robbins 1989: 2-6). In this analysis the evidence is drawn primarily from Homer. This raises a number of interesting and unresolved questions about socio-rhetorical analysis, Robbins's term for his emerging comprehensive method (Robbins 1991; Robbins 1993 for recent statements about this method), and these questions can also furnish a focus for the other three essays to which I am responding.

Dibelius's confusion of paradigm and pronouncement story (chreia) resulted from a number of problematic steps. Initially he located almost the sole context for early Christian sayings creativity in the Sermon. Second, he confused function and form, and third, he understood the shift to be from sermon (orality) to reading (literacy).[1] In regard to the first issue, New Testament scholarship has not made significant progress. Our imaginations have been weak. Yet there are important indications that we may be able to advance on this project. Helmut Koester has argued that a common wisdom source underlies Paul, Q, and Thomas (Koester 1990:55-64; John Dominic Crossan's cluster analysis offers a way to understand the intrinsic development of the Jesus tradition [Crossan 1983] but see Robbins's [1993] helpful critique). Koester and Crossan do not represent two poles but two correlating avenues to the same problem. Koester has begun to attack the issue from the point of view of form external to the material itself. Crossan offers an internal formal method. It is not an

---

[1] Bultmann himself is not innocent on these matters, but is outside the scope of this response.

either/or, but a both/and. Robbins in his research on the chreia has taken the next theoretical step from the inception of writing in the tradition. The chreia is the hellenistic rhetorical form in which the tradition is rehearsed first in writing. Therefore the gospels are not the first efforts to write the Christian tradition.

The confusion of form and function is a continuing issue. Andersen and Robbins are surely correct that the paradigm is (1) a function; (2) based on inductive logic; (3) referring to a particular situation; (4) in support of a speaker, thesis, or some part of the argument. A chreia, on the other hand, is a form that can be used in a variety of functions, including as a paradigm. Even more, a paradigm can be used in a chreia. To fall back on a Saussurean distinction, function exists at the level of *parole* while form exists at the level of *langue*. One can only identify function in an actual *parole*, whereas form can be identified regardless of its function in *parole*. A proverb is a proverb regardless of its social function. Likewise, since social context is more of an issue in *parole* than *langue*, function primarily raises the issue of social world. This issue has plagued New Testament studies ever since Bultmann incorrectly tied form to *Sitz im Leben*. Douglas Oakman begins his paper with the observation "that texts require social context for interpretation." That is true if one means text as *parole*; it is less true in the case of text as form. Rhetoric deals with both function and form and needs to be clear in its distinction between the two. This makes the appropriateness of the "socio" in *socio*-rhetorical problematic.

Avery-Peck's paper, "Rhetorical Argumentation in Early Rabbinic Pronouncement[2] Stories," illustrates this point. While the chreia is a recognized form, it is also a secondary form in that it tends to employ other forms (e.g., proverbs, maxims, etc.) and is used in differing rhetorical functions. The first chreia (Sifre Deuteronomy 38) in illustrating #6, "Statement from Example" clearly exemplifies the paradigm as worked out by Andersen and Robbins. The concluding argument, "Now if Abraham" is an inductive argument from a single example. Its weakness is the weakness of all inductive arguments: does it apply and will the receiver understand the connection? Hermogenes deals not with form but function. The reluctance of rhetorical critics to develop a new language and their preference instead to continue borrowing from the ancients obscures the analytical process. Is it helpful for chreia to designate both form and differing functions? Does this not indicate that Dibelius's confusion has its origin in the ancient discussion?

---

[2] Why don't rhetorical critics agree to abandon the term pronouncement story as belonging to an earlier day of New Testament scholarship and use *chreia* exclusively? It would reduce the clutter and confusion.

Andersen and Robbins's choice of Homer as an example of the paradigm raises an important issue about rhetorical method. Rhetorical method claims to be an emic method, i.e., it is a description from the native's point of view using their terms to describe the phenomenon. Model usage in the social sciences tends to be etic description (from outside) and the use of the emic description in etic models is an effort to overcome the hermeneutical gap (Malina 1986: 190). Did Homer know he was singing a paradigm? This is an especially interesting question given the nearly universal consensus by Homerian scholars that Homer was an oral singer (Kirk 1985: xxiii). The patterns described by Andersen and Robbins are highly abstract and therefore not compatible with the normal thought modes of an oral society (Havelock 1963; Havelock 1986).

Since the analysis of Andersen and Robbins seems convincing, the following questions occur. Is this form of rhetorical analysis etic, not from the author's point of view, but the point of view of later rhetoricians? Or did the ancient rhetoricians discover in their own Greek *parole* a structure or organization that belongs intrinsically to an agonistic culture? Since oral culture tends to be agonistic (Ong 1982: 43-5), does the persuasive and aggressive character of rhetoric derive from the peculiar blend of oral and scribal (I would prefer literate) culture that Robbins describes as "rhetorical culture" (Robbins 1991; 1993)? George Kennedy would appear to argue that it is a universal phenomenon "which is conditioned by the basic working of the human mind and heart and by the nature of all human society" (Kennedy 1984: 10). This statement seems far too grand and makes the ancient rhetoricians proto-structuralists, but points to an area demanding more research.

The paper by Avery-Peck analyzing rabbinic chreiai, addresses this point directly. Some of these seem quite oral and very similar to Homer; for example, the very first one. The Ben Dosa example has the appearance of a saying for which a context was created, but still seems part of the normal elaboration of an oral culture (Crossan 1991:153-56). The more elaborate chreiai, which constitute the majority in this collection, would appear to demand a level of abstraction more normal in a literate (rhetorical) culture (e.g., the two chreiai used as rationales).

Since Greek rhetorical method is based on analysis of Greek practice in an agonistic culture, that rhetorical analysis quickly becomes a feedback loop creating the distinctive rhetorical culture described by Robbins, the interaction of oral and written composition. "[A] rhetorical culture is aware of written documents, uses written and oral language interactively, and composes both orally and scribally [literately] in a rhetorical manner" (Robbins 1993: 118). It soon "rhetorizes" the culture; these features become practiced. To what extent does this "rhetorized" culture extend beyond the Greek language? Avery-Peck's conclusion would seem to indicate that it does not extend very far. "[W]hile subject to interpretation within the rhetorical categories developed by Theon and Hermogenes, the rabbinic evidence does not suggest a knowledge of or conscious attempt to utilize those patterns." Thus Avery-Peck's analysis is etic, not emic. This raises two important questions. Belonging to the Greco-Roman world does not automatically place one in the Greek rhetorical loop. Does using Greek accomplish this? Or is it the writing of Greek? This has important implications for understanding the development of the Jesus tradition, since it belongs both to the same trajectory that produced rabbinic chreiai and to the school of work typified by Theon and Hermogenes.

Marston Speight's paper on the Hadith literature of Islam likewise helps expand this issue. He notes that "although Arabic rhetoric and literary theory owe nothing fundamental to the Greeks, the extensive cross-cultural exchanges during the flowering of the Islamic Empire resulted in the borrowing from Hellenism of a number of literary motifs, conventions and definitions." It is perhaps to the point to note that Greek literature largely was preserved through their efforts. Speight's conclusion is similar to Avery-Peck's: "What they do show is that transmitters of Hadith used material that corresponds closely in form to the chreiai of the Hellenist rhetoricians, and that some of the features of argumentation described by Theon and Hermogenes can be seen in the reports handed down from the first generation of Muslims." Both rabbinic and Islamic literature are to a certain extent a part of the feedback loop that characterizes a rhetorical culture, even if the direct lines may be difficult to observe. Furthermore, they belong, along with Hellenism, to Mediterranean culture, which anthropologists increasingly describe in a single unit of analysis (Gilmore 1987; Malina and Neyrey 1991: 69-72). This increases the research agenda. Is Kennedy correct in his universal ascription of rhetorical forms? What is the relation of the rhetorical forms to the Greek language? To an agonistic culture? To the Mediterranean world?

Andersen and Robbins's paper raises issues concerning where rhetorical analysis fits into the overall conception of a unifying method. I would suggest that it belongs in the elementary tier that attempts to bridge authorial intention (what was the author seeking to do with this arrangement of the material) and reception (how an ancient audience would respond to that arrangement). The first aspect of this bridge frequently raises the suspicions of literary critics for whom authorial intention is anathema, because they are concerned with the text qua text, as a literary (i.e., artistic or poetic) artifact. Likewise, I would suggest that an analysis even more primary than rhetorical analysis is one of sound: how sound organizes the text, since in the ancient world both writing and reading are *recitatio*. They were meant to be done out loud. Thus a sound analysis and a rhetorical analysis together constitute an elementary analysis. A secondary analysis would involve a literary and an ideological analysis. Secondary and primary are not hierarchical nor sequential but ranges of application. The point of entrance into a text may well vary, and need not be singular.

Douglas Oakman's social-systemic analysis of the Fig Tree and Robbers' Den pronouncement stories offers an interesting parallel and contrast to these issues. He eschews a rhetorical analysis for what he calls a social-systemic perspective. The addition of "systemic" I take to mean that his method entails a systems view of the text and social context. While this essay demonstrates the ultimate importance of social science method in understanding a (con)text, it also points out its limitations as the dominant or guiding methodology. What then is its status? I would suggest that it is an auxiliary method, that it comes to the aid of the four listed above. In Iser's terms, the social sciences describe the textual repertoire (Iser 1978: 53-85). Without a proper understanding of a text's repertoire a text remains decontextualized, a problem Oakman correctly lays against much literary criticism which in its concern for the intratextual reality of a text denies or ignores its extratextual reference.

The problem with making social sciences the dominant method is clearly illustrated in a recurring problem with the paper. Despite the first footnote, which seeks to disarm the reader in a clear rhetorical gesture, one cannot use Jesus, Jesus tradition, and Mark interchangeably without loss of precision. Oakman's analysis of the cursing of the fig tree identifies a primary and secondary structure. He appears to identify the primary structure with tradition and the secondary structure with redaction, although he is not consistent in this. I would observe that the primary structure is paratactic and the secondary subordinate, which combined with rhetorical analysis might have confirmed Oakman's observations. His reference to the Lucan parallel is telling in that its paratactic structure is similar, but also quite different. It is the differences that count. The similarities point to the type of narrative structure A.J. Greimas has analyzed (Greimas 1983). Oakman follows Bultmann's argument that the non-separated Matthean form of the cursing is more original. But this is extremely problematic. The simplicity of a form does not necessarily indicate its originality, as studies on the chreia's elaboration have shown. Nor does what he calls the "Appendix" necessarily predate Mark because it is in Matthew. This is a quite circular argument. The so-called "Appendix" is only the completion of an action chreia well described by Theon. Furthermore, since Oakman argues that Mark 11:22, a part of the appendix, is a Markan construction, and Matthew takes it over in a typically Matthean rewrite, the appendix must be Markan. A rhetorical analysis could have shown that neither the Markan chreia nor Matthew's rewriting of it is at all unusual. There is much to commend Oakman's essay. I am in agreement with its main points about the kingdom and the social context. But had he begun with a rhetorical analysis of the material, he could have ordered his material in a much more coherent fashion as he explained by means of social analysis the repertoire of the text.

These essays raise many interesting questions and point to the need for reflection on and unification of our methodological procedures.

WORKS NOTED

Crossan, John Dominic
    1983   *In Fragments: The Aphorisms of Jesus*. San Francisco: Harper & Row.
    1991   *The Historical Jesus: The Life of a Mediterranean Jewish Peasant*. San Francisco: Harper San Francisco.

Dibelius, Martin
    1934   *From Tradition to Gospel*. Trans. Bertram Lee Woolf. New York: Charles Scribner's Sons.

Gilmore, David D.
    1987   *Honor and Shame and the Unity of the Mediterranean*. Publication No. 22 of the American Anthropological Association. Washington: American Anthropological Association.

Greimas, A.J.
    1983   *Structural Semantics: An Attempt at a Method*. Translated by Daniele McDowell. Lincoln: University of Nebraska Press.

Havelock, Eric Alfred
    1963   *Preface to Plato*. Cambridge: Harvard University Press.
    1986   *The Muse Learns to Write, Reflections on Orality and Literacy from Antiquity to the Present*. New Haven: Yale University Press.

Iser, Wolfgang
    1978   *The Act of Reading: A Theory of Aesthetic Response*. Baltimore: The Johns Hopkins University Press.

Kennedy, George A.
    1984   *New Testament Interpretation through Rhetorical Criticism*. Studies in Religion. Ed. Charles H. Long. Chapel Hill: The University of North Carolina Press.

Kirk, G.S.
    1985   *The Iliad: A Commentary*. Vol. 1. Cambridge: Cambridge University Press.

Koester, Helmut
　1990　　*Ancient Christian Gospels.* Philadelphia: Trinity Press International.

Mack, Burton L. and Vernon K. Robbins
　1989　　*Patterns of Persuasion in the Gospels.* Foundations and Facets. Sonoma, CA: Polebridge Press.

Malina, Bruce J.
　1986　　*Christian Origins and Cultural Anthropology: Practical Models for Biblical Interpretation.* Atlanta: John Knox.

Malina, Bruce J. and Jerome H. Neyrey
　1991　　"First-Century Personality: Dyadic, Not Individualistic." Pp. 67-96 in *The Social World of Luke-Acts: Models for Interpretation.* Ed. Jerome H. Neyrey. . Peabody, MA: Hendrickson.

Ong, Walter J.
　1982　　*Orality and Literacy, The Technologizing of the Word.* New Accents. Ed. Terence Hawkes. London and New York: Methuen.

Robbins, Vernon K.
　1991　　"Writing as a Rhetorical Act in Plutarch and the Gospels." Pp. 142-168 in *Persuasive Artistry: Studies in New Testament Rhetoric in Honor of George A. Kennedy.* Ed. Duane F. Watson. Sheffield: JSOT Press.
　1993　　"Progymnastic Rhetorical Composition and Pre-Gospel Traditions: A New Approach." Pp. 111-147 in *The Synoptic Gospels. Source Criticism and the New Literary Criticism.* BETL 110. Ed. Camille Focant. Leuven: Leuven University Press.

PERSUASIVE PRONOUNCEMENTS:
AN EVALUATION OF RECENT STUDIES ON THE CHREIA

Burton L. Mack
Claremont Graduate School
Institute for Antiquity and Christianity

This is a remarkable set of studies. It documents a full ten years of persistent scholarly labor on the rhetoric of the chreia and illustrates the new knowledge achieved by a group of scholars under the direction of Vernon Robbins. I want to celebrate this increase in our understanding of the chreia and acknowledge our indebtedness to Vernon whose analytical skills have succeeded in marking several advances in the rhetoric of pronouncement stories. As a standard for evaluating the new insights reflected in these studies, I am using as benchmarks the issue of *Semeia* edited by Robert Tannehill on "Pronouncement Stories" (1981), a number of articles on pronouncement stories by Vernon Robbins from 1981 to 1988, and the work Vernon and I did in the mid 1980s published in *Patterns of Persuasion* (1989). Within the present volume, the essays I have been asked to review are those by Dean-Otting and Robbins, Parrott, Salyer, Blount, and Branham.

The major advance has been an increased clarity about the ways in which chreiai were used to rhetorical advantage. In his introduction to the volume, Robbins distinguishes between the rhetorical "expansion" of a chreia and its elaboration. He also distinquishes two ways of elaborating a chreia which he calls "first" and "second level" elaborations. His distinctions are helpful and clean up a considerable bit of fuzziness in my own earlier attempts to trace what I called the "elaboration pattern" in early Christian pronouncement stories and other smaller units of argumentation.

Two insights in this regard are especially important. One is that the difference between the two kinds of elaboration he calls "levels" can be generally correlated with two different classifications of "arguments" in the rhetorical handbooks. Robbins's "second level" elaboration uses the list of arguments in the elaboration of the chreia by Hermogenes, roughly equivalent to "the complete argument" in the *Ad Herennium*. His "first level" elaboration, on the other hand, generally prefers "topics" or what some of the rhetorical handbooks called *kephalaia* ("headings"). Describing a typology of chreia elaboration by distinguishing between two classes of argument and two ways of constructing an argumentation is a great advance. Gregory Salyer uses this distinction to fine advantage in his study of two rhetorical units in Mark 7:1-23.

One might want to question Robbins's use of the term "level," which could suggest layers in some developmental sequence, a thesis Robbins does not propose or, I suspect, intend. He apparently has in mind something like the level of complexity or degree of approximation to the "complete argumentation." I suppose I should be satisfied with that, having made so much of "the complete argument" pattern in my own studies. But Robbins's work on the many ways in which the chreia could be turned into a small unit of argumentation is compelling and has the effect of dethroning "the complete argument" as a standard for judging a degree of rhetorical achievement. So, while the phenomenal distinction he designates is surely right, I wonder whether the term "level" is the right word for it.

The second insight marking the major advance as I see it, concerns the rationale for a phenomenon over which Vernon and I used to puzzle. The phenomenon has to do with the position given to the major pronouncement of a pronouncement story among the arguments brought to it in the course of its amplification and elaboration. Robbins helps us see that the pointed saying of a chreia could be placed up front or at the end, depending upon the rhetorical strategy and narrative location of an expanded or elaborated chreia. That is a very helpful observation.

He also makes the point that the flow of argumentation is frequently reversed when one moves from one to the other type of amplification (his "expanded" versus "elaborated"). This is also very helpful and alerts us again to the difference between school handbook paradigms and conventional compositional practices. Without the handbooks (*progymnasmata*) we may never have gotten started on the project of analyzing the rhetoric of elaborated chreiai. But the discussions in these handbooks and in the technical grammars of ancient rhetoric are written in shorthand and thus too condensed to enlighten us about the full range of compositional techniques in common practice. Robbins has consistently worked both sides of the street, carefully checking his critical observations on compositional features of the pronouncement stories against the rhetorical handbooks in order to be sure of the match. Thus many of the observations about rhetorical strategies commonly used at the time are actually to his own credit even when, after pursuing the handbooks, it finally appears that the ancients also recognized the practice and had a name for it.

A second major advance is announced in the essay by Dean-Otting and Robbins which takes up the question of scriptural citation in elaborated chreiai. The incidence of scriptural citation has long been noted and discussed, but usually under the rubric of "precedent judgment." This beginning was not exactly wrong, for it did fit what one might expect the general rhetorical classification of this type of material to have been, and it often seemed to fit the function of a citation within the (essentially "deliberative") pattern of elaboration called the complete argument. But since the latter was not always the case with a citation, and since citations that did occur in that arrangement did not always seem to have the weightiness one expected of a "precedent" legal or literary "judgment," these earlier observations frequently did not lead to critical understanding. The study by Dean-Otting and Robbins takes us several steps beyond that impasse.

Their contribution is the result of shifting attention to another species of rhetoric (the judicial) and another category of rhetorical classification, namely that of the "artistic" in distinction from the "inartistic" element in the construction of a judicial case. This I see as an extremely clever move. It courts our long-standing assumptions about the "authority" of the Jewish scriptures (one of which has been that the scriptures counted as "law"), and so obliquely puts those assumptions to the test. In a judicial speech, the rhetor distinguished between "inartistic" facts (either "exhibits" belonging to the facts of the case, or "laws" automatically pertaining to the case, and therefore "given" without the rhetor needing to "invent" them) and "artistic" arguments ("crafted," "invented," thus arguments for which the rhetor was responsible). Dean-Otting and Robbins do not set up their investigation exactly in this way, preferring to look for signs that the text of a given scriptural reference had been treated "artistically" in the citation in order to shape it for a rhetorical function. I am not sure all of the controls were in place that one might wish, especially keeping track of the odd notion of "legal" precedent that results when the scripture is treated as law and used as a precedent judgment in a nonjudicial (deliberative) elaboration. But that aside, the results of the investigation are very enlightening. They show that Jesus people treated the scriptures both "inartistically," as citations of precedent judgment that counted as given (whether "authoritative" or "well-known"), and "artistically," namely as taken from a culturally given reservoir of images available to be manipulated rhetorically. The tendency, in fact, was to treat the scriptures "artistically." To establish the fact of such *rhetorical freedom* in the citation of the scriptures is surely an important advance in our quest to understand the authorities that may have been operant in the early Jesus movements.

A third advance is illustrated best in the essay by Rod Parrott. It is the use of rhetorical analysis to instigate and control the question of a unit's compositional history. By using the elaboration pattern as a paradigm of argumentation, Parrott was able to assess the logic of several options for the compositional history of the pronouncement story about eating/plucking grain on the sabbath. I find his study rigorous and uncommonly thorough, his reasoning clear and delightfully crisp, and his conclusions compelling. Many of us have assumed that the pronouncement stories must have had a history of elaboration and that a knowledge of the rhetoric of elaboration might help us unearth moments in a given history. Parrott has developed such a knowledge and thus provided us with a model for the analysis of other stories. It need not be the case that all will yield to such an analysis, and of those that do that the result always puts us in touch with an earlier stage in the history of a story and its logics. But now that Parrott has demonstrated that such an approach has been rewarding in one case, it should be tried in others.

I should also like to make a comment about the way in which rhetorical analysis has been linked to the social location of texts. This is a focus which several of the essays share and it speaks to one of the promises of rhetorical criticism that many of us have hoped to see fulfilled. However, with the exception of a helpful insight here or there, I do not think that the studies in this volume mark a clear advance in this direction. This is not intended as a major criticism, for no claims were made in this regard. And yet, where there was an obvious reflection of a social context in a text under discussion, that context has indeed been taken seriously in many of these studies, in order to elucidate the point of a rhetoric's persuasion. So, promises aside, the practice of seeking some social location for a text is about to become standard procedure. What bothers me is that, and again there are a few exceptional remarks here and there, the quality of a rhetoric itself has seldom been used to gain purchase on the (social and) rhetorical situation. The tendency has been to accept the picture painted of the social context and to think the implicit charges against the opposition justified, on the one hand, and let the (often outrageous) rhetoric of the (Christian) speakers stand, on the other. This shows, I think, that taking up a socio-rhetorical method is no guarantee against Christian bias in the imagination of social situations in early Christian history. The Christian investment in this literature is deep and pervasive in the field of biblical studies, as everyone knows. But just for that reason, the academic quest to understand the first-century issues of social and ideological moment apart from Christian evaluation should set the controls at every turn. It does not appear to me that all of the authors in this volume have understood or achieved that.

I'd like to end on a positive note, and I can because of a brilliant essay not yet mentioned. Branham's study of Lucian's *Demonax* lays out the logic and social function of the Cynics' style of humor. It is a marvelous explication and it is extremely helpful as an introduction to the rhetoric of Cynic chreiai. Branham does not apply his insight in the nature of Cynic humor to the chreiai and pronouncement stories of Jesus, but he could. Were he to do so, I am convinced that we would never be able to read them the same way again. Because there is logic to the Cynics' humor, as Branham shows, seeing the humor in the Jesus chreiai would not threaten our work on their rhetorical compositions. But the humor in the logic may often have been the feature that made the point. Seeing that has been much more difficult for us than working out the arguments. If we ever do catch on to the humor, I think our picture of Jesus and his first followers may change again as drastically as it did when the pronouncement stories turned into elaborated chreiai.

So bravo for Robbins's skillful analyses, for the many contributions to the rhetoric of pronouncement stories in this volume, and for the promise of humor that Branham's study portends. The volume documents a real shift in our discourse about these stories, and it points toward the time when we might be able to take a deep breath, read the gospels as stories with human interest, and occasionally look for a chuckle when the logic alone fails to close the rhetorical gaps.

TELLING THE OTHER STORY: A LITERARY RESPONSE TO SOCIO-RHETORICAL CRITICISM OF THE NEW TESTAMENT

Mark Ledbetter
Huntingdon College

INTRODUCTION

I have been asked to respond to four very fine essays in this *Semeia* volume from the perspective of a contemporary literary critic. While in many ways and for many years the tasks and methods of biblical critics and literary critics have been quite similar in their tasks and goals, the two areas of criticism have nonetheless often been at odds with one another. Each deals with texts, the language of texts, and narrative's nature and function, and yet, when the critic of the bible (The small case "b" is intentional) does "literary criticism" the professional literary critic finds fault, usually in the biblicist's concern with the history behind the text, which seems, to the literary critic, to give priority to the wrong story. The literary critic has no better fortune when he/she attempts to do biblical criticism; then, the bible scholar sees an obvious failure of the literary critic to address all the important issues concerning the text. The literary critic, suggests the biblical critic, is naive to assume that these texts were formed in a language vacuum, with no historical or cultural influences. The text can be read from the 20th century but not only within the 20th century.

Reading the essays of Brian Blount, David Gowler, Robert Tannehill, and Gregory Salyer have taught me as a literary critic a great deal. While on the one hand many of my initial reservations about the literary exercise in socio-rhetorical analysis remain—I think as a product of hard-headedness and training–on the other hand, I am equally convinced that the biblical critic's reservations about contemporary literary criticism are valid. Nonetheless, I am not about to ask that each of us becomes more like the other in our critical methodologies, though I do encourage what is happening in both fields of study, as demonstrated by this volume's essays. I see a willingness to entertain and to use each other's "ways of seeing" texts to bring vitality and energy to the critical exercise of reading.

I am about to ask that each of us remember that having done our textual criticism, from the perspectives we have chosen, there is always another critical story to tell. No methodology or methodologies have claim to **the** interpretation, but only **an** interpretation. Text critics, whether of biblical or secular texts, must move beyond the language of a right or wrong interpretation and work more within the context of responsible interpretation.

Two critical questions of this approach are: Having established my methodological parameters, have I been responsible to them? and Have I made claims of methodological purity which exclude other ways of understanding the text? Until the first question is answered yes and the second question no, literary critics and biblical critics will continue their turf battles over texts and methodologies and learn little from one another. I propose that there is room for both socio-rhetorical criticism and contemporary literary criticism in their purest forms, as long as when the day's critical work is done, each critic remembers that s/he has told only her/his story and that there remains another story to tell. Furthermore, I suggest that there is room for an exciting interaction between these complementary methodologies as long as neither attempts to consume the other in an attempt to lay claim to any **one** reading of a biblical text. These observations represent only a few of the good things I have learned from the essays by Blount, Gowler, Tannehill, and Salyer.

In my remaining comments, I wish to be more detailed in my literary response to these essays and briefly explore the nature and function of literary criticism in each essay, pointing out a relationship that develops within each essay between socio-rhetorical analysis and literary criticism. While a variety of interesting "literary" issues are at work in each essay, for the sake of clarity and brevity I have chosen to develop only one major issue in response to each essay (though I shall allude to others). In this process, I shall make suggestions as to the other story that each critic might have told, had he chosen an-other critical approach. Please remember, my criticisms of each essay are not suggestions that it is wrong in its approach (in fact, having established perspectives and goals, each reading is quite successful in its approach) but rather reminders that there are other approaches/methodologies.

I shall conclude my literary response with a brief "pure" literary reading of Mark 1 and 3—the Beelzebul controversy—(since there are no such readings in these essays), not as an attempt to show a "correct" literary analysis of a biblical text, but rather to be self-critical and demonstrate that a reading of a biblical text without historical and cultural analysis serves to remind us that the literary reading, alone, like the socio-rhetorical reading, alone, allows for, even requires an-other approach.

A Socio-Rhetorical Analysis

Brian Blount's essay, "A Socio-Rhetorical Analysis of Simon of Cyrene," is the most historically oriented of the four essays, and he gives us an excellent understanding of the text(s) behind the Simon of Cyrene narratives found in Mark, Matthew, and Luke, with insightful and helpful references to Theon's *Progymnasmata,* Cicero's *De Inventione* and *Ad Herennium,* and Quintilian's *The Institutio Oratoria.* This intertextual exercise, though he never uses this critical term, is sound evidence of not only the social community of the gospel narratives, but also of the rather high level of literary sophistication among the gospel writers.

And yet, as a literary critic, I am somewhat confused as to which text is important to Blount. Is he really interested in the Simon stories? Or is he interested in the story of the social community beneath or behind the Simon texts? Blount masterfully creates another text(s) in relation to the Simon text, a text of pre-biblical narrative, which focuses on a social community that emphasizes discipleship, ethnography, and inclusion, for example. In other words, the literary text, for Blount, becomes a tool with which to garner historical information, which information becomes his primary text.

In fairness to Blount, he says such material from the Graeco-Roman world serves to "highlight" (Blount: 25) the biblical text, but notice the progression of his own text. He moves not from the Graeco-Roman background material to the text but from a verse, Luke 23:28, to the Graeco-Roman world.

> A careful reading establishes a parallel whereby a short, pithy saying such as verse 28 is elaborated into an expanded statement. A study of one such rhetorical example will illustrate that Luke has followed the pattern almost exactly. (Blount: 25)

At this point Blount talks extensively about Theon and not about the Lukan narrative. In fact, at several points in Blount's essay, I read for pages with only a general reference to the biblical text. Again, Blount is writing and reading a pre-text to the gospel narratives, which seems to have taken priority.

Is Blount's meta-text approach valuable? I think so. The reader becomes amazed at the intertextual community of the gospel writers, their cultural influences, and the far reaching scope of the period's ideology. Blount might have written another narrative in terms of ideology. The essay could explore, in relation to the structure and language of the text, Simon of Cyrene's ideology—not Rome's and not Luke's, Matthew's, or Mark's. In other words, is there an ideological function in the text that is only in the gospel texts? I suggest that there is. Should Blount have written this story, as well? I suggest no. But a caveat to his essay, concerning the other story's existence, would be helpful.

SOCIO-RHETORICAL/LITERARY ANALYSIS

David Gowler's essay, "Hospitality and Characterization in Luke 11: 37-54: A Socio-Narratological Approach," is guided more by contemporary literary theory than Blount's. His use of the narrative element, character, becomes a literary device, a reminder, that his essay is about persons in the biblical text. And, in turn, Gowler gives us a closer reading of his biblical story.

And yet either because Gowler, like Blount, has a pre-text to the biblical narrative, a text about the role of hospitality in Luke's social world, which offers some sense of interpretive security, or because he is dealing with traditional, Christian canon, he appears to have an implicit trust in the Lukan narrative. I want Gowler to be more suspicious of the biblical text, to believe not only that there are interpretations other than his own, but also to suspect that there are interpretations of situations other than Luke's.

Let me begin with Gowler's epigraph from Macrobius' *Saturnalia*: "Augustus hardly ever refused hospitality; and having been entertained to a very frugal, and, so to speak, everyday dinner, he just whispered in his host's ear, as he was saying goodby after the poor and ill-appointed meal: 'I didn't think that I was so close a friend of yours'" Gowler reads this comment as sarcasm, perhaps insult. I could as easily read the comment as humility. Since the comment is lifted out of context, certainly knowing something of its history could shed more light on the saying's meaning. And yet, knowing its context may solve little, for why can it not be the exception that proves the rule?

If I appear to be begging a point, I have sincere intentions. While Gowler has written what I think is an excellent literary interpretation of the Lukan passage, he more often than not accepts Luke's text at face value as being authoritative and true and gives little power to the language of the text to seduce and mislead. Furthermore, this implicit trust of Luke's narrative reverberates into Gowler's trust of his own interpretation; that is, if I can trust Luke, I can trust my interpretation of Luke.

I am fascinated with and impressed by Gowler's introduction, in particular his line, "People of the first century had a fascination with, and fear of, the power of words to form character." Why? Gowler would suggest because they understood the meaning of words all too well. Let me suggest another possiblity. First century persons knew language's ability to deceive and to be ambiguous. Of course, these are not either/or options; in fact, I suggest that neither interpretation is **the** correct understanding of language in the first century. Still, each is a valuable understanding that leads to a different way of interpreting texts.

Gowler's trust in the narrator of Luke's gospel is well intended. He asks that the critic let, "the text speak for itself." But he precedes this comment with statements such as, "The Gospel of Luke contains three voices of absolute authority for the reader." Such blanket claims resist all further interpretations of the gospel and lead to almost confessional comments such as, "Jesus, as the authoritative Lord (11:39), has the final words of censure, correction, and prophetic insight." Is this comment according to Luke, to the text, to Jesus, to Gowler? I am not suggesting that Gowler is writing confessionally, but his certainty of interpretation and lack of suspicion of the text's language often suggests such a reading. Other such claims exist: "Jesus is the hero of the story." Well, not to the Pharisees. Or, "the reader of Luke therefore produces meaning, but only participating in a complex of socially constructed practices with which the text inherently interacts." Was there no meaning in the text before anyone knew of these socially constructed practices?

Gowler closes his essay with a "plea" for merger of disciplines, where narrative critics take social, cultural, political situations more seriously and cultural critics take narrative texts more seriously. And yet the merger becomes "socio-narratological criticism" and concludes that "only" with this "merger" can we arrive at responsible criticism.

I find no fault with Gowler's interpretation of Luke's story; it is creatively conceived and well thought out. The other story he might have told would have trusted Luke less and perhaps de-centered Jesus. To the literary critic, biblical text need not be canon, and occasionally, Jesus may be the "bad" person in the story. Allowing other characters to be at the center of the text may only require our placing them there, which in turn reads the story over against the ideological stance of the narrator and, in turn, gives us another story. I would suggest, to use Gowler's terms, that "the texts themselves inherently request" this, too.

LITERARY/SOCIO-RHETORICAL ANALYSIS

Robert Tannehill's essay, "The Story of Zacchaeus as Rhetoric: Luke 19:1-10," works more closely with the biblical narrative than either Blount or Gowler. While he too is interested in the rhetorical styles and structures which precede Luke's narrative, Tannehill seems more concerned with how they shed light on the meaning found in the rhetorical function of the Zacchaeus narrative. The nuance here is subtle but important.

The critics doing socio-rhetorical criticism in the previous essays, by the fashion in which they structure their arguments, bring meaning to bear on the biblical text from texts outside the biblical text. Tannehill begins with Luke's narrative, its rhetorical posture and meaning, and then he turns to ancient rhetoricians. He is over half-finished with his essay before he begins a discussion of the relation of classical rhetoricians to the text. What does the rhetoric of the Zacchaeus narrative have to tell us? is the question of priority for Tannehill.

There is, though, more than a little irony in Tannehill's approach. On the one hand, he suggests by the structure of his essay that each narrative unit of the biblical text, whether Luke or a pericope in Luke, has rhetorical autonomy, and that the critic should read each narrative on its own terms before moving outside the text. On the other hand, when faced with interpretive conundrums in the Zacchaeus narrative, he resorts to the entire Lukan narrative to settle interpretive problems. The question becomes then, are the parts equal to the whole? I suggest that the answer is no; in fact; as a literary critic, I would suggest that the whole must be held accountable to its parts. Problematic readings of gospel pericopes need not be consumed by some thematic consistency in the larger text. Perhaps the text's fissure, its ambiguity located only in one pericope, is the text's most profound rhetoric, where language postures itself over against religious, political, social ideology.

Tannehill refers to earlier narratives in Luke's gospel that are similar for an interpretive key. When faced with another interpretive challenge that is not "clear" to the modern reader, he suggests that "we will be on the safest ground if we can supply the missing premises from the work that we are studying or the cultural context from which it comes. Or, he adds at another point, "missing parts" can be supplied from the rest of Luke-Acts. I am not convinced that textual problems, at least in relation to interpretation, can be solved by what might be surface plottings of a larger narrative, nor by cultural reference. I think that language, in this case narrative, has the power to resist interpretation, perhaps language's inherent rhetorical posturing. The interpretive trick, at this point, is to let ambiguity, contrast, and the illogical stand on their own. Tannehill's other story, then, is to interpret Zacchaeus within the context of the singular narrative, Luke 19:1-10, and when those moments of interpretive resistance to larger Lukan themes occur, point them out, interpret them in terms of their resistance, and grant their otherness a rhetorical power of their own.

Socio-Rhetorical and Literary Analysis

Greg Salyer's essay, "Rhetoric, Purity, and Play: Aspects of Mark 7:1-23" "plays" well over against David Gowler's essay. Where Gowler wants to merge critical methodologies under the rubric of a socio-narratological method, Salyer is content to do socio-rhetorical criticism of his biblical text, acknowledging pre-textual influence from classical rhetoric, and to arrive at the conclusions of a socio-rhetorical critic. He then stops and begins criticism again from a postmodern, literary perspective. While the two methodological approaches reach somewhat similar conclusions, there is little mistaking that we are working with two very different approaches, both insightful and both beneficial, with neither making claim for priority of interpretation.

My criticisms of the socio-rhetorical section of Salyer's essay would be repetitive. I find the same interesting movement from text to text, though again without reference to intertextuality, that I found in Blount's essay. I find the same wonderfully articulate and insightful references to anthropology and to cultural ethos concerning purity that I found in Gowler's commentary on hospitality. And I find the same keen and critical textual awareness of language's rhetorical power to posture that I found in Tannehill's narrative criticism. As a literary critic, I would raise the same questions concerning the first three fourths of Salyer's essay that I raised with the preceding essays.

And yet here is the interesting note, to me, on Salyer's essay; only four pages of thirty-five are devoted to a literary approach to his pericope. Whether intentional or not, here lies the tension between doing history—a social science—and doing literature. While literary critics have always fought tooth and nail over methodologies and interpretations of texts, what remained as the outcome of their work was nonetheless an awareness that their interpretations were never more than interpretations. Social science, history, sociology, anthropology, and other social sciences, traditionally have not merely interpreted from texts alone, but from artifact, and in many ways, historical texts are artifacts.

I find both approaches informative and valid. In other words, I find the first three fourths of Salyer's essay no more or no less important than the final fourth. Each is equally revealing of a way of reading texts; each is an interpretive act. Salyer's other story, then, would be to make his deconstructive reading the larger section of the essay and posture it over against all the other essays in the volume.

Where Salyer suggests that "rhetoric and deconstruction have much to offer and much in common" because "both are highly sensitive to both language and social constructs in which language operates," I would add that they are more than similar; they are the same (a claim with which I believe Salyer agrees). Because each is a strategy of persuasion, each is rhetoric, whose usage depends on the culture of origins: on the one hand, the origin(s) of the text(s), and, on the other hand, the origin(s) of the interpreter. These cultures may merge, as suggested by Gowler, the historian cum literary critic, and by Tannehill, the literary critic cum historian, or these cultures may remain separate, as suggested by Blount, the historian, and Salyer, the historian/literary critic. More important, each perspective has something valuable to offer the reader of texts, as each of the preceding essays has demonstrated. To rely on any one methodological approach is to tell only one of many stories, and therefore deprive ourselves of a rich variety of interpretive approaches, each legitimate and crucial in its own right.

A Literary Response: A Literary Approach

I wish to conclude, now, with a brief essay on Mark 1 and 3. My approach is strictly literary, with few if any references to the historical and cultural location of the text. While I would argue that my reading is a rhetorical exercise, it is not a socio-rhetorical exercise. I deal only with the language of the text, its structure or lack of structure, and its internal rhetoric, that is, the narrative's attempt to posture an ideological position. I include this essay as an attempt to suggest that my own methodological approach, that of a contemporary literary critic, is only an interpretive process and not the interpretive process. When my critical exercise is complete, for me, there remains another story to be told.

"The Erasure of [The] Evil [One]: The Locus of Power in Mark 1 and 3" Or, "It Takes One to Know One"

I suggest that a close look at the Gospel of Mark, chapters 1 and 3, reveals extreme ambiguity in the relationships/identities of Satan/Beelzebul and Jesus. The narratives themselves are more about the rhetoric of power, that is, who tells the story, than about characterizing a good person (Jesus) over against an evil person (Beelzebul). In fact, at every moment a trace of each character is found in the other. The identity of one is totally dependent upon identifying the other in relation to who holds center stage at any given moment in the text. The ambiguity itself becomes powerful, taking reader, writer, and character to the point of erasing the Evil One, whose language, authority, and power are now embodied in/by Jesus. In other words, evil and good become not things within themselves but rather the embodiment of a rhetoric which requires us to ask: "Who is in control in/of the text?"

Perhaps the most revealing characteristics of Jesus are not those moments when he is so acutely and clearly set over against Beelzebul but instead those moments when he is Beelzebul, or at least indistinguishable from the Evil One, moments where language blurs as the locus of power transfers from one character to another. At this point, the narrative (author?) has little choice but to attempt to erase or make absent [the] evil [one] in order to empower Jesus. Nonetheless, a trace of the other remains as the defining characteristic of the central character and reminds the reader, narrator, and the narrative's characters of the frightening implications of an assent to the Holy/Evil One.

I wish to begin with the rather ambiguous statement in Mark 1:24, in which the man with an unclean spirit says to Jesus: "What have you to do with us, Jesus of Nazareth?" From this statement I wish to read "about" in chapter 1 as I develop my comments about the Beelzebul texts.

Are the unclean man's comments an invitation to Jesus to prove himself worthy of association with the world of the unclean? Is the statement an acknowledgement that Jesus stands totally over against and other than the world of the unclean? Unlike other gospel stories, when we look, again, at Mark 1:12, we are reminded that there is no comment in the text that Jesus withstood the temptation by Satan. Of course, there is no reference to the fact that Satan was successful in his temptation of Jesus. How curious that Jesus is with both wild beasts—could this be Beelzebul's world?—and with angels—signifying the world of good (Mark 1:13). The point being that the narrative is, in its only unmistaken certainty, ambiguous. Therefore, perhaps the unclean spirit's comment, "What have you to do with us?," recognizes Jesus' complicity in the world of darkness and is, therefore, a comment of inclusion.

The question, then, has a double meaning reflected by language's play; that is, the unclean spirit recognizes one of its own—an unclean spirit. At the same time, the narrative (narrator?) and reader know that this Jesus is also the story's hero. So, the question, "What have you to do with us?" is not only a reference to complicity but also an assertion that Jesus is not one of the unclean spirits. The narrative equivocates, needing to have it both ways. Therefore, "Have you come to destroy us?" reflects the narrative's dual intentions and how Jesus is now "at play" with the unclean spirits. He is both one of them and worthy of their invitation and not one of them and his presence will destroy them. Such an observation makes the act of destruction, "Have you come to destroy us?," itself possess tremendous irony. At this point, for Jesus to destroy the unclean spirit is to destroy self and self's sameness with the possessed.

Perhaps I could argue that Jesus' encounter with the man with the unclean spirit represents the conclusion of the temptation scene. But it is not the neat conclusion narrative desires; rather, Jesus rebukes the unclean spirit, requiring silence, lest we and the narrative's audience are "let in" on this game—even war—of words and therefore learn who Jesus is—Beelzebul or the Holy One of God. That the spirit is chased from or chooses to leave the man at Jesus' command serves only to make the story even more undecipherable. Is the unclean spirit cast out (by the holy one of God) or merely responding to the request of his superior (Beelzebul)? The irony, of course, is that in either case the unclean spirit responds to a superior—that is, "a new teaching—with authority" (Mark 1:27), who "commands even the unclean spirits, and they obey him." All the time, language leaves us wondering who Jesus is and where to locate the power of good and evil.

This observation brings us back to the beginning of the temptation scene in Mark 1:12, the most fascinating comment of which is, "the spirit (no adjective, such as holy) drove him (we assume Jesus) out into the wilderness. The verb here, *ekballo*,—meaning to force or drive out, expel and a word I associate with aggression, even violence—is the same as the verb used to describe the "casting out" of demons elsewhere in Mark, as well as elsewhere in the gospels (The word is used 18 times in Mark. Every time it is used in chapters 1 and 3, it is in relation to demons, except this time.).

The narrative at this point, then, no less struggles for power than the characters in the narrative. Mark's gospel is marked by violence and destruction, and the tone of the gospel is one of confusion. The spirit tears apart the heavens and drives Jesus into the wilderness (Mark 1:10, 12). I have no trouble associating these events with either the diabolical world or the Kingdom of God. For, in Mark 1 each moment of violence is mediated by a "softening touch," the dove in the baptismal scene and the angels "waiting" on Jesus in the temptation scene. Still again, I am confused by narrative's play. The Kingdom of God is violent and peaceful? The world of the Evil One is violent and peaceful? We are not told with which characteristics to associate either one. Rhetorically, each world is seductive, and, I suggest, the two paradoxically exist simultaneously; in fact, they are so intimate with one another that to choose one is to embrace both.

The language of our texts blurs the distinctions between Jesus and the Evil One not out of some attempt to make Jesus into the "strong man" in the text. But what we know is that Jesus is the "strong man" of the text. This ambiguity in description comes about quite naturally, I think. Jesus, on the one hand, is not Beelzebul; his intent, his mission, and his very presence are not the same as the evil one. On the other hand, Jesus must at least be Beelzebul. If the question is one of authority, of who has the power in the story, Jesus may at some point move beyond his adversary, but the transition requires moving through the identity of the adversary; at least, I think that is the way Mark's gospel presents this entanglement.

At any moment in which the character of Jesus is described, the narrative reminds the reader and audience of the unclean/Beelzebul. In other words, Jesus depends on Beelzebul for his own personal identity, particularly as it relates to his powers to control his mission and those persons intimately involved with it. The flip side is, of course, that Beelzebul always possesses a trace of this "Holy One from God" as the most defining characteristic of his experience and identity.

This merger of identities raises a critical point. Jesus, along with his followers and the crowd at large, recognizes unclean spirits, but the unclean spirits, alone, recognize Jesus. The most telling and profound line for me, in Mark I, is found in verse 34, "because they knew him." These lines, in which the demons recognize Jesus, are the fissures in the text, where the text, not the heavens, is torn apart. And I think these moments represent Mark's (the gospel narrative's) genius. Not only is Jesus cautious of his identity, telling all not to tell who he is, but also the inter-play of language so violently turns on itself that none of us, reader or audience, and I would argue author, knows who Jesus is. And perhaps we might venture so far as to question Jesus' certainty as to his identity. The ambiguity of the text itself suggests to me that Jesus is violated by his own lack of certainty as to who he is and who/what guides his ministry. These moments of uncertainty, where power is disguised and manipulated by character, reader, author, and audience, are those moments I find most trustworthy in their description of who Jesus is and of what he says.

I wish now to turn to Mark 3 to obfuscate, even further, the Jesus/Beelzebul characterization. I wish to focus particularly on Mark 3:19-30, but again I shall read all about in chapter three.

If I am the most frightened by the unknown, then, the ability to name the unknown, and make it known, is my most powerful language-tool. Rhetorically, the task is set. I need not name correctly; I need merely to persuade myself and my audience of the utility of the name. Therefore, I am not surprised that in Mark 3:2—and I think it interesting that this chapter, too, begins in the synagogue—persons are waiting for and watching Jesus that "they might accuse him." And when Jesus restores the hand that is withered, the Pharisees join with the Herodians "to destroy him" (Mark 3:6). Remember, in Mark 1 the comment is that Jesus has come to destroy the unclean spirits. Now, the tables are turned.

Why do they wish to destroy him? I suggest for two reasons, intimately bound together. One, Jesus is demonic; "He has Beelzebul, and by the ruler of the demons he casts out demons" (Mark 3:22). If naming is a product of known experience, I must believe the text; the scribes see in Jesus characteristics which are associated with the evil one. Their rhetoric would have no power of persuasion otherwise. Therefore, even if they knowingly falsely accuse Jesus, there must be some validity to their claims or they lose any access to authority.

In the withered hand episode the narrative convolutes the issue by reducing the onlookers to silence, an inability to name the acts of Jesus as either good or bad. Again, the text's audience cannot name/recognize Jesus, but in verse 11 all the unclean spirits "saw him ... and shouted, 'You are the Son of God!'" They clearly recognize Jesus and yet, while Jesus is angry that his followers' "hardness of heart" prevents recognition and definition, he orders the demons not "to make him known."

Here, I would argue, is the pivotal transition of power. The narrative self-consciously allies Jesus with the ruler of demons because here rests the rhetorical power of the text. Jesus resists names which place him over against the Beelzebul figure, the ruler of demons, because at this point there is little power in being the "Son of God." This authority resides with the Pharisees, the Herodians, and the scribes; they are the religiously powerful at this moment in the text. "New teaching" with great authority rests outside traditional god-talk, in the world of demons—which Jesus embraces and destroys at the same time, as he establishes his own rhetorical strategy to place himself in a position of power. This position is best described in the parable of Satan casting out Satan.

The parable is wonderfully confusing. Jesus is accused of "having Beelzebul," an accusation which he does not deny. The parable, "How can Satan cast out Satan? If a kingdom is divided against itself that kingdom cannot stand" (Mark 3:23, 24), perhaps can be read as denial, even conundrum. I prefer to read the parable as an affirmation of allegiance with Satan and as the pivotal moment in which Jesus is other than Satan. The text reads true on both counts. On the one hand, the "strong man" is the locus of power embodied in the Pharisees and scribes. Jesus clearly comes to "plunder" their world. Only as Beelzebul, from a house undivided, can he do this. The answer then to the question, "How can Satan cast out Satan?" is that he cannot and that Satan's end cannot come until Jesus has assumed a position of power over against existing authority. The fascinating shift is that their becoming the "strong man" is the moment when Jesus moves through the Satan character, where he is no longer the Beelzebul figure, for the scribes and Pharisees assume the role of the Evil One.

Now Jesus becomes other than Beelzebul. The divided house is that moment which separates Jesus from the power mongers who hold positions in the temple; they now represent the text's Satan figures. The language shifts; where once Jesus was the accused, he now accuses his opponents for their blasphemy, this time against the Holy Spirit (Mark 3:28-9)—is this Jesus?—for having suggested that he had "an unclean spirit" (Mark 3:30). This moment is the only time Jesus has denied his association with the world of demons, which suggests that the locus of power has changed.

Nonetheless, the text remains ambiguous enough to refuse the assigning of any certainty to who Jesus is. The writer, reader, and audience are now held in tension by the trace of the other. Jesus is and is not Beelzebul; Beelzebul is and is not Jesus. Kelber's language of insider/outsider in Mark is only marginally helpful to making a distinction (Kelber: 27-29). I am convinced that there are no insiders. Even Jesus himself is tainted by the rhetoric of power required on his part to move from one without authority to one with authority, a person with the new teaching, for in doing so he sides with the "other world," a world other than the existing place of power at any given moment in the text. When the scribes and Pharisees are in power, he is Beelzebul with the trace of the "Holy One of God" ever present. Yet when power shifts to his favor, he is the "Holy One of God" standing over against the "strong man's" house, but even then ever present is the trace of Beelzebul; the trace of the other being the only means, at any given moment, of self-recognition, and at which time he can issue an invitation to belief from the surrounding community.

Within such confusion, I believe, exist the words of Jesus, those words nebulous and confusing which require an assent to faith in both the Holy/Evil One, at the same time. Of course, with assent Evil is erased as the only way in which to empower the new teaching. And still the trace remains, which places any assent to faith on rather shaky ground. "Whenever the unclean spirits saw him, they fell down before him and shouted, 'You are the Son of God!' But he sternly ordered them not to make him known," (Mark 3:11-12).

POSTSCRIPT: *APOLOGIA PRO MODUM SUA*

The task I have just put at hand is an important and good one, even a fun one. "What are/were the *very* words of Jesus, himself?" will always be an important question. Did I achieve my goal? Particularly with only a literary approach to the text? Well, only to the degree that I was responsible to the text and to the approach I chose to take, and more important, only to the extent that I am willing to entertain stories other than my own as ways of access to my goals.

My other story? It is to include the socio-rhetorical criticism that would shed new light on my understanding of the Beelzebul controversy, the language of the community that produced the story, its other texts about similar ideas and figures. I need neither to accept this other methodology nor use it in conjunction with my own, but as members, together, of an interpretive community, I must affirm the other's success as a methodology. From such affirmation, I am drawn closer to it, and I just might, in turn, learn a great deal from it.

Finally, I wish to suggest that we as critics must be cautious in our careful and detailed dissection of the text(s) and in our additions, subtractions, and impositions of text(s) in order to achieve a prescribed goal so that we do not violate what is, in essence, a pretty good story(ies). I say this not as a participant in faith, someone who is concerned with personal acts of religious belief, but as someone who is concerned with narrative and language and the power of story. In other words, I would make the same observation about a study of Faulkner or Toni Morrison.

In our attempts to find **the** story, we create other stories with our literary and rhetorical theories, and our historical and social methods. Personally, I like this; such work lends an element of excitement to what we do, which is why I think that this volume of *Semeia* is not only exciting but also necessary. Anyhow, I do not think that there is **a** story. I simply suggest that we not forget that with every story we create, stories devised of our various methods, that there remains the other story(-ies) with which we began our task. While it is much fun to play the role of Tatian and seek the one true, continuous narrative, let us also enjoy and have fun with the variety and difference found in these many good stories.

WORKS CONSULTED

Beare, Frank W.
    1962   *The Earliest Records of Jesus*. Nashville: Abingdon.

Kelber, Werner H.
    1979   *Mark's Story of Jesus*. Philadelphia: Fortress.

Mack, Burton
    1988   *A Myth of Innocence*. Philadelphia: Fortress.

Malbon, Elizabeth Struthers
    1986   *Narrative Space and Mythic Meaning in Mark*. San Francisco: Harper and Row.

Myers, Ched
    1988   *Binding the Strong Man: A Political Reading of Mark's Story of Jesus*. New York: Orbis Books.

Oakman, Douglas E.
    1988   "Rulers' Houses, Thieves, and Usurpers: The Beelzebul Pericope," *Foundations and Facets Forum* 4:109-122.

Robbins, Vernon K.
    1989   Ed. *Ancient Quotes and Anecdotes*. Sonoma: Polebridge.
    1992   *Jesus The Teacher: A Socio-Rhetorical Interpretation of Mark*. Minneapolis: Fortress.

Sellew, Philip
    1988   "Beelzebul in Mark 3: Dialogue, Story, or Sayings Cluster?" *Foundations and Facets Forum* 4:93-108.

www.ingramcontent.com/pod-product-compliance
Lightning Source LLC
Chambersburg PA
CBHW020056020526
44112CB00031B/196